Lecture Notes in Computer Science 8216

Commenced Publication in 1973
Founding and Former Series Editors:
Gerhard Goos, Juris Hartmanis, and Jan van Leeuwen

Alfredo Cuzzocrea   Sofian Maabout (Eds.)

Model and Data Engineering

Third International Conference, MEDI 2013
Amantea, Italy, September 25-27, 2013
Proceedings

 Springer

Volume Editors

Alfredo Cuzzocrea
ICAR-CNR and University of Calabria
Via P. Bucci, 41 C
87036 Rende, Italy
E-mail: cuzzocrea@si.deis.unical.it

Sofian Maabout
LaBRI, University of Bordeaux
351 cours de la libération
33405 Talence, France
E-mail: maabout@labri.fr

ISSN 0302-9743   e-ISSN 1611-3349
ISBN 978-3-642-41365-0   e-ISBN 978-3-642-41366-7
DOI 10.1007/978-3-642-41366-7
Springer Heidelberg New York Dordrecht London

Library of Congress Control Number: 2013949409

CR Subject Classification (1998): D.2, H.2, D.3, I.6, K.6, I.2

LNCS Sublibrary: SL 2 – Programming and Software Engineering

Typesetting: Camera-ready by author, data conversion by Scientific Publishing Services, Chennai, India

Printed on acid-free paper

Springer is part of Springer Science+Business Media (www.springer.com)

Preface

This volume contains the papers presented at the third International Conference on Model & Data Engineering (MEDI 2013), held in Amantea, Calabria, Italy, during September 25–27, 2013. MEDI conference was launched as an initiative of researchers from Euro-Mediterranean countries. Its aim is to promote the creation of scientific networks, projects, and faculty/student exchanges, as well as to provide a forum for the dissemination of research accomplishments and to encourage the interaction and collaboration between the modeling and data management research communities. The previous editions of MEDI were held in Obidos, Portugal, during September 2011, and Poitiers, France, during October 2012.

MEDI specifically focuses on model engineering and data engineering, with special emphasis on most recent and relevant topics in the areas of model-driven engineering, ontology engineering, formal modeling, security, and database modeling.

This year MEDI received 61 submissions from over 16 countries. Most papers were reviewed by 3 Program Committee members. After rigorous selection, the Program Committee decided to accept 19 long papers and 3 short papers. We are thankful to all the researchers that helped in the review process and made this event successful. The conference program featured two invited talks, namely, "Analyzing Massive Streaming Heterogeneous Data: Towards a New Computing Model for Computational Sustainability" by Dimitrios Gunopulos, National and Kapodistrian University of Athens, Greece, and "Model Engineering as a Social Activity: The Case of Business Processes" by Gottfried Vossen, University of Münster, Germany and University of Waikato, New Zealand.

We are very grateful to our sponsors and institutions that actively supported the organization of the conference. This year, these were:

- DIMES - Dipartimento di Ingegneria Informatica, Modellistica, Elettronica e Sistemistica, University of Calabria
- ICAR-CNR - Istituto di Calcolo e Reti ad Alte Prestazioni, Italian National Research Council

We would also like to acknowledge the EasyChair software team for making available their conference management tool which was of great help during the review process as well as for finalizing the present proceedings.

September 2013

Alfredo Cuzzocrea
Sofian Maabout

Organization

Program Committee

El Hassan Abdelwahed	University Cadi Ayyad Marrakech, Morocco
Alberto Abello	Universitat Politècnica de Catalunya, Spain
Yamine Ait Ameur	ENSEEIHT/IRIT, France
Jose F Aldana Montes	University of Malaga, Spain
Marie-Aude Aufaure	Ecole Centrale Paris, France
Franck Barbier	LIUPPA, France
Salima Benbernou	Université Paris Descartes, France
Rafael Berlanga	Universitat Jaume I, Spain
Jorge Bernardino	Polytechnic Institute of Coimbra, Portugal
Sandro Bimonte	IRSTEA, France
Alexander Borusan	TU Berlin / Fraunhofer FIRST, Germany
Azedine Boulmakoul	University of Mohammedia, Morocco
Omar Boussaid	University of Lyon, France
Stephane Bressan	National University of Singapore, Singapore
Francesco Buccafurri	DIIES - Universita' Mediterranea di Reggio Calabria, Italy
Coral Calero	Universidad de Castilla-La Mancha, Spain
Damianos Chatziantoniou	Athens University of Economics and Business, Greece
Mandy Chessell	IBM, UK
Alain Crolotte	Teradata Corporation, USA
Alfredo Cuzzocrea	ICAR-CNR and University of Calabria, Italy
Florian Daniel	University of Trento, Italy
Jérôme Darmont	Université de Lyon, France
Roberto De Virgilio	Università Roma Tre, Italy
Habiba Drias	USTHB University, Algeria
Johann Eder	University of Klagenfurt, Austria
Mostafa Ezziyyani	University Abdelmalk Esaadi, UAE
Jamel Feki	Université de Sfax, Tunisia
Pedro Furtado	Univ. Coimbra / CISUC, Portugal
Matteo Golfarelli	DEIS - University of Bologna, Italy
Daniela Grigori	University Paris-Dauphine, France
Stephane Jean	LISI/ENSMA and University of Poitiers, France
Eleanna Kafeza	Athens University of Economics and Business, Greece
Panagiotis Karras	Rutgers University, USA
Jens Lechtenbörger	University of Münster, Germany

Additional Reviewers

Table of Contents

Modeling and Simulation of Hadoop Distributed File System in a Cluster of Workstations

Longendri Aguilera-Mendoza and Monica T. Llorente-Quesada

University of Informatics Science,
Havana City, Cuba
{loge,mllorente}@uci.cu
http://www.uci.cu

Abstract. Considering the increased hard disk capacity on desktop PCs, we examine, by the modeling and simulation technique, the feasibility of exploiting the idle computational storage in a large Cluster of Workstations (COW). The model built is architecturally based on the Hadoop Distributed File System (HDFS) and was implemented in the CPN Tools using the Coloured Petri Nets combined with the CPN ML programming language. To characterize the workstations' availability in the model, a statistical study was realized by collecting data from computer laboratories in our academic institution over a period of 40 days. From the simulation results, we propose a small modification in the source code of HDFS and a specific number of replicas in order to achieve a reliable service for writing and reading files despite the random failures due to the turning on and off of the computers in a COW with hundreds of machines.

Keywords: Modeling, Simulation, Distributed File System, Hadoop, Coloured Petri Nets, Cluster of Workstations.

1 Introduction

Nowadays, the available storage capacity in hard disk has increased from gigabytes to terabytes. As a consequence, it is a common issue to find a high amount of unused space in the workstations of an institution [1,2]. In order to face this problem of wasted resources, a combination of hardware and software known as distributed file systems [3] have been developed to take advantages through the network of this available storage capacity. However, the design of these systems is a challenge keeping in mind that the hard disks fail, the desktop computers may be shutdown, the network can collapse, the applications stop and despite this the users always want a reliable service.

There are numerous distributed file systems that aggregate the idle space of various PCs to offer a storage service [4,5]. One of the most popular at this moment is the Hadoop distributed file system (HDFS), a software component of the open-source Hadoop product developed by the Apache Software Foundation. Hadoop has been designed to run on commodity hardware and some well-known

A. Cuzzocrea and S. Maabout (Eds.): MEDI 2013, LNCS 8216, pp. 1–12, 2013.

companies such as Yahoo and Facebook have deployed HDFS to save a large volume of data in a conglomerate of dedicated computers [6,7].

HDFS is fault tolerant and to ensure the availability of files it replicates the data by making several copies on different nodes. This has been well tested in some environments where the computers are dedicated to the cluster, but we wonder how well it will work in a Non-Dedicated Distributed Environment (NDDE) [8] where the number of available machines is random at certain time and the computers can suddenly be restarted or shutdown causing loss of nodes and data. The answer will depend on the replication strategy implemented in the system, the number of machines available in the environment during the day and the length of the time interval in which those PCs are idle.

An example of a NDDE can be seen in an academic institution, where the computers in laboratories (workstations) generally have no individual owner and are used by students or professors in arbitrary interval times. Assuming that the status is idle when the machines are not being used by users, then there is a great opportunity having a distributed file system like HDFS in such academic institutions.

In this work, we were motivated to study the feasibility of exploiting the academic computers laboratories in order to collect the unused storage of each desktop PC. The main goal is to predict the behavior of a distributed file system based on HDFS in a large[1] Cluster of Workstation (COW) using the modeling and simulation techniques. Since the modeling and simulation allow experimentation and validations of new configurations of the system without disruptions to existing academic institutions.

2   Modeling HDFS Using Coloured Petri Nets

The model of the HDFS in a COW was built using the Coloured Petri Nets (CPN) [9,10] and the CPN Tools (v3.4.0) available at http://cpntools.org/. There are many reasons for using the CPN modeling language [11]. Basically, we consider that CPN is suitable for modeling since it is a graphical oriented language that combines its strength with CPN ML programming language for design, specification, simulation and verification of systems. Also, the CPN Tools supports the implementation, debugging, and analysis of a CPN model [12,13,14].

The CPN model was designed and hierarchically structured by analyzing the architecture [15] and the source code of HDFS. Figure 1 shows the top page with the three main modules of the model: the *ClientNode*, the *NameNode* and the *DataNode*. In the followings subsections a zoom into these modules is described. All of them are substitution transitions that share the same place representing the network to allow the communication between them. The colour set *Network-Data* represents the messages interchange through the communication medium and it is modeled as:

---

[1] A large cluster means a conglomerate of hundreds or more workstations.

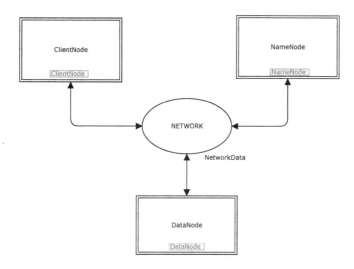

Fig. 1. The top module

```
colset DataCenter = index center with 0..pNumOfDataCenter;
colset Rack = index rack with 0..pNumOfRack;
colset Host = index host with 0.. pNumOfHostsPerRack;
colset MachineID = product DataCenter * Rack * Host;
colset NodeType = with CNode | DNode | NNode;
colset Source = product MachineID * NodeType;
colset Destiny = product MachineID * NodeType;
colset OpType = with create| addBlock| connect| abandonBlock
                | complete| write| read| register
                | setHeartBeat| reportBlocks| getBlocks;
colset Operation = product OpType * INT;
colset Args = list STRING;
colset Answer = list STRING;
colset NetworkData = product Source * Destiny * Operation
                            * Args * Answer timed;
```

Note that *pNumOfDataCenter*, *pNumOfRack*, *pNumOfHostsPerRack* are parameters for the specification of the number of data centers, racks and hosts per racks, respectively. The identification of each machine (*MachineID*) is a ternary cartesian product which models the physical locations of each workstation in the cluster. The colour set *OpType* denotes the possible operations to be sent from one node to another. The definition of these operations is based on the java interfaces *ClientProtocol*, *DataTransferProtocol* and *DatanodeProtocol* that governing the communication among the three main components of the HDFS. Finally, the *NetworkData* contains the operations and arguments to be processed by the destiny node and the answer returned to the source node.

2.1 Modeling the ClientNode

The *ClientNode* generates randomly the request to read and write files on behalf of the users. Also, it simulates the user interface program that interacts with the Hadoop file system through the Java API. In the substitution transition *User*

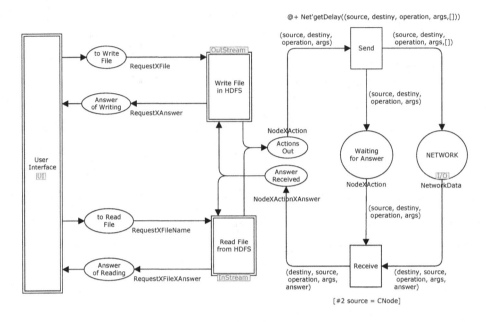

Fig. 2. The *ClientNode* module

Requests (Fig. 2), the writing and reading requests are generated. The generation process occurs using an exponential random distribution function to determine the time at which the next request will arrive.

On one hand, the writing requests are handled in the substitution transitions *Write File in HDFS* (Fig. 2). First, a client establishes a connection to create a new file entry in the *NameNode's File System Namespace*. Later, the file to write is split into data packets and each packet is written into an internal data queue. The packets in the data queue are extracted to allocate new files blocks in the *NameNode's File System Namespace*. For each block allocated, the *NameNode* returns the suitable *DataNodes* that form a pipeline to copy a replica of the block in all of them. The pipeline is formed finding the shortest path that starts from the *ClientNode* and traverses all *DataNodes* so as to reduce the communication overhead. Finally, when the blocks have been sent to the *DataNodes* and the acknowledgments have been received, a signal to complete file is sent to the *NameNode*.

On the other hand, the reading requests are handled in the substitution transitions *Read File from HDFS* (Fig. 2), where the file is opened and the location of blocks is determined by consulting the *NameNode*. The locations comprise the addresses of the *DataNodes* that have a copy for each block. The addresses returned by the *NameNode* are sorted according to their proximity to the *ClientNode* so as to reduce the communication overhead. When the blocks are read back to the client from the *DataNodes*, then a message is sent to the *NameNode* to close the file.

As shown in the right side of the figure 2, the transition *Send*, as the name suggests, sends the messages to the network creating a copy on the place *Waiting for Answer* for those that are waiting for answer. When the answer is received then the waiting message is removed from the place *Waiting for Answer* and the substitution transition *User Request* is notified through the places *Answer of Writing* and *Answer of Reading* to store the answers. Note that the function *Net'getDelay* invoked in the time delay inscriptions attached to the transition *Send* is applied to the message token in the network. A time delay means that the message token might be consumed by the destiny only after the model time is equal to the time stamp of the message token.

2.2   Modeling the Namenode

The *NameNode* implements the logic of the server which manages the File System Namespace (FSN). The FSN is modeled as:

```
colset DataNodeID = product DataCenter * Rack * Host;
colset DataNodeIDList = list DataNodeID;
colset BlockID = union blk:INT;
colset BlockSizeMB = int with 0..pBlockSizeMB;
colset Block = product BlockID * BlockSizeMB;
colset BlockList = list Block;
colset BlockInfo = record block:Block * fileName:FileName
                        * sourceDNs:DataNodeIDList
                        * scheduledDNs:DataNodeIDList ;
colset BlockInfoList = list BlockInfo;
colset BlockXTargets = product Block * DataNodeIDList;
colset BlocksToReplicate = list BlockXTargets ;
colset FileInfo = record name:FileName * fSize: INT
                        * isOpen:BOOL * blocks:BlockList;
colset FileInfoList = list FileInfo;
colset HeartBeat = product INT * INT * INT
                        (*freeSpace, usedSpace, threadLoad*);
colset DataNodeInfo = record dnID:DataNodeID * heartBeat:HeartBeat
                            * lastUpdate:INT * nBlkScheduled: INT
                            * storedBlk:BlockList
                            * blksToReplicate:BlocksToReplicate
                            * blksToInvalidate: BlockList;
colset DataNodeInfoList = list DataNodeInfo;
colset DataNodeMap = list DataNodeInfoList;
colset UnderReplicated = product Block * INT;
colset UnderReplicatedList = list UnderReplicated;
colset PendingReplication = product Block * INT * INT;
colset PendingReplicationList = list PendingReplication;
colset FSN = record fileMap:FileInfoList * blkMap:BlockInfoList
                    * dnMap:DataNodeMap
                    * neededReplications: UnderReplicatedList
                    * pendingReplications: PendingReplicationList
                    * dfsMetrics: DFSMetrics;
```

The colour set FSN is a record that contains the list of *FileInfo* (*fileMap*), the list of *BlockInfo* (*blkMap*), the bidimensional map of all *DataNodes* in the cluster (*dnMap*), the priority queue of the blocks that need replication (*neededReplications*), the list of the blocks that are being replicated (*pendingReplications*) and the collected metrics (*dfsMetrics*): free space, used space and thread load of the system. For the accessing and modification of the data defined in the FSN, there are various functions implemented in the CPN ML programming language

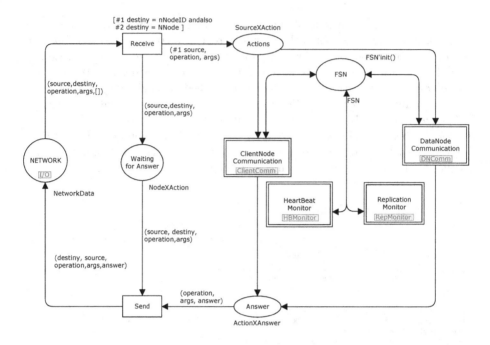

Fig. 3. The *NameNode* module

which are used in the expressions and code segments of the model. The replication strategy adopted by HDFS was codified in functions as well.

Note that the *fileMap* and *blkMap* represent the information in the FSN associated with files and their blocks, respectively. The bidimensional data structure *dnMap* is a list of lists. The first list corresponds to the racks and the second list to the *DataNodes* located in each rack. The colour set *DataNodeInfo* has the information mapped about the *DataNodes*. This information consists in the identifier (*dnID*), the *heartBeat* with the free space, used space and thread load, the time stamp at which the last update occurs (*lastUpdate*), the number of blocks scheduled to be written (*nBlkScheduled*), the list of blocks stored in the node (*storedBlk*), the list of blocks scheduled to be replicated by the node (*blksToReplicate*) since they are under-replicated and the list of blocks scheduled to be deleted by the node (*blksToInvalidate*) since they are over-replicated.

Figure 3 shows the *NameNode* module. The transition *Receive* occurs when a token message is taken from the place *Network* whose destiny is the *NameNode*. The message received contains an operation and it is processed by the substitution transition *ClientNode Communication* or *DataNode Communication* depending on who sends the message, the *ClientNode* or *DataNode*. Also, there are two other substitution transitions named *HeartBeat Monitor* and *Replication Monitor*. The *HeartBeat Monitor* periodically checks the last update time stamp of the *DataNodes* to get the dead ones. These are the *DataNodes* considered to be out of service because the *NameNode* has not received any *HeartBeats* during an interval time specified as parameter. Moreover, the *Replication Monitor* periodically computes replication work by scanning the blocks in the priority queue *neededReplications* of the FSN and assigning the under-replicated blocks to the *blksToReplicate* of the selected nodes according to the implemented placement policy in HDFS.

2.3   Modeling the DataNodes

The Figure 4 shows the *DataNode* module. This module sends and receives messages with actions and answer to other nodes. For instance, the messages received from the *ClientNode* allow the reading of stored-blocks or writing of new ones. The *DataNode* also sends messages like heartbeats[2] and report of blocks to the *NameNode* from time to time (those time intervals are specified as parameters), and may get in response some instrupctions to delete or replicate blocks. In the case of writing by means of a pipeline, each *DataNode* stores the block and forwards it to the other *DataNode* through the *Network*.

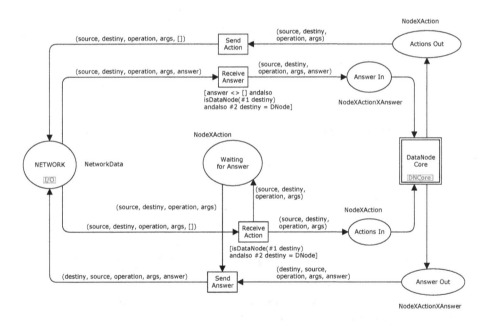

Fig. 4. The *DataNode* module

All the incoming and outgoing messages of the *DataNode* module are processed and generated in the substitution transition *DataNode Core*. This substitution transition uses the colour set *DataNode* shown below to model the workstations that store data blocks.

---

[2] The datanodes are considered by the Namenode as out of service if they do not send any heartbeat during an specific interval time.

```
colset OnOff = with On | Off;
colset DataNode = record dnID:DataNodeID * registered: BOOL
                        * freeMB:INT * usedMB:INT * status:OnOff
                        * blocks:BlockList * threadLoad:INT
                        * lastHeartBeat: INT * lastReport: INT;
```

Note that the colour set *DataNode* is a record consisting of an identifier (*dnID*), a boolean (*registered*) that specifies if the *DataNode* has been registered in the *NameNode* or not, the free space (*freeMB*), the used space (*usedMB*), the status *On* or *Off* depending on the availability, the list of stored blocks (blocks), an integer indicating the thread load (*threadLoad*) and the time at which the heartbeat (*lastHeartBeat*) and the report of the blocks (*lastReport*) were sent. The instances of the colour set *DataNode* were randomly generated according to the characteristics of our academic environment.

3   Considering the Workstations Availability

The HDFS splits files into blocks which are going to be stored in several nodes of the COW. These types of nodes will not always be ready for immediate use during the simulations. Therefore, in order to model the availability of the workstations we perform a study in which some metrics were collected from 128 computers of our institution by a client/server application running 24 hours a day. These measurements were taken from November 1st to December 10th, 2012.

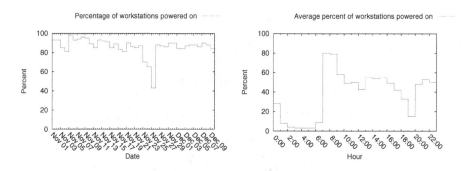

Fig. 5. Percentage of workstations powered on over the 40 days (left) and the average percent over the 24 hours a day (right)

The figures 5(a) (left) and 5(b) (right) show the percentage of workstations powered on in our computers laboratories during the 40 days and the average percent computed for 24 hours a day, respectively. As can be seen in the figure 5(a) the lower percentages correspond to the weekends, and more than 80 percent of workstations are powered on in most days. While the figure 5(b) indicates that availability of machines depends on the time of the day. This is because users frequently turn off the computers before leaving the university campus to fulfill the electric energy saving policy. Thus, we have modeled the machines powered on as follows.

Let X_{ij} be a Bernoulli random variable that takes the values:

$$X_{ij} = \begin{cases} 1 \text{ if the workstation } i \text{ is powered on at hour } j \\ 0 \text{ otherwise} \end{cases} \tag{1}$$

for $j = 0, 1, 2 \ldots, 23$ and $i = 1, 2, \ldots, N$; where N is the total number of workstations. Denoting p_j as the probability of a computer is powered on at hour j, then the probability of success is $Prob(X_{ij} = 1) = p_j$ and the probability of failure is $Prob(X_{ij} = 0) = 1 - p_j$.

Now suppose that the random variable $\hat{X}_j$ that represents the total number of workstations powered on at hour j is defined as:

$$\hat{X}_j = \sum_{i=1}^{N} X_{ij} \tag{2}$$

Note that the random variable $\hat{X}_j$ is said[3] to have a Binomial distribution with parameter N and p_j, denoted by $B(N, p_j)$. For that reason, we are going to use the Binomial random distribution functions to generate the number of workstations powered on at a given hour. Here, the parameters p_j were estimated based on the data collected and the Maximum Likelihood Estimation (MLE).

There is still an important issue related with availability and it is the random generation of the idle time at a given hour. As we were interested in predicting the behavior of the system in a chaotic environment, the Uniform random distribution function was selected to generate the period in seconds (on the interval $(0, 3600]$) during which the workstations remain powered on.

4   Simulation Results

In this section we study the behavior of the modeled system by running several simulations. Various parameters were configured taking into account the study described in section 3 and the characteristics of our academic environment. Some of them were the initial hour (*pHourInit* = 8:00), end hour (*pHourEnd* = 12:00), the minimum and maximum values to randomly generate the initial free space of the *DataNodes* (*pMinDiskFreeMB* = 1024, *pMaxDiskFreeMB* = 10*1024), the blocks size (*pBlockSizeMB* = 64), the minimum and maximum values to randomly generate the size of the files (*pMinFileSizeMB* = 500, *pMaxFileSizeMB* = 1000), probability of erasing a hard disk when the workstation is reset (*pProbOfErasingHD* = 0.2), the replication factor (*pReplicationFactor*) that was gradually increased to gain fault tolerance, the number of requests to write (*pNumOfReadingRequest* = 100), the number of requests to read (*pNumOfWritingRequest* = 100), the number of data centers (*pNumOfDataCenter* =

---

[3] A Binomial random variable can be considered as a sum of n Bernoulli random variables.

1), the number of racks ($pNumOfRack = 6$) and the number of hosts per racks ($pNumOfHostsPerRack = 100$).

Figure 6 shows one of the simulation results, that is the percentage of request for writing and reading files that were answered successfully while the replication factor increases. It can be clearly seen that the successful answers of reading go up and, on the contrary, successful answers of writing go down.

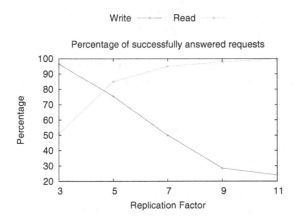

Fig. 6. The satisfactory response rate for the requests generated during the simulations

We found that the reliability of the writing requests falls because of a constraint implemented in the HDFS source code. This constraint is due to the *ClientNode* rejection of the pipeline sent from the *NameNode* with the suitable nodes to copy the newly allocated blocks, if at least one of the *DataNodes* is not available and the pipeline is interrupted. When this happens, the *ClientNode* goes back to the *NameNode* for a new list of replica locations of the block and raises an error if the number of retries specified as parameters ($pNumOfTriesInAllocatingBlock = 3$) is reached. Note that in a NDDE the probability of finding a not-connectable pipeline increases as the length of pipeline increases (replication factor) and this is the main reason of the low percentage in the writing process.

It seems that a relaxation of the mentioned constraint is needed to achieve good reliability in the writing process for a chaotic environment where the machines change their status (On/Off) randomly. To this end, we modify the model and instead of rejecting the pipeline if one of the *DataNode* is out of service, the *ClientNode* accepts the pipeline if the number of available *DataNodes* to copy the blocks is greater than a threshold specified as 1 in this study. After, the failed *DataNodes* are removed from the pipeline and the data blocks are copied in those that are on-line. This can be done without affecting dramatically the reading process thanks to the replication strategy implemented in HDFS, where the *NameNode* detects the under-replicated blocks and arranges further copies of those blocks on other *DataNodes*. Figure 7 presents the rise achieved

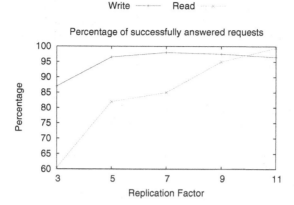

Fig. 7. The satisfactory response rate once some modifications were performed in the model

in the successful response rate of writing requests, without affecting the reading process, once the suggested modifications were implemented in the model. The parameters related with the success of this new behavior were configured to send the heartbeats every 5 minutes, the report of blocks every 10 minutes while the replication and heartbeat monitors (figure 3) ran every 5 and 15 minutes respectively.

5   Conclusions

We have built a Coloured Petri Nets model that can be seen as a framework to explore and test new configurations and alternative strategies different from those that are implemented by default in the Hadoop Distributed File System (HDFS). With this model, several simulation were realized to examine the behavior of the system in a Cluster of Workstation, where the number of computers powered-on at a given hour and the idle time were generated by the Binomial and Uniform random distribution functions, respectively. The simulation results show that a critical constraint related with the acceptance or rejection of the pipeline returned by the *NameNode*, which works well in a cluster of dedicated machines, has to be relaxed to achieve a high (over 95%) percentage of satisfactory responses for the requests of writing and reading files in a Non-Dedicated Distributed Environment with chaotic conditions of workstation availability. It seems also that the data blocks have to be replicated eleven times to get a good quality service in the modeled system.

References

1. Bolosky, W.J., Douceur, J.R., Ely, D., Theimer, M.: Feasibility of a serverless distributed file system deployed on an existing set of desktop pcs. SIGMETRICS Perform. Eval. Rev. 28(1), 34–43 (2000)

2. Anderson, D.P., Fedak, G.: The computational and storage potential of volunteer computing. In: Proceedings of the Sixth IEEE International Symposium on Cluster Computing and the Grid. CCGRID 2006, pp. 73–80. IEEE Computer Society, Washington, DC (2006)

3. Levy, E., Silberschatz, A.: Distributed file systems: concepts and examples. ACM Comput. Surv. 22(4), 321–374 (1990)

4. Thanh, T., Mohan, S., Choi, E., Kim, S., Kim, P.: A taxonomy and survey on distributed file systems. In: Fourth International Conference on Networked Computing and Advanced Information Management, NCM 2008, vol. 1, pp. 144–149 (2008)

5. Bai, S., Wu, K.: The performance study on several distributed file systems. In: 2011 International Conference on Cyber-Enabled Distributed Computing and Knowledge Discovery (CyberC), pp. 226–229 (2011)

6. Shvachko, K., Kuang, H., Radia, S., Chansler, R.: The hadoop distributed file system. In: 2010 IEEE 26th Symposium on Mass Storage Systems and Technologies (MSST), pp. 1–10 (2010)

7. Borthakur, D., Gray, J., Sarma, J.S., Muthukkaruppan, K., Spiegelberg, N., Kuang, H., Ranganathan, K., Molkov, D., Menon, A., Rash, S., Schmidt, R., Aiyer, A.: Apache hadoop goes realtime at facebook. In: Proceedings of the 2011 ACM SIGMOD International Conference on Management of data. SIGMOD 2011, pp. 1071–1080. ACM, New York (2011)

8. Novaes, R.C., Roisenberg, P., Scheer, R., Northfleet, C., Jornada, J.H., Cirne, W.: Non-dedicated distributed environment: A solution for safe and continuous exploitation of idle cycles. In: Proceedings of the Workshop on Adaptive Grid Middleware, pp. 107–115 (2003)

9. Jensen, K.: An introduction to the practical use of coloured petri nets. In: Reisig, W., Rozenberg, G. (eds.) APN 1998. LNCS, vol. 1492, pp. 237–292. Springer, Heidelberg (1998)

10. Kristensen, L.M., Christensen, S., Jensen, K.: The practitioner's guide to coloured petri nets. International Journal on Software Tools for Technology Transfer 2, 98–132 (1998)

11. Jensen, K.: An introduction to the theoretical aspects of coloured petri nets. In: de Bakker, J.W., de Roever, W.-P., Rozenberg, G. (eds.) REX 1993. LNCS, vol. 803, pp. 230–272. Springer, Heidelberg (1994)

12. Vinter Ratzer, A., Wells, L., Lassen, H.M., Laursen, M., Qvortrup, J.F., Stissing, M.S., Westergaard, M., Christensen, S., Jensen, K.: CPN tools for editing, simulating, and analysing coloured petri nets. In: van der Aalst, W.M.P., Best, E. (eds.) ICATPN 2003. LNCS, vol. 2679, pp. 450–462. Springer, Heidelberg (2003)

13. Jensen, K., Kristensen, L.M., Wells, L.: Coloured petri nets and cpn tools for modelling and validation of concurrent systems. International Journal on Software Tools for Technology Transfer. 2007 (2007)

14. Wells, L.: Performance analysis using cpn tools (2006)

15. Borthakur, D.: The Hadoop Distributed File System: Architecture and Design. The Apache Software Foundation (2007)

Analysis of Twitter Data Using a Multiple-level Clustering Strategy

Elena Baralis, Tania Cerquitelli, Silvia Chiusano,
Luigi Grimaudo, and Xin Xiao

Dipartimento di Automatica e Informatica Politecnico di Torino - Torino, Italy
{elena.baralis,tania.cerquitelli,silvia.chiusano,
luigi.grimaudo,xin.xiao}@polito.it

Abstract. Twitter, currently the leading microblogging social network, has attracted a great body of research works. This paper proposes a data analysis framework to discover groups of similar twitter messages posted on a given event. By analyzing these groups, user emotions or thoughts that seem to be associated with specific events can be extracted, as well as aspects characterizing events according to user perception. To deal with the inherent sparseness of micro-messages, the proposed approach relies on a multiple-level strategy that allows clustering text data with a variable distribution. Clusters are then characterized through the most representative words appearing in their messages, and association rules are used to highlight correlations among these words. To measure the relevance of specific words for a given event, text data has been represented in the Vector Space Model using the TF-IDF weighting score. As a case study, two real Twitter datasets have been analysed.

Keywords: clustering algorithms, association rules, social networks, tweets.

1 Introduction

Recently, social networks and online communities, such as Twitter and Facebook, have become a powerful source of knowledge being daily accessed by millions of people. A particular attention has been paid to the analysis of the User Generated Content (UGC) coming from Twitter, which is one of the most popular microblogging websites. Different approaches addressed the discovery of the most relevant user behaviors [1] or topic trends [2,3,4].

Twitter textual data (i.e., tweets) can be analysed to discover user thoughts associated with specific events, as well as aspects characterizing events according to user perception. Clustering techniques can provide a coherent summary of tweets, which can be used to provide summary insight into the overall content of the underlying corpus. Nevertheless clustering is a widely studied data mining problem in the text domain, clustering twitter messages imposes new challenges due to their inherent sparsness.

This paper proposes a data analysis framework to discover, in a data collection with a variable distribution, cohesive and well-separated groups of tweets. Our

A. Cuzzocrea and S. Maabout (Eds.): MEDI 2013, LNCS 8216, pp. 13–24, 2013.

framework exploits a multiple-level clustering strategy that iteratively focuses on disjoint dataset portions and locally identifies clusters. The density-based DBSCAN algorithm [5] has been adopted because it allows the identification of arbitrarily shaped clusters, is less susceptible to noise and outliers, and does not require the specification of the number of expected clusters in the data. To highlight the relevance of specific words for a given tweet or set of tweets, tweets have been represented in the Vector Space Model (VSM) [6] using the TF-IDF weighting score [6]. The cluster content has been compactly represented with the most representative words appearing in their tweets based on the TF-IDF weight. Association rules representing word correlations are also discovered to point out in a compact form the information characterizing each cluster. To our knowledge, this work is the first study addressing a jointly exploitation of a multiple-level clustering strategy with association rules for tweet analysis.

As a reference case study, the proposed framework has been applied to two real datasets retrieved from Twitter. The results showed that, starting from a tweet collection, the framework allows the identification of clusters containing similar messages posted on an event. The multiple-level strategy iterated for three levels compute clusters that progressively contain longer tweets describing the event through a more varied vocabulary, talking about some specific aspects of the event, or reporting user emotions associated with the event.

The paper is organized as follows. Section 2 presents a motivating example. Section 3 describes the proposed framework and describes its building blocks, while the results obtained for the two real datasets are discussed in Section 4. Finally, Section 5 analyses previous related work and Section 6 draws conclusions and future work.

2   Motivating Example

Tweets are short, user-generated, textual messages of at most 140 characters long and publicly visible by default. For each tweet a list of additional features (e.g., GPS coordinates, timestamp) on the context in which tweets have been posted is also available.

This paper focuses on the analysis of the textual part of Twitter data (i.e., on tweets) to provide summary insight into some specific aspects of an event or discover user thoughts associated with specific events. Clustering techniques are used to identify groups of similar tweets. Cluster analysis partitions objects into groups (clusters) so that objects within the same group are more similar to each other than those objects assigned to different groups [7]. Each cluster is then compactly described through the most representative words occurring in their tweets and the association rules modeling correlations among these words. Association rules [8] identify collections of itemsets (i.e., sets of words in the tweet analysis) that are statistically related in the underlying dataset. Association rules are usually represented in the form $X \rightarrow Y$, where X and Y are disjoint itemsets (i.e., disjoint conjunctions of words).

A simplified example of the textual part of two Twitter messages is shown in Figure 1. Both tweets regard the Paralympic Games that took place in London in year 2012. As described in Section 3.1, to suit the textual data to the subsequent data mining steps, tweets are preprocessed in the framework by removing links, stopwords, no-ascii chars, mentions, and replies.

Our proposed framework assigns the two example tweets to two different clusters, due to their quite unlike textual data. Both example tweets contain words as $\{paralympics, olympic, stadium\}$, overall describing the paralympics event. In addition, $\{fireworks, closingceremony\}$ and $\{amazing, athletics\}$ are the representative word sets for Tweets 1 and 2, respectively, reporting the specific subject of each message. The association rules $\{closingceremony \rightarrow fireworks\}$ and $\{amazing \rightarrow athletics\}$ model correlations among representative words in the two tweets. They allow us to point out in a compact form the representative information characterizing the two messages. While the first tweet talks about a specific event in the closing ceremony (i.e., the fireworks), the second one reports a positive opinion of people attending the event.

```
TWEET 1 - text: {Fireworks on! paralympics closingceremony at Olympic Stadium}
TWEET 2 - text: {go to Olympic Stadium for amazing athletics at Paralympics}
```

Fig. 1. Two simplified example tweets

3   The Proposed Multiple-level Clustering Framework

The proposed framework to analyse Twitter data is shown in Figure 2 and detailed in the following subsections.

The textual content of Twitter posts (i.e., the tweets) is retrieved through the Twitter Stream APIs (Application Programming Interfaces) and preprocessed to make it suitable for the subsequent mining steps. The multiple-level clustering approach is then applied to discover, in a dataset with a variable distribution, groups of tweets with a similar informative content. The DBSCAN algorithm has been exploited for the cluster analysis.

Clustering results are evaluated through the Silhouette [9] quality index, balancing both intra-cluster homogeneity and inter-cluster separation. To analyse tweets contained in the cluster set, each cluster has been characterized with the most representative words appearing in its tweets and the association rules modeling correlations among these words. We validated both the meaning and the importance of the information extracted from the tweet datasets with the support of news available on the web. This allows us to properly frame the context in which tweets were posted.

3.1   Twitter Data Collection and Preprocessing

Tweet content and their relative contextual data are retrieved through the Stream Application Programming Interfaces (APIs). Data is gathered by establishing and maintaining a continuous connection with the stream endpoint.

To suit the raw tweet textual to the following mining process, some preliminary data cleaning and processing steps have been applied. The textual message

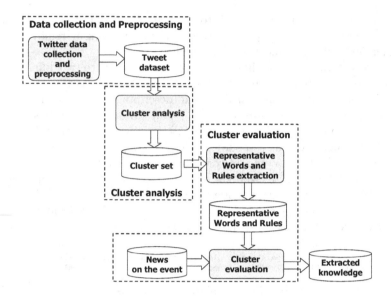

Fig. 2. The proposed multiple-level clustering framework for tweet analysis

content is first preprocessed by eliminating stopwords, numbers, links, non-ascii characters, mentions, and replies. Then, it is represented by means of the Bag-of-Word (BOW) representation [6].

Tweets are transformed using the Vector Space Model (VSM) [6]. Each tweet is a vector in the word space. Each vector element corresponds to a different word and is associated with a weight describing the word relevance for the tweet. The Term Frequency (TF) - Inverse Document Frequency (IDF) scheme [6] has been adopted to weight word frequency. This data representation allows highlighting the relevance of specific words for each tweet. It reduces the importance of common terms in the collection, ensuring that the matching of tweets is more influenced by discriminative words with relatively low frequency in the collection. In short-messages as tweets, the TF-IDF weighting score could actually boild down to a pure IDF due to the limited word frequency within each tweet. Nevertheless, we preserved the TF-IDF approach to consider also possible word repetitions.

The tweet collection is then partitioned based on trending topics, identified by analysing the most frequent hashtags. A dataset partition is analyzed as described in the following sections.

3.2 Cluster Analysis

Differently from other clustering methods, density-based algorithms can effectively discover clusters of arbitary shape and filter out outliers, thus increasing cluster homogeneity. Additionally, the number of expected clusters in the data is not required. Tweet datasets can include outliers as messages posted on some specific topics and clusters can be non-spherical shaped. Besides, the expected number of clusters can be hardly guessed a priori, because our aim is discovering groups of similar tweets through an explorative data analysis. For these reasons, the DBSCAN density-based method has been selected for tweet cluster analysis.

In the DBSCAN algorithm [5], clusters are identified as dense areas of data objects surrounded by an area of low density. Density is evaluated based on the user-specified parameters Eps and $MinPts$. A dense region in the data space is a n-dimensional sphere with radius Eps and containing at least $MinPts$ objects. DBSCAN iterates over the data objects in the collection by analyzing their neighborhood. It classifies objects as being (i) in the interior of a dense region (a core point), (ii) on the edge of a dense region (a border point), or (iii) in a sparsly occupied region (a noise or outlier point). Any two core points that are close enough (within a distance Eps of one another) are put in the same cluster. Any border point close enough to a core point is put in the same cluster as the core point. Outlier points (i.e., points far from any core point) are isolated.

One single execution of DBSCAN discovers dense groups of tweets according to one specific setting of the Eps and $MinPts$ parameters. Tweets in lower density areas are labeled as outliers and not assigned to any cluster. Hence, different parameter settings are needed to discover clusters in datasets with a variable data distribution as the one considered in this study.

In application domains where data collections have a variable distribution, clustering algorithms can be applied in a multiple-level fashion [10]. In this study we coupled a *multiple-level clustering* approach with association rule mining to discover representative clusters and the information characterizing them. Our approach iteratively applies the DBSCAN algorithm on different (disjoint) dataset portions. The whole original dataset is clustered at the first level. Then, at each subsequent level, tweets labeled as outliers in the previous level are re-clustered. The DBSCAN parameters Eps and $MinPts$ are properly set at each level by addressing the following issues. To discover representative clusters for the dataset, we aim at avoiding clusters including few tweets. In addition, to consider all different posted information, we aim at limiting the number of tweets labeled as outliers and thus unclustered.

The cosine similarity measure has been adopted to evaluate the similarity between tweets represented in the VSM model using the TF-IDF method. This measure has been often used to compare documents in text mining [6].

3.3 Cluster Evaluation

The discovered cluster set is evaluated using the Silhouette index [11]. Silhouette allows evaluating the appropriateness of the assignment of a data object to a cluster rather than to another by measuring both intra-cluster cohesion and inter-cluster separation.

The silhouette value for a cluster C is the average silhouette value on all its tweets. Negative silhouette values represent wrong tweet placements, while positive silhouette values a better tweet assignments. Clusters with silhouette values in the range [0.51,0.70] and [0.71,1] respectively show that a reasonable and a strong structure have been found [11]. The cosine similarity metric has been used for silhouette evaluation, since this measure was used to evaluate tweet similarity in the cluster analysis (see Section 3.2).

Each cluster has been characterized in terms of the words appearing in its tweets and the association rules modeling strong correlations among these words. News available on the web are used to properly frame the context in which tweets were posted and validate the extracted information. Specifically, the most representative words for each cluster are highlighted. These words are the relevant words for the cluster based on the TF-IDF weight. They occur with higher frequency in tweets in the cluster than in tweets contained in other clusters.

The quality of an association rule $X \to Y$, with X and Y disjoint itemsets (i.e., sets of words in this study), is usually measured by rule support and confidence. Rule support is the percentage of tweets containing both X and Y. Rule confidence is the percentage of tweets with X that also contain Y, and describes the strength of the implication. To rank the most interesting rules, we also used the lift index [7], which measures the (symmetric) correlation between sets X and Y. Lift values below 1 show a negative correlation between sets X and Y, while values above 1 indicate a positive correlation. The interest of rules having a lift value close to 1 may be marginal. In this work, to mine association rules representing strong word correlations, rules with high confidence value and lift grater than one have been selected.

4   First Experimental Validation

This section presents and discusses the preliminary results obtained when analysing two real collections of twitter messages with the proposed framework.

4.1   Datasets

We evaluated the usefulness and applicability of the proposed approach on two real datasets retrieved from Twitter (http://twitter.com). Our framework exploits a crawler to access the Twitter global stream efficiently. To generate the real Twitter datasets we monitored the public stream endpoint offered by the Twitter APIs over a 1-month time period and tracked a selection of keywords ranging over two different topics, i.e., Sport and Music. The crawler establishes and maintains a continuous connection with the stream endpoint to collect and store Twitter data.

For both Twitter data collections, we analyzed the most frequent hashtags to discover trending topics. Among them, we selected the following two reference datasets for our experimental evaluation: the *paralympics* and the *concert* datasets. The *paralympics* dataset contains tweets on the Paralympic Games that took place in London in year 2012. The *concert* dataset contains tweets on the Madonna's concert held in September 6, 2012, at the Yankee Stadium located at The Bronx in New York City. Madonna is an American singer-songwriter and this concert was part of the "Mdna 2012 World Tour". Tweets in each dataset are preprocessed as described in Section 3.1. Hashtags used for tweets selection have been removed from the corresponding dataset, because appearing in all its tweets.

The main characteristics of the two datasets are as follows. The paralympics dataset contains 1,696 tweets with average length 6.89. The concert dataset contains 2,960 tweets with average length 6.38. Datasets used in the experiments are available at [12].

4.2 Framework Configuration

In the proposed framework, the procedures for data transformation and cluster evaluation have been developed in the Java programming language. These procedures transform the tweet collection into the VSM representation using the TF-IDF scheme and compute the silhouette values for the cluster set provided by the cluster analysis. The DBSCAN [5] and FPGrowth [8] algorithms available in the RapidMiner toolkit [13] have been used for the cluster analysis and association rule extraction, respectively.

To select the number of iterations for the multiple-level clustering strategy and the DBSCAN parameters for each level, we addressed the following issues. We aim at avoiding clusters including few tweets, to discover representative clusters, and at limiting the number of unclustered tweets, to consider all posted information. For both datasets we adopted a three-level clustering approach, with each level focusing on a different dataset part. The Eps and $MinPts$ values at each iteration level for the two datasets are reported in Section 4.3.

To extract association rules representing strong correlations among words appearing in tweets contained in each cluster, we considered a minimum confidence threshould greater than or equal to 80%, lift greater than 1, and a minimum support threshold greater than or equal to 10%.

4.3 Analysis of the Clustering Results

Starting from a collection of Twitter data related to an event, the proposed framework allows the discovery of a set of clusters containing similar tweets. The multiple-level DBSCAN approach, iterated for three levels, computed clusters progressively containing longer tweets, that (i) describe the event through a more varied vocabulary, (ii) focus on some specific aspects of the event, or (ii) report user emotions and thoughts associated with the event.

First-level clusters contain tweets mainly describing general aspects of the event. Second-level clusters collect more diversified tweets that describe some specific aspects of the event or express user opinions about the event. Tweets become progressively longer and more focused in third-level clusters, indicating that some additionally specific aspects have been addressed. Since at each level clusters contain more specific messages, a lower number of tweets are contained in each cluster and the cluster size tends to reduce progressively. By further applying the DBSCAN algorithm on the subsequent levels, fragmented groups of tweets can be identified. Clusters show good cohesion and separation as they are characterized by high silhouette values. Both the meaning and the importance of the information extracted from the two datasets has been validated with the support of news on the event available on the web.

Cluster properties are discussed in detail in the following subsections. Tables 1 and 2 report, for each first- and second-level cluster in the two datasets, the number of tweets, the average tweet length, the silhouette value, and the most representative words. Representative association rules are also reported, pointing out in a compact form the discriminative information characterizing each cluster. Clusters are named as C_{i_j} in the tables, where j denotes the level of the multiple-level DBSCAN approach providing the cluster and i locally identifies the cluster at each level j.

Tweet Analysis in the Paralympics Dataset. First-level clusters can be partitioned into the following groups: clusters containing tweets that (i) post general information about the event (clusters C_{1_1} and C_{2_1}), (ii) regard a specific discipline (C_{3_1}) or team (C_{4_1} and C_{5_1}) among those involved in the event, (iii) report user emotions (C_{6_1}), and (iv) talk about the closing ceremony (C_{7_1}).

Specifically, clusters C_{1_1} and C_{2_1} mainly contains information about the event location (rule $\{london\} \rightarrow \{stadium, olympics\}$). Clusters C_{4_1} is about the Great Britain team taking part in the Paralympics event (rule $\{teamgb\} \rightarrow \{olympic\}$). Clusters C_{3_1} and C_{6_1} focus on the athletics discipline. While cluster C_{3_1} simply associates athletics with the Olympic event, users in cluster C_{6_1} express their appreciation on the athletics competitions they are attending (rule $\{athletics\} \rightarrow \{amazing, day\}$). Finally, tweets in cluster C_{7_1} talk about the seats of people attending the final ceremony (rule $\{closingceremony, stadium\} \rightarrow \{seats\}$).

Second-level clusters contain more diversified tweets. The following categories of clusters can be identified: clusters with tweets posting information on (i) specific events in the closing ceremony (clusters C_{1_2} and C_{2_2}), (ii) specific teams (cluster C_{3_2}) or competitions (cluster C_{4_2}) in Paralympics, and (iii) thoughts of people attending Paralympics (cluster C_{5_2}).

More in detail, cluster C_{1_2} focuses on the flame that was put out on the day of the closing celebration (rule $\{stadium, london\} \rightarrow \{flame, closingceremony\}$), while cluster C_{2_2} is on the fireworks that lit up London's Olympic stadium in the closing ceremony (rule $\{stadium, closingceremony\} \rightarrow \{fireworks\}$). Cluster C_{3_2} is about the Great Britain team taking part to athletics discipline (rule $\{teamgb, park\} \rightarrow \{athletics\}$). Tweets in cluster C_{4_2} address the final basketball competition in the North Greenwich Arena. They contain the information about the event location and the German women's team involved in the competition (rules $\{final\} \rightarrow \{north, germany\}$ and $\{final\} \rightarrow \{basketball, germany\}$). Tweets in cluster C_{5_2} show an enthusiastic feeling on Paralympics (rule $\{stadium, olympic\} \rightarrow \{london, fantasticfriday\}$) and the desire to share pictures on them (rule $\{pic, dreams\} \rightarrow \{stadium, time\}$).

Third-level clusters (with DBSCAN parameters $MinPts = 15$, $Eps = 0.65$) show a similar trend to second-level clusters. For example, clusters contain tweets on some specific aspects of the closing ceremony, as the participation of the ColdPlay band (rule $\{london\} \rightarrow \{coldplay, watching\}$), or tweets about a positive feeling on the Paralympics event (rules $\{love\} \rightarrow \{summer, olympics\}$ and $\{gorgeous\} \rightarrow \{day\}$). By stopping the multiple-level DBSCAN approach at this level, 808 tweets labeled as outliers remain unclustered, with respect to the initial collection of 1,696 tweets.

Tweet Analysis in the Concert Dataset.   Among first-level clusters, we can identify groups of tweets mainly posting information on the concert location (clusters C_{1_1}, C_{2_1}, and C_{3_1} with rule $\{concert, mdna\} \rightarrow \{yankee\}$). The remaining clusters talk about some aspects of the concert. For example, cluster C_{4_1} regards the opening act (rule $\{yankee, stadium\} \rightarrow \{opening, act\}$). Cluster C_{5_1} is on the participation of the Avicii singer (rule $\{wait\} \rightarrow \{yankee, avicii\}$), cluster C_{6_1} on the "forgive" writing on Madonna's back (rule $\{forgive\} \rightarrow \{stadium, nyc\}$), and cluster C_{7_1} is about the raining weather (rule $\{rain\} \rightarrow \{yankee, stadium\}$). Finally, cluster C_{8_1} regards people sharing concert pictures (rule $\{queen\} \rightarrow \{instagram\}$).

In second-level clusters, tweets focus on more specific aspects related to the concert. For example tweets in cluster C_{2_2} refer to Madonna with the "madge" nickname typically used by her fans (rule $\{singing\} \rightarrow \{stadium, madge\}$).

Similar to the paralympics dataset, also in the concert dataset third-level clusters (with DBSCAN parameter $Eps=0.77$ and $MinPts=23$) show a similar trend to second-level clusters. For example, clusters contain tweets regarding some particular songs. At this stage, 1660 tweets labeled as outliers remain unclustered, with respect to the initial collection of 2,960 tweets considered at the first level.

4.4   Performance Evaluation

Experiments were performed on a 2.66 GHz Intel(R) Core(TM)2 Quad PC with 8 GB main memory running linux (kernel 3.2.0). The run time of DBScan at the first, second, and third level is respectively 2 min 9 sec, 1 min 9 sec, and 48 sec for the paralympics dataset, and 4 min 4 sec, 1 min 53 sec, and 47 sec for the concert dataset. The run time progressively reduces because less tweets are considered at each subsequent level. The time for association rule extraction is about 24 sec for the cluster set at each level.

5   Related Work

The application of data mining techniques to discover relevant knowledge from the User Generated Content (UGC) of online communities and social networks has become an appealing research topic. Many research efforts have been devoted to improving the understanding of online resources [14,15], designing and building query engines that fruitfully exploit semantics in social networks [1,16], and identifying the emergent topics [17,18]. Research activity has been carried out to on Twitter data to discover hidden co-occurrences [19] and associations among Twitter UGC [2,3,4], and analyse Twitter UGC using clustering algorithms [20,21,22].

Table 1. First- and second-level clusters in the paralympics dataset (DBSCAN parameters $MinPts$=30, Eps=0.39 and $MinPts$=25, Eps=0.49 for first- and second-level iterations, respectively)

First-level clusters					
Cluster	Tweets	Avg Length	Avg Sil	Words	Association Rules
C_{1_1}	70	3	1	olympic, stadium	olympic→ stadium
C_{2_1}	30	7.33	0.773	olympics, london, stadium	london→ stadium, olympics
C_{3_1}	124	4.47	0.603	london, park, athletics, day	london, day→ athletics olympic→ park, athletics
C_{4_1}	30	6.67	0.710	heats, teamgb, olympic	teamgb→ olympic heats→ teamgb
C_{5_1}	30	5.67	0.806	mens, olympic, stadium	mens→ olympic
C_{6_1}	40	6	0.620	day, pic, amazing, athletics	athletics→ amazing, day day, pic→ stadium
C_{7_1}	36	5.72	0.804	closingceremony, seats, park, stadium	closingceremony, stadium→ seats olympic, park→ closingceremony
Second-level clusters					
Cluster	Tweets	Avg Length	Avg Sil	Words	Association Rules
C_{1_2}	90	5.67	0.398	flame, closingceremony, london, stadium	stadium,london→ flame,closingceremony
C_{2_2}	36	6.67	0.616	fireworks, closingceremony, hart, stadium	stadium,closingceremony→ fireworks fireworks, hart→ stadium
C_{3_2}	26	6.08	0.722	teamgb, athletics, park, olympic, london	teamgb, park→ olympic teamgb, park→ athletics olympic, park→ teamgb, london
C_{4_2}	34	9.65	0.502	greenwich, north, arena, basketball germany, final, womens	final→ north, germany final→ basketball, germany final→ womens, germany
C_{5_2}	40	6.5	0.670	fantasticfriday, dreams, time, pic olympic, london, stadium	pic, dreams→ stadium,time stadium,olympic→ london, fantasticfriday

Specifically, in [19] frequently co-occurring user-generated tags are extracted to discover social interests for users, while in [4] association rules are exploited to visualize relevant topics within a textual document collection. [3] discovers trend patterns in Twitter data to identify users who contribute towards the discussions on specific trends. The approach proposed in [2], instead, exploits generalized association rules for topic trend analysis. A parallel effort has been devoted to studying the emergent topics from Twitter UGC [17,18]. For example, in [18] bursty keywords (i.e., keywords that unexpectedly increase the appearance rate) are firstly identified. Then, they are clustered based on their co-occurrences.

Research works also addressed the Twitter data analysis using clustering techniques. [20] proposed to overcome the short-length tweet messages with an extended feature vector along with a semi-supervised clustering technique. The wikipedia search has been exploited to expand the feature set, while the bisecting k-Means has been used to analyze the training set. In [21], the Core-Topic-based Clustering (CTC) method has been proposed to extract topics and cluster tweets. Community detection in social networks using density-based clustering has been addressed in [22] using the density-based OPTICS clustering algorithm.

Unlike the above cited papers, our work jointly exploits a multiple-level clustering technique and association rules mining to compactly point out, in tweet collections with a variable distribution, the information posted on an event.

Table 2. First- and second- level clusters in the concert dataset (DBSCAN parameters $MinPts$=40, Eps=0.41 and $MinPts$=21, Eps=0.62 for the first- and second-level iterations, respectively)

First-level clusters					
Cluster	Tweets	Avg Length	Avg Sil	Words	Association Rules
C_{1_1}	148	5.05	0.817	concert, mdna, yankee, stadium	concert, yankee→ stadium concert, mdna→ yankee
C_{2_1}	340	4	1	bronx, yankee, stadium	yankee, stadium→ bronx
C_{3_1}	160	3	1	yankee, stadium	stadium→ yankee
C_{4_1}	40	6	0.950	opening, act, mdna, yankee, stadium	act→ opening yankee, stadium→ opening, act
C_{5_1}	60	6	0.779	avicii, wait, concert	wait→ yankee, avicii
C_{6_1}	84	6.19	0.794	forgive, nyc, mdna, stadium	forgive→ stadium, nyc
C_{7_1}	40	7	0.986	rain, yankee, stadium	rain→ yankee, stadium
C_{8_1}	40	6	0.751	queen, instagram, nyc	queen→ instagram
Second-level clusters					
Cluster	Tweets	Avg Length	Avg Sil	Words	Association Rules
C_{1_2}	60	6.67	0.523	raining, mdna, stop	raining→ mdna, stop
C_{2_2}	40	7	0.667	madge, dame, named, singing	singing→ stadium, madge madge, singing, named→ stadium, dame
C_{3_2}	44	7.64	0.535	surprise, brother, birthday, avicii, minute	yankee, stadium, surprise→ birthday
C_{4_2}	22	8.55	0.893	style, way, vip, row livingthedream	style→ vip, livingthedream

6   Conclusions and Future Work

This paper presents a framework for the analysis of Twitter data aimed at discovering, in a compact form, the information posted by users about an event as well as the user perception of the event. Our preliminar experimental evaluation performed on two real datasets shows the effectiveness of the approach in discovering interesting knowledge.

Other interesting future research directions to further improve the performance of our framework will be considering also the additional features (e.g., GPS coordinates) available in Twitter data. Furthermore, a real-time and distributed analysis of Twitter data can be addressed to support the analysis of huge data collection, also regarding parallel events.

References

1. Bender, M., Crecelius, T., Kacimi, M., Michel, S., Neumann, T., Parreira, J., Schenkel, R., Weikum, G.: Exploiting social relations for query expansion and result ranking. In: IEEE 24th Int. Conf. on Data Engineering Workshop, pp. 501–506 (2008)
2. Cagliero, L., Fiori, A.: Generalized association rule mining from Twitter. Intelligent Data Analysis 17(4) (2013)
3. Cheong, M., Lee, V.: Integrating web-based intelligence retrieval and decision-making from the twitter trends knowledge base. In: 2nd ACM Workshop on Social Web Search and Mining, pp. 1–8 (2009)
4. Lopes, A.A., Pinho, R., Paulovich, F.V., Minghim, R.: Visual text mining using association rules. Comput. Graph. 31(3), 316–326 (2007)

5. Ester, M., Kriegel, H.-P., Sander, J., Xu, X.: A density-based algorithm for discovering clusters in large spatial databases with noise. In: Knowledge Discovery and Data Mining (KDD), pp. 226–231 (1996)

6. Steinbach, M., Karypis, G., Kumar, V.: A comparison of document clustering techniques. In: KDD Workshop on Text Mining (2000)

7. Pang-Ning, T., Steinbach, M., Kumar, V.: Introduction to Data Mining. Addison-Wesley (2006)

8. Han, J., Pei, J., Yin, Y.: Mining frequent patterns without candidate generation. In: SIGMOD 2000, Dallas, TX (May 2000)

9. Rousseeuw, P.J.: Silhouettes: a graphical aid to the interpretation and validation of cluster analysis. Computational and Applied Mathematics, 53–65 (1987)

10. Antonelli, D., Baralis, E., Bruno, G., Cerquitelli, T., Chiusano, S., Mahoto, N.: Analysis of diabetic patients through their examination history. Expert Systems with Applications 40(11) (2013)

11. Kaufman, L., Rousseeuw, P.J.: Finding groups in data: An introduction to cluster analysis. Wiley (1990)

12. DBDMG (2013), http://dbdmg.polito.it/wordpress/research/analysis-of-twitter-data-using-a-multiple-level-clustering-strategy/

13. Rapid Miner Project, The Rapid Miner Project for Machine Learning (2013), http://rapid-i.com/ (last access on January 2013)

14. Li, X., Guo, L., Zhao, Y.: Tag-based social interest discovery. In: 17th Int. Conf. on World Wide Web, pp. 675–684 (2008)

15. Yin, Z., Li, R., Mei, Q., Han, J.: Exploring social tagging graph for web object classification. In: 15th ACM SIGKDD Int. Conf. on Knowledge Discovery and Data Mining, pp. 957–966 (2009)

16. Heymann, P., Ramage, D., Garcia-Molina, H.: Social tag prediction. In: 31st Int. ACM SIGIR Conf. on Research and Development in Information Retrieval, pp. 531–538 (2008)

17. Alvanaki, F., Michel, S., Ramamritham, K., Weikum, G.: See what's enblogue - real-time emergent topic identification in social media. In: 15th Int. Conf. on Extending Database Technology, pp. 336–347 (2012)

18. Mathioudakis, M., Koudas, N.: Twittermonitor: trend detection over the twitter stream. In: ACM Int. Conf. on Management of Data, pp. 1155–1158 (2010)

19. Li, X., Guo, L., Zhao, Y.E.: Tag-based social interest discovery. In: 17th Int. Conf. on World Wide Web, pp. 675–684 (2008)

20. Chen, Q., Shipper, T., Khan, L.: Tweets mining using wikipedia and impurity cluster measurement. In: Int. Conf. Intelligence and Security Informatics, pp. 141–143 (2010)

21. Kim, S., Jeon, S., Kim, J., Park, Y.-H.: Finding core topics: Topic extraction with clustering on tweet. In: IEEE Int. Conf. on Cloud and Green Computing, pp. 777–782 (2012)

22. Subramani, K., Velkov, A., Ntoutsi, I., Kroger, P.: Density-based community detection in social networks. In: IEEE Int. Conf. on Internet Multimedia Systems Architecture and Application, pp. 1–8 (2011)

Persistent Meta-Modeling Systems as Heterogeneous Model Repositories

Youness Bazhar[1], Yassine Ouhammou[1], Yamine Aït-Ameur[2],
Emmanuel Grolleau[1], and Stéphane Jean[1]

[1] LIAS/ISAE-ENSMA and University of Poitiers, Futuroscope, France
{bazhary,ouhammoy,grolleau,jean}@ensma.fr
[2] IRIT/INP-ENSEEIHT, Toulouse, France
yamine@enseeiht.fr

Abstract. Model persistence has always been one of the major interests of the model-driven development community. In this context, Persistent Meta-Modeling Systems (PMMS) have been proposed as database environments dedicated to meta-modeling and model management. Yet, if existing PMMS store meta-models, models and instances, they provide mechanisms that are sometimes insufficient to accomplish some advanced model management tasks like model transformation or model analysis. In this paper we validate the work achieved in [5] by exploiting the support of user-defined operations in PMMS in order to perform model transformations and model analysis.

Keywords: meta-modeling, model management, database.

1 Introduction

Recently, the use of model-based engineering technologies and modeling tools has widely increased especially in industrial contexts. This generates very often, in case of an excessive use, large scale models which raise the issue of scalability as one of the major weaknesses of applying modeling in real industrial contexts. Moreover, industries need also to share and exchange voluminous models and data, and a simple file exchange may sometimes be insufficient. These issues are industrial and scientific challenges and consequently, we need platforms to (i) overcome issues of scalability, (ii) surmount problems related to the heterogeneity of models, and (iii) provide a common repository for model sharing. Thus, Persistent Meta-Modeling Systems (PMMS) have been proposed as the leading solution that satisfy all these requirements. Indeed, a PMMS is a meta-modeling and model management system equipped with (1) a database that stores meta-models, models and instances, and (2) an associated exploitation language that possesses meta-modeling and model management capabilities. But, if existing PMMS support the definition and the storage of meta-models, models and instances, they provide mechanisms that are not adapted to accomplish some advanced model management tasks like model transformation, code generation, model analysis, etc. This is due to the lack of developed behavioral semantics

A. Cuzzocrea and S. Maabout (Eds.): MEDI 2013, LNCS 8216, pp. 25–37, 2013.

in PMMS since current PMMS offer mechanisms that are either specific to the database or to the domain the PMMS is dedicated to. Thus, in a recent work [5], we have proposed an extension of PMMS with the support of behavioral semantics with wide programming capabilities. Indeed, this proposition consists of introducing dynamically user-defined operations that can be implemented by web services and external programs written in any language (e.g., Java, C++). These operations can manipulate complex types (e.g., classes and meta-classes) as well as simple types (e.g., string, integer). This work has been validated with an application for handling derived ontologies concepts [6]. The contribution of this paper is to show how model transformations and model analysis can be achieved in PMMS using the approach presented in [5]. This application is prototyped with an implementation on the OntoDB/OntoQL PMMS [9].

The remainder of this paper is organized as follows. Section 2 introduces a motivating example that raises the need of operations in PMMS for model management. Section 3 gives an overview on the state of the art. Section 4 exposes the OntoDB/OntoQL PMMS on which our approach is based. Section 5 presents our approach for extending PMMS with the support of user-defined operations. Section 6 presents a model transformation and a model analysis case studies that show the usefulness of extending PMMS with operations. Finally, Section 7 is devoted to a conclusion.

2   A Motivating Example

This section presents an example of a real-time system that we use throughout this paper. The aim of this example is to design an uniprocessor system with three periodic tasks ($T1$, $T2$ and $T3$). Each task is characterized by a period P, a deadline D, and a worst-case execution time ET. The system scheduling follows the EDF (Earliest Deadline First) scheduling policy. This system is defined as a set of tasks: $S =< T1, T2, T3 >$, where:

$T1 =< P = 29ms, D = 29ms, ET = 7ms >$
$T2 =< P = 5ms, D = 5ms, ET = 1ms >$
$T3 =< P = 10ms, D = 10ms, ET = 2ms >$

This kind of systems can be designed using languages dedicated to design real-time and embedded systems like AADL [4] (see Figure 1) or MARTE [2]. Indeed, AADL (Architecture Analysis and Design Language) is an architecture description language dedicated to describe components and their hierarchical composition, while MARTE (Modeling and Analysis of Real Time and Embedded systems) is a modeling language dedicated to design both software and hardware aspects of real-time and embedded systems and supports schedulability analysis.

AADL and MARTE could express the system of our example using different constructors and following different methodologies. One of the major differences between these two languages is that AADL is more oriented towards architecture description and does not offer the capability to analyze the schedulability of systems, while MARTE meets this need. Here, we can already see the problem

```
system embsys                                          thread Task
end embsys;                                             end Task;
system implementation embsys.Impl                       thread implementation Task.Impl1
  subcomponents                                            properties
    cpu: processor cpu_embsys.Impl;                          Dispatch_Protocol => Periodic;
    proc: process process_embsys.Impl;                      Compute_Execution_Time => 7 Ms .. 7 Ms;
  properties                                                 Deadline => 29 Ms;
    Actual_Processor_Binding =>  reference cpu applies to proc;   Period => 29 Ms;
end embsys.Impl;                                        end Task.Impl1;
processor cpu_embsys                                    thread implementation Task.Impl2
end cpu_embsys;                                           properties
processor implementation cpu_embsys.Impl                    Dispatch_Protocol => Periodic;
  properties                                                Compute_Execution_Time => 1 Ms .. 1 Ms;
    Scheduling_Protocol => EDF;                             Deadline => 5 Ms;
end cpu_embsys.Impl;                                        Period => 5 Ms;
process process_embsys                                  end Task.Impl2;
end process_embsys;                                     thread implementation Task.Impl3
process implementation process_embsys.Impl                properties
  subcomponents                                             Dispatch_Protocol => Periodic;
    T1: thread Task.Impl1;                                  Compute_Execution_Time => 2 Ms .. 2 Ms;
    T2: thread Task.Impl2;                                  Deadline => 10 Ms;
    T3: thread Task.Impl3;                                  Period => 10 Ms;
end process_embsys.Impl;                                end Task.Impl3;
```

Fig. 1. The system S of our example expressed with AADL

of heterogeneous modeling that appears in the design of complex systems. Thus, analyzing an AADL model schedulability must go through a model transformation to MARTE.

Our objective is to be able to share the system of our example independently of the formalism used to express it. For this, the PMMS shall provide mechanisms to be able to transform AADL models to MARTE ones and vice versa. Moreover, we would like to be able to analyze the schedulability of our system regardless the formalism used to design it. Achieving these model management tasks require operators.

Next section presents existing PMMS and discusses their capabilities and limitations concerning behavioral semantics.

3   Related Work

In our study of the state of the art, we have classified model persistence systems into two types: model repositories and their exploitation languages that only serve to store and retrieve models, and database environments for meta-modeling and model management. This section presents and discusses these two model persistence systems.

3.1   Model Repositories and Their Exploitation Languages

Some meta-modeling systems are equipped with persistent repositories that are dedicated to store meta-models, models and instances [7]. These repositories use many back ends to store the different abstraction layers such as relational, NoSQL or XML databases. Main examples of these model repositories are dMOF [8], MDR [19], EMFStore [18] and Morsa [10]. These repositories store MOF

[1] and UML [3] models, and focus mainly, like in [11], on the architecture of the repository. As a consequence, they serve only as model warehouses in the sense that they do not offer a persistent environment for meta-modeling nor model management since all meta-modeling and model management tasks require loading models and instances from the repository and processing them in main memory.

Persistent model repositories are equipped with declarative query languages restricted only to querying capabilities. Main examples of model repositories query languages are mSQL [23], P-OQL [13], SQL/M [17], iRM/mSQL [22] and MQL [12]. These languages do not possess neither meta-modeling nor model management capabilities, and thus they remain high-level query languages only.

Persistent model repositories and their associated query languages do not offer persistent environments for meta-modeling and model management.

3.2   Persistent Model Management Systems

To manage models inside the database, several PMMS have been proposed like ConceptBase [15], Rondo [21], Clio [14] and OntoDB/OntoQL [9]. These PMMS handle the structural semantics of models by offering constructors of (meta-)classes, (meta-)attributes, etc. Yet, they provide hard-encoded mechanisms to express behavioral semantics such as predefined operators (like in Rondo and Clio), or use classic database procedural languages (e.g., PL/SQL) which cannot manipulate complex types (e.g., meta-classes or classes). The most advanced PMMS remain ConceptBase since it gives the possibility to introduce user-defined functions with external implementations. However, these implementations can only be done in the Prolog language. Besides external programs have to be stored in a special and internal file system, and requires restarting the server (cold start) in order to support the function newly introduced [16].

As the previous overview of the state of the art shows, current PMMS do not support the definition on the fly of model management operations that can be implemented using external programs and web services hence the necessity to extend PMMS with such capabilities.

Next section presents the OntoDB/OntoQL PMMS that we use to implement our approach.

4   The OntoDB/OntoQL Persistent Meta-Modeling System

OntoDB/OntoQL [9] is a four-layered persistent meta-modeling system where only the meta meta-model is hard-encoded (see Figure 2) so that we can extend on the fly the meta-model layer in order to integrate different meta-modeling formalisms (warm start). This system is equipped with the OntoDB model repository and the OntoQL exploitation language that we present in the next subsections.

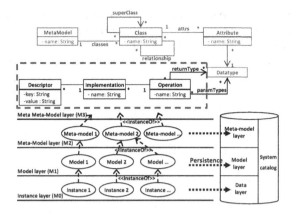

Fig. 2. The architecture of OntoDB/OntoQL

4.1   The OntoDB Model Repository

The OntoDB model repository architecture consists of four parts (Figure 2). The *system catalog* and *data layer* parts are the classical parts of traditional databases. The *system catalog* part contains tables used to manipulate the whole data stored in the the database, and the *data layer* part stores instances of models. The *meta-model layer* and *model layer* parts store respectively meta-models and models. Note that OntoDB respects the separation of the different storage layers and preserves the conformity of models and instances.

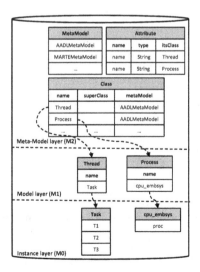

Fig. 3. Data representation in the OntoDB model repository

OntoDB stores data in relational tables since it is implemented on the Post-greSQL RDBMS. Figure 3 shows the representation of some concepts of our example. The meta-model layer contains three main tables: MetaModel, Class and Attribute that store respectively meta-models, classes and attributes. Each class is associated to a corresponding table at the model layer that stores class instances. Similarly, each concept at the model layer is associated to a corresponding table at the data layer to store instances.

4.2 The OntoQL Meta-Modeling Language

OntoQL has been defined in order to facilitate the exploitation of model repositories. OntoQL is a declarative and object-oriented language owning meta-modeling and querying capabilities. Indeed, OntoQL has been proposed to create and manipulate meta-models, models and data without any knowledge of the structure of tables and their relationships. One of the benefits of OntoQL is that it guarantees a large flexibility of expressiveness so that we can create meta-models and models on the fly. This subsection shows how we can create meta-models and models using OntoQL.

Meta-Model Definition. the meta-model part of the OntoDB model repository can be enriched to support new meta-models using the OntoQL language. Below we give some of the OntoQL statements for defining the AADL meta-model (Listing 1.1).

Listing 1.1. A subset of OntoQL statements for creating the AADL meta-model

```
CREATE ENTITY #Property (
    #name STRING,
    #value STRING);

CREATE ENTITY #ProcessSubComponent;

CREATE ENTITY #ThreadClassifier UNDER #ProcessSubComponent;

CREATE ENTITY #ThreadType UNDER #ThreadClassifier (
    #name STRING
    #extends REF (#ThreadType));

CREATE ENTITY #ThreadImpl UNDER #ThreadClassifier (
    #name STRING,
    #properties REF (#Property) ARRAY,
    #implements REF (#ThreadClassifier),
    #extends REF (#ThreadImpl));
```

Model Definition. once a meta-model is defined and supported by the OntoDB/OntoQL platform, we become able to create models conforming to that meta-model. Next statements create the AADL model of our example.

```
CREATE #ThreadType Task;

CREATE #ThreadImpl Task.Impl1
PROPERTIES (
```

```
            Dispatch_Protocol = Periodic ,
            Compute_Execution_Time = 7 Ms . . 7 Ms ,
            Deadline = 29Ms,
            Period = 29Ms)
IMPLEMENTS Task ;
```

OntoQL possesses also querying capabilities so that it makes possible to query the different layers. Moreover, OntoQL supports the other persistence basics (UPDATE and DELETE) for meta-models, models and instances.

Limitations of OntoDB/OntoQL. at this level, we only obtain an AADL model of our system. And if we need to derive the corresponding MARTE model of our system, this requires (1) storing the MARTE meta-model in OntoDB and (2) defining a model transformation from AADL to MARTE using operations. The first step is feasible as OntoDB/OntoQL supports the definition on the fly of meta-models and models. Yet, the second step cannot be accomplished since OntoDB/OntoQL does not support the definition of operations on meta-models and models elements. Moreover, OntoDB/OntoQL cannot allow us to analyze the schedulability of our system for the same reason. Indeed, we need an operator that computes the schedulability by invoking an analysis test. Thus, OntoDB/OntoQL has to be extended in order to overcome this limitation. Next section presents the extension of OntoDB/OntoQL to support behavioral semantics.

5 Extending Persistent Meta-Modeling Systems with Behavioral Semantics

In order to handle behavioral semantics in PMMS, we have extended the meta meta-model supported by the OntoDB/OntoQL PMMS with the concepts of *Operation*, *Implementation* and *Descriptor* as shown in the dotted box of Figure 2. They represent respectively a function or a procedure, its associated implementations and implementations descriptors. The extension of the OntoDB/OntoQL system took place in two main stages detailed in next subsections.

5.1 Extending the OntoDB Model Repository

The first stage concerns the extension of the meta meta-model layer at repository level with tables that store operations definitions, implementations and implementations descriptions. Figure 4 shows the main tables resulted from the extension of the meta meta-model layer of OntoDB. The Operation, Implementation and Descriptor tables store respectively operations signatures (the operation name, inputs and outputs), implementations and descriptions of these implementations.

5.2 Extending the OntoQL Meta-Modeling Language

The second stage of our PMMS extension consists in enriching the OntoQL language with the capability to create and exploit operations and implementations.

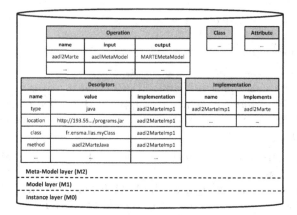

Fig. 4. The extension of the meta meta-model layer of OntoDB

OntoQL has been enhanced with CRUD (CREATE, READ, UPDATE and DELETE) basics permitting to create, read, delete and update operations and implementations. An example of the established OntoQL syntax is shown through the following statements.

```
CREATE OPERATION #rule1
INPUT  (REF (#SystemType),
        REF (#SystemImpl))
OUTPUT (REF (#saAnalysisContext),
        REF (#gaResourcesPlatform));

CREATE IMPLEMENTATION #rule1JavaImp
DESCRIPTORS (
    type = 'java',
    location = '193.55.../programs.jar',
    class = 'fr.ensma.lias.AadlToMarte',
    method = 'rule1Imp')
IMPLEMENTS #rule1;
```

The first statement creates an operation that has an AADL `System` and `SystemImpl` input, and a MARTE `saAnalysisContext` and `gaResourcesPlat-form` model output. The second statement defines an implementation of the operation previously defined by providing a set of meta-data of a remote Java program stored outside the database implementing this operation. This meta-data is exploited to run the remote program.

The other aspect of extending of the OntoDB/OntoQL PMMS was to set up mechanisms that make the mapping between data types of the OntoDB/On-toQL system, and data types of the external implementations. Thus, we have set up a behavior API (Application Programming Interface) that serves as an intermediate layer between the OntoDB/OntoQL world and the external world. In particular, it provides generic infrastructures to specify data types correspondences between the two worlds, and to execute remote programs and services.

6   Managing Models within PMMS

This section is devoted to show the usefulness, for model management, of extending PMMS with behavioral semantics. We firstly show how we can define transformation operations of AADL models to MARTE ones, and then we show how we can use operations for real-time models analysis.

Table 1. AADL to MARTE transformation rules

	AADL	**MARTE**
rule 1	`SystemType` and `SystemImpl`	`saAnalysisContext` and `gaResourcesPlatform` stereotypes
rule 2	`SystemClassifier` subcomponent	Specified by `Resources` tagged value of `gaResourcesPlatform`
rule 2.1	`ProcessType` and `ProcessImpl`	`MemoryPartition` and `Scheduler`
rule 2.2	`ProcessorType` and `ProcessorImpl`	`hwProcessor` stereotype
rule 2.3	`ProcessorImpl` properties `scheduling_protocol` property	Specified by the `schedPolicy` tagged value of `Scheduler` stereotype.
rule 2.3.1	`ProcessClassifier` subcomponent	`SchedulableResources` tagged value of `Scheduler` stereotype
rule 2.3.1.1	`ThreadType` and `ThreadImpl`	`swSchedulableResource` and `saStep`
rule 2.3.1.2	`ThreadImpl` properties: - `dispatch_protocol` and `period` - `deadline` - `compute_execution_time`	Tagged values of `swSchedulableResource` - Specified by `type` tagged value (a type of `ArrivalPattern`) In this case: tagged values of `saStep` - Specified by `deadline` tagged value - Specified by `execTime` tagged value
rule 2.4	`SystemImpl` properties - `actual_procesor_binding`	Specified by `processingUnits` tagged value of `Scheduler` stereotype

AADL to MARTE Transformation: while AADL is dedicated to design system architectures, MARTE is structured around two main concerns: one to model the features of real-time and embedded systems and the other to annotate application models in order to support analysis of system properties.

Table 1 summarizes the different concept mappings from AADL to MARTE. These transformation rules are introduced in order to justify the operations, we define later in the paper, for transforming AADL models to MARTE ones.

6.1   Using Operations for Model Transformation

We precise that our objective is not to propose a new transformation approach, neither to guarantee a safe transformation from AADL to MARTE. Several works have addressed the transformation form AADL to MARTE.

As it has been stressed before, our objective is to use the possibility to introduce operations on the fly in the OntoDB/OntoQL system in order to transform AADL models into MARTE ones. Indeed, we firstly create model transformation operations that will transform AADL concepts to MARTE ones, then we create corresponding implementations. These two steps are explained below in detail.

Definition of Transformation Operations: the definition of AADL to MARTE transformation operations consists of specifying for each operation its name, its eventual input and output types. The following statements define some of the essential transformation operations based on rules defined in Table 1.

Listing 1.2. AADL to MARTE transformation operations

```
CREATE OPERATION #rule1
INPUT (REF (#SystemType),          // AADL source elements
      REF (#SystemImpl))
OUTPUT (REF (#saAnalysisContext),  // MARTE target elements
      REF (#gaResourcesPlatform));

CREATE OPERATION #rule2
INPUT (REF (#SystemSubComponent) ARRAY)
OUTPUT (REF (#Resource) ARRAY);

CREATE OPERATION #rule2.1
INPUT (REF (#ProcessType),
      REF (#ProcessImpl))
OUTPUT (REF (#MemoryPartition),
      REF (#Scheduler));

CREATE OPERATION #rule2.2
INPUT (REF (#ProcessorType),
      REF (#ProcessorImpl))
OUTPUT (REF (#hwProcessor));
```

The `#rule1` operation transforms a `SystemType` and its associated `System-Impl` of an AADL model to their corresponding concepts in MARTE (`saAnalysisContext` and `gaResourcesPlatform`). The `#rule2` operation transforms `SystemClassifier` subcomponents of an AADL model to `Resouce` elements of the `gaResourcesPlatform`.

Definition of Implementations: once we have defined model transformation operations, we establish their associated implementations descriptions. The following statements define implementations descriptions of the operations previously defined.

```
CREATE IMPLEMENTATION #rule1JavaImp
DESCRIPTORS (
    type = 'java',
    location = '193.55.../programs.jar',
    class = 'fr.ensma.lias.AadlToMarte',
    method = 'rule1Imp')
IMPLEMENTS #rule1;


CREATE IMPLEMENTATION #rule2JavaImp
DESCRIPTORS (
    ...
    method = 'rule2Imp')
IMPLEMENTS #rule2;

CREATE IMPLEMENTATION #rule2.1JavaImp
DESCRIPTORS (
    ...
    method = 'rule2.1Imp')
IMPLEMENTS #rule2.1;
```

```
CREATE IMPLEMENTATION #rule2.1JavaImp
DESCRIPTORS (
    ...
    method = 'rule2.2Imp')
IMPLEMENTS #rule2.2;
```

Exploiting Defined Operations: after defining operations and their implementations descriptions, we become able to invoke the defined operations in order to transform AADL concepts to MARTE ones. For instance, we can use the established operations for obtaining our AADL source model expressed in the MARTE formalism. We can also transform the same model to a MARTE model in order to have two representations of our system.

```
CREATE #saAnalysisContext marte_embsys
AS SELECT #rule1 (embsys, embsys.Impl)
   FROM #SystemClassifier;

CREATE #gaResourcesPlatform marte_embsys
AS SELECT #rule1 (embsys, embsys.Impl)
   FROM #SystemClassifier;

CREATE #MemoryPartition marte_memory
AS SELECT #rule2.1 (proc_embsys, proc_embsys.Impl)
   FROM #ProcessClassifier;

CREATE #Scheduler marte_scheduler
AS SELECT #rule2.1 (proc_embsys, proc_embsys.Impl)
   FROM #ProcessClassifier;

CREATE #gaResourcesPlatform marte_embsys_cpu
AS SELECT #rule2(embsys_cpu) FROM #Processor;
```

The first statement selects the MARTE system resulted from the transformation of the AADL model of our example, while the second statement reads the resulted MARTE memory and scheduler concepts from the transformation of the **proc_embsys** process element of the AADL model of our system. Whereas, the last statement creates a **gaResourcesPlatform** instance from the resulting transformation of the **embsys_cpu** processor of the AADL model.

These are only examples of the multiple transformation operations and operation invocations we have written in order to permit a complete transformation and mapping from AADL to MARTE. This eases accessing, updating, deleting and transforming AADL models even if we do not adopt AADL as a main language for designing real-time and embedded system. We can also go further by setting up an operation that analyzes the schedulability of our AADL model that we detail in the next subsection.

6.2   Using Operations for Model Analysis

Once the MARTE model is obtained after this transformation, it becomes possible to trigger scheduler analysis on these MARTE models.

So, to analyze the schedulability of the system of our example, we define an operation whose objective is to analyze the schedulability of our system. To achieve this task, we create an operation **isSchedulable** that takes as input a MARTE model and returns as output a boolean value which states whether the systems is schedulable or not. This operation is implemented with a Java program that invokes the MAST analysis tool [20].

```
CREATE OPERATION #isSchedulable
INPUT (REF (#MARTEModel))
OUTPUT (BOOLEAN);

CREATE IMPLEMENTATION #isSchedulableJavaImp
DESCRIPTORS (
       type = 'Java',
       location = '193.55.../programs.jar',
       class = 'fr.ensma.lias.Analyzer',
       method = 'isSchedulerImp')
IMPLEMENTS #isSchedulable;
```

Now, it becomes possible to run the analysis by invoking the previous operation in the following statement.

```
SELECT #isSchedulable(#aadl2Marte(embsys.Impl)) FROM #SystemImpl
```

This statement asserts whether the embsys system, transformed from AADL to MARTE by the #aadl2Marte operation, is schedulable or not. Here, we analyze the schedulability of the corresponding MARTE model of our system. Note also that the invocation of the isSchedulable operation requires providing a MARTE model as input and thus, we provide an operation invocation as an argument of the #isSchedulable operation since OntoDB/OntoQL supports such manipulation. The previous statement invokes the isSchedulable analysis operation which is specific to MARTE, using an AADL resource hiding the transformation process to the user.

7   Conclusion and Perspectives

In this paper, we have validated our approach presented in [5] by using operations in PMMS for model transformation and model analysis. The use of operations enables particularly sharing models regardless of the language used to design them.

The work presented in this paper opens many perspectives. We expect to enhance our approach by integrating membership constraints so that operations can be defined only for a specific class like in object-oriented programming. Another perspective consists of defining an object constraint language to express static semantics in persistent meta-modeling systems by storing and evaluating the expression of invariants, contracts, and so on that can be associated to classes and operations.

References

1. Meta object facility (mof). Technical report, Object Management Group (August 2011)
2. Uml profile for marte : Modeling and analysis of real-time embedded systems. Technical report, Object Management Group (June 2011)
3. Unified modeling language (uml). Technical report, Object Management Group (August 2011)

4. Architecture analysis & design language (aadl). Technical report, SAE International (September 2012)
5. Bazhar, Y., Ameur, Y.A., Jean, S.: Bemore: a repository for handling models behaviors. In: SEKE (June 2013)
6. Bazhar, Y., Chakroun, C., Ameur, Y.A., Bellatreche, L., Jean, S.: Extending ontology-based databases with behavioral semantics. In: OTM Conferences, vol. 2, pp. 879–896 (2012)
7. Philip, A.: Bernstein and Umeshwar Dayal. An overview of repository technology. In: VLDB, pp. 705–713 (1994)
8. Cooperative Research Centre for Distributed Systems Technology (DSTC). dMOF version 1.1 user guide (2000)
9. Dehainsala, H., Pierra, G., Bellatreche, L.: OntoDB: An ontology-based database for data intensive applications. In: Kotagiri, R., Radha Krishna, P., Mohania, M., Nantajeewarawat, E. (eds.) DASFAA 2007. LNCS, vol. 4443, pp. 497–508. Springer, Heidelberg (2007)
10. Espinazo Pagán, J., Sánchez Cuadrado, J., García Molina, J.: Morsa: A scalable approach for persisting and accessing large models. In: Whittle, J., Clark, T., Kühne, T. (eds.) MODELS 2011. LNCS, vol. 6981, pp. 77–92. Springer, Heidelberg (2011)
11. Espinazo-Pagán, J., García-Molina, J.: A homogeneous repository for collaborative mde. In: Proceedings of the 1st International Workshop on Model Comparison in Practice, IWMCP 2010, pp. 56–65. ACM, New York (2010)
12. Hearnden, D., Raymond, K., Steel, J.: Mql: A powerful extension to ocl for mof queries. In: EDOC, pp. 264–277 (2003)
13. Henrich, A., Praktische Informatik Fachbereich Elektrotechnik: P-oql: an oql-oriented query language for pcte. In: Proc. 7th Conf. on Software Engineering Environments, pp. 48–60. IEEE Computer Society Press (1995)
14. Hernández, M.A., Miller, R.J., Haas, L.M.: Clio: A semi-automatic tool for schema mapping. In: SIGMOD Conference (2001)
15. Jarke, M., Jeusfeld, M.A., Nissen, H.W., Quix, C., Staudt, M.: Metamodelling with datalog and classes: ConceptBase at the age of 21. In: Norrie, M.C., Grossniklaus, M. (eds.) Object Databases. LNCS, vol. 5936, pp. 95–112. Springer, Heidelberg (2010)
16. Jeusfeld, M.A., Quix, C., Jarke, M.: ConceptBase .cc User Manual. Tilburg University, RWTH Aachen (February 2013)
17. Kelley, W., Gala, S., Kim, W., Reyes, T., Graham, B.: Schema architecture of the UniSQL/M multidatabase system. In: Modern Database Systems, pp. 621–648. ACM Press/Addison-Wesley Publishing Co., New York (1995)
18. Koegel, M., Helming, J.: Emfstore: A model repository for emf models. In: ICSE (2), pp. 307–308 (2010)
19. Matulla, M.: Netbeans Metadata Repository (2003)
20. Medina, J.L., Pasaje, J.L.M., Harbour, M.G., Drake, J.M.: Mast real-time view: A graphic uml tool for modeling object-oriented real-time systems. In: The 22nd IEEE Real-Time Systems Symposium (RTSS 2001), pp. 245–256 (2001)
21. Melnik, S., Rahm, E., Bernstein, P.A.: Rondo: A programming platform for generic model management. In: SIGMOD Conference (2003)
22. Petrov, I., Jablonski, S., Holze, M., Nemes, G., Schneider, M.: iRM: An OMG MOF based repository system with querying capabilities. In: Atzeni, P., Chu, W., Lu, H., Zhou, S., Ling, T.-W. (eds.) ER 2004. LNCS, vol. 3288, pp. 850–851. Springer, Heidelberg (2004)
23. Petrov, I., Nemes, G.: A query language for mof repository systems. In: OTM Conferences (1), pp. 354–373 (2008)

OLAP*: Effectively and Efficiently Supporting Parallel OLAP over Big Data

Alfredo Cuzzocrea[1], Rim Moussa[2], and Guandong Xu[3]

[1] ICAR-CNR & University of Calabria, Italy
cuzzocrea@si.deis.unical.it
[2] LaTICE Laboratory, University of Tunis, Tunisia
rim.moussa@esti.rnu.tn
[3] Advanced Analytics Institute, University of Technology, Sydney, Australia
guandong.xu@uts.edu.au

Abstract. In this paper, we investigate *solutions relying on data partitioning schemes for parallel building of OLAP data cubes*, suitable to novel *Big Data environments*, and we propose the framework *OLAP**, along with the associated benchmark *TPC-H*d*, a suitable transformation of the well-known data warehouse benchmark *TPC-H*. We demonstrate through performance measurements the efficiency of the proposed framework, developed on top of the ROLAP server Mondrian.

1 Introduction

Decision Support Systems (DSS) are designed to empower the user with the ability to make effective decisions regarding both the current and future activities of an organization. One of the most powerful and prominent technologies for knowledge discovery in DSS environments are *Business Intelligence* (BI) Suites and particularly *On-line Analytical Processing* (OLAP) [1] technologies. The BI market continues growing and information analysts embrace well OLAP concepts and technologies. Gartner's view [2] is that the market for BI platforms will remain one of the fastest growing software markets in most regions.

OLAP relies heavily upon a data model known as the *multidimensional databases* (MDB) [3]. Compared to relational databases, MDB increase performance by storing aggregated data and enhance data presentation. Indeed, MDB systems, offer the following three advantages:

- *Presentation*: MDB enhance data presentation and navigation by intuitive spread-sheet like views,
- *Ease of Maintenance*: MDB are very easy to maintain, because data is stored in the same way as it is viewed,
- *Performance*: MDB systems increase performance. Indeed, OLAP operations (e.g. slice, dice, drill down, roll up, and pivot) allow intuitively the analyst to navigate through the database and screen very fast for a particular subset of the data.

A. Cuzzocrea and S. Maabout (Eds.): MEDI 2013, LNCS 8216, pp. 38–49, 2013.

MDB schema contains a logical model, consisting of OLAP data cubes, where each data cube is a set of data organized and summarized into a multidimensional structure defined by facts, measures and dimensions. Building the data cube can be a massive computational task. Indeed, data warehouses tend to be extremely large. Also, the workload is composed of *business questions* (queries), which tend to be complex and ad-hoc, and do often require computationally expensive operations such as star joins, grouping and aggregation. There are also, hurdles commonly known as the *four V-dimensions*, respectively for *Volume*, *Velocity*, *Variety*, and *Variability*. Given this, we are interested in developing strategies for improving query processing in data warehouses by exploring the applicability of parallel processing techniques.

Dealing with huge data sets, most OLAP systems are I/O-bound and CPU-bound. First, this is due to hard drives I/O performances, which do not evolve as fast as storage, computing hardware (*Moore Law*) and network hardware (*Gilder Law*). Second, OLAP systems require high computing capacities. Since the 80's with RAID systems, both practitioners and experts admitted that the more we divide disk I/O across disk drives, the more storage systems outperform. In order to achieve high performance and large capacity, database systems and distributed file systems rely upon data partitioning, parallel processing and parallel I/Os. Besides high capacity and complex query performance requirements, these applications require scalability of both data and workload. It is well approved that the *Shared-Nothing architecture* [4], which features independent processors interconnected via high-speed networks, is most suited for requirements of scalability of both data and workload. Other architectures do not scale due to contention for the shared memory. Following these considerations, in this paper, we investigate *solutions relying on data partitioning schemes for parallel building of OLAP data cubes*, and we propose the framework *OLAP**, suitable to novel *Big Data environments* [5–7], along with the associated benchmark *TPC-H*d*, an appropriate transformation of the well-known data warehouse benchmark TPC-H [8]. We demonstrate through performance measurements the efficiency of the proposed framework, developed on top of the *ROLAP server Mondrian* [9].

The paper is organized as follows. In Section 2, we overview related work we highlight contributions of our research. In Section 3, we provide some theoretical results in the context of *data warehouse fragmentation* (e.g., [10–12]) for supporting optimal building of OLAP data cubes these principles are the basis of the proposed *OLAP** framework. In Section 4, we provide principles and architecture of our proposed framework OLAP* and the associated *TPC-H*d* benchmark. In Section 5, we provide experimental results and analysis of our framework. Finally, we conclude the paper and present novel research perspectives.

2 Related Work

Within the OLAP context and multidimensional views of massive data sets, building the data cube can be a massive computational task. Next, we first overview related work, with a particular interest on key design features of the data partitioning schemes of data warehouses and implementations of OLAP middlewares.

2.1   Physical Design Techniques of Distributed Data Warehouses

Data partitioning aims at minimizing (i) the cost of execution time of the OLAP workload through enabling *intra-query parallelism* and *inter-query parallelism*. We recall that *inter-query parallelism* consists in simultaneously processing different queries in distinct nodes, and *intra-query parallelism* is obtained when multiple nodes process the same query at the same time; (ii) the cost of maintenance of the data warehouse through targeted and parallel refresh operations; and (iii) the cost of ownership of a data warehouse through the use of commodity hardware with a shared-nothing architecture rather than expensive server architectures. Hereafter, we overview partitioning schemes,

First type of partitioning scheme is based on a *fully replicated Data Warehouse*, where the data warehouse is replicated on a database cluster. Load balancing of the workload among nodes enables inter-query parallelism, and consequently decreases the delay required to process a query. This schema does not reduce the time to execute the query. In order to enable intra-query parallelism, Akal et al. propose *Simple Virtual Partitioning* (SVP) [13]. SVP consists in fully replicating a database over a set of nodes, and breaking each query in sub-queries by adding predicates. Each node receives a sub-query and consequently processes a different subset of data items, such that each subset is called a virtual partition. Notice that SVP assumes that the DBMS embeds an efficient query optimizer. Otherwise, a sub-query execution time will be comparable to the query execution time. Besides, the DBMS robustness, SVP efficiency relies on a partitioning attribute producing equal sizes virtual partitions. For fully replicated data warehouses, Lima et al. propose A*daptive Virtual Partitioning* (AVP) [14], where the query optimizer is responsible for the best virtual partition size set-up.

Second type of partitioning schemes, performs primary horizontal partitioning of the fact table and replicates all dimensions [15].

Third type of partitioning schemes proposes derived horizontal partitioning (DHP) of the fact table along selected dimension tables. Consequently, a new issue emerges which is the choice of the dimension tables. The problem is denoted as the *referential horizontal partitioning problem*, and proved NP-hard [16]. Hereafter, we present heuristics used for the selection of dimension tables.

- A simple solution for select a dimension table to referential partition the fact table, is to choose the biggest dimension table. This selection is based on the following motivations: First, joins are expensive operations, particularly when the relations involved are substantially larger than main memory. Consequently, DHP of the fact table along the biggest table will reduce the cost of joining these two relations. Second, the fragmentation of the biggest dimension table will save storage costs.
- The second solution is to choose the most frequently used dimension table(s). The frequency of a dimension table is calculated by counting its appearance

in the workload. This selection is based on reducing the time to join the most frequent dimension table to the fact table.

- The third solution is to choose the dimension table having the minimal share with the fact table [16]. An OLAP workload is composed of star-join queries, which feature multiple and sequential joins (resulting into right or left -deep execution trees) to the fact table and implies finding out a cost of effective order for joining dimension tables to the fact table. As in join ordering problem [17], the best choice of dimension table should reduce the size of intermediate results of the most important join star queries. Based on this analysis, the solution consists in perform referential partition the fact table reducing the size of intermediate results.

Fourth type of data warehouse partitioning is based on range and list-partitioning of the fact table along attributes belonging to hierarchy levels of the dimension tables. Stohr et al. [18] propose *multidimensional hierarchical fragmentation* called MDHF for partitioning the fact table. MDHF allows choosing multiple fragmentation attributes from different hierarchy levels of the dimension tables, with each fragmentation attribute refers to a different dimension.

2.2   Middleware for Distributed OLAP Workload Processing

In this Section, we overview state-of-the-art middlewares for distributed OLAP workload processing.

PowerDB (2000) Röhm et al. [15] evaluated TPC-R benchmark in a database cluster. They compare the execution of OLAP queries in a fully replicated database system to a hybrid one combining partial replication with partitioning. Their partitioning scheme consists in partitioning the biggest table *LineItem* and in replicating all other tables. The system architecture is 3-tier, clients, DBMSs and a coordinator. The coordinator is responsible for processing TPC-R SQL workload.

cgmOLAP (2006) Chen et al. [19] claim that *cgmOLAP* is the first fully functional parallel OLAP system able to build data cubes at a rate of more than 1 Terabyte per hour. The *cgmOLAP* system consists of an application interface, a parallel query engine, a parallel cube materialization engine, metadata and cost model repositories, and shared server components that provide uniform management of I/O, memory, communications, and disk resources.

ParGRES(2008) Paes et al. [20] implemented *ParGRES middleware*. The main features of *ParGRES* are: automatic parsing of SQL queries to allow for intra-query parallel execution; query processing with inter- and intra-query parallelism; virtual dynamic partition definition; result composition; update processing; and dynamic load balancing.

SmaQSS DBC middleware(2009) Lima et al. [21] propose distributed database design alternatives which combine physical/virtual partitioning with partial replication. They adopt partial replication of data partitions using *Chained Declustering*. Finally, they assessed their partitioning schemes with the implementation of a prototype system *SmaQSS DBC middleware* (Smashing Queries while Shrinking disk Space on a DataBase Cluster) and using data of TPC-H benchmark, as well as a subset of the workload of TPC-H Benchmark, namely Q1, Q4-Q6, Q12, Q14, Q18 and Q21.

2.3   Contribution of this Work

Significant research has been published on physical design of distributed data warehouses and distributed OLAP workload processing. However, no research work reported and released a middleware handling a truly OLAP workload with distributed cube building using the most prominent TPC-H benchmark. Our current research investigates opportunities for high performance data cube computation, with a particular emphasis upon contemporary shared-nothing relational database environments. In this paper, an innovative parallel framework for the computation of a data cube, *OLAP**, is presented, along with its experimental evaluation on the benchmark *TCP-H*d*. The associated parallel query engine uses the standardized multidimensional query language MDX (*Multi-Dimensional eXpressions*) [22].

3   Data Warehouse Fragmentation Theoretical Results for Supporting Optimal Building of OLAP Data Cubes

In this Section, we provide some theoretical results in the context of data warehouse fragmentation for supporting optimal building of OLAP data cubes. These principles are the basis of the proposed OLAP* framework. We consider a data warehouse schema, with one fact table F and n dimension tables $(D_1, D_2, \ldots, D_n)$, such that (i) each fact joins to one and only one dimension member, and a single dimension member can be associated with multiple facts and (ii) each fact references the n dimensions. We define SF as the scale factor of the data warehouse. We assume that the size of F is $\alpha \times SF$ Bytes and the size of each dimension D_i is either $\alpha_i \times SF$ Bytes (i.e., SF dependent) or α_i Bytes (i.e., SF independent). It is important to weigh the space/time trade-offs. These trade-offs are dependent on many parameters some of which are (1) number of dimensions, (2) sizes of dimensions, (3) cardinalities of dimensions' members and (4) degree of sparsity of the data cubes. Hereafter, we compare the storage (3.1) and multidimensional analysis (3.2) of four proposed schemas, namely, *Schema 1*, *Schema 2*, *Schema 3* and *Schema 4*, which are characterized as follows:

- *Schema 1*: the data warehouse is not fragmented and not replicated.
- *Schema 2*: the data warehouse is fully replicated over N nodes.
- *Schema 3*: the fact table F is fragmented along Primary Horizontal Partitioning (PHP) and all dimensions are fully replicated over N nodes.
- *Schema 4*: every dimension D_i which size is SF independent is fully replicated; a selected dimension table D_k is fragmented along primary horizontal partitioning (PHP), all tables in hierarchical relationship with D_k, including the fact table are fragmented using derived horizontal partitioning along D_k. Finally, other tables are replicated.

Table 1. Data Warehouse Volume for the four Schemas

	Volume
Schema 1	$\alpha \times SF + \sum \alpha_i \times SF + \sum \alpha_j \times SF$
Schema 2	$N \times (\alpha \times SF + \sum \alpha_i \times SF + \sum \alpha_j \times SF)$
Schema 3	$\alpha \times SF + N \times (\sum \alpha_i \times SF + \sum \alpha_j \times SF)$
Schema 4	$\alpha \times SF + N \times (\sum \alpha_i \times SF + \sum \alpha_j \times SF) - (N-1) \times (\sum \alpha_k \times SF)$

Table 2. Cube Characteristics at each Node

	Cube Size	Cube Density
Schema 1		$\dfrac{\beta \times SF}{\prod \alpha_i' \times SF \prod \alpha_j'}$
Schema 2	$\prod \alpha_i' \times SF \prod \alpha_j'$	
Schema 3		$\dfrac{\beta \times SF}{N \times \prod \alpha_i' \times SF \prod \alpha_j'}$
Schema 4	$\dfrac{\prod \alpha_i' \times SF \prod \alpha_j'}{N}$	$\dfrac{\beta \times SF}{\prod \alpha_i' \times SF \prod \alpha_j'}$

3.1 Storage Overhead Analysis

Table 1 summarizes the results of storage overhead analysis, for the four different schemas. Notice that *Schema 3* overhead in storage is less than the overhead for *Schema 4*. In general, every candidate schema maximizing the number of partitioned dimension tables will produce a smaller storage overhead.

3.2 Multidimensional Analysis

Table 2 summarizes the results of our multidimensional analysis, for the four different schemas. Hereafter, $\alpha' \times SF$ denotes the number of facts within F. Idem, α_i' denotes the number of rows within dimension D_i and α_j' denotes the number of rows within dimension D_j (being SF independent). The cube density is measured as the ratio of the actual cube data points to the product of the cardinalities of the dimension hierarchies. Below, we consider an OLAP data cube, built with one measure and from all dimension tables, such that it includes each dimension primary key table as a member and fragmented dimension tables are evenly distributed among all nodes. For an OLAP data cube, the cross product of dimensional members, form the intersections for measure data. But, in reality most of the intersections will not have data. This leads to density (inversely to sparsity). We assume that, for the OLAP data cube we consider (along with its dimensions), the number of non empty intersections depends on SF, and is equal to $\beta \times SF$. Notice that, Schema 3 produces OLAP data cubes more sparse than Schema 1, while Schema 4 produces OLAP data cubes N times smaller than Schema 1 and Schema 3, and might have same density than Schema 1.

4   The OLAP* Framework: Parallel OLAP over Big Data

Following the results deriving from the analysis provided in Section 4, in order to accomplish different requirements posed by these analysis, we designed and implemented a *middleware for parallel processing of OLAP queries*. Figure 1 depicts the logical architecture of OLAP*. Summarizing, this architecture is devoted to query routing and cubes post-processing and encompasses some emerging components like Mondrian (ROLAP server) and MySQL (Relational DBMS). It can be easily interfaced to other classical OLAP clients at the front-end side (e.g. JPivot), thanks to suitable APIs.

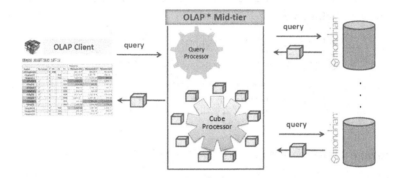

Fig. 1. OLAP* Middleware Logical Architecture

4.1   TPC-H*d Benchmark

In order to assess the effectiveness of our framework *OLAP** in comparison with the ones of other proposals, we designed an innovative benchmark targeted to multidimensional data, called *TPC-H*d* benchmark, which is inspired to the well-known TPC-H benchmark [8], the most prominent *decision support benchmark*. TPC-H benchmark consists of a suite of *business oriented complex ad-hoc queries* and *concurrent data modifications*. The workload and the data populating the database have been chosen to have broad industry-wide relevance. The workload is composed of 22 SQL queries with a high degree of complexity. Existing TPC-H implementation allows the generation of raw data stored into eight *TBL files*, namely *Region, Nation, Customer, Supplier, Part, PartSupp, Orders, LineItem*, by using a specific scale factor SF (1, 10, ..., 100000). The latter determines the final TPC-H data size (1GB, 10GB, ..., 100TB). Basically, *TPC-H*d* is a suitable transformation of the TPC-H benchmark into a multi-dimensional OLAP benchmark. Indeed, each business question of TPC-H workload is mapped into an OLAP cube, and a temporal dimension (Time table) is added to the data warehouse. Also, we translated the TPC-H SQL workload into an MDX workload.

Table 3. TPC-H*d Fragmentation Schema

Relation	Schema
Customer	PHPed along $c\_custkey$
Orders	DHPed along $o\_custkey$
LineItem	DHPed along $l\_orderkey$
PartSupp, Supplier, Part, Region, Nation, Time	Replicated

Table 3 shows the fragmentation schema of *TPC-H*d* relational data warehouse, where PHP stands for *Primary Horizontal Partitioning* and DHP stands for *Derived Horizontal Partitioning* (e.g., [18,21,23]), which both are well-known data warehouse partitioning strategies.

With respect to the partitioning scheme shown in Table 3, typical business queries of TPC-H [8] can be in turn partitioned into three different types of queries, and three corresponding different executions to handle. These query classes are the following:

- *Class 1*: as result of replication, business queries which involve only replicated tables are executed by any node.
- *Class 2*: business queries which involve only the partitioned tables are executed on one database node as result of partitioning.
- *Class 3*: business queries which involve both partitioned and replicated tables are executed on all database nodes. In this class, we distinguish two types of cubes' post-processing, namely:
  - *Sub-Class 3.1*: cubes built at edge servers have completely different dimension members, consequently the result cube is obtained by operating the *UNION ALL* of cubes built at edge servers;
  - *Sub-Class 3.2*: cubes built at edge servers present shared dimension members, consequently the result cube requires operating specific aggregate functions over measures, respectively sum over sum measures, sum over count measures, max over max measures, and so forth.

4.2 Experimental Assessment

Hereafter, we provide experimental results and analysis of our framework *OLAP** over our proposed benchmark *TPC-H*d* in comparison to the well-known ROLAP server Mondrian [9]. Mondrian is an open source ROLAP server of *Pentaho BI suite*, written in Java. It executes queries written in the MDX language, by reading data from a relational database (RDBMS), and presents the results in a multidimensional format (a.k.a. *pivot table*) via a Java API [24].

In our experimental framework, the client sends a stream of MDX queries in a random order to the database tier, and measures performance of MDX queries for two different workloads. The first workload stream is a *Query Workload*. It is composed of TPC-H queries translated into MDX, while the second

Table 4. Performance results of *OLAP* - MySQL/ Mondrian* with TPC-H*d benchmark for SF = 10: single DB backend vs. 4 MySQL DB backends

	MDX Workload (sec)			Parallel MDX Workload (sec)			Parallel+ MDX Workload (sec)		
	Query Workload	Cube-then-Query Workload		Query Workload	Cube-then-Query Workload		Query Workload	Cube-then-Query Workload	
		Cube	Query		Cube	Query		Cube	Query
Q1	2,147.33	2,778.49	0.29	485.73	862.77	0.19	1.10	1.32	0.25
Q2	1,598.54	2,346.92	1,565.51		985.07	1,896.03	n/a^{*1}	n/a^{*1}	-
Q3	n/a^{*1}	n/a^{*1}	-		n/a^{*2}	n/a^{*2}	n/a^{*2}	2,106.23	n/a^{*2}
Q4	1,657.60	7,956.45	5.33	523.67	1,657	1.54	0.06	0.07	0.05
Q5	54.53	3,200.64	0.46	12.96	1,219.19	0.19	0.12	0.99	0.06
Q6	282.11	371.80	0.53	72.58	131.70	0.37	0.42	0.77	0.37
Q7	260.23	617.20	0.06	36.01	195.24	0.06	0.08	0.95	0.06
Q8	50.63	2,071.00	4.61	13.38	716.10	2.70	0.07	3.83	0.23
Q9	n/a^{*1}	n/a^{*1}	-		n/a^{*1}	n/a^{*1}	n/a^{*2}	n/a^{*2}	-
Q10	7,100.24	n/a^{*2}		2,654.20	13,674.02	1,599.47	127.67	9545.68	5.16
Q11	2,558.21	3,020.27	1,604.10	535.75	990.75	505.2	587.99	875.33	497.67
Q12	456.81	735.67	123.43	223.6	467.9	45.7	0.06	0.13	0.06
Q13	n/a^{*2}	n/a^{*2}	-		n/a^{*2}	n/a^{*2}	0.08	0.16	0.05
Q14	391.06	946.16	0.06	112.41	356.8	0.05	0.06	0.13	0.05
Q15	13,005.27	32,064.90	12,413.74	2870.56	7,832.22	1,945.7	0.05	0.45	0.03
Q16	414.82	461.90	4.62	640.59	615.77	9.27	3.15	5.25	0.71
Q17	1,131.37	5,711.14	2.03	279.56	1,150.86	2.05	0.10	0.12	0.05
Q18	n/a^{*2}	n/a^{*1}	-	12,331.92	13,111.99	8,272.76	0.02	0.05	0.02
Q19	598.9	727.72	37.57	296.18	330.07	15.57	4.89	6.78	0.45
Q20	14,662.53	n/a^{*3}	-	11,842.90	n/a^{*5}	-	2909.71	n/a^{*6}	-
Q21	578.09	855.46	0.15	185.10	272.39	0.21	2.04	25.12	0.71
Q22	68.74	402.16	39.33	8.19	98.71	13.67	6.7	60.4	3.67

- n/a^{*1}: java.lang.OutOfMemoryError: GC overhead limit exceeded,
- n/a^{*2}: java.lang.OutOfMemoryError: Java heap space,
- n/a^{*3}: Mondrian Error:Size of CrossJoin result (200,052,100,026) exceeded limit (2,147,483,647),
- n/a^{*4}: Mondrian Error:Size of CrossJoin result (200,050,000,000) exceeded limit (2,147,483,647),
- n/a^{*5}: Mondrian Error:Size of CrossJoin result (199,940,270,958) exceeded limit (2,147,483,647),
- n/a^{*6}: Mondrian Error:Size of CrossJoin result (199,935,171,300) exceeded limit (2,147,483,647).

is a *Cube-then-Query Workload*. It is composed of TPC-H*d cubes MDX statements followed by queries MDX statements (denoted by $C_i - Q_i, C_j - Q_j, \ldots$). Second workload type should allow query result retrieval from built cubes and consequently, it is expected to lead to better performance results. Table 4 shows detailed performance results for scale factor equal to SF=10, comparing *TPC-H*d* workload performances of a single DB backend to a cluster composed of 4 DB backends. We also report performance results for N=4, with usage of derived data, namely,

- *Aggregate tables* for business questions Q1, Q3-Q8, Q12-Q20, and Q22. The corresponding OLAP cubes' sizes are scale factor independent or very sparse (e.g. C15 and C18).
- *Derived attributes* for business questions Q2, Q9-Q11 and Q21. The corresponding OLAP cubes' sizes are scale factor dependent. For these business questions, Aggregate tables tend to be very big.

The hardware system configuration used for performance measurements are Suno nodes located at Sophia site of GRID5000. Each node has 32 GB of memory, its CPUs are Intel Xeon E5520, 2.27 GHz, with 2 CPUs per node and 4 cores per CPU, and run Squeeze-x64-xen-1.3 Operating System. Response times are measured over three runs, and the variance is negligible.

Table 5. Derived Attributes Calculus for TPC-H*d with SF = 10: single DB backend vs. 4 MySQL DB backends

	Single DB (sec)	OLAP*, N = 4 (sec)
ps_isminimum	862.40	862.40
L_profit	4,377.51	1,288.31
o_sumlostrevenue	1,027.98	217.71
n_stockval	20.22	19.88
p_sumqty, p_countlines	1139,94	331.01
ps_excess_YYYY	18,195.48	1,461.99
s_nbrwaitingorders	299.15	71.24

Table 6. Aggregate tables building times for TPC-H*d with SF = 10: single DB backend vs. 4 MySQL DB backends

	Nbr of Rows	Data Volume	Single DB (sec)	OLAP*, N = 4 (sec)
agg_C1	129	16.62KB	343.91	71.63
agg_C3	2,210,908	103.32MB	173.45	39.52
agg_C4	135	5.22KB	138.45	32.92
agg_C5	4,375	586.33KB	822.29	198.6
agg_C6	1,680	84.67 KB	148.29	42.67
agg_C7	4,375	372.70KB	720.26	187.8
agg_C8	131,250	12.77MB	2894.38	818.82
agg_C12	49	3.15KB	186.68	43.94
agg_C13	721	26.33KB	9,819.46	2,272.45
agg_C14	84	6.33KB	367.88	146.76
agg_C15	28	3.84KB	10,904.00	852.84
agg_C16	187,495	10.03MB	63.05	62.26
agg_C17	1,000	45.92KB	3,180.26	435.52
agg_C18	624	37.56KB	905.16	212.32
agg_C19	854,209	80.65MB	88.57	26.10
agg_C22	25	1.73KB	6.25	1.15

Experiments show that,

– For some queries, cube building is not improving performances such Q2. The corresponding MDX statements include new members calculus (i.e., measures or named sets), or perform filtering on levels' properties. This constrains the system to build a new pivot table for the query,

– For SF=10, most cubes allow fast data retrieval after their deployment. Nevertheless, the system under test was unable to build cubes related to business questions: Q3, Q9, Q10, Q13, Q18 and Q20, either for memory leaks or systems constraints. Overall, for SF=10, improvements vary from 42.78% to 100%, for Q1, Q4-Q8, Q12-Q14, Q16-Q17, Q19 and Q21.

– *OLAP** demonstrates good performances for N=4. Indeed, except Q3 and Q9 for which, the system was unable to run MDX statements for memmory leaks, the rest of queries were improved through parallel cube building. Experimental results clearly confirm the benefits deriving from our proposed framework.

- Reponse times of business questions of both workloads, for which aggregate tables were built, namely Q1, Q3-Q8, Q12-Q20, and Q22, were improved. Indeed, most cubes are built in a fraction of a second, especially for those corresponding aggregate tables are small (refer to Table 6 for aggregate tables' sizes).
- The impact of derived attributes is mitigated. Performance results show good improvements for Q10 and Q21, and small impact on Q11. For Q2, the system under test was unable to build the cube using *ps_isminimum* derived attributes.
- The calculus of derived data, namely aggregate tables reported in Table 6 and derived attributes in Table 5 is improved, except for not fragmented tables.

5 Conclusions and Future Work

In this paper, we have proposed and experimental assessed *OLAP**, a novel framework for efficiently supporting parallel OLAP in modern data-intensive infrastructures, along with the associated benchmark *TPC-H*d*, a suitable transformation of the well-known data warehouse benchmark TPC-H. Experiments have clearly demonstrated the superiority of *OLAP** over Mondrian, a state-of-the-art ROLAP server. Future work is mainly oriented towards devising a novel version of *OLAP** capable of supporting the challenges posed by so-called big multidimensional data processing [7].

References

1. Gray, J., Chaudhuri, S., Bosworth, A., Layman, A., Reichart, D., Venkatrao, M., Pellow, F., Pirahesh, H.: Data cube: A relational aggregation operator generalizing group-by, cross-tab, and sub-totals. Data Min. Knowl. Discov. 1, 29–53 (1997)
2. Nicole, L.: Business intelligence software market continues to grow (2011), http://www.gartner.com/it/page.jsp?id=1553215
3. Vassiliadis, P.: Modeling multidimensional databases, cubes and cube operations. In: Proceedings of the 10th International Conference on Scientific and Statistical Database Management, SSDBM 1998, pp. 53–62. IEEE Computer Society (1998)
4. DeWitt, D.J., Madden, S., Stonebraker, M.: How to build a high-performance data warehouse (2005), http://db.lcs.mit.edu/madden/highperf.pdf
5. Agrawal, D., Das, S., El Abbadi, A.: Big data and cloud computing: current state and future opportunities. In: Proceedings of the 14th International Conference on Extending Database Technology, EDBT/ICDT 2011, pp. 530–533. ACM (2011)
6. Thusoo, A., Sarma, J.S., Jain, N., Shao, Z., Chakka, P., Zhang, N., Anthony, S., Liu, H., Murthy, R.: Hive - A petabyte scale data warehouse using hadoop. In: ICDE (2010)
7. Cuzzocrea, A., Song, I.Y., Davis, K.C.: Analytics over large-scale multidimensional data: the big data revolution! In: Proceedings of the ACM 14th International Workshop on Data Warehousing and OLAP, DOLAP 2011, pp. 101–104. ACM (2011)
8. Transaction Processing Council: TPC-H benchmark (2013), http://www.tpc.org/tpch

9. Pentaho: Mondrian ROLAP Server (2013), http://mondrian.pentaho.org/
10. Bellatreche, L., Cuzzocrea, A., Benkrid, S.: $\mathcal{F\&A}$: A methodology for effectively and efficiently designing parallel relational data warehouses on heterogenous database clusters. In: Bach Pedersen, T., Mohania, M.K., Tjoa, A.M. (eds.) DAWAK 2010. LNCS, vol. 6263, pp. 89–104. Springer, Heidelberg (2010)
11. Bellatreche, L., Benkrid, S., Ghazal, A., Crolotte, A., Cuzzocrea, A.: Verification of partitioning and allocation techniques on teradata DBMS. In: Xiang, Y., Cuzzocrea, A., Hobbs, M., Zhou, W. (eds.) ICA3PP 2011, Part I. LNCS, vol. 7016, pp. 158–169. Springer, Heidelberg (2011)
12. Bellatreche, L., Cuzzocrea, A., Benkrid, S.: Effectively and efficiently designing and querying parallel relational data warehouses on heterogeneous database clusters: The f&a approach. Journal of Database Management (JDM), 17–51 (2012)
13. Akal, F., Böhm, K., Schek, H.-J.: OLAP query evaluation in a database cluster: A performance study on intra-query parallelism. In: Manolopoulos, Y., Návrat, P. (eds.) ADBIS 2002. LNCS, vol. 2435, pp. 218–231. Springer, Heidelberg (2002)
14. Lima, A.A.B., Mattoso, M., Valduriez, P.: Adaptive virtual partitioning for olap query processing in a database cluster. JIDM 1, 75–88 (2010)
15. Röhm, U., Böhm, K., Schek, H.-J.: OLAP query routing and physical design in a database cluster. In: Zaniolo, C., Grust, T., Scholl, M.H., Lockemann, P.C. (eds.) EDBT 2000. LNCS, vol. 1777, pp. 254–268. Springer, Heidelberg (2000)
16. Bellatreche, L., Woameno, K.Y.: Dimension table driven approach to referential partition relational data warehouses. In: Proceedings of the ACM Twelfth International Workshop on Data Warehousing and OLAP, DOLAP 2009, pp. 9–16. ACM (2009)
17. Steinbrunn, M., Moerkotte, G., Kemper, A.: Heuristic and randomized optimization for the join ordering problem. The VLDB Journal 6, 191–208 (1997)
18. Stöhr, T., Martens, H., Rahm, E.: Multi-dimensional database allocation for parallel data warehouses. In: Proceedings of the 26th International Conference on Very Large Data Bases, VLDB 2000, pp. 273–284 (2000)
19. Chen, Y., Rau-Chaplin, A., Dehne, F., Eavis, T., Green, D., Sithirasenan, E.: cgmOLAP: Efficient parallel generation and querying of terabyte size rolap data cubes. In: Proceedings of the 22nd International Conference on Data Engineering, ICDE 2006, pp. 359–370 (2006)
20. Paes, M., Lima, A.A., Valduriez, P., Mattoso, M.: High-performance query processing of a real-world OLAP database with pargres. In: Palma, J.M.L.M., Amestoy, P.R., Daydé, M., Mattoso, M., Lopes, J.C. (eds.) VECPAR 2008. LNCS, vol. 5336, pp. 188–200. Springer, Heidelberg (2008)
21. Lima, A.A., Furtado, C., Valduriez, P., Mattoso, M.: Parallel OLAP query processing in database clusters with data replication. Distrib. Parallel Databases 25, 97–123 (2009)
22. Microsoft: Multi-dimensional expressions language (2013),
    http://msdn.microsoft.com/enus/library/aa216779(SQL.80).aspx
23. Stöhr, T., Rahm, E.: Warlock: A data allocation tool for parallel warehouses. In: Proceedings of the 27th International Conference on Very Large Data Bases, VLDB 2001, pp. 721–722 (2001)
24. JPivot: OLAP client (2013), http://jpivot.sourceforge.net/

Centrality Indices for Web Search Engine Results Understanding

Roberto De Virgilio

Dipartimento di Ingegneria
Università Roma Tre, Rome, Italy
dvr@dia.uniroma3.it

Abstract. Searching relevant information from Web may be a very te-
dious task. Usually Web search engines return search results in a global
ranking making it difficult to the users to browse in different topics or
subtopics that they query. If people cannot navigate through the Web
site, they will quickly leave. Thus, designing effective navigation strategies on Web sites is crucial. In this paper we provide and implement
centrality indices to guide the user for an effective navigation of Web
pages. Such indices support users gaining more relevant results to their
query and then group the search results into categories according to the
different meanings of this query. We get inspiration from well-know location family problems to compute the center of a graph: a joint use of
such indices guarantees the automatic selection of the best starting point
for each cluster. To validate our approach, we have developed a system
that implements the techniques described in this paper on top of an engine for keyword-based search over RDF data. Such system exploits an
interactive front-end to support the user in the visualization of both annotations and corresponding Web pages. Experiments over widely used
benchmarks have shown very good results.

1   Introduction

The original perception of the Web by the vast majority of its early users was as
a static repository of unstructured data. This was reasonable for browsing small
sets of information by humans, but this static model now breaks down as programs attempt to dynamically generate information, and as human browsing is
increasingly assisted by intelligent agent programs. With the size and availability
of data constantly increasing, a fundamental problem lies in the difficulty users
face to find and retrieve the information they are interested in [15]. To this aim,
search engines are an inestimable tool for retrieving information on the Web.
Users place queries as they insert keywords, and then the search engines return
a list of results ranked in order of relevance to these queries. However, a relevant
problem is that using a search engine probably the retrieved pages are not always what user is looking for. To give an example, let us consider Wikipedia and
type "`Kenneth Iverson Language`", i.e., we would retrieve information about
the developer of programming languages.

A. Cuzzocrea and S. Maabout (Eds.): MEDI 2013, LNCS 8216, pp. 50–64, 2013.

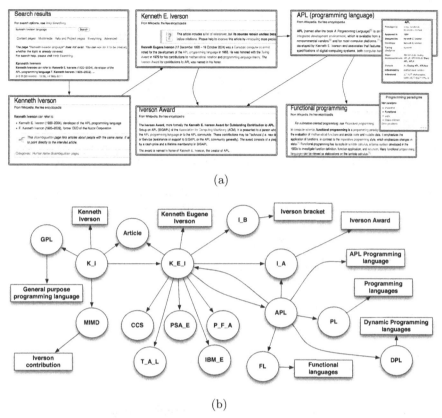

(a)

(b)

Fig. 1. (a) Searching *Kenneth Eugene Iverson*, developer of the *APL programming language*, and (b) Semantic Annotation of *Kenneth Iverson* wikipedia pages

As shown Fig. 1.(a), the user has to browse the list of all Kenneth Iverson, then manually to solve the disambiguation (i.e., selecting *Kenneth Eugene Iverson*) and finally to consume the information about development of APL programming language following the link in the Web page. Such task is time consuming and in case of a long chain of links to follow it could convince the user to quickly leave the Web site. Moreover, as discussed in [12], users frequently modify a previous search query in hope of retrieving better results. Most reformulation strategies result in some benefit to the user. The work in [12] proved that certain strategies like add/remove words, word substitution, acronym expansion and spelling correction are more likely to cause clicks, especially on higher ranked results. In [13] studying the Dogpile.com logs reported that 37% of search queries were reformulations when ignoring same queries. A study of Altavista logs [14] identified that 52% of users reformulated their queries. Therefore an organization of the results in topics or sub-topics could support the user to refine the search. To this aim Semantic Web helps encoding properties and relationships between objects represented by information stored on the Web. It envisions that authors of pages include semantic information along with human-readable Web content,

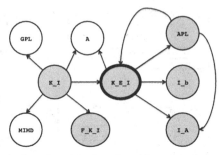

Fig. 2. Semantic Search engine result to "`Kenneth Iverson Language`"

perhaps with some machine assistance in the encoding. Referring to the example of Fig. 1.(a), we could annotate the corresponding Web pages with the following RDF triples

```
<rdf:Description rdf:about="wiki:Kenneth_Iverson">
 <rdf:type rdf:resource="wiki:Article"/>
 <wiki:redirectsTo rdf:resource="wiki:Kenneth_E._Iverson"/>
 <wiki:redirectsTo rdf:resource="wiki:F._Kenneth_Iverson"/>
       ...
</rdf:Description>

<rdf:Description rdf:about="wiki:Kenneth_E._Iverson">
 <rdf:type rdf:resource="wiki:Article"/>
 <wiki:internalLink rdf:resource="wiki:APL_programming_language"/>
 <wiki:internalLink rdf:resource="wiki:Iverson_Award"/>
 <wiki:internalLink rdf:resource="wiki:Iverson_bracket"/>
       ...
</rdf:Description>
```

Therefore we can build a possibly big RDF graph as depicted in Fig. 1.(b). Due to the huge amount of RDF data available on the Web (currently around 7 billion RDF triples and 150 million RDF links), keywords search based systems (e.g., [6]) are increasingly capturing the attention of researchers, implementing IR strategies on top of traditional database management systems with the goal of freeing the users from having to know data organization and query languages. The aim of such approaches is to query semantic annotations (in terms of RDF graphs [1]) instead of making a deep analysis of a large number of Web pages. The result is a set of RDF subgraphs linked to the Web pages of interest. For instance Fig. 2 shows a complete RDF subgraph matching the query "`Kenneth Iverson Language`". For the sake of simplicity, we used only initials of URIs and marked matching nodes in gray.

However most of the proposals do not analyze in depth how to exploit the resulting RDF annotation to navigate the pages of interest. The user manually has to analyze the RDF graph, selecting the starting node from which begins the navigation of the corresponding Web pages. Of course, in this situation semi-automatic tools would support the analysis but the risk is to guide the user to select a wrong starting point, so far from the most interesting Web pages. For instance looking at the RDF graph of Fig. 2, a semi-automatic tool could select K_I as starting point (i.e., it is the source of the graph): in this case we reconduct the user to the same situation of Fig. 1.(a). The best choice would be

K_E_I linking to the Web page of *Kenneth Eugene Iverson*. Due to the different interpretations of the query, a second issue is to provide solutions grouped in topics or subtopics. In this way the user can filter the semantics not of interest. To this aim a clustering Web search engine can be useful as they provide faster subtopic retrieval following the desired topic instead of browsing the whole list of the results. Usually for clustering web search results a two stage approach is followed: in the first step the retrieval is done based on a query and at the second step the clustering is performed. Usually, the clustering system groups the ranked results and gives the user the ability to choose the groups of interest in an interactive manner. Assuming that there is a logical topic structure in the result set, the output of a search results clustering algorithm is a set of labelled clusters representing it in various ways as flat partitions, hierarchies etc. For instance the query "Kenneth Iverson Language" matches two semantics: (i) the user would retrieve all information about Kenneth Iverson as language developer or (ii) information about Programming languages, with particular reference to the APL programming language of Kenneth Eugene iverson.

In this paper we provide and implement centrality indices to guide the user for an effective navigation of Web pages. In particular, we propose a clustering web search system by exploiting novel techniques and proposing the trade-off time for qualitatively better results. We get inspiration from well-know location family problems to compute the center of a graph; in particular we provide two kinds of centers: (i) *structural* centers to get able the user to reach all parts of the graph and (ii) *semantic* centers to get able the user to reach directly the parts of the graph matching the query. A joint use of such indices guarantees the automatic selection of the best starting point. Such indices support the clustering of results: solutions sharing the same centers expose the same semantics, therefore they could be grouped in the same cluster. To validate our approach, we have developed a system that implements the techniques described in this paper on top of an engine for keyword-based search over RDF data [4,6]. Such system exploits an interactive front-end to support the user in the visualization of both annotations and corresponding Web pages. Experiments over widely used benchmarks have shown very good results, in terms of both effectiveness and efficiency. The rest of the paper is organized as follows. In Section 2 we discuss the related research. In Section 3 we present our centrality indices. Finally Section 4 illustrates the experimental results, and in Section 5, we draw our conclusions and sketch future works.

2   Related Work

Clustering Web Search Engines. in the plethora of clustering web search engines, we can find a vast literature. carpineto et al. [5] survey different approaches in designing clustering web search engines, providing a taxonomy of different algorithms; all of these approaches are based on the analysis of web pages content, exploiting data-centric and description-centric methods to extract the most meaningful terms (i.e. matching the user query). in our approach we would exploit semantic annotations and reconduct the problem to facility location analysis, as follows.

Location Analysis. Facility location analysis deals with the problem of finding optimal locations for one or more facilities in a given environment. Location problems are classical optimization problems with many applications in industry and economy. The spatial location of facilities often take place in the context of a given transportation, communication, or transmission system, which may be represented as a network for analytic purposes. A first paradigm for location based on the minimization of transportation costs was introduced by Weber [23] in 1909. However, a significant progress was not made before 1960 when facility location emerged as a research field. There exist several ways to classify location problems. According to Hakimi [9] who considered two families of location problems we categorize them with respect to their objective function. The first family consists of those problems that use a minimax criterion. As an example, consider the problem of determining the location for an emergency facility such as a hospital. The main objective of such an emergency facility location problem is to find a site that minimizes the maximum response time between the facility and the site of a possible emergency. The second family of location problems considered by Hakimi optimizes a *minisum* criterion which is used in determining the location for a service facility like a shopping mall. The aim here is to minimize the total travel time. A third family of location problems described for example in [20] deals with the location of commercial facilities which operate in a competitive environment. The goal of a competitive location problem is to estimate the market share captured by each competing facility in order to optimize its location. Our focus here is not to treat all facility location problems. The interested reader is referred to a bibliography devoted to facility location analysis [7]. The aim of this paper is to introduce three important vertex centralities by examining location problems. Then we can introduce a fourth index based not only on "spatial" properties (such as the other centrality indices) but also on the semantics. The definition of different objectives leads to different centrality measures. A common feature, however, is that each objective function depends on the distance between the vertices of a graph. In the following we focus on G as connected directed graph with at least two vertices and we suppose that the distance $d(u, v)$ between two vertices u and v is defined as the length of the shortest path from u to v. These assumptions ensure that the following centrality indices are well defined. Moreover, for reasons of simplicity we consider G to be an unweighted graph, i.e., all edge weights are equal to one. Of course, all indices presented here can equally well be applied to weighted graphs.

3   Web Navigation

As said in the Introduction, user is supported by different approximate query processing methods to improve the search of information on the Web. In particular Semantic Web was introduced to annotate the semantics involved into a Web

---

Algorithm 1. Center computation by eccentricity

Input : The graph G
Output: The center c_E

1 $n \leftarrow V.length$;
2 $L_E \leftarrow \text{InitializeArray}(n)$;
3 $M \leftarrow \text{FloydWarshall}(G)$;
4 **for** $i \leftarrow 0$ **to** n **do**
5 $\quad \lfloor \quad L_E[i] \leftarrow \text{Max}(M[i])$;
6 $i_{min} \leftarrow \text{MinIndex}(L_E)$;
7 $c_E \leftarrow V[i_{min}]$;
8 **return** c_E;

---

page, making more automatic the interoperability between applications and machines and improving the effectiveness of the results. However a significant issue is to exploit the result (annotation) of the query processing to navigate the corresponding Web pages in an effective way. Formally, the result can be modeled as a labelled directed graph G. It is a six element tuple $G = \{V, E, \Sigma_V, \Sigma_E, L_G, \omega\}$ where V is a set of vertices and $E \subseteq V \times V$ is a set of ordered pairs of vertices, called edges. Σ_V and Σ_E are the sets of vertices and edge labels, respectively. The labelling function L_G defines the mappings $V \to \Sigma_V$ and $E \to \Sigma_E$, while the weight function ω assigns a (positive) score to each node by defining the mapping $V \to \mathbb{N}$. Then, centrality indices can be computed to quantify an intuitive feeling that in the result some vertices or edges are more central than others. Such indices can support the user to navigate directly the part of the result that best fits the query provided by the user.

3.1 Center Indices

In the following we get inspiration from well-know location family problems to compute the center of G.

Eccentricity. The aim of the first problem family is to determine a location that minimizes the maximum distance to any other location in the network. Suppose that a hospital is located at a vertex $u \in V$. We denote the maximum distance from u to a random vertex v in the network, representing a possible incident, as the eccentricity $e(u)$ of u, where $e(u) = max\{d(u, v) : v \in V\}$. The problem of finding an optimal location can be solved by determining the minimum over all $e(u)$ with $u \in V$. In graph theory, the set of vertices with minimal eccentricity is denoted as the center of G. Hage and Harary [10] proposed a centrality measure based on the eccentricity $c_E(u) = \frac{1}{e(u)} = \frac{1}{max\{d(u,v):v \in V\}}$ This measure is consistent with the general notion of vertex centrality, since $e(u)^{-1}$ grows if the maximal distance of u decreases. Thus, for all vertices $u \in V$ of the center of G: $c(u) \geqslant c_E(v)$ for all $v \in V$. Based on such method, we define a procedure to compute the center of the graph as described in the Algorithm 1.

In the algorithm, by using the function `InitializeArray`, we initialize the eccentricity vector L_E (line[2]). Such vector has length n (the number of nodes in V): for each node with index i we calculate the maximum distance from the

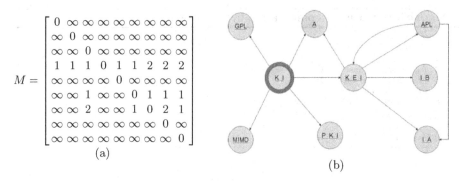

$$M = \begin{bmatrix} 0 & \infty & \infty & \infty & \infty & \infty & \infty & \infty & \infty \\ \infty & 0 & \infty & \infty & \infty & \infty & \infty & \infty & \infty \\ \infty & \infty & 0 & \infty & \infty & \infty & \infty & \infty & \infty \\ 1 & 1 & 1 & 0 & 1 & 1 & 2 & 2 & 2 \\ \infty & \infty & \infty & \infty & 0 & \infty & \infty & \infty & \infty \\ \infty & \infty & 1 & \infty & \infty & 0 & 1 & 1 & 1 \\ \infty & \infty & 2 & \infty & \infty & 1 & 0 & 2 & 1 \\ \infty & \infty & \infty & \infty & \infty & \infty & \infty & 0 & \infty \\ \infty & \infty & \infty & \infty & \infty & \infty & \infty & \infty & 0 \end{bmatrix}$$

(a)

(b)

Fig. 3. Eccentricity computation: (a) Floyd-Warshall Matrix and (b) center

nodes of G (lines[4-5]). The distances from each couple of nodes are computed in a matrix M (line[3]) by using the Floyd-Warshall algorithm [18], that is a graph analysis algorithm for finding shortest paths in a weighted graph. If there does not exist a path between two nodes we set the distance to ∞. Finally we select the index i_{min} in L_E corresponding to the minimum value (line[6]). The center c_E corresponds to the node with the index i_{min} in V. For instance let us consider the graph of Fig. 1.(b). The matrix computed by Floyd-Warshall algorithm is shown in Fig. 3.(a), where idx(GPL) = 1, idx(MIMD) = 2, idx(A) = 3, idx(K_I) = 4, idx(F_K_I) = 5, idx(K_E_I) = 6, idx(APL) = 7, idx(I_b) = 8 and idx(I_A) = 9. Then the eccentricity vector L_E is $\begin{bmatrix} \infty & \infty & \infty & 2 & \infty & \infty & \infty & \infty & \infty \end{bmatrix}^t$. In L_E the minimum value is 2, corresponding to the index 4: in this case the center c_E is K_I, as shown in Fig. 3.(b).

Closeness. Next we consider the second type of location problems - the minisum location problem, often also called the median problem or service facility location problem. Suppose we want to place a service facility, e.g., a shopping mall, such that the total distance to all customers in the region is minimal. This would make traveling to the mall as convenient as possible for most customers. We denote the sum of the distances from a vertex $u \in V$ to any other vertex in a graph G as the total distance $\sum_{v \in V} d(u, v)$. The problem of finding an appropriate location can be solved by computing the set of vertices with minimum total distance. In social network analysis a centrality index based on this concept is called closeness. The focus lies here, for example, on measuring the closeness of a person to all other people in the network. People with a small total distance are considered as more important as those with a high total distance. Various closeness-based measures have been developed, see for example [2,3,16,19] and [22]. The most commonly employed definition of closeness is the reciprocal of the total distance $c_C(u) = \frac{1}{\sum_{v \in V} d(u,v)}$. In our sense this definition is a vertex centrality, since $c_C(u)$ grows with decreasing total distance of u and it is clearly a structural index. Before we discuss the competitive location problem, we want to mention the radiality measure and integration measure proposed by Valente and Foreman [22]. These measures can also be viewed as closeness-based indices. They

---

Algorithm 2. Center computation by closeness

    Input : The graph G
    Output: The center c_C

1 $n \leftarrow V.length$;
2 $L_C \leftarrow$ InitializeArray(n);
3 $M \leftarrow$ FloydWarshall(G);
4 **for** $i \leftarrow 0$ **to** n **do**
5 $\lfloor$ $L_C[i] \leftarrow \sum_{j=0}^{n-1} M[i][j]$;

6 $i_{min} \leftarrow$ MinIndex(L_C);
7 $c_C \leftarrow V[i_{min}]$;
8 **return** c_C;

---

were developed for digraphs but an undirected version is applicable to undirected connected graphs, too. This variant is defined as $c_R(u) = \frac{\sum_{v \in V}(\triangle_G + 1 - d(u,v))}{n-1}$, where $\triangle_G$ and n denote the diameter of the graph and the number of vertices, respectively. The index measures how well a vertex is integrated in a network. The better a vertex is integrated the closer the vertex must be to other vertices. The primary difference between c_C and c_R is that c_R reverses the distances to get a closeness-based measure and then averages these values for each vertex. Based on such method, we define a procedure to compute the center of the graph as described in the Algorithm 2. As for the eccentricity, we initialize the closeness vector L_C and calculate the matrix M. Then for each node with index i we calculate the sum of distances from the other nodes (lines[4-5]). Finally, as for the eccentricity, we calculate the index i_{min} of the minimum value in L_C. Such index corresponds to the center c_C in G. Referring again to our example, given the matrix M by the Floyd-Warshall algorithm, we have the following closeness vector $L_C = \begin{bmatrix} \infty & \infty & \infty & 11 & \infty & \infty & \infty & \infty & \infty \end{bmatrix}^t$. Since the minimum value is 11, i_{min} is 4: also in this case the center is K_I.

Centroid Values. The last centrality index presented here is used in competitive settings. Suppose each vertex represents a customer in a graph. The service location problem considered above assumes a single store in a region. In reality, however, this is usually not the case. There is often at least one competitor offering the same products or services. Competitive location problems deal with the planning of commercial facilities which operate in such a competitive environment. For reasons of simplicity, we assume that the competing facilities are equally attractive and that customers prefer the facility closest to them. Consider now the following situation: a salesman selects a location for his store knowing that a competitor can observe the selection process and decide afterwards which location to select for her shop. Which vertex should the salesman choose? Given a connected undirected graph G of n vertices. For a pair of vertices u and v, $\gamma_u(v)$ denotes the number of vertices which are closer to u than to v, that is $\gamma_u(v) = |\{w \in V : d(u,w) < d(v,w)\}|$. If the salesman selects a vertex u and his competitor selects a vertex v, then he will have $\gamma_u(v) + \frac{1}{2}(n - \gamma_u(v) - \gamma_v(u)) = \frac{1}{2}n + \frac{1}{2}(\gamma_u(v) - \gamma_v(u))$ customers. Thus, letting $f(u,v) = \gamma_u(v) - \gamma_v(u)$, the competitor will choose a vertex v which minimizes

---

Algorithm 3. Center computation by centroid values

      Input : The graph G
      Output: The center c_F

```
 1  n ← V.length;
 2  C ← InitializeMatrix(n,n);
 3  min ← InitializeArray(n);
 4  M ← FloydWarshall(G);
 5  for i ← 0 to n do
 6      for j ← 0 to n do
 7          if i == j then
 8              C[i][j] ← ∞;

 9          else
10              for h ← 0 to n do
11                  if h ≠ i ∧ h ≠ j then
12                      if M[i][h] < M[j][h] then
13                          C[i][j] ← C[i][j] +1;

14                      else if M[i][h] > M[j][h] then
15                          C[i][j] ← C[i][j] -1;


16  for i ← 0 to n do
17      min[i] ← Min(C[i]);
18  imax ← MaxIndex(min);
19  cF ← V[imax];
20  return cF;
```

$f(u, v)$. The salesman knows this strategy and calculates for each vertex u the worst case, that is $c_F(u) = min\{f(u,v) : v \in V - u\}$. $c_F(u)$ is called the centroid value and measures the advantage of the location u compared to other locations, that is the minimal difference of the number of customers which the salesman gains or loses if he selects u and a competitor chooses an appropriate vertex v different from u. Based on such method, we define a procedure to compute the center of the graph as described in the Algorithm 3. In the algorithm, we initialize the centroid vector min and the centroid matrix C, i.e., $n \times n$, where each value [i,j] corresponds to $f(i,j)$. We fill C (lines[5-15]) by using the matrix M, calculated by the Floyd-Warshall algorithm. Then for each row i of C we copy the minimum value in $min[i]$ (lines[16-17]). Finally we calculate the index i_{max} corresponding to the maximum value in min (line[18]). The center c_F correspond to the node in V with index i_{max}. Referring again to our example, Fig. 4.(a) shows the centroid matrix C. From C we compute the following vector $min = \begin{bmatrix} -7 & -7 & -7 & 0 & -7 & 0 & -3 & -7 & -7 \end{bmatrix}^t$. In this case the maximum value is 0, corresponding to two indexes: 4 and 6. This means that we have two centroids, i.e., K_I and K_E_I, as shown in Fig. 4.(b).

3.2 Semantic Center of a Search Result

The methods discussed above compute the center of a graph with respect to the topology information on the nodes. Referring to the example in Fig. 1.(b), in any method we have the center K_I (the centroid method reports K_E_I also). In this case such center allows to reach all nodes of the graph, but the navigation

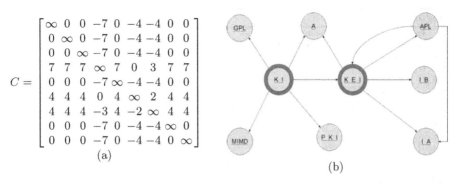

$$C = \begin{bmatrix} \infty & 0 & 0 & -7 & 0 & -4 & -4 & 0 & 0 \\ 0 & \infty & 0 & -7 & 0 & -4 & -4 & 0 & 0 \\ 0 & 0 & \infty & -7 & 0 & -4 & -4 & 0 & 0 \\ 7 & 7 & 7 & \infty & 7 & 0 & 3 & 7 & 7 \\ 0 & 0 & 0 & -7 & \infty & -4 & -4 & 0 & 0 \\ 4 & 4 & 4 & 0 & 4 & \infty & 2 & 4 & 4 \\ 4 & 4 & 4 & -3 & 4 & -2 & \infty & 4 & 4 \\ 0 & 0 & 0 & -7 & 0 & -4 & -4 & \infty & 0 \\ 0 & 0 & 0 & -7 & 0 & -4 & -4 & 0 & \infty \end{bmatrix}$$

(a)

(b)

Fig. 4. Centroid computation: (a) Centroid Matrix and (b) center

starting from such center is not effective: K_I corresponds to the Web page with all Kenneth Iverson. The best starting point would be K_E_I that is the Kenneth Iverson directly linked to the APL programming language page. Therefore beyond the center based on the spatial information of the graph, we need a "center of interest", i.e., some vertex that is more closed to the significant pages than others. In other words we need the node, with no-zero score, that is close to the nodes having high scores (i.e., matching the keywords). Therefore, we define a procedure to compute the center of interest as described in the Algorithm 4.

Algorithm 4. Center of interest

Input : The graph G
Output: The center of interest c

```
1   n ← V.length;
2   D ← InitializeArray(n);
3   M ← FloydWarshall(G);
4   min ← 0;
5   for i ← 0 to n do
6   |   D[i] ← 0;
7   |   if ω(V[i]) > 0 then
8   |   |   for j ← 0 to n do
9   |   |   |   if ω(V[j]) > 0 then
10  |   |   |   |   D[i] ← D[i] + M[i][j];
11  |   |   D[i] ← D[i]/ω(V[i]);
12  |   else
13  |   |   D[i] ← ∞;
14  i_min ← MinIndex(D);
15  c ← V[i_min];
16  return c;
```

In the algorithm, we calculate the closeness of each node, that is the sum of distances from the others but we normalize it with respect to the score of the node (lines[5-13]): the center of interest will have the minimum closeness with the highest score (i.e., ω refers to the function in [6]). If the node with index i we are considering has score 0 then the closeness is ∞. We store all values into

Algorithm 5. Compute Clusters

Input : The set S of solutions, the query Q
Output: The set of Clusters CL

1 $CL \leftarrow \emptyset$;
2 **while** S *is not empty* **do**
3 $\quad S - \{S_i\}$;
4 $\quad$ **if** $\exists cl_j \in CL, S_j \in cl_j: D(S_j) = D(S_i) \lor \texttt{Keywords}(D(S_j), Q) = \texttt{Keywords}(D(S_i), Q)$ **then**
5 $\quad\quad cl_j \leftarrow cl_j \cup \{S_i\}$;
6 $\quad$ **else**
7 $\quad\quad cl_j \leftarrow \emptyset$;
8 $\quad\quad cl_j \leftarrow cl_j \cup \{S_i\}$;
9 $\quad\quad CL \leftarrow CL \cup \{cl_j\}$;
10 **return** CL;

the vector D, initialized by `InitializeArray`(line[2]). Finally we calculate the index i_{min} corresponding to the minimum value in D and the center of interest c will be the node in V with index i_{min}. Referring again to our example we have the vector $D = \begin{bmatrix} \infty & \infty & \infty & \frac{8}{2} & \frac{12}{1} & \frac{6}{2} & \frac{9}{1} & \frac{10}{1} & \frac{9}{1} \end{bmatrix}^t$. Since the minimum value is 3 (i.e., $\frac{6}{2}$), the center of interest has index 6 (i.e., K_E_I). Therefore computing both structural and semantic centers we obtain the node K_E_I that is both a structural and semantic center for the result: it is the best starting point to reach the information of interest. In this way, the joint use of the center calculated by spatial methods and the center of interest allows an effective navigation.

3.3   Effective Navigation of Web Pages

A relevant step in Web search is the computation of a useful partition of results in clusters, such that solutions in the same cluster are semantically "homogeneous". For instance let us consider Fig. 5. Suppose the set of solutions, *i.e.* Web search engine results, to the query "Kenneth Iverson Language": $S = \{S_1, S_2, S_3\}$. As the reader can see, S_1 and S_3 highlight Iverson as key semantics, whereas S_2 focuses on Language as key semantics. All the solutions $match^1$ the keywords of the query but they provide different interpretations of user request. Grouping such solutions, w.r.t the semantics they represent, can support the user to navigate the information he is looking for. As shown in Fig. 5, we can group the solutions in two clusters: $CL_1 = \{S_1, S_3\}$, *i.e.* Iverson is the key semantics, and $CL_2 = \{S_2\}$, *i.e.* Language is the key semantics. In this way the user can choose which semantics to expand and, therefore, which results to navigate, *i.e.* filtering some results.

To this aim, the indices discussed above support the clustering of results. Let us denote the matching relationship between values with $\approx$. Given a solution S and a query $Q = \{q_1, q_2, \ldots, q_m\}$, we say that S matches a keyword $q_i \in Q$ iff there exists a node $n_S \in S$ such that $n_S \approx q_i$. Moreover we indicate with

---

[1] We follow the traditional Information Retrieval approach to value matching adopted in full text search.

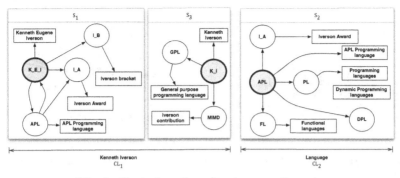

Fig. 5. Clustering of results via semantic center

$D(S)$ the center of interest in S. For instance referring to Fig. 5, the centers of interest of S_1, S_2 and S_3 are double marked and indicated in gray, *i.e.* $D(S_1) =$ K_I, $D(S_2) =$ APL and $D(S_3) =$ K_E_I. The idea is to group solutions matching the same semantics. In this case, solutions having the same center of interest or whose center of interest matches the same keywords in Q belong to the same clusters. Algorithm 5 shows the procedure to compute clusters. The algorithm takes as input the set of solutions $\mathcal{S}$ and the query Q. First of all we initialize the set $\mathcal{CL}$ as an empty set (line [1]). We have to analyze each element S_i in $\mathcal{S}$ (line [3]). If there exists an element S_j in a cluster cl_j of $\mathcal{CL}$ such that S_i and S_j expose the same semantics then S_i is inserted into cl_j (line [5]). Otherwise we build a new cluster cl_j, we insert S_i into cl_j and cl_j into $\mathcal{CL}$ (lines [7-9]). Two solutions expose the same semantics iff they present the same center of interest, *i.e.* $D(S_i) = D_{(S_j)}$, or their centers of interest match the same set of keywords in the query Q (line [4]). The latter test is performed by the procedure Keywords. This procedure takes as input a node n_S and a query $Q = \{q_1, q_2, \ldots, q_m\}$; Keywords returns a set K of keywords q_i such that $n_S \approx q_i$. Referring to Fig. 5, we first create the cluster cl_1 containing the solution S_1. In this case S_1 provides K_I as center of interest, *i.e.* $D(S_1)$, whose set of matching keywords K is {Kenneth, Iverson}. Then we extract the second solution S_2 having $D(S_2) =$ APL and $K =$ {Language}; in this case there does not exist any cluster in $\mathcal{CL}$ exposing an element with the same semantics of S_2, *i.e.* S_1 and S_2 have different centers of interest and sets of matching keywords. In this case a new cluster cl_2, containing S_2, is built and inserted into $\mathcal{CL}$. the last solution S_3 has $D(S_3)$ = K_E_I and $K =$ {Kenneth, Iverson}; S_1 and S_3 share the same semantics: they have different centers of interest but such centers expose the same set of matching keywords. Hence, S_3 is inserted into cl_1.

4 Experimental Results

We implemented our framework in a Java tool[2], according to a client-server architecture. At client-side, we have a Web interface based on GWT that provides

---

[2] A video tutorial is available at http://www.youtube.com/watch?v=CpJhVhx3r80

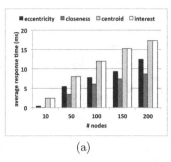

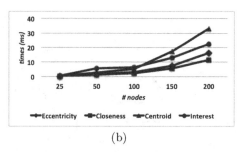

(a)   (b)

Fig. 6. (a) Performance of the approach for the query "algorithm 1999" and (b) Scalability to compute centers

(i) support for submitting a query, (ii) support for retrieving the results and (iii) a graphical view to navigate the Web pages via the resulting annotation. At server-side, we have the core of our query engine: we used YAANII [4,6], a system for keyword search over RDF graphs. We have executed several experiments to test the performance of our tool. Our benchmarking system is a dual core 2.66GHz Intel with 2 GB of main memory running on Linux. We have used Wikipedia3, a conversion of the English Wikipedia into RDF (i.e. it is available at http://labs.systemone.at/wikipedia3). This is a monthly updated data set containing around 47 million triples. The user can submit a keyword search query Q to YAANII that returns the top-100 solutions. Each solution is a connected subgraph of Wikipedia3 matching Q.

Performance. Getting inspiration from the benchmark in [11], we formulated ten queries. Using YAANII, we executed ten runs of each query and then we computed the centrality indices, described in Section 3. Due to space constraints, we refer the user to [4] for efficiency tests of YAANII itself. In Fig. 6.(a) we show the performance of our system to compute the centrality indices on top of the results coming from executing Q_1 = "algorithm 1999". In particular we measured the average response time (ms) to calculate the center in any method w.r.t. to the increasing number of nodes in the single solution. The query Q_1 is much general and provides many results whose sizes, i.e. number of nodes, grow from 10 to 200 nodes. We recall that such graphs are solutions coming from executing a query. Therefore 200 nodes is a huge size; on the average a good solution should be 10 or 15 nodes at most. As expected the computation of centroids and centers of interest represents the more complex task, but in a reasonable time. The other queries expose a similar behavior, but the times for Q_1 represent an upper bound. The Figure shows the relevant efficiency of indices computation that does not invalidate the efficiency of the entire process. In particular we can appreciate the scalability of the indices computation on top of all queries, as shown in Fig. 6.(b). In this case we have the average response time to compute indices in all strategies for all queries w.r.t. the increasing number of nodes in a solution. The figure shows a polynomial trend of all strategies w.r.t. to the size of a solution. The clustering step is trivial; therefore we do not report times to compute clusters, i.e. few milliseconds.

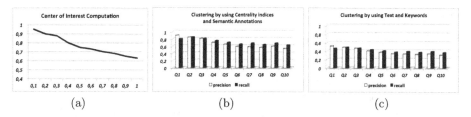

Fig. 7. Effectiveness: (a) center of interest, (b) clustering by indices and (c) clustering by text and keywords

Effectiveness. Then, publishing the system on the Web, we asked to several and different expert users (i.e., about 100 people between researchers and professors in computer science) to test the tool by providing the set of ten keyword search queries and to indicate if the centers are really effective. In particular we asked to indicate which structural and semantic centers are effective for each solution: the navigation is effective if the page of interest is distant at most two nodes from the computed centers. In this way we calculate the interpolation between precision and recall to compute the center of interest, as shown in Fig. 7.(a). This results validates the feasibility and effectiveness of our approach: the precision is in the range $[0.68, 0.95]$ w.r.t. the increasing recall. Similarly we measured precision and recall of our clustering for each query. As for centrality indices, we asked to each user the topics to group the solutions, *i.e.* the sets of keywords identifying each group. In particular we employed AISEARCH [21], SNAKET [8], and LINGO [17] as competitors. Fig. 7.(b) shows the results of our technique while Fig. 7.(c) the average trend of all competitors (i.e. AISEARCH performs worse while SNAKET and LINGO show a behavior quite similar to the figure). As expected, the recall of our clustering is in the range $[0.63, 0.8]$ while the precision is in the range $[0.53, 0.9]$. Referring to the recall, we have a good average value: our system is able to recognize the topics of interest for the user. With respect to the precision, the values are more varying: consequently we have *noise*; the system produces overlapping or useless clusters. On the other hand, our technique outperforms all competitors, providing upper bounds of both precision and recall lower than lower bounds of our approach.

5   Conclusion and Future Work

In this paper we discussed and implemented an approach for an effective navigation of Web pages by using semantic annotations. The approach is based on defining and implementing centrality indices, allowing the user to automatically select the starting point from which to reach the Web pages of interest. Experimental results demonstrate how significant it is the use of semantic annotations for surfing the Web effectively. In particular, an effective visualization of the annotation matching the user request improves the quality of the navigation. For future work, we are investigating new methods to determine the starting point and more sophisticated techniques to produce clusters. Moreover we are studying an implementation for distributed architectures (e.g., mobile environments).

References

1. Angles, R., Gutierrez, C.: Querying RDF data from a graph database perspective. In: Gómez-Pérez, A., Euzenat, J. (eds.) ESWC 2005. LNCS, vol. 3532, pp. 346–360. Springer, Heidelberg (2005)
2. Bavelas, A.: Communication patterns in task oriented groups. Journal of the Acoustical Society of America 22(6), 271–282 (1950)
3. Beauchamp, M.A.: An improved index of centrality. Behavioral Science 10(2) (1965)
4. Cappellari, P., De Virgilio, R., Maccioni, A., Roantree, M.: A path-oriented RDF index for keyword search query processing. In: Hameurlain, A., Liddle, S.W., Schewe, K.-D., Zhou, X. (eds.) DEXA 2011, Part II. LNCS, vol. 6861, pp. 366–380. Springer, Heidelberg (2011)
5. Carpineto, C., Osinski, S., Romano, G., Weiss, D.: A survey of web clustering engines. ACM Comput. Surv. 41(3) (2009)
6. De Virgilio, R., Cappellari, P., Miscione, M.: Cluster-based exploration for effective keyword search over semantic datasets. In: Laender, A.H.F., Castano, S., Dayal, U., Casati, F., de Oliveira, J.P.M. (eds.) ER 2009. LNCS, vol. 5829, pp. 205–218. Springer, Heidelberg (2009)
7. Domschke, W., Drexl, A.: Location and Layout Planning: An International Bibliography. Springer, Berlin (1985)
8. Ferragina, P., Gulli, A.: The anatomy of a hierarchical clustering engine for webpage, news and book snippets. In: ICDM, pp. 395–398 (2004)
9. Hakimi, S.L.: Optimum location of switching centers and the absolute centers and medians of a graph. Operations Research 12(2), 450–459 (1964)
10. Harary, F., Hage, P.: Eccentricity and centrality in networks. Social Networks 17(1), 57–63 (1995)
11. He, H., Wang, H.: J.Yang, Yu, P.S.: Blinks: ranked keyword searches on graphs. In: SIGMOD, pp. 305–316 (2007)
12. Huang, J., Efthimiadis, E.N.: Analyzing and evaluating query re- formulation strategies in web search logs. In: CIKM, pp. 77–86 (2009)
13. Jansen, B.J., Spink, A., Blakely, C., Koshman, S.: Defining a session on web search engines. Journal of the American Society for Information Science and Technology 58(6), 862–871 (2007)
14. Jansen, B.J., Spink, A., Pedersen, J.: A temporal comparison of altavista web searching. Journal of the American Society for Information Science and Technology 56(6), 559–570 (2005)
15. Li, W.S., Candan, K.S., Vu, Q., Agrawal, D.: Retrieving and organizing web pages by "information unit". In: WWW, pp. 230–244. ACM Press (2001)
16. Moxley, R.L., Moxley, N.F.: Determining point-centrality in uncontrived social networks. Sociometry 37(1), 122–130 (1974)
17. Osinski, S., Stefanowski, J., Weiss, D.: Lingo: Search results clustering algorithm based on singular value decomposition. In: Intelligent Information Systems, pp. 359–368 (2004)
18. Rosen, K.H.: Discrete Mathematics and Its Applications. Addison Wesley (2003)
19. Sabidussi, G.: The centrality index of a graph. Psychometrika 31(4), 581–603 (1966)
20. Smart, C., Slater, P.J.: Center, median and centroid subgraphs. Networks 34(4), 303–311 (1999)
21. Stein, B., Eissen, S.M.Z.: Topic identification: Framework and application. In: I-KNOW (2004)
22. Valente, T.W., Foreman, R.K.: Measuring the extent of an individual's connectedness and reachability in a network. Social Networks 20(1), 89–105 (1998)
23. Weber, A.: Uber den Standort der Industrien. J. C. B. Mohr, Tubingen (1909)

Generation of Reliable Randomness via Social Phenomena

Roberto De Virgilio and Antonio Maccioni

Dipartimento di Ingegneria
Università Roma Tre, Rome, Italy
{dvr,maccioni}@dia.uniroma3.it

Abstract. Randomness is a hot topic in computer science due to its important implications such as cryptography, gambling, hashing algorithms and so on. Due to the implicit determinism of computer systems, randomness can only be simulated. In order to generate reliable random sequences, IT systems have to rely on hardware random number generators. Unfortunately, these devices are not always affordable and suitable in all the circumstances (*e.g.,* personal use, data-intensive systems, mobile devices, etc.). Human-computer interaction (HCI) has recently become bidirectional: computers help human beings in carrying out their issues and human beings support computers in hard tasks. Following this trend, we introduce RANDOMDB, a database system that is able to generate reliable randomness from social phenomena. RANDOMDB extracts data from social networks to answer random queries in a flexible way. We prototyped RANDOMDB and we conducted some experiments in order to show the effectiveness and the advantages of the system.

1 Introduction

Randomness has been studied in many fields, from philosophy to psychology, from physics to social sciences. Analogously, mathematics and computer science have studied randomness under many aspects. In this context, randomness is considered to be the extent that allows us to obtain numbers and sequences of numbers (generally referred to as *random data*) in a non-predetermined and unpredictable manner. It means that every single number is equally probable to be drawn and the completion of a sequence cannot be inferred by correlation with previous sequences. The generation of random data has to be really accurate and therefore it is performed by complex agents, the so-called *Random Number Generators* (*RNGs*). They allow computer systems to reach the "realism", precluded by deterministic procedures. Although at first glance the generation of random numbers can appear as simple as throwing a dice, it is a sensitive task for automatic agents. In fact, automatic agents are deterministic systems able to generate data only by processing machine-instructions and computing formulas. In case, it is possible to provide pseudo-randomness by executing an algorithm with a *secret* input, called *seed*. It means that, despite the user perception of a random generation, the randomness is only simulated. Moreover, the choice of a

A. Cuzzocrea and S. Maabout (Eds.): MEDI 2013, LNCS 8216, pp. 65–77, 2013.

seed is a hard task because, if it is revealed, random data becomes predictable. Researchers and companies are still investigating ways to improve both *RNGs* and the choice of effective seeds. Most of the generators are *Pseudo Random Number Generators* (*PRNGs*) able to reach only pseudo-randomness. In critical applications a *PRNG* is not good enough (and therefore not even allowed in some cases such as gambling applications). They can be cryptographically insecure, present a poor dimensional distribution, suffer some form of periodicity and use an unbounded size of memory. Therefore, using a *True Random Number Generator* (*TRNG*) is often required. Even if there is no exact way to determine if a *RNG* is *true* or *pseudo*, the *TRNGs* are those that gather information from entropic sources without using any sort of algorithm. For instance, they extract information from physical phenomena such as radioactive decay, thermal noise, micro-states of atoms and molecules. *TRNGs* are often implemented in expensive hardware devices and have a lower throughput than *PRNGs*. Therefore different kind of true random generators would be desiderale.

Motivation. HCI features are becoming more and more prominent in many computer science's areas. Unaware human decisions have recently became part of algorithms and computational processes in order to help computers in solving hard computational operations. The *reCAPTCHA* [15] project digitalizes books, newspapers and old time radio shows by exploiting the *CAPTCHA*[1] tasks, which were initially proposed for distinguishing human beings from computer bots. *Duolingo*[2] aims at translating the Web pages using language course exercises. Micro-tasks of any kind are widely managed and solved through the use of crowd-sourcing and collaborative platforms such as *Mechanical Turk Machine*[3]. In the database area, *CrowdDB* [5] uses people for answering queries. Following this trend, we try to solve the problem of reliable random number generation in a crowd-like way. Whereas a single human being shows a high degree of determinism when generating a random sequence of numbers [13], studies made by *sociophysics* (see [6] for survey) show that the society is a chaotic system and thus, some social phenomena follow entropic and physical behavior that are not ruled by determinism. Even entropy definitions such as the one in the second law of thermodynamics are likened to psychology [8] and to economics [3].

Contribution. From the motivations above, we can consider the collective behavior an entropic source and consequently, social networks (*e.g.,* Facebook, Twitter, Flickr, etc.) the virtual places where social phenomena take place. Nowadays social networks constantly produce huge amounts of data that reflect and capture the behavior of millions of people. Therefore, on the one hand, these social data comprise entropic data; on the other hand, due to the significant amount of data, they need a persistent storage, *i.e.* DBMS technology. For this purpose we propose a database system, called RANDOMDB, that, by exploiting social data, produces "good" randomness overcoming many drawbacks of exist-

---

[1] Completely Automated Public Turing test to tell Computers and Humans Apart.
[2] http://duolingo.com/
[3] http://www.mturk.com/

ing *RNGs*. Therefore, RANDOMDB can be used as a reliable *RNG*, replacing the current state of the art.

Organization. The paper is organized as follows: in Section 2 we discuss related work, in Section 3 we overview the RANDOMDB showing the architecture and the system at work. In Section 4 we show the assessments of a developed prototype. Finally, we sketch conclusions and future evolutions in Section 5.

2   Related Work

RNGs are commonly classified into *PRNGs* and *TRNGs*. Famous *PRNGs* are the Linear Congruential Generator, Lehmer Random Number Generator, the Mersenne Twister [10], Blum Blum Shub, CryptGenRandom[4] (a.k.a. Microsoft CAPI) and Yarrow. *PRNGs* are easily predictable [2] and therefore in many critical applications we are forced to use systems from the plethora of *TRNGs*. Random.org[5] exploits atmospheric noise and offers random data through Web APIs. Lavarnd[6] selects a true random seed by taking pictures of floating material in lava lamps and then uses a *PRNG* to generate random data. HotBits[7] employs radioactive decays. Intel DRNG[8] generates random data at a high-rate from the thermal noise within the silicon. Finally, Protego[9] exploits quantum physics and GRANG [14] computes the thermal noise together with a Poisson arrival time for better efficiency. The main disadvantages of these methods are the high cost of ad-hoc devices and, often, their inability to reach an expected random data output rate. To this aim, work has been done in order to extract randomness from other contexts (*e.g.,* [12,4,7]). In [12] and [4] the authors exploit the entropy generated by human beings using mouse and keyboard. Since these methods are not always applicable and present dangerous vulnerabilities [16], the work in [7] aims to produce pseudo-random data with the conjunct use of extractors and people playing videogames.

3   System Overview

In this section we sketch how RANDOMDB works and overview its architecture.

System Architecture. As shown in Fig. 1, RANDOMDB is composed by three main components: (i) the *Query Processor* (QP), (ii) the *Mapper* (MP) and (iii) the *Generator* (GN). The MP and GN components are supported by a DBMS to store *Data* and *Metadata*.

In particular the *Data store* contains the social data concerning social phenomena. In a start-up phase, the administrator selects all data sources from

---

[4] http://technet.microsoft.com/en-us/library/cc962093.aspx
[5] http://www.random.org/
[6] http://www.lavarnd.org/
[7] http://www.fourmilab.ch/hotbits/
[8] http://software.intel.com/
[9] http://www.protego.se/

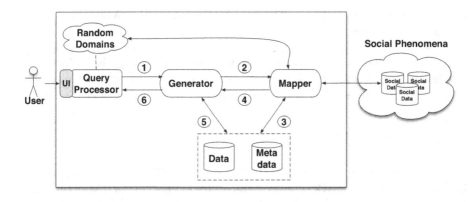

Fig. 1. RANDOMDB architecture

which to extract all social data. Then such data are stored in a database with respect to a certain source domain and the *Metadata store* will contain all information useful to map source domains and target domains, as we will describe later. The QP component provides an interface to interact with the *external world*.

System At Work. The working process is to map data from a *source* domain to a *target* domain. Source domains refer to data from social phenomena[10]. For example, let us consider people expressing preferences on a picture or on a topic (*i.e.* the iLike feature of many social networks); in this case the source domain S is represented by data that measures this liking (*e.g.*, natural numbers). The target domains correspond to random data domains that users and applications require. A target domain is associated to a query (*random query*) to perform in RANDOMDB. For example a *rand*()-like function of the C programming language is a random query that can be submitted to RANDOMDB. In this case the target domain refers to all real numbers in the range $(0, 1]$. Therefore, in order to generate a random real number in the range $(0, 1]$, our system has to use a mapping function $\mathcal{M}$ that maps a source S in $T = (0, 1]$, *i.e.* $\mathcal{M} : S \rightarrow T$. A user or an agent, through a *random query*, selects to generate random data in a particular target domain (*e.g.*, a real number, in case in a particular range). Then, the request is transferred to the GN component (*i.e.* Fig. 1, step ①). GN is responsible to generate the final random data fitting the user request. Such component has a central role in RANDOMDB architecture since it communicates with all the other components. GN communicates with MP (*i.e.* Fig. 1, step ②) to know which mapping has to be computed from one or more source domains associated to the selected target domain. MP is the component which is aware of the source domains and it is in charge of mapping them to the target domains. Such mappings are implemented in stored procedures on the underlying data store as will be explained in the next Section 4. MP exploits metadata (*i.e.* Fig. 1,

---

[10] In this paper we do not delve into considerations about what is a social phenomenon and when it can be considered *entropic*.

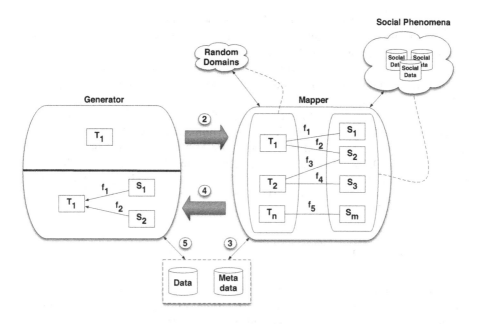

Fig. 2. RANDOMDB generation process

step ③) in order to return a query to GN; such query will be executed over the underlying social data stored in our database (*i.e.* Fig. 1, step ④ and step ⑤). The procedure selects social data of interest and then, in case, applies some *transformations* on such data. A transformation could be a simple operation, *e.g.*, a casting operation, or a more complex task, *e.g.*, *mod* operation, to provide data correctly in the range of the target domain. In this last example, we are aware that a transformation can ruin the uniform distribution of the target domain interval. In the case of the mod, we have to be sure that the source domain interval is much larger than the target domain interval, *e.g.*, we cannot map a natural number in the range $[0, 1]$ into a natural number in the range $[0, 2]$. This *intelligence* is already embedded in MP that checks statistical metadata of the social data such as variance, covariance, standard deviation, minimum and maximum values, etc. Finally, the random data is returned to QP that will output the result (*i.e.* Fig. 1, step ⑥).

Fig. 2 sketches the working process of both MP and GN. Let us consider several target domains, *i.e.* $T_1, T_2, \ldots, T_n$ and source domains, *i.e.* $S_1, S_2, \ldots, S_m$. A target domain can be associated to one or more source domains, *e.g.*, a real number within $(0, 1]$ can be extracted from different phenomena. In this case we have a target domain, *i.e* T_1, corresponding to the set of real numbers within the range $(0, 1]$ and two source domains, *i.e* S_1 and S_2, corresponding for instance, to a Facebook phenomena and a Flickr phenomena, respectively. Given the mapping $\mathcal{M}' : \langle S_1, S_2 \rangle \to T_1$, to generate an element of T_1 the mapping can use an element of S_1 or of S_2, or a composition of elements from both S_1 and S_2.

Use of the System. RANDOMDB can be configured on top of common DBMSs and used in two scenarios. In the former is used by a human user that wants to get a random data upon request, while in the latter case is used embedded into an application where QP is a programmable interface to allow an automatic communication between RANDOMDB and the application itself (*i.e.* API). In this last scenario, contrary to common *RNGs*, we can exploit RANDOMDB to work with the active domain of existing database instances (the actual content of the database). The active domain of the database can, even dynamically, form target domains. For example, if we have a table containing cities, RANDOMDB would be able to directly retrieve randomly a city. This operation can be simply computed by enumerating tuples (or values) and after that, generating a number in the range $[1, \ldots, t]$, where t is the number of objects in the range of the target domain.

4   System Evaluation

This section evaluates the prototype of RANDOMDB that we have implemented. First, we explain how it was created and then we provide the evaluation in terms of efficiency and effectiveness. This also shows the feasibility to implement randomness generation processes using a DBMS.

Implementation. RANDOMDB is implemented in Java and exploits a procedural language for SQL procedures to implement all mappings and transformations. In particular PL/pgSQL, since we used PostgreSQL 9.1 as RDBMS. Java is used to implement a set of wrappers and different programmatic accesses to social phenomena in several social networks. At the moment, we consider the following social networks.

- *Flickr*[11]: we extracted the most recent photos (500 at a time) via the Flickr API. Let us consider Fig. 3 that, on the left side, shows an extract from Flickr and, on the right side, shows the retrieved information. They contain lot of different information that can be considered random. In particular, we extract values from the fields `secret`, `owner` and `title`. In future work we can extend the extraction by considering also information extracted from the pixel values of the photos.
- *Twitter*[12]: we used the tags associated to the photos extracted by Flickr to search the most recent 100 tweets.
- *Facebook*[13]: similarly to Twitter, we used the tags associated to the photos extracted by Flickr to search the most recent 200 posts.

Fig. 4 shows the schema we implemented to test our system. In particular we have three main relations: (i) DOMAINS, (ii) MAPPINGS and (iii) SOCIALDATA. The first two tables belong to the *Metadata store* while the third to the *Data*

---

[11] http://www.flickr.com/services/api/

[12] https://dev.twitter.com/

[13] http://developers.facebook.com/

Fig. 3. Extraction of social data from Flickr

store. The relation DOMAINS collects all meta information about the domains (both source and target) considered in RANDOMDB. In particular we store an identifier, *id* that is the key of the relation, the *name* of the domain and the *domain_type*, whose value is s (for source) or t (for target). The attribute *data_type* indicates which type of data is associated to the domain. Then we store an attribute *range*, indicating the range of the domain.

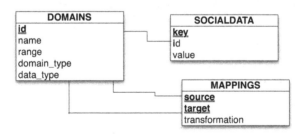

Fig. 4. Database schema in RANDOMDB

The relation MAPPINGS collects all mappings between domains; in particular the attributes *source* and *target* refer to identifiers in DOMAINS whose types have values s and t, respectively. The attribute *transformation* stores an identifier of a stored procedure that is needed to retrieve correctly the requested random data. Finally, we have the relation SOCIALDATA containing all data values extracted from the social phenomena. In particular each entry of SOCIALDATA provides an auto-increment primary key, *i.e. key*, an identifier *id* corresponding to the identifier in the relation DOMAINS, *i.e.* it is a foreign key, and the data

Domains

id	name	range	domain_type	data_type
S_1	Flickr	[-32768, 32767]	s	smallint
S_2	Facebook	[-999999, 999999]	s	int
S_3	Flickr	[a,z]	s	char
S_4	Twitter	[0, 4294967295]	s	uint
T_1	Target1	(0,50]	t	int
T_2	Target2	[a,z]	t	char
T_3	Target3	(0, 1]	t	real
...	...	...	...	...

SocialData

key	id	value
7898	S_4	78999
7899	S_2	770328
8000	S_1	124
8001	S_3	b
8002	S_1	23456
8003	S_2	-1793,89
...	...	...

Mappings

source	target	transformation
S_1	T_1	f_1
S_2	T_1	f_2
S_2	T_2	f_3
...	...	...

Fig. 5. An instance of tables in RANDOMDB

value in the domain, *value*. For instance, Fig. 5 shows an example of instance corresponding to the schema of Fig. 4. In this case we have four source domains extracted from Flickr, Twitter and Facebook. Then we define several mappings to generate random data. Let us consider the mapping $\mathcal{M}' : \langle S_1, S_2 \rangle \rightarrow T_1$. In this case we can generate random data for the target domain Target1 from Facebook and/or Flickr. Each mapping is processed by a PL/pgSQL procedure to generate the corresponding queries. In this case we have to select the first available value from the source domains (*i.e.* S_1 and S_2), as we can see in the following query:

```
SELECT id, value
FROM SocialData
WHERE id = S1 OR id = S2
ORDER BY key
LIMIT 1
```

Considering the instance tables in Fig. 5, the query returns the pair <S_2, 770328>. Then, another query selects the *transformation* that we have to execute on the retrieved *value* for the given mapping:

```
SELECT transformation
FROM Mappings
WHERE source = S2 and target = T1
```

The identifier f_2 is returned to individuate a built-in operation or another stored procedure. For instance, let us suppose that f_2 = CAST(MOD(value,50) as int). Now the final query can compute the transformation f_2 on the value 770328:

Table 1. Throughput of *TRNG*s

TRNG	Throughput
PROTEGO	16 KB/s (*)
GRANG	50 MB/s (*)
INTEL DRNG	500 MB/s (*)
HOTBITS	100 B/s (*)
RANDOMDB	400 KB/s

* Declared by the vendor

```
SELECT CAST(MOD(770328,50) AS INT)
```

The answer 28 is returned to the user. Once we generated the random data, we delete the entry in the table SOCIALDATA used for the generation. Our system will enrich periodically the *Data store* by extracting new values from the social phenomena that will be appended in the table SOCIALDATA. Note that the extracted data in the *Data store* are sequentially ordered on the exact time of generation. In this way the simulation of the system is the same as if the whole process was computed online.

Efficiency Evaluation. The efficiency of RANDOMDB is based on two factors: (i) extraction of social data and (ii) query processing on the database. The former is dependent from the bandwidth and access policy of the social networks. The latter is based on the physical design of the database and on the speed of the machine where RANDOMDB is deployed. We compared the throughput of RANDOMDB against the most used *TRNG*s in Table 1. We used the declared rates by the vendors because as said before, these systems are commercial (and expensive), so we couldn't test them by ourself. We did not consider the *PRNG*s for the efficiency, which however is similar to RANDOMDB (*i.e.* mostly it depends on the the power of the machines). We used a commodity laptop with a dual core 2.5 GHz Intel and 4 GB of memory, running Linux Ubuntu. We measured the throughput of RANDOMDB posing a loop of random queries for the integer numbers target domain.

Under this aspect, we perform better than some of the *TRNG*s. Note that we can improve the performance if we use a faster machine. However, the high rate throughput *TRNG*s are expensive hardware devices.

Effectiveness Evaluation. Evaluating the effectiveness of random data generation is a very complex task, probably even harder than the generation itself. Currently, empirical statistical tests are considered the best way to evaluate a *RNG* [11]. Since *"Building a RNG that passes all statistical tests is an impossible dream"*, as famously stated by Pierre L'Ecuyer, the goodness of a *RNG* is evaluated on the number of passed tests among a battery of many statistical significance tests [9]. These tests define, on the next random data to be generated, hypotheses enclosed in confidence intervals $[\alpha, 1 - \alpha]$, where α is usually set to 0.05 or to 0.01. The hypotheses are based on criteria over previous generated data. For example, a criteria can consider if the sum of a sequence of numbers is constant. Therefore, for a better evaluation one should compute a set of

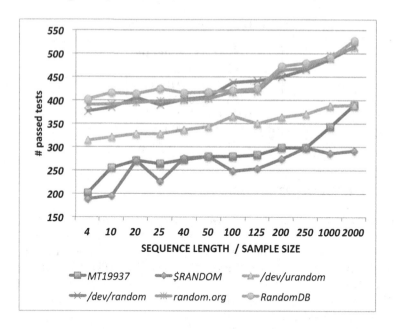

Fig. 6. RNGs comparison with Dieharder's tests

different tests over random generated sequences. The result of a test is summarized by the *p-value* which represents a probability (in fact *p-value* $\in [0, 1]$) to measure the support for randomness hypothesis. The test is considered passed, *i.e.* the sequence is not predictable on the basis of the given hypotheses, if $|p\text{-}value-1| \geq \alpha$, *i.e.* $abs(p\text{-}value-1) \geq \alpha$, otherwise the test is failed. Note that two different sequences generated with the same *RNG* can return different *p-values*. This is the reason why, for the same *RNG*, the tests are executed many times over different sequences. Among the existing statistical tests for *RNGs*, the Diehard battery tests of George Marsaglia[14] and the NIST [1] test collection are the most common. They both implement the principles explained above and, in particular, the last one is becoming the de-facto standard battery test since it is required in many critical applications. In order to assess RANDOMDB we used the Dieharder test suite[15] that is included in the GNU Scientific Library (GSL). It comprises both the Marsaglia's tests (*e.g.*, the *birthday spacings test* that, based on the birthday paradox, checks if the spacings between the numbers are asymptotically exponentially distributed) and some of the NIST tests (*e.g.*, the *serial tests* that check if the overlappings of patterns across a sequence are equally probable). The suite can exploit *RNGs* of the GSL, or takes in input a sequence of bits or numbers. We conducted two different experimental campaigns, the first to compare RANDOMDB against other *RNGs* (both *pseudo* and *true*) and the second to evaluate the probability distribution of the elements in a target domain. For the first campaign we compared RANDOMDB with the

---

[14] http://www.stat.fsu.edu/pub/diehard/
[15] http://www.phy.duke.edu/~rgb/General/dieharder.php

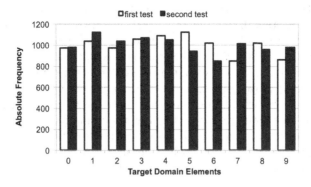

Fig. 7. Frequency distribution for [0,9] integers in RANDOMDB

MT19937 variant of the Mersenne Twister algorithm [10], the Linux shell random number generator ($RANDOM) and the Linux random number generator /DEV/URANDOM as *PRNG*s. We also used the RANDOM.ORG[16] and the Linux /DEV/RANDOM as *TRNG*s. With every *RNG*, we generated 10 sequences of 1000 numbers, 10 of 5000 numbers and 10 of 10000 numbers. For a more comprehensive evaluation, each sequence has been tested with 4 different sample sizes (5, 40, 100, 250). The ratio between the sequence length and the sample size (*i.e.* $\frac{seq.\ length}{sample\ size}$) defines a test case. This ratio is also an indicator of the complexity to predict a random number since a larger sample size brings a smaller *p-value*, for more details see [1]. Every test case has been tested with each of the 57 different tests within the Dieharder library and with $\alpha = 0.005$ (so making the tests harder than the default ones with $\alpha = 0.05$). Then, we counted the times that an *RNG* test case passed the verification out of the 570 launched tests, as shown in Fig. 6.

We can see that in general the *TRNG*s perform better than the *PRNG*s. RANDOMDB performs almost always better than the others. For sure, we can say that it exhibits a reliable behavior, as if it is a *TRNG*. The second campaign has been conducted to see if, in RANDOMDB, every number is equally probable. We computed the frequency distribution of the target domain [0, 9]. We made two extractions (*i.e.* we call them *first test* and *second test*) of 10000 numbers and we counted the frequency. In Fig. 7 we show the frequency of each number. It shows that the probability of all the numbers is uniform, i.e. we can consider every element of the range equally probable.

5   Conclusions and Future Work

In this paper we presented RANDOMDB, a database system to generate reliable randomness via social phenomena. It exploits human-computer interaction (HCI) and the data generated in social networks. RANDOMDB is highly flexible and easily embeddable in software applications. We prototyped RANDOMDB

---

[16] http://www.random.org/

and we conducted some experiments in order to show the effectiveness and the advantages of the system. Experiments showed that RANDOMDB is reliable as a *TRNG* in generating random data. Our first design of RANDOMDB is basically constructed upon social Web data. We are individuating other fields that will be used to "feed" RANDOMDB. For example data from sensor networks, since they are more and more deployed on cities and environments to measure natural phenomena. This opens future directions to data-recycling in many other contexts. Moreover we are considering to introduce crowd sourcing techniques to improve the effectiveness of our system. From a practical point of view, we are working on the prototype in order to test it with the official NIST benchmark. In this way RANDOMDB can be proposed for a wide-usage.

References

1. Bassham III, L.E., Rukhin, A.L., Soto, J., Nechvatal, J.R., Smid, M.E., Barker, E.B., Leigh, S.D., Levenson, M., Vangel, M., Banks, D.L., Heckert, N.A., Dray, J.F., Vo, S.: A statistical test suite for random and pseudorandom number generators for cryptographic applications. SP 800-22 Rev. 1a (2010)
2. Boyar, J.: Inferring sequences produced by pseudo-random number generators. J. ACM 36(1), 129–141 (1989)
3. Chen, J.: The Physical Foundation of Economics: An Analytical Thermodynamic Theory. World Scientific Publishing Company (2005)
4. Dorrendorf, L., Gutterman, Z., Pinkas, B.: Cryptanalysis of the random number generator of the windows operating system. ACM Trans. Inf. Syst. Secur. 13(1) (2009)
5. Franklin, M.J., Kossmann, D., Kraska, T., Ramesh, S., Xin, R.: CrowdDB: answering queries with crowdsourcing. In: SIGMOD, pp. 61–72 (2011)
6. Galam, S.: Sociophysics: A Physicist's Modeling of Psycho-political Phenomena. Springer (2012)
7. Halprin, R., Naor, M.: Games for extracting randomness. In: SOUPS (2009)
8. La Cerra, P.: The First Law of Psychology is the Second Law of Thermodynamics: The Energetic Evolutionary Model of the Mind and the Generation of Human Psychological Phenomena. Human Nature Review 3, 440–447 (2003)
9. L'Ecuyer, P., Simard, R.J.: TestU01: A C library for empirical testing of random number generators. ACM Trans. Math. Softw. 33(4) (2007)
10. Matsumoto, M., Nishimura, T.: Mersenne twister: A 623-dimensionally equidistributed uniform pseudo-random number generator. ACM Trans. Model. Comput. Simul. 8(1), 3–30 (1998)
11. Maurer, U.M.: A universal statistical test for random bit generators. J. Cryptology 5(2), 89–105 (1992)
12. de Raadt, T., Hallqvist, N., Grabowski, A., Keromytis, A.D., Provos, N.: Cryptography in openbsd: An overview. In: USENIX Annual Technical Conference, FREENIX Track, pp. 93–101 (1999)
13. Rapoport, A., Budescu, D.V.: Randomization in Individual Choice Behavior. Psychological Review 104(3), 603–617 (1997)
14. Saito, T., Ishii, K., Tatsuno, I., Sukagawa, S., Yanagita, T.: Randomness and genuine random number generator with self-testing functions (2010), http://csrc.nist.gov/rng/rng2.html

15. Von Ahn, L., Maurer, B., McMillen, C., Abraham, D., Blum, M.: reCAPTCHA: Human-based character recognition via web security measures. Science 321(5895), 1465–1468 (2008)
16. Yilek, S., Rescorla, E., Shacham, H., Enright, B., Savage, S.: When private keys are public: Results from the 2008 Debian OpenSSL vulnerability. In: Proceedings of IMC 2009, pp. 15–27. ACM Press (November 2009)

A Measured Evolution of Database Integrity

Hendrik Decker*

Instituto Tecnológico de Informática, Universidad Politécnica de Valencia, Spain

Abstract. Inconsistency in large database systems is commonplace and therefore must be controlled in order to not get out of hand. Consistency in database systems is encoded by integrity constraints. Inconsistency thus corresponds to constraint violations. Database system services need to function in spite of extant integrity violations, but inconsistency should not increase beyond control in the course of the evolution of such systems. Evolution is effected by updates that may involve insertions and deletions of relational facts as well as schema updates. We show how to determine the causes of violations. Knowledge about such causes can be used to control inconsistency: an increase of integrity violations by updates can be prevented, while tolerating extant inconsistencies, even if the database schema is altered, and even if the schema is unsatisfiable.

1 Introduction

Whenever a database or its schema is updated, its integrity should be checked. In case the update would cause the violation of an integrity constraint, it should either be rejected, or a warning should be issued such that the user or the application may modify the update, so that consistency will be preserved.

However, integrity is not always checked, be it out of neglect, or for trading off consistency for performance, or due to the incompatibility of legacy data with constraints, or for other reasons. Hence, inconsistency tolerance is needed, while an increase of integrity violations by updates should be avoided. Unfortunately, conventional integrity checking methods are not meant to be applied in the presence of inconsistency. They all require that integrity be totally satisfied in the state before the update, in order to check efficiently if integrity remains satisfied in the updated state.

Example 1. Consider the two constraints $I = \leftarrow married(x, y), male(x), male(y)$ and $I' = \leftarrow married(x, y), female(x), female(y)$ in a database system D of a civil registry office. They deny cosexual marriages (which is technically more convenient than stating and processing that the partners of each married couple must be of opposite gender). Yet, suppose D contains the fact $married(jay, pat)$, where *jay* and *pat* are both male, perhaps due to a gender reversal after nuptials. Clearly, that amounts to a violation of I. Thus, conventional integrity checking methods are no longer applicable for updates of D, since they require that D does not violate integrity before checking any update for integrity preservation.

---

* Supported by ERDF/FEDER and the Spanish MEC grant TIN2012-37719-C03-01.

A. Cuzzocrea and S. Maabout (Eds.): MEDI 2013, LNCS 8216, pp. 78–91, 2013.

Obviously, that is unnecessarily restrictive, in general. For instance, consider the update $U = insert\ married(joe, susan)$, which should be acceptable, because it is independent of the extant violation of I and does not cause any new violation.

Similarly, also schema updates, such as, e.g., inserting the constraint $I'' = \leftarrow married(x, y), married(x, z), y \neq z$, which forbids bigamy, is traditionally not considered to be efficiently checkable in the presence of extant constraint violations, even if I'' is not violated by any tuple in D.

In [15,16], we have shown that, contrary to common belief, most, though not all integrity checking methods are inconsistency-tolerant, i.e., the total satisfaction requirement can simply be waived without incurring any penalty. In other words, there is no problem with checking updates such as U in Example 1 in the presence of inconsistency, provided the used method is inconsistency-tolerant.

More precisely, we show in [15,16] that each inconsistency-tolerant method guarantees the preservation of the satisfaction of all 'cases' (instances of constraints) that were satisfied in the old state, even if other instances are violated. Hence, such methods make sure that inconsistency never increases across checked updates of base facts and view definitions, while tolerating extant inconsistencies.

In [6], we have shown that case-based inconsistency tolerance is possible also for schema updates. There, we have also seen that integrity violation can be controlled by inconsistency-tolerant methods if new or modified constraints are checked only against current and future updates, but not against legacy data. Moreover, we have shown in [6] that inconsistency tolerance can guarantee a reliable handling of hard and soft constraints through schema updates.

In [8], we have shown that, for *definite* databases and constraints, essentially the same guarantees of integrity preservation can be made if, instead of *cases* of constraint violations, the increase of *causes* of violations across updates of base facts and view definitions is checked. Causes as defined in [8] are minimal sets of database clauses, the presence or absence of which is responsible for integrity violations. As opposed to cases, causes also provide a basis for computing answers that have integrity in spite of extant violations, as shown in [9].

In [10], we have shown that cause-based inconsistency tolerance is also possible for updates of relational databases that involve schema updates, and that all advantages obtained by case-based inconsistency-tolerant methods for schema updates also are achieved by cause-based methods. However, the minimality condition for causes as defined in [8,10] does not scale up to non-monotonic negation. For instance, $\emptyset$ but not $\sim q$ would be a cause for the answer *no* to the query $\leftarrow p$ in $D = \{p \leftarrow q\}$.

In this paper, we are going to see that the generalization of causes in [9] to justify the integrity of positive and negative answers in definite and non-definite databases works as well also for controlling the evolution of integrity, i.e., for updates including schema alterations. Moreover, the generalized definition in [9] is formalized in a much simpler and less circumstantial manner in this paper.

2   Preliminaries

Our terminology and notation largely adhere to *datalog* [1]. In particular, for each database D, the well-known completion [4] of D is denoted by *comp*(D), and $\models$ denotes logical consequence, i.e., truth in all Herbrand models. We assume a universal underlying language $\mathcal{L}$, of which $\mathcal{L}^c$ be the set of constant terms in $\mathcal{L}$ and $\mathcal{H}_\mathcal{L}$ the Herbrand base of $\mathcal{L}$.

In 2.1, we recapitulate some database fundamentals. In 2.2, we characterize the updates that we are going to deal with. In 2.3, we abstractly define the concept of integrity checking as implemented by conventional integrity checking methods. Later, in 3.3, that definition will be generalized in terms of inconsistency tolerance, based on a concept of causes, to be introduced in Section 3.

2.1   Basics

Each *database schema* (in short, *schema*) consists of a set T of *table definitions*, a set V of *view definitions* and a set IC of *integrity constraints*, a.k.a. *integrity theory*. Each table in T uniquely corresponds to a *base predicate* with some arity. Each view in V corresponds to a *view predicate*, defined by a set of clauses of the form $A \leftarrow B$ where A is an atom and B a conjunction of literals with predicates that recur on base predicates. Each constraint in IC is a first-order predicate logic sentence. Unless explicitly stated otherwise, each constraint be represented in the form of a *denial*, i.e., a clause without head whose body is a conjunction of literals.

A *database* is a pair $D = (S, E)$ where S is a schema and E is an *extension* of the table definitions in S, i.e., a set of ground base predicate facts. As usual, we assume that, for each schema $S = (T, V, IC)$ and each database $D = (S, E)$, $V \cup E$ determines a unique minimal Herbrand model, sometimes called the *standard model* of D.

For a database D, an integrity theory IC and $I \in IC$, let $D(IC) = sat$ (resp., $D(I) = sat$) denote that IC (resp., I) is satisfied in D, and $D(IC) = vio$ (resp., $D(I) = vio$) that it is violated. 'Consistency' and 'inconsistency' are synonymous to 'satisfied' and, resp., 'violated' integrity.

From now on, let D always denote a database, IC the integrity theory of the schema of D, I a constraint in IC, E the extension of D, and U an update.

We may use ';' as a delimiter between elements of sets, for avoiding confusion with the use of ',' which also symbolizes conjunction of literals in the body of clauses.

2.2   Updates

Updates map databases to databases. For a database D with view definitions V and an update U, let D^U denote the database into which D is mapped by U, V^U the views of D^U and IC^U the integrity theory of D^U. D is also called the *old* database and D^U the *new* database. If $IC^U = IC$, U is called a *conventional update*. Let U_c denote the maximal subset of U that is a conventional update. Moreover, if $V^U = V$ and $IC^U = IC$, U is called an *extensional update*.

2.3   Integrity Checking

From now on, let $\mathcal{M}$ always denote an integrity checking method (in short, *method*). Each $\mathcal{M}$ can be formalized as a function that maps pairs (D, U) to $\{ok, ko\}$, where ok means that $\mathcal{M}$ sanctions U and ko that it does not. The computation of $\mathcal{M}(D, U)$ usually involves less access to E, and thus is more efficient than a *brute-force* check, i.e., a plain evaluation of all constraints against the entire database, without any simplification.

For simplicity, we only consider methods $\mathcal{M}$ and classes of pairs (D, U) such that the computation of $\mathcal{M}(D, U)$ terminates. That can always be achieved by a timeout mechanism with output ko.

Below, Definition 1 captures the conventional concept of soundness and completeness of integrity checking methods for updates including schema updates.

Definition 1. (*Conventional Integrity Checking*)
$\mathcal{M}$ is called *sound* or, resp., *complete* if, for each (D, U) such that $D(IC) = sat$, the implication (1) or, resp., (2) holds.

$$\mathcal{M}(D, U) = ok \;\; \Rightarrow \;\; D^U(IC^U) = sat \tag{1}$$

$$D^U(IC^U) = sat \;\; \Rightarrow \;\; \mathcal{M}(D, U) = ok \tag{2}$$

Both (1) and (2) relate the output ok of $\mathcal{M}$ to integrity satisfaction. We omit symmetric relationships of ko and integrity violation, since soundness and, resp., completeness for ko and violation is equivalent to (2) and, resp., (1).

Example 2.
Let $IC = \{I, I'\}$ and U be as in Example 1, and suppose that $D(IC) = sat$. Most methods $\mathcal{M}$ evaluate the simplified constraints $\leftarrow male(joe)$, $male(susan)$ and $\leftarrow female(joe)$, $female(susan)$, and output $\mathcal{M}(D, U) = ok$ if joe is registered as male and $susan$ as female (and, curiously, also if joe would be registered as female and $susan$ as male). Otherwise, $\mathcal{M}(D, U) = ko$.

3   Causes

In this section, we first revisit the definitions of causes for integrity violation in definite databases [8] and for constraints with negation in relational databases [10]. Then, we extend them to non-definite databases and constraints by simplifying a previous generalization in [9].

Informally speaking, causes are minimal explanations of why an answer is given or why a constraint is violated. In 3.1, we formalize this idea in a homogeneous form for definite databases, queries and constraints, as well as for constraints with negation in relational databases. In 3.2, we generalize the preceding definitions for 'normal' deductive databases, queries and constraints with non-monotonic negation in the body of clauses, as well as for negative answers. In 3.3, we outline the use of causes for inconsistency-tolerant integrity checking, which is the cornerstone for an inconsistency-tolerant control of the evolution of databases, and particularly of schema updating, as addressed in Section 4.

3.1   Simple Causes

For the definition below, suppose that D is definite. Also, recall that the violation of a constraint of the form $\leftarrow B$ corresponds to a non-empty answer to the query $\leftarrow B$.

Definition 2. (*Causes for Definite Databases, Queries and Constraints*)
Let V be the view definitions and E the extension of a database D, V^* the set of all ground instances of V, B a conjunction of atoms and θ an answer to $\leftarrow B$ in D. A subset C of $V^* \cup E$ is called a *cause* of θ, and also a *cause* of $\forall(B\theta)$ in D, if $C \models \forall(B\theta)$ and there is no proper subset C' of C with that property. If $\leftarrow B$ is a constraint, we also call C a *cause of the violation* of $\leftarrow B$ in D.

Example 3.
Let D be as in Example 1. Clearly, $\{married(jay, pat),\ male(jay),\ male(pat)\}$ is a cause of the violation of I in D.

Causes according to Definition 2 can be computed straightforwardly, and essentially come for free, by tracing SLD refutations of denials [9]. However, due to the non-monotonicity of database negation, both the definition and the computation of causes become much more involved for causes of negative answers, and for causes of answers and constraint violations in databases with clauses that may contain negative literals in their body.

Small first steps into that direction had been taken in Section 6 of [8] and [10], for negative answers as well as queries and constraints with negative literals, but only for flat relational databases. A variant of the corresponding definition which likens it more to Definition 2 is reproduced below.

Definition 3. (*Causes for Negation in Relational Databases*)
Let D be a relational database, B a conjunction of literals and θ an answer to $\leftarrow B$ in D. A set C of ground literals such that $comp(D) \models C$ is called a *cause* of θ, and also a *cause* of $\forall(B\theta)$ in D, if $C \models \forall(B\theta)$ and there is no proper subset C' of C with that property. If $\leftarrow B$ is a constraint, we also call C a *cause of the violation* of $\leftarrow B$ in D.

Example 4. Let $I^\sim = \leftarrow married(x,y),\ male(x),\ \sim female(y)$ and D as in Example 1. Clearly, a cause of the violation of $I^\sim$ in D is $\{married(jay, pat),\ male(jay),\ \sim female(pat)\}$.

In fact, the definition in [8] is somewhat more general than Definition 3, in that $\leftarrow B$ is replaced by an arbitrary first-order sentence. Yet, for queries, both versions of the definition are fairly bland, since each answer in a flat relational database essentially explains itself. Thus, the computation of causes in relational databases is even simpler than the computation of causes in the definite case. However, Definition 3 is as interesting as Definition 2 for explaining the violation of constraints, since the facts that cause violations can be used for explanations [11] and repairs [12].

3.2 General Causes

Due to the non-monotonicity of database negation, the definitions in 3.1 do not generalize to explanations of negative answers, nor of answers and constraint violations for *normal* databases, queries and integrity theories, where negative literals may occur in the body of clauses. An extension of the definition of causes in [8] in order to cope with database negation had first been proposed in [9]. Below, we present a less complicated but equivalent version of that extension.

First, we recall that $comp(D)$ essentially consists of the if-and-only-if completions (in short, completions) of all predicates in $\mathcal{L}$. For a predicate p in $\mathcal{L}$, let p_D denote the completion of p in D.

Definition 4. Let D be a database, p a predicate in $\mathcal{L}$, n the arity of p, $x_1, \ldots, x_n$ the $\forall$-quantified variables in p_D and θ a substitution of $x_1, \ldots, x_n$. For $A = p(x_1, \ldots, x_n)\theta$, the *completion* of A in D is obtained by applying θ to p_D and is denoted by A_D. Further, let $comp(D) = \{A_D \mid A \in \mathcal{H}_\mathcal{L}\}$, and $if(D)$ and $only\text{-}if(D)$ be obtained by replacing $\leftrightarrow$ in each $A_D \in comp(D)$ by $\leftarrow$ and, resp., $\rightarrow$. Finally, let $iff(D) = if(D) \cup only\text{-}if(D)$. The usual equality axioms of $comp(D)$ that interpret $=$ as identity be associated by default also to $iff(D)$.

Clearly, $if(D)$ is equivalent to the set of all ground instances of clauses in D. Moreover, $comp(D)$, $\overline{comp(D)}$ and $iff(D)$ clearly have the same logical consequences. However, the characterization of causes in Definition 5 below by minimal subsets of $iff(D)$ is more precise than it could be if subsets of $comp(D)$ were used instead.

Definition 5. (*Causes for Normal Databases, Queries and Constraints*)
Let D be a normal database, B a conjunction of literals and θ an answer to $\leftarrow B$ in D. A subset C of $iff(D)$ is called a *cause* of θ, and also a *cause* of $\forall(B\theta)$ in D, if $C \models \forall(B\theta)$ and there is no proper subset C' of C with that property. If $\leftarrow B$ is a constraint, we also call C a *cause of the violation* of $\leftarrow B$ in D.

For easy reading, we may represent elements of $only\text{-}if(D)$ in a simplified form, in subsequent examples. Simplifications are obtained by replacing ground equations with their truth values and by common equivalence-preserving rewritings for the composition of subformulas with *true* or *false*. Also, we may identify D with (V, E), while representing constraints or integrity theories explicitly, and omitting T.

Example 5.

a) Let $D = \{p(x) \leftarrow q(x), r(x); \ q(1); \ q(2); \ r(2); \ s(1); \ s(2)\}$. The only cause of the violation of $\leftarrow s(x), \sim p(x)$ in D is $\{s(1); \ p(1) \rightarrow q(1) \wedge r(1); \ \sim r(1)\}$.

b) Let $D = \{p \leftarrow q(1, x); \ q(2, y) \leftarrow r(y); \ r(1)\}$. The only cause of the violation of $\leftarrow \sim p$ in D is $\{p \rightarrow \exists x \, q(1, x)\} \cup \{\sim q(1, i) \mid i \in \mathcal{L}^c\}$.

c) Let $D = \{p \leftarrow q(x, x); \ q(x, y) \leftarrow r(x), s(y); \ r(1); \ s(2)\}$. Each cause of $\sim p$ in D contains $\{p \rightarrow \exists x \, q(x, x)\} \cup \{q(i, i) \rightarrow r(i) \wedge s(i)) \mid i \in \mathcal{L}^c\} \cup \{\sim r(2); \ \sim s(1)\}$ and, for each $j > 2$ in $\mathcal{L}^c$, either $\sim r(j)$ or $\sim s(j)$, and nothing else.

d) Let $D = \{p \leftarrow q;\ p \leftarrow \sim q\}$, $D' = D \cup \{q\}$ and $I = \leftarrow p$. Clearly, D is a cause of the violation of I in D and in D'. Another cause of p in D is $\{p \leftarrow \sim q;\ \sim q\}$. Another cause of p in D' is $\{p \leftarrow q;\ q\}$.

e) Let $D = \{p \leftarrow \sim q;\ q \leftarrow \sim r;\ r \leftarrow \sim s;\ r \leftarrow \sim t\}$. The two causes of the violation of $\leftarrow p$ in D are $\{p \leftarrow \sim q;\ q \rightarrow \sim r;\ r \leftarrow \sim s;\ \sim s\}$ and $\{p \leftarrow \sim q;\ q \rightarrow \sim r;\ r \leftarrow \sim t;\ \sim t\}$.

f) Let $D = \{p(x) \leftarrow r(x);\ r(1)\}$ and $I = \exists x(r(x) \wedge \sim p(x))$. A denial form of I is $\leftarrow vio$, where vio is defined by $\{vio \leftarrow \sim q;\ q \leftarrow r(x), \sim p(x)\}$, where q is a fresh 0-ary predicate. Thus, the causes of the violation of I in D are the causes of vio in $D' = D \cup \{vio \leftarrow \sim q;\ q \leftarrow r(x), \sim p(x)\}$. Thus, for each $\mathcal{K} \subseteq \mathcal{L}^c$ such that $1 \in \mathcal{K}$, $\{vio \leftarrow \sim q\} \cup \{p(i) \leftarrow r(i) \mid i \in \mathcal{K}\} \cup \{q \rightarrow \exists x(r(x) \wedge \sim p(x))\} \cup \{\sim r(i) \mid i \notin \mathcal{K}\}$ is a cause of vio in D'.

3.3   Cause-Based Inconsistency Tolerance

By common sense, an update U should be rejected only if U would cause the violation of a constraint, independent of the presence or absence of violations that are independent of U. However, conventional methods require that all constraints be satisfied before any update could be checked for integrity preservation.

Example 6. As in Example 1, let us assume a database D with constraints for preventing bigamy, married minors and other unlawful relationships. Yet, D may contain entries of persons married twice, underage spouses, etc. Such integrity violations may be due to omissions (e.g., an unrecorded divorce), neglect (e.g., integrity checking switched off for schema evolution) or other irregularities (e.g., a changed marriage legislation). Although new marriages that satisfy all constraints can be entered without problems into D, such updates have traditionally been considered to be not checkable by conventional methods if D contains facts that violate integrity.

As opposed to conventional approaches, cause-based integrity checking, as defined below, is inconsistency-tolerant, since it may sanction updates that do not increase the amount of causes of integrity violation, no matter how high the amount of inconsistency is before the update is executed. As we are going to see in Example 11, Definition 6 entails that even each unsatisfiable schema is tolerable, for updates that do not violate any constraint.

Definition 6. (*Cause-based Integrity Checking*)
a) Let $cv(D, I) = \{C \mid C$ is a cause of violation of I in $D\}$ denote the set of all causes of the violation of I in D, *modulo renamings of variables.*

b) A method $\mathcal{M}$ is called *sound* and, resp., *complete* for cause-based inconsistency-tolerant integrity checking if, for each tuple (D, U), implication 3 or, resp., 4 holds.

$$\mathcal{M}(D, U) = ok \ \Rightarrow \ cv(D^U, I) \subseteq cv(D, I) \text{ for each } I \in IC \tag{3}$$

$$cv(D^U, I) \subseteq cv(D, I) \text{ for each } I \in IC \ \Rightarrow \ \mathcal{M}(D, U) = ok \tag{4}$$

Definition 6 is going to be illustrated by examples 7 and, later, 8–12. Examples 7 and 12 feature extensional updates. Examples 8–10 are schema updates involving changes of tables, view definitions or integrity constraints. Example 12 also features the method in [17], which is not inconsistency-tolerant.

Example 7. For a table p, $I = \leftarrow p(x, y), p(x, z), y \neq z$ is a primary key constraint on the first column of p. Updates such as $U = insert\ p(a, b)$ can be accepted by each cause-based inconsistency-tolerant method $\mathcal{M}$, unless another p-tuple with the same key, e.g., $p(a, c)$, is in the database. In that case, $\{p(a, b), p(a, c)\}$ would be a new cause that violates I, and $\mathcal{M}$ would have to reject U. Otherwise, $\mathcal{M}$ can accept U, independent of any extant violation of I, e.g., by stored facts $p(b, b)$ and $p(b, c)$. Then, $\{p(b, b), p(b, c)\}$ is a cause of the violation of I, but no new cause of the violation of I is introduced by U. Since U does not increase the amount of causes of inconsistency, U can be accepted.

In [16], *case-based* inconsistency-tolerant integrity checking is studied. Case-based methods make sure that the amount of violated cases of constraint does not increase across updates. In [15,16], we have shown that many, though not all methods in the literature are sound for case-based inconsistency tolerance. An analogous result for cause-based methods is

Theorem 1. Each method shown to be sound for case-based integrity checking in [15,16] also is sound for cause-based inconsistency-tolerant integrity checking of conventional updates.

Proof. Theorem 1 follows from the more general result that each case-based method whatsoever is cause-based for conventional updates and updates of view definitions. That has been shown for definite databases and denials in [8], but that proof generalizes straightforwardly to normal databases and arbitrary integrity constraints.

In the remainder of this paper, we are going to show that the results for checking arbitrary schema updates with case-based methods in [6] continue to hold also for cause-based methods.

4   Inconsistency-Tolerant Schema Updating

In 4.1 we are going to show that cause-based methods that are inconsistency-tolerant for checking conventional updates in normal databases with normal constraints can also be used for schema updates involving changes in the integrity theory. We illustrate that result for table alterations in 4.2, for updates of integrity theories in 4.3, and for updates of view definitions in 4.4. In 4.3, we also propose an inconsistency-tolerant checking policy that makes schema updates more efficient. In 4.4, we also show that cause-based integrity checking even tolerates unsatisfiable schema definitions. In 4.5, we show that cause-based inconsistency tolerance is applicable to control the preservation of integrity for safety-critical schema updates in evolving databases.

4.1   Cause-Based Checking of Schema Updates

Most conventional integrity checking methods are not conceived for insertions or alterations of integrity constraints. (No checking is needed for the deletion of constraints since that may never cause any integrity violation.) However, to check new or altered constraints cannot take advantage of the incrementality of checking updates of base facts or view definitions. Rather, new or altered constraints usually are evaluated brute-force against the updated state, in order to check whether they are violated or not.

The following result states that methods that are cause-based for conventional updates continue to be inconsistency-tolerant according to Definition 6 for arbitrary schema updates, involving table alterations, updates of view definitions and integrity theories.

Theorem 2.
Each method $\mathcal{M}$ that is sound for cause-based integrity checking of conventional updates also is sound for cause-based integrity checking of schema updates.

Proof. For updates that involve only base facts and view definitions, the result follows from the generalization of the result in [8], as mentioned in the proof of Theorem 1. For updates involving changes in the integrity theory, the result can be shown by verifying (3) and (4) of Definition 6 by induction on the number of constraints inserted by U, assuming that each $I \in IC^U \setminus IC$ is evaluated brute-force in D^U.

Theorem 2 addresses the *soundness* of cause-based methods for schema updates. With regard to scaling up the *completeness* of cause-based methods from conventional updates to schema updates including modifications of the integrity theory, a somewhat surprising result is going to be presented in 4.3.

In the following subsections, we illustrate Theorem 2 by examples of checking various kinds of schema updates with cause-based methods: table alterations in 4.2, modifications of integrity theories in 4.3, alterations of view definitions and updates of databases with an unsatisfiable schema in 4.4, and updates by safety-critical applications in 4.5.

4.2   Inconsistency-Tolerant Table Alterations

Example 8 is going to illustrate that the amount of causes of violation never increases whenever any table alteration is checked by an inconsistency-tolerant method. It may even decrease, since some causes of violation may disappear by altering tables. Thus, cause-based inconsistency-tolerant methods support *inconsistency-tolerant partial repairs* [12], i.e., updates that reduce the amount of violated causes, while surviving violations are tolerated.

Example 8. Let $I = \leftarrow q(x, x, y)$ constrain q to be void of tuples the first and second arguments of which coincide. Let $q(a, a, a)$, $q(a, a, b)$ be the only facts in D that match $q(x, x, y)$. Clearly, each of them is a cause of the violation of I. Hence, conventional integrity checking refuses to handle the update U which alters the definition of q by swapping the second and third columns. As opposed to that, each complete cause-based inconsistency-tolerant method $\mathcal{M}$ will admit U and output ok if D contains no fact matching $q(x, y, x)$ such that $x \neq a$, and ko otherwise (e.g., if $q(b, a, b) \in D$). Thus, a sanctioned U does not only contain, but even diminish $cv(D, I)$.

4.3   Inconsistency-Tolerant Integrity Updates

As seen in 4.1, inconsistency tolerance of each cause-based method $\mathcal{M}$ for arbitrary schema updates U in databases D can be achieved by computing $\mathcal{M}(D, U_c)$ and evaluating each inserted or modified constraint brute-force against D^U. (For deleted constraints, no checking is needed. For example, to delete I and I' in Example 1 clearly cannot cause any integrity violation.)

Example 9. Assume U and $IC = \{I\}$ as in Example 7, and let U' consist of U and the insertion of the constraint $I' = \leftarrow p(x, x)$. Further, let us assume that U does not cause any violation of I. Thus, a brute-force evaluation of I' against D^U will result in $\mathcal{M}(D, U) = ok$ if $D(I') = sat$, and $\mathcal{M}(D, U) = ko$ if not, e.g., if (c, c) is a row in p.

Yet, brute-force evaluation is inefficient, inflexible and possibly unfeasible. For instance, if, in Example 9, (c, c) is a row in p, then the cause $p(c, c)$ of the violation of $\leftarrow p(x, x)$ in D^U is not tolerated if I' is checked brute-force. Of course, that is sound, since U' would increase the amount of violations.

However, in a database $D = ((T, V, IC), E)$ that is operational while undergoing schema updates, it may be impossible to delay operations until inserted constraints are evaluated entirely against possibly huge volumes of legacy data. Then, it should be advantageous to check an arbitrary schema update U by computing $\mathcal{M}(((T, V, IC^U), E), U_c)$. That is, inserted constraints are not evaluated brute-force, but are just checked against the update and future updates. Thus, updated constraints are not checked against legacy data, and the current and all future updates are prevented from introducing new causes of violation, at the expense of having to tolerate possible violations of inserted constraints by legacy data. If needed, they can be dealt with at less busy times, e.g., during night runs.

The following theorem reveals another advantage of using this policy: it may achieve completeness, while brute-force checking of inserted constraints cannot.

Theorem 3.
No method $\mathcal{M}$ that checks inserted constraints brute-force is complete for cause-based integrity checking.

Proof. If, in Example 9, no fact matching $p(a, y)$ is in D and $p(c, c)$ is the only fact that violates I', then, for each $\mathcal{M}$ that evaluates I' brute-force, $\mathcal{M}(D, U) = ko$ holds. However, condition (4) in Definition 6 warrants the output ok, since $U'_c = U$ clearly does not cause any violation of IC^U. Hence, $\mathcal{M}$ is not complete.

Example 10. (Example 9, continued).
If $\mathcal{M}$ checks U' by computing $\mathcal{M}(((T, V, IC^{U'}), E), U_c')$, it will output *ok*, since $U_c' = U$ and I' is not relevant for U. Thus, causes such as $p(c, c)$ of the violation of I' in D are tolerated by $\mathcal{M}$.

Clearly, checking inserted constraints only with regard to U_c is much more efficient than evaluating them against the whole database. By the way, the latter is advocated in the SQL99 standard (cf. [19]), while the former lacks standardization, but is common practice.

4.4   View Modification and Unsatisfiability

Cause-based methods guarantee that all cases satisfied in the old state will remain satisfied in the new state, and that the set of causes of constraint violations does not grow larger. In fact, that continues to hold even if the given schema is unsatisfiable. Thus, inconsistency-tolerant methods are also unsatisfiability-tolerant. Hence, also the standard premise that the schema be satisfiable can be waived. We illustrate that by the following example where the modification of a view causes the unsatisfiability of the schema.

Example 11. Let $\{p(x, y) \leftarrow q(x, y), q(y, z);\ q(x, y) \leftarrow r(x, y);\ q(x, y) \leftarrow s(x, y)\}$ be the view definitions in D, and $IC = \{\leftarrow p(x, x);\ \exists x, y\ r(x, y)\}$. Clearly, the schema is satisfiable. Let (a, a), (a, b) be all tuples in s. Thus, $\leftarrow p(a, a)$ is a violated case. There are no more violated ground cases of $\leftarrow p(x, x)$ if and only if neither $r(b, a)$ nor any fact matching $r(x, x)$ is in D. Moreover, $\exists x, y\ r(x, y)$ is a violated case if and only if the extension of r is empty. Now, let U be the insertion of $q(x, y) \leftarrow r(y, x)$. Clearly, U makes the schema unsatisfiable. However, each inconsistency-tolerant method $\mathcal{M}$ can be soundly applied to check U for preserving satisfied cases. It is easy to see that $\mathcal{M}(D, U) = ko$ if and only if there is any tuple of form (A, B) in r such that (B, A) is not in r and (A, B) matches neither (b, a) nor (x, x). Otherwise, all cases of $\leftarrow p(x, x)$ that are violated in D^U are already violated in D, hence $\mathcal{M}(D, U) = ok$.

Although, in Example 11, the updated schema is unsatisfiable, it makes sense to accept further updates of D^U that do not violate any satisfied case. Such updates may even lower the number of violated cases, e.g., $U' = delete\ s(a, a)$.

4.5   Updating Safety-Critical Integrity Theories

As already seen, inconsistency tolerance is desirable. Yet, the need of safety-critical applications to have a set of 'hard' integrity constraints that are totally satisfied at all times should not be lightheartedly compromised. Hence, methods are called for that can guarantee total satisfaction of all hard constraints for dynamic schema maintenance. Fortunately, each inconsistency-tolerant method is capable of providing such a service. To see this, we first define the following reliability property, then infer Theorem 4 from it, and then interpret the definition and the result in terms of a dynamic maintenance of safety-critical applications.

Definition 7. $\mathcal{M}$ is called *reliable for hard constraints* if, for each pair (D, U) and each subset IC_h of IC such that each I in IC_h is a *hard* constraint, i.e., I must always be satisfied, i.e., $D(I) = sat$, the following implication holds.

$$\mathcal{M}(D, U) = ok \quad \Rightarrow \quad D^U(IC_h) = sat. \tag{5}$$

Theorem 4. Each cause-based method is reliable for hard constraints.

Proof. Let $\mathcal{M}$ be a cause-based method, and $IC_h \subset IC$. Then, (5) follows by applying Definition 6, property (3) and Definition 7.

By definition, each reliable method for hard constraints can maintain the total satisfaction of IC_h across updates, even if $IC \setminus IC_h$ is violated. However, for methods that are not inconsistency-tolerant, e.g., the one in [17], (5) may not hold, i.e., they may not be reliable. Example 12 shows that.

Example 12. Let $IC = \{\leftarrow q(a), r(x,x), \ \leftarrow q(b), r(x,x)\}$, $IC_h = \{\leftarrow q(b), r(x,x)\}$, and $D(IC_h) = sat$. Further, let $q(a)$ and $r(b, b)$ be the only facts in D that cause a violation of $\leftarrow q(a), r(x, x)$ in D, and $U = insert\ q(b)$. To check U, the method $\mathcal{M}_G$ in [17] drops $q(b)$ in $\leftarrow q(b), r(x, x)$, since U makes it *true*, thus obtaining the simplification $\leftarrow r(x, x)$. Since $\leftarrow q(a), r(x, x)$ is not relevant for U, the assumption of $\mathcal{M}_G$ that $D(IC) = sat$ wrongly entails that $D^U(\leftarrow q(a), r(x, x)) = sat$. Now, assume that D is distributed, q is locally accessible and r is remote. Then, $\mathcal{M}_G$ infers that also $D^U(\leftarrow r(x, x)) = sat$, since $q(a)$ is *true* in D^U. Hence, it unreliably outputs *ok*, although $D^U(IC_h) = vio$. As opposed to that, $\mathcal{M}(D, U) = ko$ holds for each cause-based inconsistency-tolerant method $\mathcal{M}$.

5 Related Work

Inconsistency tolerance is a subject of increasing importance [3]. Also inconsistency-tolerant integrity checking has received considerable attention recently [16]. The work in [16] is not based on causes, but on cases, i.e., instances of constraints that are relevant for given updates. In [8], it is shown that each case-based method is inconsistency-tolerant wrt causes, for updates of base facts and view definitions, but that the converse does not hold in general.

In general, causes are a smarter basis for inconsistency-tolerant integrity checking than cases, as argued in [7,8]. Among others, the concept of completeness is less problematic for causes than for cases. As outlined in [8,9], another advantage of causes over cases is that causes also provide a basis for computing answers that have integrity in inconsistent databases. The latter are similar to, though different from consistent query answers [2]. The relationship of the latter to cases is discussed in [9,16], and their relationship to causes in [8]. Moreover, causes offer advantages over cases with regard to partial repairs [12], and an automation of integrity checking for concurrent transactions [14].

Case-based inconsistency-tolerant schema updates are the theme of [6]. This paper upgrades the latter, by having causes take the place of cases, and by generalizing from definite to normal databases and constraints.

The concept of causes as proposed in [18] is much more complicated and involved than ours. The one in [18] is meant for explaining answers to human agents, but not, as in this paper, to programmed agents, e.g., modules that cater for integrity checking, repairing, query answering with integrity, or more.

The work in [5] is related to this paper by the topic of integrity updates. Like this paper, it is application-oriented, and additionally focuses also on issues such as database migration and web information systems, which we do not address, due to space limitation. However, inconsistency tolerance is not an issue in [5].

6 Conclusion

We have outlined how to extend conventional approaches to database schema update management. We have proposed a cause-based approach that can deal with arbitrary schema updates, including changes of the integrity theory. We have shown that such updates can be dealt with efficiently and reliably, without compromising hard integrity requirements for safety-critical applications.

As illustrated by Example 12, the advantages of our cause-based approach could not be obtained by employing any integrity checking method that is not inconsistency-tolerant. Thus, for updates U of integrity constraints, legacy data can safely be left alone only if the method used for checking U is inconsistency-tolerant.

Fortunately, the usual requirements of the total satisfaction of each database state and the satisfiability of the database schema can simply be waived, for most methods, without incurring any penalty. In fact, the power-to-mechanism ratio of our concept of inconsistency tolerance is exceedingly high, since no special mechanism is needed at all for achieving what has been disregarded by most researchers in the field until recently: inconsistency tolerance is provided for free by most methods, as argued in [15,16]. The main contribution of this paper is to have shown that cause-based inconsistency tolerance generalizes straightforwardly to updates than involve insertions or alterations of views and integrity constraints.

Ongoing work is concerned with applying a more general (not just case- or cause-based) metric approach to integrity checking of conventional updates, as presented in [13], also to schema updates. Moreover, we are working on the inconsistency-tolerant preservation of integrity across concurrent schema updates in distributed and replicated databases. A further topic of growing importance that is an objective of our current investigations is the metric-based control of consistency deterioration in cloud databases.

References

1. Abiteboul, S., Hull, R., Vianu, V.: Foundations of Databases. Addison-Wesley (1995)
2. Arenas, M., Bertossi, L.E., Chomicki, J.: Consistent query answers in inconsistent databases. In: Proceedings of PODS, pp. 68–79. ACM Press (1999)

3. Bertossi, L., Hunter, A., Schaub, T. (eds.): Inconsistency Tolerance. LNCS, vol. 3300. Springer, Heidelberg (2005)
4. Clark, K.: Negation as failure. In: Gallaire, H., Minker, J. (eds.) Logic and Data Bases, pp. 293–322. Plenum Press (1978)
5. Curino, C., Moon, H., Deutsch, A., Zaniolo, C.: Update rewriting and integrity constraint maintenance in a schema evolution support system: Prism++. PVLDB 4, 117–128 (2010)
6. Decker, H.: Towards a dynamic inconsistency-tolerant schema maintenance. In: Song, I.-Y., et al. (eds.) ER Workshops 2008. LNCS, vol. 5232, pp. 89–98. Springer, Heidelberg (2008)
7. Decker, H.: Basic causes for the inconsistency tolerance of query answering and integrity checking. In: Proc. 21st DEXA Workshops, pp. 318–322. IEEE CSP (2010)
8. Decker, H.: Toward a uniform cause-based approach to inconsistency-tolerant database semantics. In: Meersman, R., Dillon, T., Herrero, P. (eds.) OTM 2010. LNCS, vol. 6427, pp. 983–998. Springer, Heidelberg (2010)
9. Decker, H.: Answers that have integrity. In: Schewe, K.-D. (ed.) SDKB 2010. LNCS, vol. 6834, pp. 54–72. Springer, Heidelberg (2011)
10. Decker, H.: Causes for inconsistency-tolerant schema update management. In: Proc. 27th ICDE Workshops, pp. 157–161. IEEE CSP (2011)
11. Decker, H.: Consistent explanations of answers to queries in inconsistent knowledge bases. In: Roth-Berghofer, T., Tintarev, N., Leake, D. (eds.) Proc. IJCAI 2011 Workshop ExaCt, pp. 71–80 (2011)
12. Decker, H.: Partial repairs that tolerate inconsistency. In: Eder, J., Bielikova, M., Tjoa, A.M. (eds.) ADBIS 2011. LNCS, vol. 6909, pp. 389–400. Springer, Heidelberg (2011)
13. Decker, H.: Measure-based inconsistency-tolerant maintenance of database integrity. In: Schewe, K.-D., Thalheim, B. (eds.) SDKB 2013. LNCS, vol. 7693, pp. 149–173. Springer, Heidelberg (2013)
14. Decker, H., de Marín, R.J.: Enabling business rules for concurrent transactions. In: Proc. Int. Conf. on P2P, Parallel, Grid, Cloud and Internet Computing, pp. 207–212. IEEE CPS (2001)
15. Decker, H., Martinenghi, D.: Classifying integrity checking methods with regard to inconsistency tolerance. In: Proceedings of the 10th International ACM SIGPLAN Conference on Principles and Practice of Declarative Programming, pp. 195–204. ACM Press (2008)
16. Decker, H., Martinenghi, D.: Inconsistency-tolerant integrity checking. IEEE Transactions of Knowledge and Data Engineering 23(2), 218–234 (2011)
17. Gupta, A., Sagiv, Y., Ullman, J.D., Widom, J.: Constraint checking with partial information. In: Proceedings of PODS 1994, pp. 45–55. ACM Press (1994)
18. Meliou, A., Gatterbauer, W., Moore, K., Suciu, D.: The complexity of causality and responsibility for query answers and non-answers. In: Proc. 37th VLDB, pp. 34–45 (2011)
19. Türker, C.: Schema evolution in SQL-99 and commercial (object-)relational DBMS. In: Balsters, H., De Brock, B., Conrad, S. (eds.) FoMLaDO 2000 and DEMM 2000. LNCS, vol. 2065, pp. 1–32. Springer, Heidelberg (2001)

A Preliminary Survey on Innovation Process Management Systems*

Claudia Diamantini, Laura Genga, and Domenico Potena

Università Politecnica delle Marche
via Brecce Bianche, 60131 Ancona, Italy
{c.diamantini,l.genga,d.potena}@univpm.it

Abstract. In last decades innovation management has turned out to be a key factor in organizations growth, thus stimulating a strong research activity about such a topic. In the present work we analyse the current state of Literature regarding innovation modelling and management, taking into account different approaches with their main features. Elaborating upon such investigation, we identify open research issues and fruitful research directions for the development of data-driven, analysis-based innovation support and management systems. Finally we introduce the main features of our own approach, based on the analysis of traces generated by innovation activities, following the principles of Process Mining methods, of which an overview is delineated.

1 Introduction

In current economic scenario, highly dynamic and uncertain, innovation management and promotion are widely recognized as required skills for organization survival and growth. More and more often to gain and maintain a significant competitive advantage organizations have to continuously innovate themselves, adapting their products, services, processes and so forth to deal with the product life cycle contraction, the changeable market demand and so on [1].

While in the past innovation was mostly regarded as an even chance, strictly dependent by the intuition of few "genius", modern theories tend toward a more systematic approach, capable of optimizing the management of an innovation process, i.e. the flow of activities involved in the production of innovation. Although such a topic is used to be addressed mainly by scholars in business and economy Literature, recently also IT experts have been interested in it, developing several contributions about automatic or semi-automatic innovation support tools.

In the present work we depict the main features of principal methodologies and tools aimed to lead and support innovation tasks. We analyse strengths and weaknesses of proposals in Literature, and then discuss about open and fruitful research directions, introducing in particular our own proposal.

---

* This work has been partly funded by the EC through the ICT Project BIVEE: Business Innovation and Virtual Enterprise Environment (FoF-ICT-2011.7.3-285746).

A. Cuzzocrea and S. Maabout (Eds.): MEDI 2013, LNCS 8216, pp. 92–103, 2013.
© Springer-Verlag Berlin Heidelberg 2013

The rest of this work is organized as follows; in section 2 we present the major trends we have recognized in Literature for innovation support, with some applicative example. In section 3 we illustrate our approach, together with an introduction of Process Mining principles we refer to. The last section is devoted to draw some conclusive considerations.

2   Innovation Management Approaches

In this section we illustrate the principal features of several approaches aimed to model and support innovation that have been proposed over time. We start by considering the earlier methodologies, especially ones belong to Systematic Innovation field, mostly developed in business and economic Literature. Then, we illustrate some approaches devoted to technology analysis and forecasting, where IT methodologies and in particular Data Mining techniques have been introduced to model the innovation process. Finally, we discuss about more recent proposals, which see innovation as a collaborative process.

2.1   Systematic Innovation

Systematic Innovation(SI) is defined as a "structured way of creating innovative ideas to solve engineering, service and management problems" [2]. Such relatively new field aims to optimize the innovation process, e.g. by minimizing the waste of resources, improving its results and so forth. More precisely, SI theories start from the assumption that the innovation skills are not a prerogative of just some talented individual, or "genius", but can instead be learned and improved in the most of the people, under an appropriate framework.

Currently several and often heterogeneous approaches are developed under the SI umbrella. However, Systematic Innovation was for a long time strictly related to, and often identified with, the *TRIZ* theory, Russian acronym for Theory of Inventive Problem Solving. Indeed many contributions tend to consider the two terms almost synonyms or, anyway, indicate TRIZ as the most important part of SI framework [2,3]. Nevertheless, many recent works are also interested in non-TRIZ theories and their integration with TRIZ ones [4]. Such a topic is gaining an important role in SI studies, which can hence more broadly intended as a "combination of the TRIZ theories, and of its evolutions, with other troubleshooting methodologies" [5].

Anyway, TRIZ remains the most well note and used approach of SI. In the following we briefly introduce the main principles of such theory, with a few examples of relevant extensions.

TRIZ Framework. The Theory of Inventive Problem Solving was developed by Altshuller and his colleagues in the URSS between 1946 and 1985; several years later it has become a hot topic in R&D department management also in the West countries. Many works have explored such theory, expanding the original methodology and application field over time. Today, TRIZ is intended as a "problem solving method based on logic and data, not intuition, which accelerates the project team's ability to solve these problems creatively" [6].

Originally, the TRIZ theoretical framework was aimed to address and solve the technical issues that affect the product development process. The main idea is that each *inventive problem* encountered during the development of innovative products is "a problem containing at least one contradiction" [7] that arises between certain parameters of the system. For instance, in the aeronautic domain, we can consider the trade-off between the speed of an aircraft and its *adaptability*, i.e. the needed length of take-off and landing strip; as one can argue, the improvement of the first cause a worsening of the other and vice versa. To each inventive problem correspond one or more *inventive solutions* able to wholly or partially eliminate the contradiction. In our example, one of the proposed solutions suggests to use *dynamics* to modify the system geometry.

A significant result of preliminary works of Altshuller consists in the discovery of some typical evolutive paths, or trends, that usually regulate a technological system evolution and hence can be applied to lead such evolution in a desired manner [8]. In particular, Altshuller conducted an extensive analysis of successful patents, in order to extract the most common inventive problems with their corresponding solutions. From such analysis he derived the so-called *40 Inventive Principles*, i.e. general principles repeatedly used in patents to solve system contradictions. Furthermore he also organized the most typical contradictions in a *Technical Contradiction Matrix*, i.e. a 39x39 matrix where each cell represents a contradiction. Such a matrix is used to map the several kinds of contradiction with the inventive principles set typically applied to solve them, thus facilitating the selection of the most suitable principles for the particular problem one is interested in.

Over time many efforts have been conducted to make the TRIZ theory more flexible and reliable, e.g. "Su-field model" and "76 Standard Solutions" [9]. In particular, the former models problems related to existing technological systems by identifying causal relationships which exist among its components. Problems occur when a causal relationship is ineffective. The latter consists in a collection of solutions grouped into five large categories (i.e. improving the system with no or little change, improving the system by changing the system, system transitions, detection and measurement, strategies for simplification and improvement). Typically, 76 Standard Solutions are applied to manage problems identified by the Su-field approach. Another example of TRIZ expansion is reported in [10], where the original contradiction matrix is extended with a further dimension to take into account also the human factors. The goal in this case is hence to adapt the original TRIZ theory in order to apply it also to non technical problems. Finally, there are many works interested in the integration of TRIZ and other problem solving methods (e.g. axiomatic design and case based reasoning), as reported in [4] and in [5].

Although the original TRIZ framework is not intended to be implemented in automatic tool, today it is possible to find several software tools based on TRIZ principles (e.g. [11]).

2.2   Technology Analysis

In last decades several efforts have been aimed to model technological trends by analysing patents, both to understand current scenarios and to *forecast* the future trends. Although there are some examples of TRIZ theories applied to technology analysis and forecasting, like in [12], such a topic has been addressed also from several contributions outside the SI framework, that we briefly introduce.

Patent analysis approaches usually make use of a patent bibliometric information, as its number, inventor, international classification and so on, applying appropriate techniques to manipulate it. Among these, one of the most known is the *patent citation analysis*, whose principles are similar to the scientific literature analysis ones [13]. Considering the amount of citations of a certain patent in subsequent patents as a relevance metric, one can apply citation-based techniques both to obtain a database of linked patents and to evaluate a patent by means of quantitative measures, like citations per patent, highly cited patent, impact index and so forth.

Nevertheless, several limitations affect citation analysis, e.g. the limited scope of the analysis and the information extracted, since only information about cited-citing are taking into account, or the little attention toward the overall relationship among the patents and so on. Therefore, an intensive research activity is being conducted in order to overcome such limitations. In particular several recent theories have introduced mining techniques, especially text-mining ones, in patent analysis, in order to deal with the patents unstructured and textual nature. For instance in [14] the authors propose to combine text-mining and network analysis techniques to investigate the patents links in a database. More precisely, the authors make use of a text-mining technique to extract a keywords vector for each patent; then they evaluate patents relationship in terms of Euclidean distance between each keyword in corresponding vectors. The outcome of such analysis is an incidence matrix, where two patents are linked only if their distance is minor that a certain predefined threshold. Starting from the incidence matrix, a patent network is constructed, where each patent is a node and edges represent patents links. Such network can then be used both to obtain a visual overall vision of patents relationship and to derive some quantitative measures.

Technology Forecasting. Another interesting use of patents analysis regards the *Technology Forecasting* (TF), which involves theories and methodologies devoted to anticipate and lead future technological innovations trends. Over time several TF approaches have been developed under two main categories, namely the *exploratory* approaches and the *normative* ones. While the first are mainly aimed to actually conduce future technology trends forecasts, the latter are more interested in identifying and aiding the development of promising and unexplored technologies. However, more recent TF contributions are especially interested in normative, experience-based methodologies, since they turned out to be more suitable to effectively aid technology development. In particular, such methodologies are typically focused on patents and scientific literature analysis.

An example of application of patent analysis in TF can be found in [15]. Here, the authors want to exploit one of the most known normative TF methods, i.e. the *morphological analysis* (MA), combining it with a text-mining technique in order to improve its results. Morphological analysis is mainly aimed to structure a problem, in order to make it easier to understand and stimulate the development of solutions. In particular, MA is typically used to recognize, given a certain subject or system, its set of *dimensions*, i.e. a set of features capable of describing it as complete as possible [16]. Each dimension can assume a certain number of values, each representing a particular instance, usually indicated in MA as a *shape*. Note that all activities in MA are based on the human expertise. Figure 1 shows an example of MA dimensions and related shapes used in [15] to describe a technology. Then the patent analysis goes on with (1) the extraction of a keywords vector for each patent related to the given technology, (2) an appropriate filtering of the keywords based on domain experts, and (3) the mapping of each keyword to a specific shape. Hence, at the end of the procedure, each patent is assigned to a certain combination of shapes on the basis of the shapes of its most frequent keywords. In such a way, we are able to identify what combinations of shapes are not-explored yet, so providing useful indications to the development of innovative technological solutions.

Table 1. Example of MA output

Process	Energy	Structure	Function	Material
Addition	Chemical	Quadrate	Drilling	Stone
Removal	Heat	Triangle	Grilling	Iron
Grouping	Biological	Circle	Turning	Gas
		Linear		Paper

2.3 Innovation as Knowledge and Social Process

One of the most important trends of innovation management Literature regards the relationship between innovation and collaboration, initially recognized by the "Open Innovation" theory [17]. Indeed in last few years more and more organizations are moving from a *closed* innovation activities conduction toward an *open* one, where the collaborative work, both intra and inter organizations, represents the real innovation engine. As a consequence, the efficient management of collaborative work, together with the improvement of the creativity of both the individual and the group her belongs to, achieved a central role in the development of methodologies aimed to innovation support.

In the IT Literature the collaboration support is a well known issue, addressed in many contributions and in particular in *Computer Support Cooperative Work* (CSCW) field [18, 19]. This one is a really broad research field, which involves several topics related to the collaborative work improvement through IT technologies; some of such topics revealed to be of interest also for innovation issues e.g. group creation (e.g. [20, 21]), group decision making (e.g. [22]) and so forth. However, only few contributions explicitly deal with the innovation support topic. Among these, in the following we briefly introduce two examples of different frameworks, respectively presented in [23] and in [24].

In the former the authors define the innovation process like a "consecutive problem-resolution", usually performed in a group context, and propose a seven-step problem resolution methodology, named *Group Model Building by Selection and Argumentation*(G-MoBSA) to improve its results. The goal is to capture the knowledge arising from group members interactions in an explicit and formal representation through the creation of so-called *models*. Firstly a model is created by a group member as an explicitation of her perception of a certain problem, possibly with her proposed solution; then the other members can support or question such a model, thus firing a discussion aimed to enrich the original model with the other members knowledge. Note that the discussion is structured by formal rules, i.e. each member can use a predefined set of statements both to question and support the model. In order to support the methodology, the authors also developed a web-based tool, named *Knowledge Breeder*. Such a tool allows the users to construct and visualize the various models developed by each actor, in the structure imposed by the adopted argumentation formalism. Moreover, it can automatically infer about the validity of a model, under the assumption that the statement composition rules were followed by the actor which developed the model.

With respect to G-MoBSA framework, the approach proposed in [24] is interested in aiding group members intuitions, instead of formalizing their interactions, making use of text mining principles on some data of interest in order to stimulate members creativity. Such idea extraction and improvement process is called *idea discovery* and involves two main tasks, i.e. a) the use of ad-hoc mining algorithm capable of organizing textual knowledge in a graph, named *scenario map*, and b) scenario-based activities aimed to enable idea generation. More precisely, the mining algorithm exploited, called *ideaGraph*, is able to extract a graph from a textual innovation document by clustering the data on the base of some ad-hoc linkage measure, with the aim of improving the human data comprehension and aiding the discovery of hidden knowledge. Anyway, its generation is just a step in the idea discovery process, illustrated by Figure 1. Subsequent steps are the *static* and *dynamic* discovery. The former uses the graph obtained to generate new ideas through combinational, analogical and reasoning thinking, while during dynamic discovery previous and actual graphs are compared to identify important changes between them that can stimulate human insights. In a group, it is possible to conduce both the discovery paths in parallel. Note that the process is inherently iterative: the new data obtained from reasoning about static or dynamic discovery are integrated with original ones and the process can restart.

2.4   Discussion

Previous approaches are focused only on some specific aspects of the innovation process. The TRIZ theory stresses the technical aspect, trying to solve new

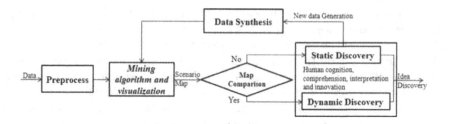

Fig. 1. Idea Discovery process

technical issues by identifying similarities with already solved problems. In this way it mostly uses patents knowledge, without considering human aspects, in particular collaboration and creativity. Although some recent SI studies propose the integration of TRIZ with other problem solving tools, to take into account more aspects than technical one, such attempts are not organized in a systematic and well-defined methodology like the original TRIZ one yet. Regard other patent-based methodologies, they are mainly dedicated to the technological scenario analysis, without considering the process that has guided the development of the patent (i.e. the innovation). Finally, collaborative support methodologies focus on the human collaboration support, by organizing group knowledge and improving their domain understanding. Hence, the innovation is not seen as an evolving process.

Furthermore, it is to be noted that the analysis of the innovation process as a structural datum can provide useful knowledge about e.g. how the enterprise works, helping to individuate bottlenecks, best practices, and so forth. Nevertheless, at the best of our knowledge such a topic has not been addressed in Literature.

3   Process Mining for Innovation Support

In order to overcome limitations of the previously discussed approaches, we propose to consider the innovation process as a whole, by identifying and linking the innovative activities set performed by an organization. In such a way we expect to obtain an innovation process model suitable to exploit some tailored business intelligence tools to investigate and improve it.

More precisely, we intend to adopt the so-called *process-driven* approach, introduced in *Process Mining*(PM) research field. This latter is a relatively new discipline usually defined as "distilling a structured process description from a set of real executions" [25]; more precisely, the goal is deriving real process schemas by exploring activities logs stored in the organization informative systems, e.g. ERP, Workflow Management Systems and so forth.

Most of PM techniques work well on traditional, well-structured business operational processes; however they have revealed some problems when applied to the so-called *Spaghetti processes*, i.e. processes with a very little or no structure.

In fact in such cases the PM outcomes are usually too complex and detailed to be used in process analysis tasks. Note that innovation processes are inherently spaghetti: they can be intended as sets of goal-driven activities, deeply influenced by human experience and behaviour, thus resulting mostly uncertain and unstructured.

In order to improve PM methods results for the spaghetti processes, several methodologies have been developed over time. As reported in [27] mostly of them try to appropriately simplify the final outcome, or by directly manipulating the log, like in [29], or by clarifying the process schema, obtained by another PM method, e.g. [30]. In the former the authors perform an iterative log clustering to obtain small and homogeneous traces clusters, then extracting for each of them a different process schema which represents a so-called process *variant* (e.g. a specific usage scenario). The final process model, called "disjunctive workflow schemas" consists in the union of all schemas. The latter approach exploits the "Fuzzy Miner" algorithm. The schema reduction is founded on two main tasks, namely the "abstraction" and the "clustering" of elements, respectively aimed at removing and aggregating schema elements, on the basis of the "significance" of each schema element, which is evaluated through a predefined, configurable metrics set.

Another approach dealing with spaghetti processes has been proposed in [33] by the authors of the present work. In contrast with previous approaches, in this work the focus is on analysing parts of the process to discover important activities patterns, instead of extracting, or simplifying, a complete process model. The proposal is based on the adoption of a graph-based hierarchical clustering technique, which will be explained in the next section. The main goal is to identify the most relevant activities patterns and, arranging them in a hierarchy, the relations between these patterns.

Note that innovation domain presents some specific challenges to deal with, first of all the already mentioned human component influence. With respect to this latter one can find some similarities with software development process, for which some mining strategies have been proposed e.g. in [26] or in [28]. However software development can usually refer to some ad-hoc design methodologies, which provide the team members with a set of well known guide lines or rules making their activities less chaotic than innovation ones.

Another important challenges to deal with consists in data gathering: data regarding innovation activities are typically very hard to collect, being raw, spread among many and heterogeneous sources and possibly concerning also informal activities typically not stored in a digital format.

Consequently, in order to explore innovation activities a tailored approach is needed, which is able to deal with data gathering and with the unstructured or loosely-structured nature of an innovation process.

3.1   Methodology

Our goal consists in the analysis of innovation activities logs in order to extract valuable knowledge about these ones. To this end three principal steps have to been conducted, namely a)data collection, b)data transformation, and c)data analysis.

Data Collection. As already mentioned the data collection is a non trivial issue. As a matter of fact, currently there are not available platforms able to track organization innovation activities and hence generate logs of these latter. Therefore, we have to explore several alternatives. Among these, currently we are focused on collection of data about a research team daily work, since it can be easily intended as an example of collaborative and creative work. Such data mainly consist in ones typically stored in PCs of team members, like file system logs, agenda notes, email and so on. Anyway we also plan to involve the team members in generation of data about informal tasks, since they cannot be automatically traced.

Furthermore we expect to use in following years the result of BIVEE[1]. It is an EU project aimed to support innovation in distributed environments. In particular, one of its goal consists in the build up of an innovation framework where all innovation activities are conducted, so allowing their automatic recording.

A third way that we have partially explored yet consists in the generation of synthetic datasets. In particular we recognized collaboration models in the Literature and implemented a methodology for generating random instances based on these models. Although they are affected from a bias due to the manually generation, such datasets are an useful way to test and compare different data analysis techniques, to identify much promising approaches for future test on real data.

Data Transformation. This second phase is aimed to obtain a single dataset containing innovation activities logs we are interested in. We identify two principal tasks to perform, i.e. a)application of preprocessing techniques and b)data integration. The former is mainly aimed to manage wrong and missing data; furthermore we plan to adopt appropriate mechanisms that allow us to deal with homogenization requirements of data regarding group activity. For instance if a meeting activity is performed by three members but only two of them have a related note in their agenda, the system has to be able to identify the presence of the third member. Data integration refers to the reconciliation of data from heterogeneous source in a single schema, for which we plan to test different integration techniques.

Data Analysis. Once traces are obtained, we can proceed with actual analysis of these ones. Such analysis can be performed by exploiting several PM techniques, e.g. the ones previously introduced. In the following, we describe our own approach. As already mentioned, we adopt a pattern discovery technique; more precisely, we transform the traces in graphs in order to make use of already

---

[1] http://www.bivee.eu

existing graph-techniques for pattern discovery. Among these, we focus on hierarchical clustering: in particular, we refer to the SUBDUE algorithm [31], which is able to discover a lattice of activities patterns. At top-level are returned patterns that have the best balance between frequency and representativeness. As a matter of fact, given two or more patterns with the same frequency the algorithm chooses the most complex one, which usually corresponds to the most significant in the domain. The low-level patterns are built starting from the upper-level ones. Figure 2 shows a simple example of lattice generated by the proposed method-

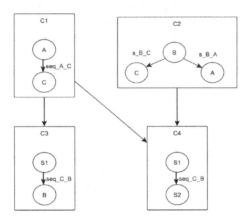

Fig. 2. Example of a simple lattice

ology: defining A, B, C specific activities and S_i patterns, in cluster C_1 and C_2 we have, respectively, graphs containing the pattern $S_1 = \{A \rightarrow C\}$, and the pattern $S_2 = \{B \rightarrow A; B \rightarrow C\}$. We can note that lower-level clusters C_3 and C_4 are an extension of the former ones, since they are obtained by extending their patterns with other specific elements. A practical example of SUBDUE application for data analysis can be found in [32]. Moreover, we have conducted some preliminary experiments on synthetic innovation data, whose results are reported in [33].

4   Conclusion

The paper examined the principal methodologies developed in Literature for the innovation process modelling and support. We firstly considered SI approaches, aimed to organize and lead inventive process by exploiting patents knowledge. Then we discussed about other patents analysis-based methodologies, mainly aimed to analyse technological trends and to identify most promising new technologies. Finally we illustrated more recent innovation theories, which stress the collaborative aspect of innovative tasks and hence are mainly focused on group knowledge extraction, organization and so forth.

From such analysis we derived major weaknesses of those approaches, mainly due to a too specific vision of innovation process, which is not able to consider all innovation aspects. As a remedy we propose to adopt a process driven approach, which refers to Process Mining field, through which we expect to be able to deal with innovation process as a whole, hence overcoming the limits of previous approaches. Since such approach is currently under development, in this work we provided an overall vision of methodology, pointing out the major challenges that we have to address in its development, e.g. data retrieval.

In the future we plan to extend our Literature analysis, to provide a more broad and complete vision about innovation management methodologies. At the same time, we intend to develop our own methodology and put it into practice, in order to demonstrate its effectiveness in innovation support.

References

1. Baregheh, A., Rowley, J., Sambrook, S.: Towards a multidisciplinary definition of innovation. Management Decision 47, 1323–1339 (2009)
2. Li, M.Y.H.: Systematic Innovation: A successful case to create innovative idea for power transformer overhaul. In: 8th International Conference on Supply Chain Management and Information Systems, pp. 1–3. IEEE Press (2010)
3. Sheu, D., Lee, H.: A proposed process for systematic innovation. Int. J. of Prod. Res. 49, 847–868 (2011)
4. Hua, Z., Yang, J., Coulibaly, S., Zhang, B.: Integration TRIZ with problem-solving tools: A literature review from 1995 to 2006. Int. J. of Bus. Inn. and Res. 1, 111–128 (2006)
5. Bandera, C., Filippi, S., Motyl, B.: A survey on systematic innovation strategies for product design and development. In: Conchieri, G., Meneghello, R., Savio, G. (eds.) International Conference on Innovative Methods in Product Design, pp. 299–306. Libreria internazionale cortina padova (2011)
6. Triz Journal, http://www.triz-journal.com
7. Stratton, R., Mann, D.: Systematic innovation and the underlying principles behind TRIZ and TOC. J. of Mat. Proc. Techn. 139, 120–126 (2003)
8. Changqing, G., Kezheng, H., Fei, M.: Comparison of innovation methodologies and TRIZ. TRIZ Journal, http://www.triz-journal.com/archives/2005
9. Savransky, S.D.: Engineering of creativity: Introduction to TRIZ Methodology of Inventive Problem Solving. CRC Press (2002)
10. Akay, D., Demiray, A., Kurt, M.: Collaborative tool for solving human factors problems in the manufacturing environment: the Theory of Inventive Problem Solving Technique (TRIZ) method. Int. J. of Prod. Res. 46, 2913–2925 (2008)
11. Ideation International Inc., http://www.ideationtriz.com/software.asp
12. Mann, D.L.: Better technology forecasting using systematic innovation methods. Tech. Forecasting and Social Change 70, 779–795 (2003)
13. Narin, F.: Patent bibliometrics. Scientometrics 30, 147–155 (1994)
14. Yoon, B., Park, Y.: A text-mining-based patent network: analytical tool for high-technology trend. J. High Technol. Managem. Res. 15, 37–50 (2004)
15. Yoon, B., Park, Y.: A systematic approach for identifying technology opportunities: Keyword-based morphology analysis. Tech. Forecasting and Social Change 72, 145–160 (2005)

16. Wissema, J.G.: Morphological analysis: its application to a company TF investigation. Futures 8, 146–153 (1976)
17. Chesbrough, H.W.: Open innovation: the new imperative for creating and profiting from technology. Harvard Business Press (2003)
18. Wilson, P.: Computer-Supported Cooperative Work. An Introduction. Springer (1991)
19. Bannon, L., Schmidt, K.: Taking CSCW seriously. Computer Supported Cooperative Work 1, 7–40 (1992)
20. Fitzpatrick, E.L., Askin, R.G.: Forming effective worker teams with multifunctional skill requirements. Comput. & Ind. Eng. 48, 593–608 (2005)
21. Wi, H., Oh, S., Mun, J., Jung, M.: A team formation model based on knowledge and collaboration. Expert Systems with Applications 36, 9121–9134 (2009)
22. Klein, M., Iandoli, L.: Supporting Collaborative Deliberation Using a Large-Scale Argumentation System: The MIT Collaboratorium (2008)
23. Adamides, E.D., Karacapilidis, N.: Information technology support for the knowledge and social processes of innovation management. Technovation 26, 50–59 (2006)
24. Wang, H., Osaka, Y.: Idea discovery: A scenario-based systematic approach for decision making in market innovation. Expert Systems with Applications 40, 429–438 (2013)
25. Van der Aalst, W.M.P., Weijters, A.J.M.M.: Process mining: a research agenda. Comp. in Industry 53, 231–244 (2004)
26. Rubin, V., Günther, C.W., van der Aalst, W.M.P., Kindler, E., van Dongen, B.F., Schäfer, W.: Process mining framework for software processes. In: Wang, Q., Pfahl, D., Raffo, D.M. (eds.) ICSP 2007. LNCS, vol. 4470, pp. 169–181. Springer, Heidelberg (2007)
27. van der Aalst, W.M.P.: Process Mining. Discovery, Conformance and Enhancement of Business Processes. Springer (2011)
28. Huo, M., Zhang, H., Jeffery, R.: A systematic approach to process enactment analysis as input to software process improvement or tailoring. In: Jalote, P. (ed.) 13th Asia Pacific Software Engineering Conference, pp. 401–410. IEEE Press (2006)
29. Greco, G., Guzzo, A., Pontieri, L., Saccà, D.: Discovering Expressive Process Models by Clustering Log Traces. IEEE Trans. on Knowledge and Data Engineering 18, 1010–1027 (2006)
30. Van der Aalst, W.M.P., Giinther, C.W.: Finding structure in unstructured processes: The case for process mining. In: Basten, T., Juhàs, G., Shukla, S. (eds.) 7th International Conference on Application of Concurrency to System Design, pp. 3–12. IEEE Press (2007)
31. Jonyer, I., Cook, D.J., Holder, L.B.: Graph-based hierarchical conceptual clustering. J. Mach. Learn. Res. 2, 19–43 (2002)
32. Diamantini, C., Potena, D., Storti, E.: Mining usage patterns from a repository of scientific workflows. In: 27th Annual ACM Symposium on Applied Computing, pp. 152–157. ACM Press (2012)
33. Diamantini, C., Genga, L., Potena, D., Storti, E.: Pattern discovery from innovation processes. In: Smari, W.W., Fox, G.C. (eds.) The 2013 International Conference on Collaborative Technologies and Systems, pp. 457–464. IEE (2013)

A Stakeholder-Centric Optimization Strategy for Architectural Documentation

J. Andres Diaz-Pace, Matias Nicoletti, Silvia Schiaffino,
Christian Villavicencio, and Luis Emiliano Sanchez

ISISTAN Research Institute, CONICET-UNICEN, Campus Universitario,
Paraje Arroyo Seco (B7001BBO) Tandil, Argentina
{andres.diazpace,matias.nicoletti,silvia.schiaffino}@isistan.unicen.edu.ar
{cvillavicencio,lsanchez}@alumnos.exa.unicen.edu.ar

Abstract. The Software Architecture is an important asset in a software development process, which serves to share and discuss the main design concerns among the project stakeholders. The architecture knowledge must be properly documented in order to be effectively used by these stakeholders (e.g., using a Wiki). However, the repository of architectural documents usually fails to satisfy the stakeholders' information needs. There are several reasons for this mismatch, namely: documentation efforts not perceived as valuable, little consideration of potential documentation consumers, or documentation generated in one single step but "late" in the lifecycle, among others. Therefore, the value of the architecture as a means for engaging stakeholders and articulating their goals within the project is diminished. To address the problem, we argue for a knowledge management strategy in which: (i) architecture documentation is created incrementally; and (ii) its contents are driven by a model of stakeholder preferences. In this work, we present an information optimization approach applied to the architecture documentation domain, derived from an existing documentation method. Specifically, we propose a tool that recommends a satisficing set of (documentation) tasks for delivering architectural contents that address the main stakeholders' needs. A preliminary evaluation of our approach has shown its potential for cost-effective information management.

Keywords: architecture knowledge sharing, documentation model, stakeholders, information needs, optimization tool.

1 Introduction

The *software architecture* is a useful model for describing the high-level structure of a system [2], at early development stages. The software architecture is also the container of the *main design decisions* for satisfying the *stakeholders' concerns* (e.g., performance, time-to-market, reliability, modifiability, cost-of-ownership, usability, etc.). The architecture knowledge must be properly documented in order to be effectively shared. The architecture is typically captured by a number of documents stored in the so-called *Software Architecture Document (or*

A. Cuzzocrea and S. Maabout (Eds.): MEDI 2013, LNCS 8216, pp. 104–117, 2013.

SAD). This information repository enables communication and knowledge sharing among the stakeholders of the project [3]. Due to the complexity and size of the SAD, it is commonly organized into views, which permit to understand and reason about the architectural solution from different perspectives.

When a software system has multiple stakeholders, having a good-quality SAD is crucial for the project success. However, producing architectural information in a *cost-effective* manner is not a straightforward activity. A first challenge is that the SAD targets multiple readers, which might have different backgrounds and information needs [7]. For example, project managers are mainly interested in high-level module views and allocation views, whereas developers need extensive information about module views and behavioral views. Many times, the documenters[1] tend to load the architectural repository with development-oriented contents that only consider a few (internal) stakeholders. Studies [10,19] have shown that individual stakeholder's concerns are addressed by a fraction (less than 25%) of the SAD, but for each stakeholder a different (sometimes overlapping) SAD fraction is needed. A second challenge is the effort for creating and updating the SAD, an expenditure that developers and managers do not wish to bear. This can be due to budget constraints, tight schedules, or pressures on developing user-visible features. As a result, the architecture knowledge is informally captured and its details only exist in the architects' minds. In addition to the stakeholders' dissatisfaction, this problem brings hidden costs such as: knowledge vaporization, re-work, and poor system quality [16].

In this context, we argue that the architecture documentation should be *planned*. This planning is a compromise between documenting those aspects that are essential for the stakeholders, and avoiding "too much" documentation, because the resources available are often limited. A *documentation strategy* to achieve this goal should: (i) produce stakeholder-centric architectural documents, and (ii) build the SAD repository in incremental versions concurrently with the design work. In this article, we propose a semi-automated approach for the generation of SAD contents, in which the production of documents is explicitly linked to the needs of its consumers (i.e, the stakeholders). To do so, we rely on the Views & Beyond (V&B) method [3], which provides a semantic model for understanding the relationships between stakeholders' interests and possible architectural views to be included in the SAD.

We have developed an information optimization tool that acts as an assistant to the documenter, and suggests her relevant *tasks* for updating the current SAD (e.g., adding a new section with a module view, adding details to an existing section). The problem of choosing the most useful tasks is a combinatorial one: we seek a new SAD version that maximizes the stakeholders' preferences without exceeding a cost constraint. This problem is cast to a knapsack problem and solved by our tool. The contributions of the approach are two-fold. First, unnecessary information will not be documented, with the consequent effort savings. Second, the (stakeholder-centric) motivation for architecture knowledge will be reinforced in the development team. We report on a preliminary tool evaluation

---

[1] This role is usually played by members of the architecture team.

with stakeholders using Wiki-based SADs. The results show that the optimization tool helps the documenter meet the stakeholders' goals with reduced costs.

The rest of the article is organized into 5 sections. Section 2 presents the main concepts behind our approach and tool, based on the principles of the V&B method. Section 3 deals with the formulation of the optimization problem. Section 4 describes the evaluation of the approach. Section 5 discusses related work. Finally, section 6 gives the conclusions and future work.

2 Supporting the Architecture Documentation Process

The software architecture of a computing system is the set of structures needed to reason about that system, which comprise software elements, relations among them, and properties of both [2]. Design decisions are an essential part of the architecture, because they record the rationale behind the solution developed by the architects [9]. Examples of decisions are the use of certain patterns, such as layers or client-server, to meet modifiability or performance qualities. The architecture serves as a blueprint in which the main concerns of the stakeholders can be discussed, at an abstraction level that is reasonably manageable, even for non-technical stakeholders. By *stakeholder* [13], we mean any person, group or organization that is interested in or affected by the architecture (e.g., managers, architects, developers, testers, end-users, contractors, auditors). In order to share the architecture knowledge among the stakeholders, it must be adequately documented and communicated. The Software Architecture Document (SAD) is the usual artifact for capturing this knowledge. The SAD format can range from Word documents to a collection of Web pages hosted in a Wiki.

The SAD is generally structured around the concept of *architectural views*, which represent the many structures that are present simultaneously in software systems. A view presents an aspect or viewpoint of the system (e.g., static aspects, runtime aspects, allocation of software elements to hardware, etc.). Therefore, the SAD consists of a collection of sections (according to predefined templates) whose contents include views (e.g., module views, components-and-connectors views, allocation views) plus textual information about the views (e.g., system context, architectural drivers, key decisions, intended audience).

The stakeholders are important actors in the documentation process, as they are the main consumers of the SAD. Moreover, a SAD is useful as long as its contents satisfy the *stakeholders' information needs*. In a typical development, the architecture is the result of an iterative design process [2], in which the solution is designed (and assessed) incrementally until it is stable enough to proceed downstream with the implementation efforts. Since this process must be supported by appropriate documentation, the documentation work must go hand in hand with the design work. Along this line, we argue that the SAD should be delivered in incremental versions to the stakeholders. The general schema of our proposal is shown in Figure 1. In previous work [14], we proposed a documentation approach for Wiki-based SADs that relies on user profiling techniques. This approach derives from a well-known documentation rule: "write the [SAD]

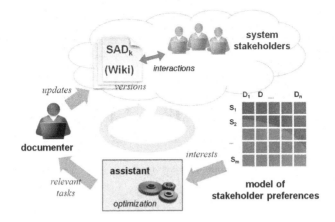

Fig. 1. Iterative architecture documentation driven by stakeholders' concerns

contents from the reader's perspective rather than from writer's perspective" [3]. Nonetheless, the work did not explore the issue of prioritizing the SAD contents (for delivery) under cost constraints, which is the main topic of this article.

2.1 The Views and Beyond Method

Views & Beyond (V&B) [3] is an architecture documentation method developed by the Software Engineering Institute. Like other documentation methods, V&B is view-centric. The basic V&B principle is that documenting a software architecture involves documenting the *relevant views*, and then documenting the information that applies to more than one view (e.g., relations between a module view and component-and-connector view, or mappings between architectural drivers and design decisions). Furthermore, V&B helps the architect identify and record the necessary architectural information during development, by providing a general SAD template and specific templates for views. The choice of the relevant views for the SAD depends on its anticipated usage by the stakeholders. To this end, V&B characterizes several types of stakeholders regarding their use of architectural views, as depicted by the matrix of Figure 2. A cell of the matrix indicates the information of view X needed by stakeholder role Y. Each column can be seen as stakeholder preferences on the contents of a particular SAD view.

The emphasis of V&B on planning for the SAD contents makes it suitable to our work. Still, an adoption barrier is that practitioners often view V&B as a heavy-duty method, due to the amount of documentation (or bureaucracy) imposed on the documenter. We believe that a way of lowering this barrier is via "intelligent" tools that operationalize the prescriptions of documentation methods. The assistant described next is an example of that position.

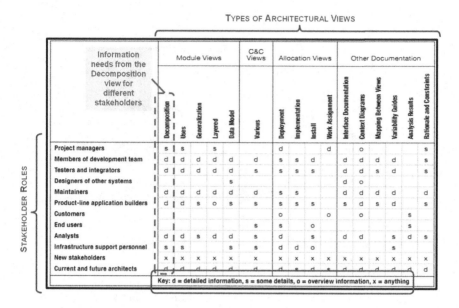

Fig. 2. V&B characterization of stakeholder preferences on architectural views [3]

2.2   Our Documentation Assistant

We assume that the increment between the current SAD version and the next one is the result of what we call documentation tasks. A *documentation task* takes a SAD section, which might include one or more views, and increases the level of detail (or completion) of that section. For example, a task can take an empty section and add contents to it (e.g., adding a "Primary presentation" according to the V&B view template). Another task can take an overview section and make it more detailed (e.g., including an "Element catalog" in V&B terminology). From the documenter's perspective, these tasks are units of work stored in some backlog, from which she can pick and apply the most relevant ones for the current SAD. In the context of a model of stakeholder preferences, like the one of Figure 2, updating a SAD section through certain task(s) makes direct contributions to the stakeholders' needs. This is a key point of our tool approach.

In an ideal setting, the documenter would analyze the stakeholder profiles and then perform all the tasks necessary for fulfilling their preferences, which in turn would produce a new (satisficing) SAD. Unfortunately, this is seldom the case, because the choice of tasks must consider factors such as: documentation efforts allocated to the tasks (e.g., person-hours), priorities of the stakeholders, or the need of incremental SAD versions to support people's work, among others. Therefore, for each SAD increment, the documenter must decide which tasks from the backlog will change SAD sections that best satisfy the stakeholders' needs. We refer to this set of tasks as an *update plan*.

As the number of stakeholders increases, so do their information needs, and they might conflict with each other. This situation is further complicated by the size of the SAD (i.e., the number of sections and views), which is likely to be large. In this scenario, determining a good update plan for the next SAD version can be a time-consuming and error-prone activity for a human, which might even discourage any documentation effort. For this reason, we envision an automated assistant to support the documenter in such an activity. To this end, we have developed a Web-based infrastructure that integrates a Wiki with a documentation assistant. On one hand, the Wiki (DokuWiki or XWiki[2]) facilitates a collaborative edition of the SAD and its access by the stakeholders. The Wiki pages are SAD sections instantiated on V&B templates[3]. On the other hand, the assistant processes the Wiki-based SAD along with the stakeholder preferences, and shows a backlog of high-priority documentation tasks to the documenter. This backlog is implemented with a to-do-list metaphor. When a specific task is chosen, the tool opens the corresponding SAD section in the Wiki and provides writing guidelines to the documenter. Examples of these guidelines are: expected contents of the section, or a brief description of the task effect on the current stakeholders' concerns. The execution of the suggested tasks on the SAD is not mandatory. The documenter makes the final documentation decisions based on her architecture expertise, domain knowledge, or past experiences.

3   Selecting Documentation Tasks as a Knapsack Problem

Let's consider the SAD as an artifact that contains n sections (Wiki pages), according to the V&B templates. Let $SAD_t = \{D_1, ..., D_n\}$ be a SAD version at time t, in which each position of the vector corresponds to a section (or document). In this vector, d_k ($1 \leq k \leq n$) is the detail level of document D_k at time t. A document can be in one of 4 possible states $DS = \{empty, overview, someDetail, detailed\}$, as illustrated in Figure 3. Given a partially-documented SAD_t, the documenter must select an update plan in order to produce a SAD_{t+1} with additional contents. Initially, we define a list with all possible tasks applicable to SAD_t. That is, $L = \{a_{11}, a_{21}, ..., a_{12}..., a_{ln}\}$ where a_{jk} ($1 \leq j \leq l, 1 \leq k \leq n$) is a feasible task for document D_k that leads to a state change $d_k \longmapsto d'_k$. The documentation assistant is constrained by a fixed-cost iteration and must recommend the most valuable tasks from L. This is a combinatorial optimization known as the *0-1 knapsack problem*.

In particular, we deal with a variant called the *multiple-choice knapsack problem (MCKP)* [17]. The MCKP is stated as follows: given n classes $[D_1, ..., D_n]$ of items to pack in some knapsack of capacity C, each item $j \in D_i$ has a benefit b_{ij} and a cost c_{ij}, and the problem is to choose one item from each class such that the benefit sum is maximized without having the cost sum to exceed C.

---

[2] DokuWiki: http://www.dokuwiki.org - XWiki: http://www.xwiki.org/
[3] V&B templates:
    http://www.sei.cmu.edu/downloads/sad/SAD_template_05Feb2006.dot

The classes $[D_1, ..., D_n]$ are mutually disjoint. In our case, these classes become the SAD sections, while the items correspond to the tasks available per section.

Let $AT = \{doOverview, addMoreDetail, complete\}$ be a set of atomic tasks. An atomic task, if applicable, increases the detail of a SAD section. This effort is quantified as the cost of the (atomic) task. Furthermore, we map these tasks to the parts of the view template provided by V&B, as depicted in Figure 3. Task *doOverview* takes an *empty* section and asks (the documenter) to fill in the "Primary presentation" part of the view. Task *addMoreDetail* takes a section (having already an overview state) and tries to add information in the "Element catalog" and "Context diagram" parts. At last, task *complete* takes a section (having already some detail) and fills out the pending parts: "Variability guide" and "Rationale". Note that this framework can be extended with other kinds of tasks, or support other templates with different parts. For instance, we might have a task that updates an already-documented section because of a change in the architecture design.

The applicable tasks depend on the actual state of the section, since we do not model "undo" tasks. Atomic tasks can be arranged in sequences to derive composite tasks. For example, if a section is in *overview*, it can only go to states *someDetail* or *detailed* by means of the task sequences $< addMoreDetail >$ (atomic task) or $< addMoreDetail, complete >$ (composite task) respectively. Along this line, the candidate tasks for a section D_k (items of a class in MCKP) are all the allowed task sequences derivable from AT that follow the state dependency chain $doOverview \rightarrow addMoreDetail \rightarrow complete$. These dependencies model the meaningful order in which atomic tasks should be performed on the V&B view template. With 4 atomic tasks and no undo, we have a total of 6 allowed tasks (not all showed in Figure 3, for the sake of clarity). This set of tasks also includes the *null task*, which means that no change is performed on a section and has zero cost (also not shown in Figure 3).

When it comes to the profit of tasks (either atomic or composite ones) in L, we compute it indirectly on the basis of the stakeholders' interests over the SAD sections (or architectural views). Let $S = \{S_1, ..., S_m\}$ be a set of stakeholders,

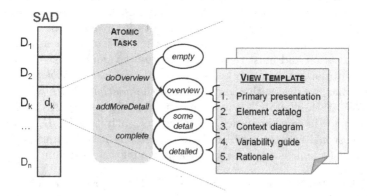

Fig. 3. Documentation tasks for a SAD section, based on the V&B view templates

each S_i with a priority p_i in the range $[0, 10]$, where 0 is the lowest priority and 10 is the highest one. For every document with state d_k, a stakeholder S_i has a value of interest (or preference) denoted by $interest(S_i, D_k) = v_{ik}$. These interests actually come from the V&B matrix (recall Figure 2), according to the role of the stakeholder and the viewtype of the section. The utility of a document with state d_k (after executing some task) is given by a function $U_k(d_k, v_{ik}) \rightarrow [0, 1]$, which models the "happiness" of stakeholder S_i with the actual detail of the document, compared to her preferred level of detail. These utility functions are specified during the setup of the problem. Utilities $U_k(d_k, v_{ik})$ can be computed for all stakeholders related to document D_k (a specific row in the V&B table of Figure 2). If we weight these utilities using the stakeholder priorities, the utility of a document state is given by Equation 1.

$$document\_utility(d_k) = \frac{\sum\limits_{j=1}^{m} U_k(d_k, v_{jk}).p_j}{\sum\limits_{i=1}^{m} p_i} \quad (all\ m\ stakeholders\ in\ S) \quad (1)$$

We see $document\_utility(d_k)$ as a proxy for the benefit of the task a_{jk} ($1 \leq j \leq l, 1 \leq k \leq n$) that makes document D_k reach state d_k. Thus, each feasible task a_{jk} in L is assigned to a $benefit(a_{jk})= document\_utility(d_k)$, for some document change. In the 0-1 MCKP formulation, the tasks a_{jk} only take values 0 or 1, depending on whether they are included in the update plan. Remember that a task can be either atomic or composing (i.e., a sequence of atomic tasks). In the former case, $cost(a_{jk})$ is a constant. In the latter case, $cost(a_{jk})$ is the sum of the costs of the constituent tasks. With all this information, the objective function is expressed by Equations 2 and 3. Note that Equation 3 indicates that only one action per class could be performed (similar to the MCKP).

$$maximize: \quad sad\_utility(SAD_t) = \sum_{k=1}^{n} \sum_{j \in D_k} benefit(a_{jk}).a_{jk} \quad (2)$$

$$subject\ to: \quad \sum_{k=1}^{n} \sum_{j \in D_k} cost(a_{jk}).a_{jk} \leq C \quad with \sum_{j \in D_k} a_{jk} = 1 \quad (3)$$

4   Evaluation

We empirically evaluated our approach with stakeholder groups accessing Wiki-based SADs. The main goal was to compare SAD increments suggested by the optimization tool against SAD versions generated in an ad-hoc manner (i.e., with no assistance). We measured the SAD utility (for the whole group of stakeholders) as well as the cost necessary to produce it. We additionally analyzed the satisfaction of individual stakeholders, according to their roles and priorities.

From the V&B matrix, we have that the satisfaction of a given stakeholder is proportional to the degree of matching between the stakeholder's preferences and the actual details of the SAD sections. In Section 3, this relationship was quantified with utility functions $U_k(d_k, v_{i,k}) \rightarrow [0, 1]$. For the experiments, those functions were implemented as indicated in Equation 4. That is, the utility of a document D_k with current detail d_k, for a stakeholder S_i who prefers v_{ik} as the detail level for D_k, is dependent on the difference between d_k and v_{ik}. We set $\varepsilon = 0.1$ as the "allowed difference" between the two detail levels. Note that $satisfaction(S_i, D_k)$ gets the maximum utility when the two levels are the same, and gives some reward if the document level is above the preferred one. We configured the same function for all stakeholders. The average utility of all SAD documents for a stakeholder S_i is given by Equation 5.

$$satisfaction(S_i, D_k) = \begin{cases} |d_k - v_{ik}| \leq \varepsilon & \rightarrow 1 \\ d_k - v_{ik} > \varepsilon & \rightarrow 0.5 \\ d_k - v_{ik} < -\varepsilon & \rightarrow 0 \end{cases} \qquad (4)$$

$$sad\_utility(S_i, SAD_t) = \frac{\sum\limits_{k=1}^{n} U_k(d_k, v_{i,k})}{n} \quad (all\ n\ documents\ in\ SAD_t) \quad (5)$$

The test subjects were undergraduate/graduate students from a Software Architecture course taught at UNICEN University, with 2-4 years of developing experience. We organized the students into 11 groups of 7 members. Each member played a distinctive stakeholder role: 3 members took the architect role, whereas the other 4 members were divided into: 1 manager, 1 evaluator (responsible for peer reviews and architectural evaluation) and 2 clients. The priorities were assigned as follows: $p_{manager} = 10$, $p_{architect} = 6$, $p_{client1} = 6$, $p_{evaluator} = 2$, $p_{client2} = 2$, in decreasing order of importance.

The architects were asked to design an architecture solution for a model problem, the Clemson Transit Assistance System[4], and use V&B to produce SADs (in DokuWiki) that should satisfy the concerns of the other stakeholders of the group. Both the design and documentation work had to be done in 3 iterations of 3 weeks, with 2 (partial) SAD versions for the first 2 iterations and a final release after 9 weeks. The managers, clients, and evaluators periodically assessed the solution and documentation quality, and gave feedback to the architects. We refer to these documentation versions as *ad-hoc SADs*, because their production strategy was not intended to address the stakeholders' concerns explicitly.

Once all the ad-hoc SAD versions were available, we contrasted their average utility with that of simulated SADs resulting from our documentation assistant. The ad-hoc SADs produced by each group were not considered as 100% complete, because some sections were unfinished or lacked details. In average,

---

[4] http://people.cs.clemson.edu/~johnmc/courses/cpsc875/resources/
Telematics.pdf

we determined the following percentages of completion: 10-25% for the first version (slice 1), 40-60% for the second version (slice 2), and 75-85% for the last version (final SAD). The percentage of completion of a version was estimated by counting the number of words and images per document (an image ≈ 200 words). The same metric was also used to estimate the cost of producing a SAD document, by considering a word as a unit of effort. Certainly, gathering good effort estimations is difficult and need to be calibrated via expert judgment.

As a baseline, we assessed the ad-hoc SADs of every group in terms of overall utility (using the V&B model of preferences) and production costs. For every group, we then executed the optimization tool on slice 1 with a cost constraint equal to the units of effort necessary to reach the completion percentage of slice 2. The same procedure was repeated for the transition from slice 2 to the final SAD. We refer to the SAD versions produced by our tool as *optimized SADs*. The vectors of Figure 4 show the evolution of the average values of utility and cost, with and without optimization. We observe that the optimized SADs achieved higher utility values in both transitions and involved lower costs in terms of tasks for generating each version. This represents a utility increment of 15-25% and a cost reduction of 10-33% when applying the optimization tool. Because of how we estimated costs, cost reductions mean that the optimization produced smaller SADs. This would suggest that the ad-hoc SADs had unnecessary contents, given the current stakeholder's needs. Another observation is that the state of a SAD version conditions the utility improvements attainable in successive versions. For example, a key stakeholder might want an overview of some section that is already detailed, but the section contents cannot be "downsized" with our tasks.

Figure 5 decomposes the global utility into the individual stakeholders. In both transitions, we notice that all the stakeholders were evenly satisfied by the ad-hoc SADs. On the contrary, the optimized SADs clearly favored high-priority stakeholders. For instance, the first transition (left chart) shows a bias towards managers and less care about evaluators, while the second transition (right chart) is mainly focused on managers and architects. Although the update plans suggested by the tool were guided by the high-priority stakeholders, the plans could have tasks that still benefit less important stakeholders. This is the case of client 2 in the left chart, who improved her satisfaction with the second SAD even being a low-priority stakeholder. In the right chart, the utility improvements were minor and only noticeable for the main stakeholders, because of the conditioning effect of precedent SAD versions mentioned above.

We performed a basic sensitivity analysis to see how tighter costs would affect the solution optimality (i.e., SAD utility). Reducing the cost constraints up to 50% of the original value made the optimality drop only a 8% in average. This evidence shows that the SAD solutions can be robust to satisfy the main stakeholders. For reductions higher than 50%, the solutions had quality problems. Anyway, an in-depth sensitivity analysis that considers possible errors (or uncertainty) in the stakeholders' preferences and in the costs of the documentation tasks is subject of future work.

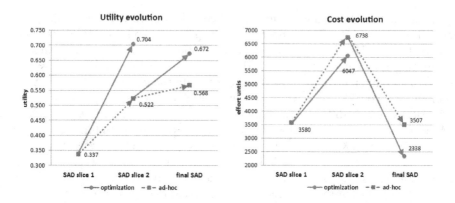

Fig. 4. Optimized versus ad-hoc SADs - Variations in overall utility and cost

Fig. 5. Optimized versus ad-hoc SADs - Satisfaction of individual stakeholders

The optimization problems were solved with an exact algorithm implemented in Java. All the tests were executed on a PC with an Intel Core i3-2310 processor and 8GB RAM memory. The performance of the algorithm was reasonably low, ranging from 60-4000 seconds in average for SADs with 12-18 sections, respectively. Since the knapsack problem is a NP-problem, the computational costs grow exponentially with the number of sections. Real-life SADs normally have 15-40 documents, depending on how critical the architecture is for the system. For such instances, we can apply constraint programming toolkits (e.g., integer linear programming) and still get exact solutions with acceptable performance. As another alternative, we envision the usage of well-known heuristics for the MCKP that tradeoff solution optimality in exchange for polynomial complexity.

5   Related Work

Several architecture documentation methods exist in the literature [3,6,11,18]. Common to all these methods is the prescription of a SAD structure (i.e., templates) and the use of views for different system viewpoints. These viewpoints might be related to stakeholders' concerns. Nonetheless, the methods do not provide guidelines for creating the documentation package, except for the steps suggested by V&B. Thus, the documenter is responsible for determining how the SAD contents will be staged for delivery.

Lattanze [12] classifies architecture documentation strategies into horizontal and vertical ones, emphasizing that both require SAD planning as well as identification of stakeholders and their information needs. In a vertical strategy, custom documents are created for specific stakeholders. These documents might have duplication or require considerable efforts, but the SAD will certainly fulfill the stakeholders' needs. V&B falls in this category, although it helps documenters save some efforts, if the method is applied in a disciplined way. In a horizontal strategy, on the contrary, the documenter creates small, isolated documents and then tries to reuse them to form documentation suites for specific stakeholders. Usually, some writing has to be added to link the documents together. Thanks to the reuse, this strategy reduces the SAD production efforts and its maintenance. Currently, our assistant implements a vertical strategy but it can accommodate a horizontal one with some modifications.

As it regards the profiling of documentation readers, Su [19] proposed an automated approach based on pieces of architectural information, called chunks. These chunks are the result of specific exploration paths followed by a user when reading a SAD. When a new user is about to navigate the SAD, a tool recommends her candidate sections by reusing previous (similar) exploration paths. This approach effectively assists readers to find information, but unlike our approach, it does not support documentation strategies.

Different authors have reported experiences with Wikis applied to architecting tasks [1,5]. Bachmann and Merson [1] discussed the role of a Wiki to record technical documentation in a collaborative setting, and specifically, how to use a Wiki with V&B documentation. Farenhorst et al. [5] built JIT AK Portal to capture architecture knowledge and share it among architects, but not among other stakeholders. Another related tool is Knowledge Architect [8], which supports the retrieval of knowledge for multiple stakeholder types, although only focused on the reader's side. Neither JIT AK Portal nor Knowledge Architect consider the process of producing architectural contents, which is the cornerstone of our tool. Graaf et al. [4] conducted an empirical study on Wiki-based SADs. The SAD is built on top of a semantic Wiki equipped with annotations, using an ontology of architecture concepts. We believe semantic Wikis are an interesting feature for boosting the "intelligence" of our documentation assistant.

6   Conclusions and Future Work

In this work, we have proposed a lightweight approach and tool for optimizing the information contents of a repository of architectural documents. Our strategy for managing the architecture knowledge is driven by the needs of the stakeholders interested in the documents, but also considers the document production efforts. The problem of producing a satisficing SAD is seen as an optimization problem and solved by our tool. In particular, we have leveraged on the concepts and guidelines of the V&B documentation model and mapped this model to an MCKP formulation, which constitutes a novel aspect of the proposal.

The results of applying our tool to a case-study with Wiki-based SADs have been encouraging. In particular, we observed a clear improvement in the quality of the SAD versions generated with the tool, when compared to SAD versions generated in an ad-hoc manner. Nonetheless, more experiments and real-word case-studies are needed in order to confirm this observation. The current optimization framework makes some simplifying assumptions. For instance, we did not consider dependencies between sections of the V&B templates. V&B also recommends to merge views addressing marginal stakeholders. The model of stakeholder preferences is static, i.e., the interests for a given role do not change over time. Unfortunately, if a person plays more than one role within an iterative development context, her interests are likely to be dynamic [12]. To cope with this scenario, we are enhancing the stakeholder profiling with text mining techniques integrated into the Wiki environment [15]. We argue that this approach can have a dual purpose, supporting the writers and the readers of the SAD. On the reader's side, a personalization tool could identify potentially-relevant SAD sections for specific stakeholders, alleviating information overload problems. Another line of work is to apply our approach to process a large information repository in order to extract small documentation suites for particular goals. This scenario would need "undo" tasks in our optimization framework.

Finally, as a long-term research goal, we want to investigate if our approach can be customized to other information domains. Along this line, we speculate that the production planning strategy can be applicable to other documentation artifacts or content-management systems, as long as some documentation structure is available and the information items can be linked to user profiles.

Acknowledgments. This work was partially supported by ANPCyT (Argentina) through PICT Project 2011 No. 0366 and PICT Project 2010 No. 2247, and also by CONICET (Argentina) through PIP Project No. 112-201101-00078.

References

1. Bachmann, F., Merson, P.: Experience using the web-based tool wiki for architecture documentation. Technical Note CMU/SEI-2005-TN-041, Software Engineering Institute, Carnegie Mellon University (2005)
2. Bass, L., Clements, P., Kazman, R.: Software Architecture in Practice, 3rd edn. Addison-Wesley Professional (2012)

3. Clements, P., Bachmann, F., Bass, L., Garlan, D., Ivers, J., Little, R., Merson, P., Nord, R., Stafford, J.: Documenting Software Architectures: Views and Beyond, 2nd edn. Addison-Wesley Professional (2010)
4. de Graaf, K.A., Tang, A., Liang, P., van Vliet, H.: Ontology-based software architecture documentation. In: Proceedings Joint Working Conf. on Software Architecture & European Conf. on Software Architecture (WICSA/ECSA), WICSA 2012, pp. 315–319. IEEE Computer Society (2012)
5. Farenhorst, R., van Vliet, H.: Experiences with a wiki to support architectural knowledge sharing. In: Proceedings of the 3rd Workshop on Wikis for Software Engineering (Wiki4SE), Porto, Portugal (September 2008)
6. Hofmeister, C., Nord, R., Soni, D.: Applied Software Architecture, 1st edn. Addison-Wesley Professional (2000)
7. ISO/IEC/IEEE: Iso/iec/ieee 42010: Systems and software engineering - architecture description (2011)
8. Jansen, A., Avgeriou, P., van der Ven, J.S.: Enriching software architecture documentation. Journal of Systems and Software 82(8), 1232–1248 (2009)
9. Jansen, A., Bosch, J.: Software architecture as a set of architectural design decisions. In: Proceedings Working Conf. on Software Architecture, pp. 109–120. IEEE Computer Society (2005)
10. Koning, H., Vliet, H.V.: Real-life it architecture design reports and their relation to ieee std 1471 stakeholders and concerns. Automated Software Eng. 13, 201–223 (2006)
11. Kruchten, P.: The 4+1 view model of architecture. IEEE Software 12(6), 42–50 (1995)
12. Lattanze, A.: Architecting Software Intensive Systems: A Practitioners Guide. Taylor & Francis (2008)
13. Mitchell, R.K., Agle, B.R., Wood, D.J.: Toward a theory of stakeholder identification and salience: Defining the principle of who and what really counts. Academy of Management Review 22, 853 (1997)
14. Nicoletti, M., Diaz-Pace, J.A., Schiaffino, S.: Towards software architecture documents matching stakeholders' interests. In: Cipolla-Ficarra, F., Veltman, K., Verber, D., Cipolla-Ficarra, M., Kammüller, F. (eds.) ADNTIIC 2011. LNCS, vol. 7547, pp. 176–185. Springer, Heidelberg (2012)
15. Nicoletti, M., Diaz-Pace, J.A., Schiaffino, S.: Discovering stakeholders' interests in wiki-based architectural documentation. In: Proceedings of the XVI Ibero-American Conference on Software Engineering, CibSE (2013)
16. Parnas, D.L.: Precise documentation: The key to better software. In: Nanz, S. (ed.) The Future of Software Engineering, pp. 125–148. Springer (2010)
17. Pisinger, D.: A minimal algorithm for the multiple-choice knapsack problem. European Journal of Operational Research 83, 394–410 (1995)
18. Rozanski, N., Woods, E.: Software Systems Architecture: Working With Stakeholders Using Viewpoints and Perspectives, 2nd edn. Addison-Wesley (2011)
19. Su, M.T.: Capturing exploration to improve software architecture documentation. In: Proceedings 4th European Conf. on Software Architecture: Companion Volume, ECSA 2010, pp. 17–21. ACM, New York (2010)

Hints from the Crowd: A Novel NoSQL Database

Paolo Fosci[1], Giuseppe Psaila[1], and Marcello Di Stefano[2]

[1] University of Bergamo, Dept. of Engineering,
Viale Marconi 5, I-24044 Dalmine (BG), Italy
{paolo.fosci,psaila}@unibg.it
[2] University of Palermo, Dept. of Computer Science Engineering,
Viale delle Scienze Ed. 6, I-90100 Palermo, Italy
marcello.distefano@unipa.it

Abstract. The crowd can be an incredible source of information. In particular, this is true for reviews about products of any kind, freely provided by customers through specialized web sites. In other words, they are *social knowledge*, that can be exploited by other customers.

The *Hints From the Crowd* (HFC) prototype, presented in this paper, is a *NoSQL* database system for large collections of product reviews; the database is queried by expressing a natural language sentence; the result is a list of products ranked based on the relevance of reviews w.r.t. the natural language sentence. The best ranked products in the result list can be seen as the best hints for the user based on crowd opinions (the reviews).

In this paper, we mainly describe the query engine, and we show that our prototype obtains good performance in terms of execution time, demonstrating that our approach is feasible. The IMDb dataset, that includes more than 2 million reviews for more than 100,000 movies, is used to evaluate performance.

1 Introduction

Reviews about products that customers can freely write on specialized web sites constitute an incredible source of information, by means of which users would like to get useful *hints*. But how could a user obtain them? Typically, the user has some wishes and would like to find products that match those wishes, based on opinions of other users. But to do that, a specialized system is necessary.

Looking at the problem from a database technology point of view, product reviews constitute a text database that has a given structure; user's wishes can be seen as natural language queries over the set of reviews and the user wants to obtain the products whose set of reviews matches the query at the highest degree; the ideal solution, is to get a ranked list, where the best ranked products can be seen as the best hints for the user based on crowd opinions (the reviews). We focus only on reviews, since every single review is a mine of unstructured information that are hard to be queried by classical techniques. In other words,

A. Cuzzocrea and S. Maabout (Eds.): MEDI 2013, LNCS 8216, pp. 118–131, 2013.

such a system is a *NoSQL* database system, where queries are natural language sentences.

Thus, the *Hints From the Crowd* (HFC) prototype is a *NoSQL* database system for large collections of product reviews; the database is queried by expressing a natural language sentence; the result is a list of products ranked based on the relevance of reviews w.r.t. the natural language sentence. Semantic tagging and term expansion (by means of WordNet) are performed, both indexing reviews and querying them.

We wanted to demonstrate that it is possible to obtain an answer to a query in acceptable time on a large set of reviews. Therefore, we tested the prototype on reviews about movies downloaded from the IMDb.com web site, that includes more than 2 million reviews for more than 100,000 movies. The study about execution times at query time is presented.

The paper is organized as follows. Section 2 presents related literature. Section 3 shows and describes the architecture of the system. Section 4 describes how the query engine works and the ranking measure. Section 5 presents the results of the performance study we conducted by means of the IMDb dataset. Finally, Section 6 draws the conclusions.

2   Related Work

Research in the database area is more and more addressing the concept of NoSQL database. Several attempts to define the concept can be found. Referring to [13], three categories of data stores are considered: *Key-Value stores*, *Document stores* and *Column Family stores*. The first category deals with datasets similar to maps or dictionaries where data are addressed by a unique key. The second category deals with sets of text documents, and our work falls into this category. The third category encompasses column oriented stores, extensible record stores and wide columnar stores. *Graph databases* can be considered as well belonging to the world of NoSQL databases [11].

One important aspect of NoSQL data stores is performance. Often, NoSQL databases are necessary due to the implicit limitation of relational databases in given application contexts, where the relational structure of data is an obstacle to obtain fast execution times. The work in [1] tries to address this perspective and presents six features of NoSQL data stores. The are: (1) the ability to horizontally scale simple operation throughput over many servers; (2) the ability to replicate and to distribute (partition) data over many servers; (3) a simple call level interface or protocol (in contrast to a SQL binding); (4) a weaker concurrency model than the ACID transactions of most relational (SQL) database systems; (5) efficient use of distributed indexes and RAM for data storage; (6) the ability to dynamically add new attributes to data records.

The ranking metrics we defined as the basis of the HFC system is inspired to the concept of itemset, developed in the area of data mining for mining frequent itemsets and association rules. Several works [6,8] adopt association rule mining for analyzing customer reviews and extract opinions from them. In [6], association rule mining is used to extract, from within customer reviews, relevant features the characterize opinions of users about products. In [8], a system to compare opinions about products is presented, where product reviews reports PROs and CONs; in particular, association rule mining is exploited to assign a positive or negative polarity to words (namely, adjectives) in product reviews, and use this polarity to rank the opinion about products. The work in [5] extracts, by means of an association rule mining technique, relevant features that summarize product reviews.

Other data mining techniques are used to analyze customer reviews. For instance, in [9] a sentence clustering technique is adopted. In [2], both supervised and unsupervised approaches are evaluated. A similar work is done in [7], where key classification techniques for opinion mining are discussed. The work in [3] presents a technique for semantic classifications of product reviews.

However, we do not propose a data mining technique and the HFC system is not a data mining system. We simply take inspiration from the concept of frequent itemset.

Proposals related with the notion of frequent itemset and association rule mining was exploited in the area of recommender systems [12]. In effect, the reader could imagine the HFC system as a kind of recommender system. However, based on the general perception about recommender systems (well presented in [10]) a recommender system builds a profile of the user and matches this profile against previous knowledge. In contrast, the HFC system does not build a profile of users; it performs a query, consciously submitted by the user, on the set of product reviews.

Furthermore, notice that certainly the our proposal has some common aspects with search engines and information retrieval techniques. However, these techniques usually model documents based on the Vector Space Model, and do not consider at all the specific features of collections of product reviews.

3   The HFC System

As stated in Section 1, *Hints From the Crowd* is a NoSQL database system that deals with collections of product reviews, that can be queried by expressing a natural language sentence (i.e. *query* in the rest of the paper).

Due to lack of space, in this Section we shortly mention system architecture and data structure underlying the *Query Engine*, that we describe in Section 4.

3.1   Architecture

The HFC system is composed by several components, each one devoted to perform a specific task as shown in Figure 1. In particular, we distinguish between the *back-end* and the *front-end*: the former is responsible for collecting, analyzing and indexing data from product reviews; the latter is the actual user interface accessed by users, that is built on top of the *Query Engine*.

Let us describe the architecture in details.

Fig. 1. Architecture of the HFC System

Back-end. In this side of the system, we find the components (rectangles) that prepares the data structure on which queries are executed. These components operate on source data and intermediate results (ovals) and upload data structures in the *Storage* box.

- *Analyzer.* This component is responsible for analyzing product reviews, identifying words and their grammar category (noun, verb, adjective or adverb). This *pos-tagging* operation is performed by the *Stanford Parser*[1]. As a result, reviews are transformed into tagged sentences, composed of *tagged terms*, i.e., a term associated to a tag that denotes the grammar category.
- *Loader.* The goal of this component is to load *Tagged Reviews* into the data structures on which queries are performed (see Section 3.2).
- *Expander.* After the loading phase has ended, tagged terms are expanded on the base of an ontology (in our case, *WordNet*), so that the *Query Engine* can exploit semantic relationships in order to capture a wider set of results related with the query.

Front-end. From the architectural point of view, the key component of the front-end is the *Query Engine*: it exploits the preliminary work performed by back-end components, and works on data structures describing occurrences of terms in product reviews. The *Web Application* component has been developed to give end users the capability to exploit the system.

3.2   Data Structure

Figure 2 graphically depicts the logical schema of the HFC data-structure.

Table `Products` describes each single product, and its schema is context-dependent, in the sense that the attributes are defined based on the application domain. For example, since we use IMDb movie data set to test the prototype, we defined attributes concerning movies, such as title, director, year, and so on.

Table `Terms` is the key table, that describes each single tagged word managed by the system. Attributes `products`, `reviews` and `occurrences` counts the number of products and the number of reviews in which a tagged term occurs, and the total number of occurrences, respectively. Notice that, while attribute

---

[1] From the *Stanford NLP Group*: http://nlp.stanford.edu/index.shtml

Terms(**id**, word, tag, taggedword, products, reviews, occurrences)
Term2Expansion(termId, expandedWordId, relation)
Occurrences(**id**, productId, termId, review, position)
Product(**id**, *domain specific attributes*)

Fig. 2. Schema of the Relational Database

`taggedword` denotes a unique element in the table, since a simple word can be associated to more than one grammar category (i.e. word *book* can be either a *noun* or a *verb*), it can appear several times in the table.

Table `Term2Expansion` represent the relations of a tagged term (by means of attribute `termId`) with another tagged term (by means attribute `expandedTermId`). Attribute `relation` denotes the typology of expansion[2], i.e., synonym, hypernym, heponym to name a few. Notice that tagging a term with its grammar category (for instance *noun*), allows us to delimit word expansion only to the relations implied by the grammar category (i.e. the concept of *meronym* can be applied to a *verb*, but not to a *noun*).

Finally, table `Occurrences` describes all occurrences of tagged terms in product reviews; in particular, notice attribute `position`, that indicates the position of the occurrence in the review.

Data storing. The previous data structure could be totally implemented on a traditional relational database, with indexes on the main searching attributes of tables. But after we implemented this solution, since our data-set is quite big (see 5), when we submitted the first query-test the *HFC System* still had to answer after one hour! So due to performance issues, part of the data resides as tables on a relational (*Postgres*) database (tables `Product`, `Terms` and `Term2Expansion`), and part on the file system (tables `Occurrences`).

Specifically, as table `Occurrences` is likely to be huge[3], it has been split in single occurrences file for each term. Each file, containing occurrences of a single term, is identified by the term id. due to the very large number of terms, files are distributed in a subdirectory tree to avoid to saturate file system limits of files per directory.

Internally, each occurrences file is organized as a binary file, where a fixed length data structure represents a term occurrence; this data structure is a 12-bytes triple *(ProductId, ReviewId, Position)*.

Furthermore, for the sake of performance study, we also have a 2nd version of the file system data structure, where occurrences are partitioned in 5 orthogonal subtrees, and each subtree describes occurrences for 1/5 of the products. This second version allows us to implement a multi-thread query engine, with 5 threads running in a parallel way (see 5.2).

---

[2] WordNet provides a set of 15 different possible expanding relations depending on word grammar category.

[3] In our test case, the size is more than 12Gb.

4   Query Engine

We now describe the key component, i.e., the query engine. Based on a natural language sentence (the query) it extracts those products whose reviews are mostly relevant for the query. Relevance is evaluated by means of a *ranking metric*; retrieved products are returned as a list sorted in reverse order of relevance. Hereafter, we describe how the ranking metric is defined.

4.1   Termsets

In this paper we consider a query q as a *set of terms* (or briefly, a *termset*). Thus, we describe a query containing a number n of terms as $q = \{t_1, \ldots, t_n\}^4$, and we investigate only those queries where $n > 1$ or, in other words, $|q| > 1$. With I, we denote a generic termset that is a subset of q for which applies $|I| > 1$. With D_q, we denote the set of termsets I derived from q. Notice that the cardinality of D_q is $|D_q| = 2^n - (n+1)$, i.e. D_q is the power set of q without the empty set and the n single terms that compose q.

With I_l we denote an l-termset of q, that is a termset composed by l terms, i.e. $|I_l| = l$. With $D_{q,l}$ we denote the set of l-termsets I_l. Notice that the cardinality of $D_{g,l}$ is $|D_{q,l}| = \binom{n}{l}$.

4.2   Termset Weight

We now define the concept of *weight* for a termset.

Definition 1: The weight of a l−termset is a function of its length and the length of the query q $(|q| = n)$ and it is denoted as $w_q(l)$.
For $n = 2$ there is only one 2-termset and its weight is $w_q(2) = 1$ by definition. For $n > 2$ the weight of the single n−termset q is, by definition, $w_q(n) = 0.5$, while for $2 < l < n$ it is $w_q(l) = w_q(l+1)/(\binom{n}{l}+1)$ and for $l = 2$ it is $w_q(2) = w_q(3)/\binom{n}{2}$.   □

The rationale behind Definition 1 is the following. The topmost termset, corresponding to the whole query, is the most important one, and its weight is equal to the overall weight of all the shorter termsets. The same principle is valid for any generic termset I_l (with $2 < l < n$), whose weight is equal to the overall weight of all lower levels termsets (even those that are not subset of I_l). In this way, reducing the size of termsets, the contribution of each level quickly decreases.

Notice, that the overall weight of all termsets is exactly 1 $(\sum_{I \in D_q} w_q(|I|) = 1)$.

Figure 3 shows the termsets levels with an example query.

4.3   Query Expansion and Semantic Coefficient

As stated in Section 3.1, reviews are processed performing several operations. Similar operations are performed on a user query in natural language as well.

---

[4]   At moment, in this stage of the project we do not consider word order or repetitions.

l	$\#I_l$	weight	termsets (I)
4	1	0.5000	{funny, great, hilarious, jokes}
3	4	0.1000	{funny, great, hilarious}
			{funny, great, jokes}
			{funny, hilarious, jokes}
			{great, hilarious, jokes}
2	6	0.0167	{funny, great} {funny, hilarious}
			{great, hilarious} {great, jokes}
			{funny, jokes} {hilarious, jokes}

Fig. 3. Termsets levels for query *great funny hilarious jokes* and corresponding weights

Pos-tagging. By means of *Stanford Parser*, each word of a user query is tagged with an attribute that denotes its grammar role (*verb, noun, adjective* to name a few) in the query.

Stopwords filtering. Stopwords are those words that are too common in reviews (such as *articles, conjunctions*); furthermore, common verbal forms like *is* or *have* (just to name a few) are treated as stopwords. Stopwords include also some very context-dependent words such as the word *actor* in a movie context. These words hold a small semantic meaning, so after pos-tagging operation *stopwords* are discarded from the query.

Thus, denoting with SW the set of possible stopwords, in the rest of the paper the notation:

$$q = \{t_1, \ldots, t_n\}$$

includes only those terms $t_i \notin SW$, and, as stated in Section 4.1, we consider only those queries q such that $|q| > 1$ (actual length without stopwords).

Term expansion. By means of *WordNet* ontology, each tagged term $t_i \in q$ is expanded with all those terms directly associated to t_i depending by its grammar tag. Thus, for example a *noun* is expanded with all its *synonyms, hypernyms* or *hyponyms* and so on, while a *verb* is expanded with all its *synonyms* or *meronyms*, to name a few. There are actually a total of 15 possible different relations between a tagged term and its expanded words.

We denote with t_i^* the generic expanded term of t_i, and with $ET(t_i)$ the set of all expanded terms of t_i. By definition, $t_i \in ET(t_i)$ with an *identity* relation, thus, $|ET(t_i)| \geq 1$.

Notice that, given a generic expanded term t^*, it can happen that $t^* \in ET(t_i)$ and $t^* \in ET(t_j)$ with $i \neq j$. In other words, we cannot state a-priori that $ET(t_i) \cap ET(t_j) = \oslash$ with $i \neq j$. As an example, the term *colour* can be an *hypernym* expansion for both terms *red* and *black*.

Query expansion. An *expanded query* q^* is each combination of $\{t_1^*, \ldots, t_n^*\}$. We consider *valid* a combination $q^* = \{t_1^*, \ldots, t_n^*\}$ only if $t_i^* \neq t_j^* \; \forall i \neq j$ Notice that the original query q is a particular q^* itself, and it is *valid* by definition.

Table 1. a) Trend of Semantic coefficient w.r.t. the cardinality of $ET(t)$. b) Semantic coefficient for a generic 2-termset where each term has two expansions.

$|ET(t)|$	$sc_t(t)$ (not expanded)	$sc_t(t^*)$ $(t^* \neq t)$
1	1.0000	—
2	0.7500	0.2500
3	0.6667	0.1667
5	0.6000	0.1000
10	0.5500	0.0500

a)

I^* (structure)	#	$sc_t(I^*)$
$\{t_1, t_2\}$	1	0.4444
$\{t_1^*, t_2\} or \{t_1, t_2^*\}$	4	0.1111
$\{t_1^*, t_2^*\}$	4	0.0278

b)

Expanded termsets. Previous considerations about query q and its expansions, are applicable to each termset I_l. With I_l^* we denote an *expanded termset* $I_l^* = \{t_1^*, \ldots, t_l^*\}$, and similarly I_l^* is *valid* only if $t_i^* \neq t_j^*$ $\forall i \neq j$.
With $EI(I)$ we denote the set of all possible expanded termset I^* that can be derived from I. The cardinality of $EI(I) = \prod_{t \in I} |ET(t)|$, that is the number of all possible combinations of the expanded terms of those terms that compose I.

Finally, with D_q^*, we denote the set of all valid expanded termsets that are included in q and all its valid expansions q^*.

Semantic coefficient. Each $t^* \in ET(t)$ has a *semantic coefficient* $sc_t(t^*)$, with $0 < sc_t(t^*) \leq 1$, that depends on the cardinality of $ET(t_i)$.

Definition 2: For each $t^* \in ET(t)$ except t, $sc_t(t^*) = 0.5/|ET(t)|$, and $sc_t(t) = 0.5 + 0.5/|ET(t)|$. □

The rationale of semantic coefficient, is the following. A term describes a semantic concept that is mostly expressed by the term itself, but receives a small contribution from expanded terms: the greater the number of expansion, the smaller the semantic contribution of a single expanded term. Notice that $\sum_{t^* \in ET(t)} sc_t(t^*) = 1$. Table 1.a shows how sc_t varies with $ET(t)$ cardinality.

With $sc_I(I^*)$ we denote the semantic coefficient for an expanded termset I^* derived from I.

Definition 3: Given an expanded termset $I^* = \{t_1^* \ldots t_l^*\}$ derived for a termset $I = \{t_1 \ldots t_l\}$, it is $sc_I(I^*) = \prod_{t_i^* \in I_l^*} sc_{t_i}(t_i^*)$. □

This way, a termset that contains only original terms gives the highest semantic contribution, while augmenting the number of expanded terms in the termset, the semantic contribution decreases.
Table 1.b shows the trend of the semantic coefficient for a 2-termset where each original term has two expansions. Notice that, according to the above definition, $\sum_{I^* \in EI(I)} sc_I(I^*) = 1$.

4.4   Product Reviews and Termsets

Consider a product p (a movie, a camera, etc.), its set of reviews is denoted by $R(p) = \{r_1, \ldots, r_k\}$. Each review is a text, i.e., a sequence of term occurrences $r_i = < t_1, \ldots, t_s >$.

With $T(R(p))$ we denote the set of terms appearing in reviews for product p, and with $T(r_i)$ the set of terms appearing in review $r_i \in R(p)$.

Definition 4: A termset I is said *relevant* for product p if $\exists r_i | I \subseteq T(r_i)$.   □

The set of relevant termsets for product p is denoted as $RD_{p,q}$. In an analogous way, $RD_{p,q}^*$ is the set of all relevant expanded termsets for product p. Notice that $RD_{p,q} \subseteq D_q$, and also $RD_{p,q}^* \subseteq D_q^*$.

4.5   Termset Average Density

In a preliminary work [4], we assumed that every termset occurrence in product reviews contribute to the *support* of the termset with the same weight, i.e. 1, since the support, by definition, is the number of reviews containing the termset on the total amount of reviews.

Given a termset I, in a single review, terms in I can be very dense or, on the opposite case, very sparse. We consider a review in which the occurrences of terms in I are dense being more relevant for the query than a review where occurrences are sparse. Thus, we introduce the concept of *Termset Density* of an termset I for a single review.

Definition 5: Consider a product p, a review $r \in R(p)$, and a termset I_l. The *Termset Review Density* $d_r(I_l)$ is defined as
$$d_r(I_l) = l/minWin_r(I_l)$$
where $minWin_r(I_l)$ is the size of the minimal window in review r that includes all the terms of termset I_l.   □

Notice that for *Termset Review Density*, it holds that $0 < d(I_l, r) \leq 1$

The next step is to define a *Termset Average Density* for a generic termset I (we omit the subscript l not to burden notation) w.r.t. a product p.

Definition 6: Consider a product p and its set of reviews $R(p)$. With $R_I(p)$ we call the subset of $R(p)$ of those reviews containing termset I. The *Termset Average Density* for product p, denoted as $ad_p(I)$, is defined as:
$$ad_p(I) = (\textstyle\sum_{r \in R_I(p)} d_r(I))/|R(p)|$$
□

The Termset Average Density is analogous to termset support, with the difference that the contribution of the occurrence of a termset I in a review r is not 1 but its density $d_r(I)$. Notice, thus, that $ad_p(I) \leq s_p(I) \leq 1$, where with $s_p(I)$ we denote the support of a termset I for a product p.

4.6   Product Ranking Metric

Finally, we can now define the *Product Ranking Metric PRM*.

Table 2. Indexed schemes

Schema	A	B	Diff %
Pos-Tagger	active	inactive	
Distinct tagged terms	1,151,827	776,852	-32.55%
Occurrences	216,345,522	216,345,522	0.00%
Analysis Time (A = Ps+Pt)	2226.80h	3.82h	-99.83%
Parsing Time (Ps)	2.11h	2.42h	+14.74%
Pos-tagging Time (Pt)	2224.69h	1.40h	-99.94%
Db Loading Time (D)	56.05h	49.76h	-11.23%
Term Expansion Time (E)	3.73h	2.67h	-28.49%
Total Time (T = A+D+E)	2286.58h	56.25h	-97.54%

Definition 7: Consider a query q, the set of termsets D_q^* derived from q, the system of the weights $w_q(|I^*|)$ and semantic coefficients $sc_q(I^*)$ for each expanded termset $I^* \in D_q^*$.

Consider a product p, the set of reviews $R(p)$ and the set of relevant expanded termsets $RD_{p,q}^*$ that can be actually extracted from $R(p)$. Given for each $I^* \in RD_{p,q}^*$ the average termset density $ad_p(I^*)$, the *Product Relevance Value* for product p is defined as

$$PRM_q(p) = \sum_{I^* \in RD_{p,q}^*} (w_q(|I^*|) \times ad_p(I^*) \times sc_q(I^*))$$

$\square$

The rationale of the above definition is the following. For each termset I^* included in the query q and actually relevant in the reviews, its contribution to the overall relevance value is given by its weight $w_q(|I^*|)$ (that depends on its size) multiplied by its *average density* $ad_{p,q}(I^*)$ and its semantic coefficient $sc_q(I^*)$.

The system of weights and semantic coefficients has been designed to obtain a $PRM_q(p) = 1$ for an *ideal* set of reviews for product p, where each review contains every expanded termset I^* that can be derived from q with a density $d_r(I^*) = 1$, and every expanded termset I^* is *valid*.

5   Evaluation

Our dataset is composed by a total of *2,207,678* user reviews for *109,221* movies downloaded from the IMDb.com web site[5]. The size of the text we downloaded is approximatively *3,091Mb*. Each movie has a number of reviews included between *1* and *4,876*, and the average number of reviews per movie is *20*.

Experiments has been run on a PC with two Intel Xeon Quad-core 2.0GHz/L3-4MB processors, 12GB RAM, four 1-Tbyte disks and Linux operating system.

---

[5] We focus on *movies* as Imdb data-set as been the first freely accesible big-data set we've found. Anyway the same approach is suitable for any set of product reviews.

5.1   Indexing

While indexing our data set, as described in the *back-end* side of HFC system architecture in 3.1, we figured out how *pos-tagging* affects the HFC system.

Disabling pos-tagging means tagging each term with a unique trivial tag, and considering for each term every possible expansion regardless of its role inside the query; in other words, disabling pos-tagging means a significant reduction of the number of managed terms because words are distinguished on the basis of their grammar category (for instance word *colour* could be both a noun and a verb); however, the counter effect is that the possible number of expansions for a termset combinatorially increases.

Table 2 reports data collected during dataset indexing. Column *A* shows data regarding indexing with pos-tagging activated (*Schema A*), while Column *B* shows data regarding indexing with pos-tagging deactivated (*Schema B*). Column *Diff %* shows the percentage variation from data of Schema A to data of Schema B (where applicable). For each *Schema*, the total number of indexed term occurrences (row *Occurrences*) and the number of identified tagged terms are shown. As said in the premises, disabling pos-tagging reduces the number of tagged terms ($\sim 33\%$). Table 2 reports, in rows, also data relative to execution time (in hours) during the indexing phase. The *Total Time* of the indexing is given by the sum of *Analysis Time*, *Db Loading Time* and *Term Expansion Time*. Moreover *Analysis Time* is split in *Parsing Time*, that is basically the time due to reading data from data set, and *Pos-tagging Time*, that considers only the execution time of *Stanford Parser* when pos-tagging is active, and instead the simple operation of labeling each term with the same tag when the pos-tagging is inactive. It is clearly evident how much the Analysis Time is affected by Pos-tagging Time using *Stanford Parser*: the more than 2200 hours needed for pos-tagging are equivalent to more than 90 days! In order to reduce this waiting time, we exploited all the 8 cores of the machine used for the experiment, parallelizing the Analysis phase in 8 independent processes, splitting data set into 8 different sub-data sets, and reducing the actual waiting time to about 13 days.

The analysis of variation of *Db Loading Time* and *Term Expansion Time* highlights how the higher number of tagged terms in *Schema A* w.r.t. *Schema B* affects the execution time of the *Loader* and the *Expander*.

5.2   Query Performance

For our query performance tests we prepared a set of 25 standard user queries[6] like *I want to know more about the history of Greece and the Persian wars*, or *All those moments will be lost in time, like tears in rain*[7].

The first test we made, compares the variation of performance of the query engine working on *Schema A* (ad described in Section 5.1) in a *single-searching-thread* version versus a *5-searching-threads* version. Table 3 shows the average

---

[6] Due to lack of space, we don't report the testing queries.

[7] From *Blade Runner* movie.

Table 3. Single-thread search engine Vs 5-threads search engine

	Single-thread	5-threads	Diff %
Average Time (T=QE+TG+TE+TM+S)	2,501.12 ms	1,994.66 ms	-20.25%
Query Expansion (QE	286.44 ms	286.40 ms	-0.01%
Thread generation (TG)	0.40 ms	1.88 ms	370.00%
Thread execution (TE ≤ O+R)	2,199.64 ms	1,691.60 ms	-23.10%
Occurrences Loading (O)	1,962.52 ms	1,639.84 ms	-16.44%
Ranking (R)	237.12 ms	75.12 ms	-68.32%
Thread merging (TM)	1.64 ms	1.80 ms	9.76%
Sorting (S)	13.00 ms	12.98 ms	-0.17%

results of the test performed on the set of 25 standard queries mentioned before. Column *Single-thread* shows performance of the single-thread search engine, while Column *5-threads* shows performance of the 5-threads search engine, and column *Diff %* shows the percentage variation from single-thread w.r.t. 5-threads search engine. For each search engine version, the average execution time per query is provided in row *Average Time*.

Basically, the query engine evaluates a query performing 4 different steps: (1) *query expansion*, (2) *occurrences loading*, (3) *product ranking*, (4) *result sorting*. Steps 2 and 3 can be parallelized (and performed in different threads), while Steps 1 and 4 must be performed by a single thread.

Row *Thread execution* of Table 3 reports the average execution time of the slowest searching threads for each query, while rows *Occurrences Loading* and *Ranking* report the average time of the slowest thread in executing respectively Step 2 and Step 3 for each query; that is why $TE \leq O + R$.

The analysis of execution times in Table 3 shows that most of the time needed to perform a query is because of *occurrences loading*: this is mostly due to our storage system based on classical hard disks. With more modern solid-state storage system, that are at least one order of magnitude faster, we are confident to dramatically improve performance.

Another issue is about threads parallelization. From the compared analysis, at first glance could seems that the 5-thread search engine version has not significantly improved performance, since there is only a 16.44% of gain in occurrences loading. However, this is mostly due to the fact that we have *de facto* a single storage system: data are transferred to main memory through a single *system bus*. We are confident that parallelized the process on different machines performance should dramatically increased. As a matter of fact, the compared analysis of ranking execution times, that do not involve disk use, tells that 5-treads search engine is 68.32% more perfoming that the single-thread search engine.

The second test we have made on our set of 25 queries, is a comparison between performance of the 5-thread search engine on the *Schema A* and *Schema B* as described in Section 5.1. Table 4 shows in column *A* data related to *Schema A*, and in column *B* data related to *Schema B*. Column *Diff %* shows the percentage variation from *Schema A* w.r.t. *Schema B*.

Table 4 provides average *data-per-query*. It can be noticed that when pos-tagger

Table 4. Pos tagging VS No-pos tagging

Schema	A	B	Diff %
Pos Tagging	active	inactive	
Total time	1,995 ms	3,480 ms	74.47%
Movies	2,067	2,994	44.85%
Occurrences	107,200	226,994	111.75%
Termsets	5,414	13,795	154.80%

is inactive there is a growing of average execution time, mostly due to the larger number of occurrences to load, and also to a larger number of termsets to analyze. On the other hands, there is larger number of movies retrieved as, actually, deactivating pos-tagging means increasing the number of expanded terms to search (causing generation of false positive movies, i.e., movies whose reviews are not actually relevant w.r.t. the original query).

6 Conclusions

The scope of this paper was to present the architecture and the query engine of *HFC NoSQL* database system. Although performance of the system can be further be improved, the considerations in 5.2 show that the approach is feasible in terms of query response time.

We are aware we did not discuss about system effectiveness, but it was beyond the scope of the paper. However the web-interface we developed is designed to collect users opinions about the system, and by means of that, in the future work we intend to deeper investigate effectiveness of the system. Moreover, as far as effectiveness is concerned, in the future work we intend to integrate term expansion with *linked-data* as a source for semantic ontology about terms, and also considering *word order* and *word repetition* in queries in our ranking model. In the end, we are also aware we have to deal with advanced semantic issues such as *negative sentences*.

References

1. Cattell, R.: Scalable sql and nosql data stores. SIGMOD Record 39(4), 12–27 (2011)
2. Chaovalit, P., Zhou, L.: Movie review mining: a comparison between supervised and unsupervised classification approaches. In: HICSS. IEEE Computer Society (2005)
3. Dave, K., Lawrence, S., Pennock, D.M.: Mining the peanut gallery: opinion extraction and semantic classification of product reviews. In: WWW, pp. 519–528 (2003)
4. Fosci, P., Psaila, G.: Toward a product search engine based on user reviews. In: Int. Conf. on Data Technologies and Applications, DATA 2012, Rome (Italy) (July 2012)
5. Hu, M., Liu, B.: Mining and summarizing customer reviews. In: Kim, W., Kohavi, R., Gehrke, J., DuMouchel, W. (eds.) KDD, pp. 168–177. ACM (2004)

6. Hu, M., Liu, B.: Mining opinion features in customer reviews. In: McGuinness, D.L., Ferguson, G. (eds.) AAAI, pp. 755–760. AAAI Press / The MIT Press (2004)

7. Lee, D., Jeong, O.-R., Goo Lee, S.: Opinion mining of customer feedback data on the web. In: Kim, W., Choi, H.-J. (eds.) ICUIMC, pp. 230–235. ACM (2008)

8. Liu, B., Hu, M., Cheng, J.: Opinion observer: analyzing and comparing opinions on the web. In: Ellis, A., Hagino, T. (eds.) WWW, pp. 342–351. ACM (2005)

9. Ly, D.K., Sugiyama, K., Lin, Z., Kan, M.-Y.: Product review summarization based on facet identification and sentence clustering. CoRR, abs/1110.1428 (2011)

10. Resnick, P., Varian, H.: Recommender systems. Communications of the ACM 40(3), 56–58 (1997)

11. Robin, H., Jablonski, S.: Nosql evaluation: A use case oriented survey. In: International Conference on Cloud and Service Computing, CSC 2011, Hong Kong, China, pp. 336–341 (December 2011)

12. Sandvig, J.J., Mobasher, B., Burke, R.D.: Robustness of collaborative recommendation based on association rule mining. In: Konstan, J.A., Riedl, J., Smyth, B. (eds.) RecSys, pp. 105–112. ACM (2007)

13. Strauch, C.: Nosql databases (2011),
http://www.christof-strauch.de/nosqldbs.pdf

Towards a Formal Approach for Verifying Temporal Coherence in a SMIL Document Presentation

Abdelghani Ghomari[1], Naceur Belheziel[1],
Fatma-Zohra Mekahlia[1], and Chabane Djeraba[2]

[1] Université of Oran
Industrial Computing and Networking Laboratory (LRIIR)
BP 1524, El-M'Naouer 31000 - Algeria
{ghomari65,belheziel,mekahlia.fzohra}@yahoo.fr
[2] University of Lille 1 Bât. M3
59655 Villeneuve D'ASCQ CEDEX - France
Chabane.Djeraba@lifl.fr

Abstract. In this paper we will present an approach based on Time Petri net (TPN) for verifying temporal coherence in a SMIL (Synchronized Multimedia Integration Language) document presentation. In our approach, we can model a SMIL document by TPN model by translation of the SMIL elements and attributes into TPN concepts. Some extension of the TPN model is made to obtain the synchronization concepts equivalence of a SMIL document like sequential and parallel. The analysis of TPN by the Tina tool allows us to verify the consistency properties and the temporal coherence of the SMIL document.

Keywords: Time Petri net (TPN), SMIL document, IMD, temporal coherence.

1 Introduction

The Interactive Multimedia Documents (IMDs) that we consider in this paper are collections of heterogeneous objects (such as video, audio, text, and image) organized in both the spatial and temporal dimensions. Moreover they support a hypertext structure to provide the reader with interaction capabilities. Several formats exist to model such documents: MHEG [11], HyTime [8], and SMIL [2] are the most well-known standards. Designing such a document is known to be a complex and error prone task for numerous reasons. Authors must handle large numbers of objects in the document, they have to deal with complex temporal information (synchronization tasks and objects duration) and they cannot easily reuse parts of existing documents.

SMIL [2] is an XML-based (Extensible MarkupLanguage) language that lets authors write interactive multimedia presentations, and supports detailed temporal synchronization semantics. Using SMIL, an author can describe the multimedia presentation's temporal behavior, associate hyperlinks with media objects, and describe the presentation's layout on a screen.

A. Cuzzocrea and S. Maabout (Eds.): MEDI 2013, LNCS 8216, pp. 132–146, 2013.

In spite of its numerous advantages, many things remain to make, particularly in the field of the formalization to be able to verify any temporal or spatial coherence of a SMIL document before its presentation [1]. Indeed, the complexity of the SMIL synchronization model is such that is difficult to guarantee the validity of a scenario using non formal methods. On the other hand, the formal techniques based on mathematical models offer a complete formal semantics and propose formal techniques for consistency checking [5], but are in general time consuming. Although many research studies were dedicated to IMDs authoring, only few of them has addressed temporal consistency checking problems. Yet, it is clear that the temporal consistency of a document has a direct impact on the quality of the presentation and consequently on the author satisfaction (consider the case of a presentation that stops playing before its end, a part of its semantics is lost). In this work, we propose an approach for modeling and validation of SMIL documents by using the TPN of Merlin [3] which is a powerful formal model of specification and validation of temporal coherence of IMDs.

In this paper, we highlight the following points: related works (Section 2), our approach of SMIL documents formalization (Section 3), and the architecture of the realized tool (Section 4). Finally, Section 5 presents some conclusions of this work.

2   Related Works

The IMDs have been largely used in several fields and are accessed over the Web. The specification of the temporal structure of IMD has been reported in several publications by the proposal of models, languages and authoring tools, for instance, IMAP [14], MADEUS [9] and SMIL [2]. The language SMIL has been proposed by the World Wide Web Consortium's (W3C) as a standard solution for the presentation of IMD over the Web. The temporal model of SMIL allows an author to describe temporal synchronization relationships. These relations constitute a set of synchronization constraints which must be satisfied at the presentation of the document. Unfortunately, an incoherence situation may occur as ("deadlock", "media never played", "reference to a media that does not exist", etc.). For these reasons, an approach that detects and corrects these inconsistencies is needed. This can be done with *Simple Temporal Constraints problems* as used in Madeus [9] (it is an authoring environment for IDMs). In this approach, an IDM is translated into a graph where nodes correspond to events such as *start* or end of a media object and *arcs* to relations between events. These relations take account of metric information (for instance, duration of task). Algorithms such as cycle detection are applied to these graphs to control coherence and other properties. Unfortunately, this framework does not suit some important characteristics of multimedia authoring process such as the presence of links in objects and objects whose duration is not controllable (typically videos).

In [13], another methodology for the design of SMIL documents based on the formal description technique RT-LOTOS is proposed. This approach presents the advantage of providing techniques for modeling the dynamic behavior of the document and its temporal non-determinism. Furthermore, a RT-LOTOS specification [5,12] is based on composition of processes; this concept allows to describe an IMD with simple media objects which can be composed. RT-LOTOS allows also giving a formal semantic to logical and temporal behavior of a document. Temporal automata derived from RT-LOTOS specification are used for temporal consistency checking (at this level, simulation techniques of RTL tool are used). In [4], a similar approach based on an enhanced Object Composition Petri Net (OCPN) [10] has been proposed to capture information of multimedia objects along with their timing and synchronization specified in SMIL.

In [6], an approach for automatic verification of SMIL documents based on temporal logic is proposed. This approach presents a tool which can assist the user in the complex task of authoring a multimedia presentation. The tool is based on a formal semantics defining the temporal aspects of SMIL elements by means of a set of inference rules. The rules, in the spirit of Hoare's semantics, describe how the execution of a piece of code changes the state of the computation of a player. If any temporal conflict is found, the system returns a message to the user pointing out the element which contains the conflict and its motivation. This helps the user to develop robust and clear code.

This paper refers to a methodology for the formal design of IMDs based on the formal description technique TPN. In particular, this paper presents an approach applied by our methodology for the automatic translation of SMIL documents into TPN specifications.

Our objective is to explore TPN's [4] capabilities to model and analyze IMDs. This paper presents an enhancement to our previous work that describes a similar formal approach [7].

3   Our Approach of SMIL Documents Formalization

3.1   SMIL

SMIL is part of the W3C's family of XML-related standards. SMIL lets authors create simple multimedia presentations and add more complex behavior incrementally. In August 2001, W3C released version 2.0 of SMIL. SMIL's features fall into five categories: media content, layout, timing, linking and adaptivity [2]. SMIL has been installed on a large number of desktops world wide, primarily because of its adoption in Real Player, Quicktime and Internet Explorer.

We focus primarily on the media object module and the timing and synchronization module for the translation process. The media object module contains elements and attributes to describe media objects, and the timing and synchronization module defines elements and attributes to coordinate and synchronize the presentation of media over time [2]. The term media covers a broad range, including discrete media types such as still images, text and vector graphics as well as continuous media types that are intrinsically time based, such as video, audio and animation [2]. The primary media object elements are <ref> (generic media reference), <img>, <audio>, <text>, <video >, <animation>

and <textstream>. The primary media object attributes are src (the value of src is the Uniform Resource Identifier (URI) of the media element, which is used for locating and fetching the associated media) and type (content type of the media referenced by the src attribute). The elements (referred to as time containers) defined in the timing and synchronization module are <seq> (container that plays child elements in a sequence), <par> (container that plays child elements in parallel), <excl> (container that plays one child at a time but does not impose order) and <priorityClass> (container defines a group of <excl> children and the pause interrupt behaviour of the children [2]. The child elements can be media object elements or other elements. If a <priorityClass> element appears as a child of an excl element then the excl element can contain only <priorityClass> elements. The primary attributes in the timing and synchronization module are begin, end, dur (these three attributes are used for timing control), endsync, min, max (these three specify extended activation), fill (specifies the object persistence), syncBehavior, syncTolerance, syncMaster (these three are used for synchronization), timeContainer and timeAction (these two are used for XML timing integration) [2].

The following examples show how timing and synchronization between media can be specified with SMIL :

```
<seq>   <audio src="audio.wav"/>   <video src="video.mpg"/></seq>
Sequential playback of an audio followed by a video.

 <par>   <audio src="audio.wav"/>   <video src="video.mpg"/></par>
Parallel playback of an audio and a video as a group.

<par endsync="first"><audio src="audio.wav"/><video src="video.mpg"/></par>
```

Parallel playback to be stopped with the first media that ends.

3.2   Incoherence in SMIL Documents

The flexibility of high level authoring models (such as SMIL) for the edition of IMDs can lead authors, in certain cases, to specify synchronization relations which could not be satisfied during the presentation of the document, thus characterizing the occurrence of temporal inconsistencies. For this reason, we need to apply a methodology which provides the formal semantics for the dynamic behavior of the IMD, consistency checking, and the scheduling of the presentation taking into account the temporal non-determinism of these IMD.

The presentation of an IMD depends on the temporal constraints defined on the objects of the document. Indeed, these relations must be well defined otherwise they can give deadlock situations. Authors of SMIL documents are free to express relationships between SMIL components without describing how they are processed. The author can incrementally modify his/her specifications by adding, or removing constraints from the current temporal constraints or replacing an object by another which may have a different duration. These modifications may imply incoherence in the temporal specified constraints. There are mainly two kinds of incoherencies:

1. **Quantitative Incoherence:** Let us suppose that a scenario defines a parallel presentation of two objects namely A and B. The element B begins 4 seconds after the *par* begins. The duration of B is 5 seconds, and then it ends at (4s + 5s) 9 seconds. The element A begins 1 second after the element B begins (i.e. at 5 seconds) and ends at 3 seconds. This is impossible. For example, we can have the following SMIL code:

```
<par> <img id="A" begin =begin (B) +1s, end= 3s />
<img id="B" begin=4s, dur="5s" /> </par>
```

2. **Qualitative Incoherence:** Let us suppose that a scenario defines a parallel presentation of two objects namely A and B. The beginning of element A depends on the beginning of element B and vice versa. Neither A nor B can begin.
For example, we can have the following SMIL code:

```
<par><img id="A" begin = begin (B) />
<img id="B" begin = begin (A) /> </par>
```

3.3   TPN (Time Petri Nets)

The Petri nets are graphical and mathematical tools applied to a number of systems. They are used to describe and study the processes of information systems which are described by competitiveness, synchronization and asynchronization, distributiveness, parallelism, determination, stochastic. As a graphical tool, they are used for visual communication. The tokens in them are used to simulate dynamic and competitive processes. As a mathematical tool, they define the state equations, algebraic equations of models for systems management.

To model time constraints of real time systems various time extensions are proposed, in the literature, for Petri nets. Among these extensions, TPN model [3] is considered to be a good compromise between modeling power and verification complexity. TPN are a simple yet powerful formalism useful to model and verify concurrent systems with time constraints (real time systems). In TPN, a firing interval is associated with each transition specifying the minimum and maximum times it must be maintained enabled, before its firing. Its firing takes no time but may lead to another marking. TPN are then able to model time constraints even if the exact delays or durations of events are not known. So, TPN are appropriate to specify time constraints of real time systems which are often specified by giving worst case boundaries.

First, we recall the definition of TPN.

Definition 1 (TPN). *A TPN is a tuple N = (P, T, W, Mo, Is) where:*

1. *P and T are nonempty finite sets of places and transitions respectively with $P \cap T = \emptyset$;*
2. *W is the arc weight function;*
3. *Mo is the initial marking;*

4. Is: $T \to Q^+ \times (Q^+ \cup \{\infty\})$ is the static interval function, where Q^+ is the set of positive rational numbers.

The *Is* function associates each transition t with a temporal static interval. The left bound and the right bound are called the static earliest firing time (sEFT) and the static latest firing time (sLFT) respectively. A marking is a function $M : P \to N$ where M (p) denotes the number of tokens at place p. The firing of a transition depends on both enabling and timing conditions.

Definition 2 (enabling). *A transition t is enabled in a marking M iff $\forall p \in P, M(p) \geq W(p, t)$. We denote by enabled (M) the set of all transitions enabled in marking M. A transition t enabled in marking M is fireable in the associated untimed Petri net but not necessarily in the TPN.*

Definition 3 (State). *A state of TPN, called interval state, is a pair $E = (M, Id)$ in which M is a marking and Id is a dynamic firing interval function. Functions Id associates with each enabled transition the time interval [dEFT, dLFT] in which the transition is allowed to fire.*

Definition 4 (Firing Condition). *Firing a transition t, at relative time θ, from state $E = (M, Id)$, is allowed iff both the following conditions hold:*

1. *The transition is enabled: $\forall p \in P, M(p) \geq W(p, t)$*
2. *The relative firing time θ, relative to the absolute time at which state E has been reached, is comprised between the dEFT of transition t and the smallest of the dLFTs among of the transitions enabled.*

Definition 5 (Firing rule). *If a transition t is fireable at the time θ from state $E = (M, Id)$, its firing leads to a new state $E' = (M', Id')$, computed as follows:*

1. *The new marking M' is defined for any place, as in Petri nets, as: $M'(p) = M(p) - W(p, t_f) + W(t_f, p)$*
2. *The new firing intervals Id' for transitions enabled by marking M' are computed as follows:*
   - *For all transitions t enabled by marking M and not in conflict with t_f, then: $Id'(t) = Max(0, dEFT(t) - \theta)), dLFT(t) - \theta)$.*
   - *All other transitions have their interval set to their static firing interval.*

3.4   Automatic Translation of SMIL Documents into TPN

Our objective is to give a formal approach to verify the coherence of SMIL documents by using TPN. Here we define the main translation patterns. A SMIL document is modeled by TPN (see Figure 1) that contains two places (initial and final place) and a start transition ts-smil constrained with a time interval equals to [0, 0]. The initial place p is associated to the <smil> tag and corresponds to the start of the presentation. The final place p_{in} is associated to the </smil> tag and corresponds to the end of the presentation. In the initial marking M_0, the place p is marked with one token.

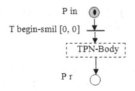

Fig. 1. An example of a SMIL document

A SMIL document describes the composition of several media objects by means of synchronization operators. To facilitate the derivation of a TPN from a SMIL document, we extend the TPN model with a 'component' concept (Figure 2). A component is the basic building block in the translation procedure. It encapsulates a TPN which describes the temporal behavior of a media object. Its input and output interfaces are respectively a set of input places and an output transition. The TPN in the Figure 2 contains a start place $P_{begin-object}$, two transitions: the transition of departure $t_{begin-object}$ and transition of the end $t_{end-object}$ and a place region $P_{r-object}$. The presence of a token in $P_{r-object}$ means that the object is in execution.

In the Figure 2 the interval SI_1 of $t_{begin-object}$ models the begin attribute and SI_2 models the attributes: *dur*, *begin* and *end*.

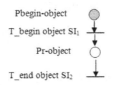

Fig. 2. Basic Media object

To summarize the formalization of SMIL documents by the TPN model, our approach consists of five phases:

1. Analysis of SMIL documents and decomposition into key words.
2. Initiate the SMIL document into TPN: During detection of the body of the document SMIL (<body>... </body>), the following objects are generated:
   - begin place (Activated)
   - begin transition ([0, 0])
   - Nd Place
3. Find the following components such as:
   - The media (<img/>, <video/>, <audio/>, <textstream/>) (Figure 2)
   - The <seq/> and <par/> operators (Figure 3)

- **The element Seq** To model the element *Seq* in a SMIL document (Figure 3.a), the input interface t_{s-seq} is the link of the first child which will be played and the output of the interface is linked to the place meet (P_{m-seq}). t_{e-seq} is the interface of the output of the sequence which contains the interval $SI_2 = [\text{dur-seq, dur-seq}]$.
- **The element Par** The modeling of the element *Par* depends on the attribute "endsync". The Figure 3-b models the element by whom the attribute contains "endsync='last' " i.e. the transition t_{e-par} that must be fired if all the childs end their playback.

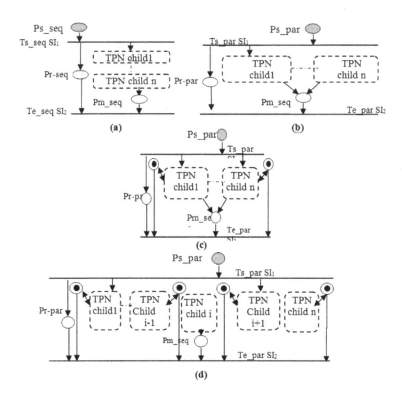

Fig. 3. The TPN modeling of the elements (a) Seq, (b) Par operator (endsync = 'last'), (c) Par operator (endsync = 'first') and (d) Par operator (endsync = 'id-object')

The Figure 3-c treats the case "endsync='first' " where we add a new place called 'disrupt'. It is an input/output place that is used when the first child ends and the transition t_{e-par} stops or inhibits the others media with 'stealing' the token of the 'disrupt'. The Figure 3-d treats the case "endsync=id-objet" such that name-object is the identifier of a child of an element par. When this child end, all the others childs are stopped.

- **The link objects** The element a or area will be modeled by a link place (circle in dotted lines) which is followed by two transitions: the first one contains an interval [0, 0] for the element a and [begin, begin] for the element area, and the second transition contains an interval [dur, dur] for both elements. According to the value of the attribute "show", the elements a and area can have three behaviors:

  - *Pause:* the activation of the link suspends the component source during the execution of the target component, and allows to resume the component source until durc-t with durc is the duration of the playback of the media source and t is the duration of the playback of the media source before it's pause. This behavior is modeled by the Figure 4-a.

  - *Replace:* the target component replaces the component source; the component source is then stopped. This is modeled by the Figure 4-b where the activation of the link causes the stop of the presentation of the element source and the presentation.

  - *New:* the target component begins in a new context, without influencing the component source. This case will be modeled by the Figure 4-c where the target element runs in an autonomous and independently of the component source.

    In every case, the run time of the target element is not counted in the time of the source presentation; the elements of links do not influence the synchronization of the element source.

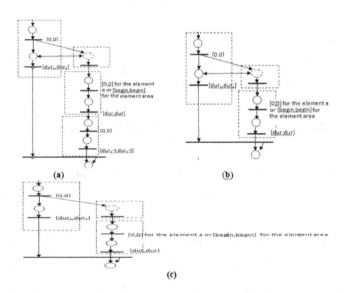

Fig. 4. The TPN modeling of the elements (a) The link objects (show=Pause), (b) The link objects (show=Replace) and (c) The link objects (show=New)

4. Translate the components to the TPN model and proceed to the jointures:
   An example of translation is as follows:

```
<par id = 'par1'> <img id = 'img' begin = '2s' dur = "4s" />
     <video d= 'vid' begin=begin (img)+"2s" end="3s" />
     <text id = 'txt' begin = begin (vid) dur = "2s" /><par/>
```

The TPN of the above SMIL document is depicted in Figure 5.

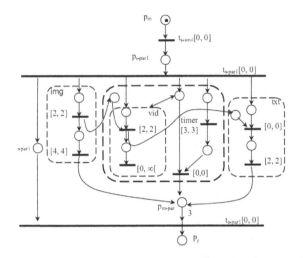

Fig. 5. TPN model of a SMIL document

5. Verification of TPN structure and properties:
   - **Verification of the intra-element coherence** Each media is verified
     from its temporal attributes *begin, dur, end*.
     `<video src = ... Begin=B dur = D end = E.../>`
     The basic rule is as follow: $T\_begin + T\_dur = T\_end \Leftrightarrow B + D = E$
     If the condition of the basic rule is not satisfied then an intra-element
     temporal incoherence is declared.
     Example 1: Incoherence on the media
     `<img src= " img1" begin = "5s" dur = "25s" end= "25s" ...>`
   - **Verification of the inter-elements coherence** If the intra-element
     coherence is verified then we proceed to verify the coherence of a media
     set included into a synchronization operator such as: Seq and Par. The
     verification is done from the temporal attributes (*begin, dur, end*) of
     each media and the attribute duration of the operator.
     Example 2: Incoherence between several media
     `... <body>    <par  dur= " 25s ">`
     `<img src= " img1"  begin = "0s" dur = "25s"...>`
     `<img src= " img2" begin = "12s" dur = "15s"...> </par></body> ...`
     Example 3: Incoherence on the operator Seq
     `... <body>    <seq  dur= " 20s " >`
     `<vid src= " video"  begin = "0s" dur = "15s" ...>`
     `<img src= " img1" begin = "0s" dur = "9s" ...> </seq></body> ...`

3.5   Case Study

Let us consider an example of an IMD of a heart medical file: in the framework of a service provided by a hospital, a doctor has the possibility to choose a multimedia service among several. For example, when consulting a heart medical file of a patient, the doctor is able, to visualize the multimedia file of the patient, thanks to temporal synchronization (Figure 6), while focusing himself on the affected bodies.

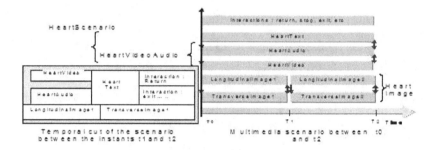

Fig. 6. An IMD of a heart medical file

The IMD of the heart medical file is composed of a textual description of the heart (a text describing the heart) and its behavior, audio and video sequence describing the beats of the heart. The audio and video sequence is synchronized with two images, describing a longitudinal and transverse cut of the heart, respectively. These two cuts evolve with the audio and video sequence of the heart. At any moment, the user can stop, represent, and return to the initial menu to choose medical files of other patients or leave completely the scenario. The user has also the possibility to activate a link E to navigate in the heart video document.

After editing the IMD of the heart medical file in the LimSee 3 editor[1], we can obtain the corresponding SMIL code as below:

```
<body>
  <par dur=15s endsync="last">
    <seq dur="18s">
      <img src=" ImageLongitudinale1.gif" begin="0s" dur="10s" end="18s"/>
      <img src=" ImageTransversale1.gif" dur="8s"/>
    </seq>
    <seq dur="18s">
      <img src=" ImageLongitudinale2.gif" begin="0s" dur="10s"/>
      <img src=" ImageTransversale2.gif" dur="9s"/>
    </seq>
    <audio src=" AudioCoeur.mp3" begin="0s" dur="18s" />
      <textstream src=" TexteCoeur.rt" begin="0s" dur="18s"/>
    < video src=" VideoCoeur.rm" begin="0s" dur="18s"/>
      <a href="lien1"dur=10 show="new" accesskey="E"/ >
    < video/>
  </par>
</body>
```

---

[1] http://limsee3.gforge.inria.fr/public-site/help/tutorial-install/
install-installing.html

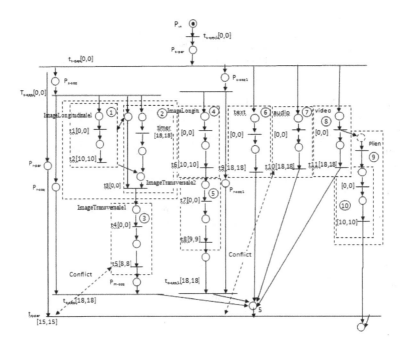

Fig. 7. An example of a TPN model of the heart medical file

The translation of this SMIL code in a TPN model is then executed by our tool by applying a set of rules already cited in section 3.3. Then, we obtain a TPN model like in the figure 7:

Beside the usual graphic editing and simulation facilities, the software tool Tina[2] may build a number of state space abstractions for TPN, preserving certain classes of properties. For TPN, that have in general infinite state spaces, they provide finite representation of their behavior, in terms of state class graphs. So, we use in our work, the Tina toolbox for analyzing the TPN of the figure 7 that corresponds to heart medical file IMD. We then detect three temporal incoherencies:

- The first one is an intra-element incoherence and it is detected on the media image 1, such as:

  `<img src=" ImageLongitudinale1.gif" begin="0s" dur="10s" end="18s" />`,

  where $begin + dur \neq end$ results in an unreasonable physical meaning.
- The second one is an inter-elements incoherence between the media: video-Coeur, audioCoeur and textCoeur and it is detected on the operator Par, such as:

---

[2] http://www.laas.fr/tina

```
<Par dur=15s endsync="last"> ...
      < video src=" VideoCoeur.rm" begin="0s" dur="18s"/>
      <audio src=" AudioCoeur.mp3" begin="0s" dur="18s" />
      <text src=" TextCoeur.txt" begin="0s" dur="18s" />
...</Par>
```

Where the duration of the element Par is smaller than the durations of the media: VideoCoeur, AudioCoeur and TexteCoeur.

- The third one is also an inter-elements incoherence between the media: ImageLongitudinale1 and ImageLongitudinale2 and it is detected on the operator *Seq* such as:

```
<Seq dur="18s">
    <img src=" ImageLongitudinale1.gif" begin="0s" dur="10s" />
    <img src=" ImageLongitudinale2.gif" dur="9s"/>
</Seq>
```

Where the duration of the element Seq is smaller than the durations of the media: ImageLongitudinale1 and ImageLongitudinale2. The inter-elements time conflict could be detected by traversing the TPN and comparing the computed firing times of its transitions.

4   The Global Architecture of Our Tool

The realized tool is implemented on HP Intel®Core I5 platform using the programming language JBuilder9, and run in a window environment [15]. According to the architecture of the tool (depicted in Fig. 8), the following components can be described: (1) Edition of SMIL documents in LimSee 3 which permits to a user to compose multimedia objects like text, image, video, audio; (2) Translation of SMIL documents into a TPN model by applying a set of rules; (3) Verifying temporal coherence of TPN by using the Tina tool; (4) Presentation of SMIL documents by using a player like: RealOne, QuickTimle, VLC, etc.

5   Conclusion

In this paper, we have presented a formal approach based on TPN for coherence control of SMIL documents. We have presented a tool to assist the user to produce SMIL documents with robust and clear code. The tool verifies the presence of temporal conflicts and, in the case of correct documents, produces as output a valid sequence for scheduling. The tool is based on a formal semantics defining the temporal aspects of SMIL by means of a set of inference rules which describe how the execution of a piece of code changes the state of the computation of a player, and analyses only but efficiently a subset of SMIL documents.

For verification, we parsed some SMIL documents into TPN data structures and then displayed the specified temporal and synchronization information graphically in the Tina toolbox [14]. The state class graph derived from TPN

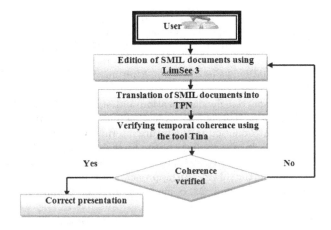

Fig. 8. The global architecture of our tool

allows to verify if a given presentation can be played until the end. Other information (such as object never played or object started and never terminated) can be extracted from the state class graph by using model checking technique. Such information is useful to correct errors in SMIL documents.

References

1. Asnawi, R., Ahmad, W.F.W., Rambli, D.R.A.: Formalization and verification of a live multimedia presentation model. International Journal of Computer Applications 20(3), 32–41 (2011)
2. Ayars, J., Bulterman, D., Cohen, A., Day, K., Hodge, E., Hoschka, P., Hyche, E., Jourdan, M., Kubota, K., Lanphier, R.: Synchronized multimedia integration language (SMIL) 2.0 specification. Work in progress. W3C Working Drafts (September 21, 2000), http://www.w3.org/TR
3. Berthomieu, B., Diaz, M.: Modeling and verification of time dependent systems using time petri nets. IEEE Trans. Software Eng. 17(3), 259–273 (1991)
4. Chung, S.M., Pereira, A.L.: Timed petri net representation of the synchronized multimedia integration language (smil) of xml. In: Proceedings of the International Conference on Information Technology: Computers and Communications, ITCC 2003, pp. 711–716. IEEE Computer Society, Washington, DC (2003)
5. Courtiat, J.-P., De Oliveira, R.C.: Proving temporal consistency in a new multimedia synchronization model. In: Proceedings of the Fourth ACM International Conference on Multimedia, MULTIMEDIA 1996, pp. 141–152. ACM, New York (1996)
6. Gaggi, O., Bossi, A.: Analysis and verification of smil documents. Multimedia Systems 17(6), 487–506 (2011)
7. Ghomari, A., Djeraba, C.: An approach for synchronization and management of multimedia scenarios in an object-oriented database. In: Loucopoulos, P., Cavarero, J.-L. (eds.) RCIS, pp. 175–182. IEEE (2010)

8. International Organization for Standardization. Information technology — hypermedia/time-based structuring language (hytime). ISO/IEC 10744 (1997)
9. Jourdan, M., Layaïda, N., Roisin, C., Sabry-Ismaïl, L., Tardif, L.: Madeus, and authoring environment for interactive multimedia documents. In: Proceedings of the Sixth ACM International Conference on Multimedia, MULTIMEDIA 1998, pp. 267–272. ACM, New York (1998)
10. Little, T.D.C., Ghafoor, A.: Synchronization and storage models for multimedia objects. IEEE Journal on Selected Areas in Communications 8(3), 413–427 (1990)
11. Price, R.: Mheg: an introduction to the future international standard for hypermedia object interchange. In: Proceedings of the First ACM International Conference on Multimedia, MULTIMEDIA 1993, pp. 121–128. ACM, New York (1993)
12. Sampaio, P.N.M., Courtiat, J.-P.: An approach for the automatic generation of rt-lotos specifications from smil 2.0 documents. J. Braz. Comp. Soc. 9(3), 39–51 (2004)
13. Sampaio, P.N.M.: Conception Formelle de Documents Multimedia: Une Approche s'appuyant sur RT-LOTOS. PhD thesis, Univ Paul Sabatier, Toulouse, France (2003)
14. Vazirgiannis, M., Boll, S.: Events in interactive multimedia applications: Modeling and implementation design. In: Proceedings of the 1997 International Conference on Multimedia Computing and Systems, ICMCS 1997, p. 244. IEEE Computer Society, Washington, DC (1997)
15. Zaza, M.: Modeling and verifying the Temporal Coherence of SMIL Documents Using Time Peti Nets. Master's thesis, University of Es Senia, Oran (September 2012)

Analyzing Massive Streaming Heterogeneous Data: Towards a New Computing Model for Computational Sustainability

Dimitrios Gunopulos

Department of Informatics and Telecommunications
National and Kapodistrian University of Athens
kddlab.di.uoa.gr/dg.html
dg@di.uoa.gr

1   Introduction

Today we are witnessing advances in technology that are changing dramatically the way we live, work and interact with the physical environment. New revolutionary technologies are creating an explosion on the size and variety of information that is becoming available. Such technologies include the development and widespread adoption of networks of small and inexpensive embedded sensors that are being used to instrument the environment at an unprecedented scale. In addition, the last few years have brought forward the widespread adoption of social networking applications. Another trend with significant ramifications is the massive adoption of smartphones in the market. The rise of the social networking applications and the always-on functionality of the smartphones are driving the rise of a part of the web that is dedicated to recording, maintaining and sharing rapidly changing data which has been termed the Live Web.

The Live Web phenomenon goes back to the development and extensive use of RSS feeds and publish-subscribe applications on the web, which allowed the distribution of information in real time. Today the Live Web comprises these parts of the web that are dedicated and used by the users to document their lives, exchange and share information with colleagues and friends, but also connect their online presence with real life considerations. The Live Web encompasses social networking sites, as exemplified by Twitter or Facebook, but also other sites that the users use to post information, experiences, and so on, including blogs, review sites that serve as a combined repository of knowledge on several topics, and which are becoming very influential on how people make decisions on several everyday problems.

The important characteristics of the Live Web are: (i) the data in the Live web typically have temporal information associated with them. The data themselves may be changing continuously (for example, the location of the user), or their relevance to a query or a task may change continually (for example, blogging about current events). For example, consider twitter: only the latest twits are easily accessible from the interface, and if a person does not respond or retransmit a twit soon after receiving it, it is very unlikely that this action will take place later.

A. Cuzzocrea and S. Maabout (Eds.): MEDI 2013, LNCS 8216, pp. 147–148, 2013.
© Springer-Verlag Berlin Heidelberg 2013

(ii) very frequently these data have spatial information as well, and this information is crucial in evaluating the data. Spatial and temporal data permeate people's lives and describe how people perform several activities. The term "spatial capital" refers to how people's location can impact and influence their lives, chances of success, etc.

(iii) One of the most important uses of the Live Web is for building networks and enabling collaborations.

In this environment we will see the emergence of novel, complex, mobile cyberphysical systems where people actively participate through personal mobile phones, in the process of sensing, instrumenting and analyzing live data. Applications may be as simple as providing alternative routing paths in a transportation application, to more sophisticated examples such as planning common carpool routes or optimizing routes in future public transportation systems, to applications with hard real-time constraints such as emergency response systems to natural or man-caused disasters. In fact new applications are moving beyond the entertainment and information sharing domains and into the emergency response and resource allocation domains, where more robust solutions are required.

In this talk we present recent research work along the trends we describe above. We also consider how such novel research results are enabling forms of computation that were not possible before. First, we focus on the specific problem of Finding Events and Trends when monitoring heterogeneous datasets. Our goal is to develop techniques which efficiently and accurately aggregate necessary information from different sources, and will orchestrate it appropriately. A fundamental problem that arises is the high diversity of the incoming data, obtained from very different sources and having different formats and scales. A second fundamental problem is developing techniques that would achieve monitoring in real-time, given that our motivation comes from applications, including emergency response and disaster management, which have strong real-time requirements. Our work is in the context of the INSIGHT FP7 project, and we consider data from sources as different as traffic sensors and Twitter streams. We also present recent work using spatiotemporal patterns to detect trends.

In the second part of the talk we consider the more general problem of how to develop and reason about the behavior of novel applications that exploit the new setting of the Live Web. Computing in this setting has the following new aspects: (i) Always on connectivity, (ii) there is a merging of virtual and real life (e.g. most twitter or facebook users use their real identities when using social media) and (iii) there exists an availability of massively distributed and human computing components. In addition, it appears necessity that we need to develop very distributed and complex mechanisms, and grassroots development and optimization may be the most general and effective approach to do so. A fundamental problem that is emerging is how to understand the implications on the design, development and deployment of new applications of these aspects. We describe initial work on the formulation of this new computing paradigm, and on describing how it can be applied for computational sustainability applications.

Toward Expressing a Preliminary Core Identity Significantly Characterized from the Social Network Temporal Dynamicity

Billel Hamadache, Hassina Seridi-Bouchelaghem, and Nadir Farah

Laboratory of Electronic Document Management LabGED
Badji Mokhtar Annaba-University, P. O. Box 12, 23000, Annaba, Algeria
{Hamadache,seridi,farah}@labged.net

Abstract. The social computing research and the data mining can be interoperated in order to provide answers to the man socialization within emergent online social network (SN). Given as a new trend in the social network analysis and Mining (SNA), the social dynamic behavior is aimed to enhance, modeling, formalizing and identifying more significantly interesting phenomena as a core structure of an emergent SN. The nature and the behaviors of such underlying social structure are surrounded by the raised question in this paper in front of this temporal dynamicity. Firstly, the internal cohesion, persistence, composition stability and the important played role in the network in time are proposed as parameters. A core identity significantly characterized, will be acquired by a grouping of individuals, if a sufficient equilibrium between these parameters is expressed within a dynamic social networked environment. Secondly, a modeling method is addressed by formalizing a weighted temporal graph model where parameters combinations characterizing the behaviors and locations of groupings (temporal overlaps) in the network are expressed. Thirdly, a sub-model is identified as a container within which, a persistent structure should be deeply encapsulated, embodying a largest group maximizing and balanced between stable composition and central role throughout an observation period. Such identity is still discussed to enhance it, toward a more significant identity characterizing a core structure around that, a developing process of dynamic SN occurs in time.

Keywords: SNAM, underlying core structure, dynamic SN, temporal dynamicity, group dynamics, temporal overlaps, composition stability, group centrality, significant core identity.

1 Introduction

In front of the growing availability of large volumes of relational data, the social networks (SN) research is being positioned as a particular area inspired from data mining based on theoretical foundations of graph mining. Boosted by the proliferation of social media web sites, the Social Network Analysis and Mining (SNAM) [1] doesn't content nowadays only to understand large social representations within a

A. Cuzzocrea and S. Maabout (Eds.): MEDI 2013, LNCS 8216, pp. 149–161, 2013.
© Springer-Verlag Berlin Heidelberg 2013

structural and static framework. New trends are aimed to modeling more and more realistic SN able to capturing more information richness (temporal dynamicity, semantic richness... etc.). This provides opportunities for useful knowledge discovery by formalizing concepts and phenomena giving more informative and meaningful answers feeding the business strategies and decisions. An underlying social structure as a core structure is an interesting phenomenon to study within a networked environment. Structural and static considerations have been addressed and remaining a starting point of a methodological debate [2] towards constitution and identification of a core structure. The question is raised about the nature and the role of a core grouping in front of new analysis dimensions? Like all dynamic systems, the SN(s) change continuously in time. This dynamic aspect can be exploited to characterize more significantly a core identity by its expressed cohesion, resistance and appearance in time. Thereby, this characterized identity will be partially introduced by the paper contribution, situating it as the intersection point between the internal structure, the role (group centrality) and dynamic of groupings in time.

Though that the SN dynamicity must be studied with real data sets, the social data richness (temporal data) from which new analysis dimensions (temporal dimension) are derived, are less expressed in available implicit or explicit social graphs. During an observation period the temporal data can be expressed by an optimal time windows resolution capturing the network dynamic behavior. By deriving parameters from the characterization concepts, a methodology for modeling and identifying is followed. A temporal weighted graph modeling a network sample will be defined. It's an evolutionary process linking network group structures at each time point. The weighting model is designed to support explicitly these parameters characterizing exclusively the temporal overlaps of successive groups in time. A sub-model is detected as the covering and heaviest groups sequence. This is a container within which a persistent grouping should be deeply encapsulated, imitating an identity embodied by a largest group, balanced between a stable and central composition during the observation period. A dynamic social context surviving in a networked environment is structured into stratums where parameters are deeply concentrated in a persistent grouping of individuals.

In the first section of paper, related works to the core conceptions, and others surrounding its proposed identity components, are discussed accompanied by motivation and objective. Second section is dedicated to preliminary concepts. The proposed methodology will be detailed in third section. Using a SN sample of a company communication network evolving in time, experiments studies are proposed showing whenever a persistent grouping character encapsulated within a detected container in the model. Finally, a last part is provided to discuss this characterized identity and what lacks to enhance it, toward as a more significant core identity.

2   Related Works

Intuitively, SN(s) are now modeled by graphs that are not random manifesting special characteristics, as including underlying social structures as a core structure. According to different viewpoints, such concept has been addressed by some works in order to formalize, identify a real core structure (periphery) in SN. Knowing that a core is a common but informal notion in SNA and other areas, it can be intuitively considered, as a dense and cohesive part in the network [2]. Some authors tried to formalize these intuitive conceptions using for example a block modeling, describing (discrete/ continuous) ideal models of a core part, based on structural foundations: link density or degree of coreness [2]. In this case, individuals forming a core region are characterized by high degrees of coreness (high centralities [3]) in network [2]. For some others, a core structure can be located as groups ((α, β)-communities) intersection zone overlapping in a static and dense SN representation [4]. However, the core identification didn't exceed the static framework, whereas in fact, the temporal dynamicity is a SN character (changes in time). Beyond structural/ static features, the following question may be asked: Compared to what? Can we say that a subset of individuals can be qualified as a core within a given SN? It's true that this is a dense region composed by central individuals, but it will be more expressive when the composition nature, behavior and location (role) of core under a group view is addressed in time.

A question about the role of a grouping considered to be a core is opened. This can be provided from its location in the network by extended metrics on social groups [5]. These're generalization method of individual metrics measuring the group centrality [5] basing on the externals individuals (Outside group) but not regarding other groups (not based on group configuration). The boundary, periphery and core notions are not considered. Thereby, a huge potential can be exploited to find central groupings and explain important phenomena related to efficiency and groups success [5] as a core group but in a static context. As new trend in SNA, The temporal dimension is aimed to identifying more realistically the SN phenomena giving more fidelity to analytical studies surrounding core structure identification. The SN dynamic nature can be observed as a network development process in time (An endogenous dynamic context) [6]. A more significant identity can be acquired by a core region in front of this temporal dynamicity. Its evolution as a group in time can be placed within the collectivity behavior evolution context in the network over time. Interesting related phenomena: persistence (durability), stability, development of groups (temporal community) in time [7] can be shown by a good formalization of dynamic SN partitioning. Many works related to community detection offering models, measures [7], and others more extended studying the quality (modularity) and grouping evolution in time. But even the recent efforts don't consider the core structure in dynamic SN neither its role as a group in time. Beyond the static context, we believe until now, that a significant characterization of core identity can be surrounded by previous concepts about related to social groupings behavior and centrality leading to define it as a cohesive resistant region having a strategic role in a dynamic social context of a networked environment.

3   Preliminaries and Principals

We characterize a core structure identity within SN by three key features:
Internal Cohesion: It's a dense region in the network, meaning a strong internal connectivity within a subset of individuals. Even in the literature some proposed approaches (in static case) are aimed to maximize core region density. This can be characterized by the whole concept of social grouping (natural cohesion) in time.

Appearance (salience/ importance): Core actors must have a certain (weight) role compared to others in the network communication. It has been shown that such actors have a high degree of coreness and equally high centralities. However, under a more global viewpoint, the role played by the grouping of these actors as a whole is more meaningful than studying independently individual strategic positions. As a group, the core role can be imitated from its individual elements. But it will not need to know individuals roles if the group role is known. The core appearance can be expressed by a central (potential/ more efficient) group in the network.

Resistance: The social representation coherence can be significantly acquired by a core structure within a dynamic context compared to the static case. This is the resistance point against the network temporal dynamicity. At the same time, it constitutes the spring change insofar the representation is dislocated in case of its core loss because of change said deep when affects this region. The core resistance will be expressed by two angles. Such structure should be the most persistent, stable grouping (composition stability) and equally presents a possible stable role (centrality stability) in time.

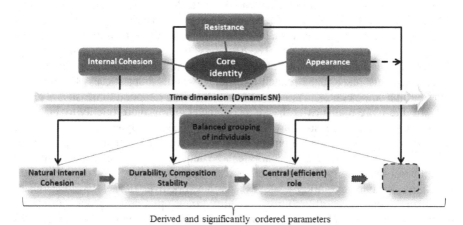

Fig. 1. Characterized core identity surrounded by key concepts embodied by derived parameters within dynamic SN

For this paper, a core identity fenced by these concepts will be modeled by a grouping of individuals able to capture and balance respectively between derived parameters: a persistent, stable and central (efficient) grouping (cohesion nature) in time.

4   Proposed Methodology and Research Orientation

The main steps of our adopted methodology will be summarized by a descriptive stack, shortly detailed to explain research orientation (Fig.2) within dynamic temporal social network analysis context.

4.1. Social Data and Temporal Information: Though this is currently the best source for SNA, for many different reasons, the expressivity degree (temporal information) in available social data from online and organizational SN (OSN) doesn't always meet to new analysis trends (temporal dimension). The SN dynamic character is generated from social behaviors changes (simultaneous influence between behavior and relationships) between the network entities. During an observation period, actors can create and equally remove new relationships with others (relationship lifetime). This has a direct impact on its position in the network, its role and its possible affiliation to one or more groups in time (chronological affiliation to groups). The temporal information allows us to give more meaning to a structure qualified as an organization SN core in front of its temporal dynamicity. As well, understanding its development process occurring around this underlying structure versus to a static model based analysis (may give misleading information).

4.2. Core Structure Identity (According to derived parameters): Basing on previous characteristics, this special identity can be acquired by a group of individuals when a certain balance is expressed during a network observation period. The cohesion, the resistance and the played role in time will be addressed from derived parameters. Each parameter represents explicitly one of these characteristics for a given group, or describes a possible implicit dependence with other parameters.

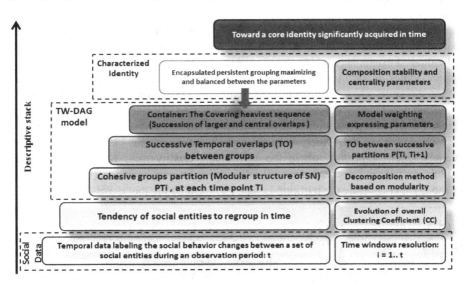

Fig. 2. A methodological modeling and identification toward characterizing significantly a core identity within dynamic SN

4.3. Modeling by Temporal Weighted Graph: After defining previous parameters, a SN model able to support explicitly these parameters characterizing the groupings of individuals in dynamic context must be firstly defined. This can be manifested by a particular graph model. A version was previously proposed to describe the phenomena of persistence and community dynamics in SN [7]. However, model formalism will be defined under our concepts and purposes. Suppose that interactions between set of social entities are observed during a period divided into time points i = 1...t, modeled by a temporal weighted (TW) direct acyclic graph (DAG), denoted by TW-DAG: ({V1, V2... Vt}, A (Ti, Ti+1), W).

It's a multiparty graph, each part Vi is a partition (structure of groups) PTi of SN at time point Ti composed by a set of groups Gx-(Ti), x = 1... X.

An arc (a ∈ A (Ti, Ti+1)) connects two groups between two successive partitions: a (Gx-(Ti), Gy-(Ti+1)) if and only if these two groups firstly overlap and the weight W (Gx-(Ti), Gy-(Ti+1)) isn't null. (i = 1...t-1). It's a temporal acyclic graph model representing a process steps (Dynamic SN). A weighted arc from Gx to Gy means that group Gx appears in a partition before Gy It's an evolutionary process of social groupings in time (It isn't connected).

A weighting W: A (Ti, Ti+1) → R, (i = 1...t-1) defines the arc weight connecting a group at Ti to another at Ti+1. W (Gx-(Ti), Gy-(Ti+1)) is essentially based on successive temporal overlap (TO) parameters between 2 groups Gx-(Ti) and Gy-(Ti+1). This is the most important component in this model and varies according to considered parameters. The model components will be shortly described:

4.3.1. Tendencies of Individuals to Regroup and Network Partition at Each Time Point Ti:

A social group evolution process is described by such model. The tendency of individuals to regroup is raised as a first question about the group structure of individuals during a network observation period. Once a certain tendency is expressed by individuals to form groups in time, the network structure can be represented by a set of possible groups at each time point Ti. The structural dimension of a representative identity characterizing a core structure is basically embodied by the composition and internal cohesion (structural parameter) of group in time, regarding the TW-DAG model. Such parameter will be expressed using a particular decomposition algorithm, where the partitioning quality must be optimized by a modularity function maximization [8] ensuring an internal cohesion (Using Louvain method) [9] [12] inside the partition groups PTi forming the model vertices at each Ti.

4.3.2. Partitioning and Weighting According to Successive Temporal overlaps of Groups between Ti, Ti+1:

When an individual socializes in a networked environment, it may be affiliated to one or more groups of different compositions in time. Therefore the groups belonging to different partitions can overlap in time. We're interested exclusively, at successive temporal overlaps between time points Ti, Ti+1. Given two successive partitions: PTi, PTi+1, composed respectively by X, Y groups. The temporal overlap between these two partitions is defined by a partition P (Ti, Ti+1): a set of groupings resulting from all possible overlaps (z = 1...k) between each group Gx-(Ti) ∈ PTi with all groups Gy-(Ti+1) ∈ PTi+1, meaning that an overlap Oz–(Ti, Ti+1) = Gx-(Ti) ∩Gy-(Ti+1).

4.3.3. Improved Weighting of TW-DAG Model

The TW-DAG model has been weighted to support increasingly parameters, in its arc weights W (A, B) concerning locally the possible successive overlaps (A∩B) between Ti, Ti+1. The model weighting W is targeted to express and balance locally between parameters combinations characterizing these local stable compositions (successive overlaps) well adapted to following investigations.

a. *Characterized core identify container (Critical pattern)*

An identity that will be expressed by individuals collectivity (denoted N) maximizing and balanced between parameters during a network observation period can be captured inside a particular container. This is the heaviest groups sequence covering t observation time points (critical pattern (CP) in the model), viewed as a temporal overlaps succession within which a persistent structure should be firstly encapsulated, imitating such core identity deeply constituted inside these stratums or layers of social grouping sequence in time.

b. *Weighting formula to improve and balance*

Parameters are incrementally expressed in weights. For a new improved weighting, a new parameter is considered or adjusted, in order to enhance an earlier version. The latest weighting version should be able to express and balance between all parameters surrounding the core identity components. Considering two groups A, B belonging respectively to two successive partitions PTi, PTi+1 in time. If the overlap (A∩B) is empty, W (A, B) = 0, else W (A, B) can be incrementally improved by:

Formula 1 (Composition stability and Centrality): An average centrality of an overlap (A∩B) between Ti, Ti+1 is firstly included in the weighting (Fig.3). It's a subset of individuals preserving its composition between Ti, Ti+1, allowing studying its group centrality in a reduced dynamic context (between two successive time points). This is the same grouping at Ti and at Ti+1, but that doesn't mean that it has the same centrality, because it belongs to two partitions at two different time points.

$$W(A, B) = \frac{GC.Ti(A \cap B) + GC.Tj(A \cap B)}{2}, \quad j = i+1, i = 1...t-1 \qquad (1)$$

The type of group (role) centrality (GC) and how to quantify it must be selected and clarified (Degree: GDC, Closeness GCC, Betweenness GBC). This weighting can be called "Temporal Overlapping groups (Degree/ Closeness/ Betweenness) centrality". It's a group centrality of temporal overlap TO-GC.

The resulting graph model according to this weighting formula is denoted by TW-DAG (TO-GC)-formula1. Thereby, the following particular cases can be cited:

- *Null centrality (stable and isolated composition):* When W (A, B) = 0, group A or B is a stable composition (A∩B = A = B), but isolated at Ti, Ti+1.
- *Singleton overlap group:* If a grouping is larger, it's more likely to playing more central role. However, it's possible that A∩B is composed by a single individual, but it has more central role between Ti and Ti+1 than that played by another overlap C∩D which is not singleton. |A∩B| = 1 << |C∩D|, but W (A, B) > W (C, D). Accordingly, the dependence between centrality and locally stable composition (its size), is not always guaranteed.

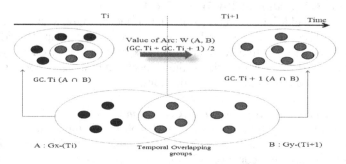

Fig. 3. Weighted arc from group A to B by the weighting formula1 (TO-GC)

- *Null centrality at a given time Ti*: It's may be that (A∩B) centrality is null at Ti, whereas, it presents more central role at Ti+1 (or vice versa).

This weighting formula will be adjusted, enhanced by new versions considering such specific cases and bringing more balance between more expressed parameters.

Formula 2 (A largest stable composition and central location)

This weighting formula is proposed to balance between expressed parameters until now guiding to a largest stable and central composition. The question is raised about weighting if is it able to balance between a stable group (A∩B) size and its centrality between Ti, Ti+1? It's to add more influence of (A∩B) size to the weighting W:

$$W(A, B) = |A \cap B| * \frac{GC.Ti(A \cap B) + GC.Tj(A \cap B)}{2}, j = i+1, i = 1...t-1 \quad (2)$$

W (A, B) becomes more dependent with overlap size |A∩B| and its centrality between Ti and Ti+1. Thereby, more balance between arcs weight regarding singletons or no singletons involved overlaps. The resulting graph model can be denoted by TW-DAG (TO-GC)-formula 2. This weighting scheme is summarized by following procedure:

```
For i = 1...t-1 do
For each overlap A∩B of P (Ti, Ti+1).
If A∩B = ∅, Then W (A, B) = 0.
Else
    // W (A, B) is calculated with formula 1 and after 2.
    If W (A, B) = 0 Then // GC.Ti (A∩B) = 0 and GC.Ti+1 (A∩B) = 0 →A∩B = A = B, isolated.
    Else
    // adjust with new added parameters:
        // Take into account the constraint: not null centrality //calculate W (A, B) with new weighting formula.
        // Take into account the centrality stability // calculate W (A, B) with new weighting formula.
```

Accordingly, the next proposed weighting must be capable to support additional constraints (not null centrality) and new parameters (centrality stability in time), using new weighting formulas.

5   Experimental Results

Dataset: Characterizing and identifying a more significant identity of core social structure must be shown within real interactions (collaborations, coordination...etc.) dynamicity modeled by the TW-DAG model expressing explicitly the temporal information. Our studies have been experimented on a dataset sample describing the Enron email communication network (in Enron Company "The Enron Energy Corporation") [3]. It's an historical of emails exchanges among a set of company employees [13] [14]. The used sample is a subset of emails exchanges between 112 employees during the year 2000. This is one of available samples (under CMX format) from Commetrix tool [10]. Our data were extracted and processed in order to submit it under (.net) format. This is a simple and powerful format supporting the temporal information and well adapted on Pajek tool (Version 3.08) [11], on which some experimental studies and proposals will be applied. The data observation period was divided into t = 12 time points (12 months). The set of 112 nodes is assumed as consistent (Each node's lifetime is [1-12]). Each created link, connects two employees and labeled by a lifetime [Ti, Tj], $1 <= i <j <= t$, beginning from the first exchange date (first link event) and ending at the last exchange date (Last link-events).

Results: Initially, the study of tendency change to regroup by nodes has been quantified at each time point by Watts-Strogatz clustering coefficient (CC) [12], showing generally that this tendency varies but doesn't vanish alluding to a network modular structure during its observation time. Thereby, modeling this dynamic SN by TW-DAG needs to define partitions PTi (using Louvain method [9] [12]): set of its vertices Gx-(Ti) at each Ti, i = 1... t., arcs connecting between groups overlapping and belonging to successive partitions. The graph arcs are weighted basing essentially on nonempty (and no singleton) temporal overlaps parameters. The constructed TW-DAG model contains 525 groups during 12 time points. Overlap rate and some reports (Statistical bi-varied Measures) between successive partitions of groups in time, were studied. Ratio of similarity (Adjuster Rand Index [12]), the Spearman correlation coefficient [12] between each PTi, PTi+1, and the information preservation rate in PTi+1 from PTi (index Rajski PTi +1 ➔ PTi), showed a remarkable dependence between groups belonging to partitions PTi, PTi+1, proving a gradually change step after step and describing a real temporal dynamicity.
A standard model has been firstly weighted from (similarity) matrix (R) offering the possible overlaps size between each group Gx-(Ti) with groups Gy-(Tj): $1 <= i <j <= 12$ (especially from matrix diagonal blocks that we're interested). The heaviest arc (G5-(T10), G5-(T11)) is identified as the largest temporal overlap. The covering and heaviest sequence of groups (A1, A2.., A12), weighted by $\sum W (Ai, Ai+1) = 144$ (i ==1...11), is detected as a critical pattern including a persistent grouping of individuals $N \subset Ai \cap Aj, \forall i, j$, j = i+1, encapsulated inside the groups sequence and deeply in their successive overlaps (within a succession of larger overlaps).

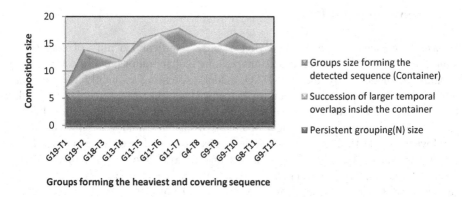

Groups forming the heaviest and covering sequence

▨ Groups size forming the detected sequence (Container)

▨ Succession of larger temporal overlaps inside the container

■ Persistent grouping(N) size

Fig. 4. Persistent and stable grouping (larger composition) encapsulated - layers view

This is the largest and perfect stable structure during the observation period (Fig.4), embodying a deep and stable layer (the composition resistance of a core identity) within the SN temporal dynamicity, but its role (its influence and efficiency) still an opened question in the network?

Thus, the model that should be enhanced in order to be able to express locally the centrality parameter has been weighted according to weighting formula 1, from weights matrix (M1) called the successive temporal overlap (the group degree centrality (GDC)) centrality matrix. In this case, a central context is expressed by the covering and heaviest detected sequence. Within which a persistent group (N) should be encapsulated, and from which its centrality can be imitated.

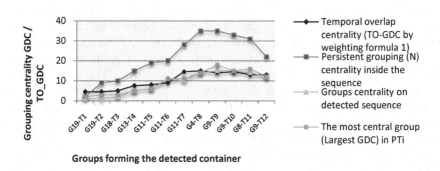

Groups forming the detected container

──◆── Temporal overlap centrality (TO-GDC by weighting formula 1)

──■── Persistent grouping (N) centrality inside the sequence

──▲── Groups centrality on detected sequence

──■── The most central group (Largest GDC) in PTi

Fig. 5. Stable grouping (N) centrality inside the successive temporal overlaps of path groups

It is remarkable (Fig.5) that groups forming the detected sequence (A1... A12) are generally the most central structures at each Ti. The centrality of their successive overlaps $(Ai \cap Aj \subset Ai, Aj)$ is approximate. And the encapsulated grouping centrality $N \subset Ai \cap Aj$ (j = i+1, i = 1...11) is generally higher during the observation period (within a succession of more central overlaps). This is the most possible stable (resistant composition) and strategic (central) structure in SN, but it's not guaranteed to be balanced between these parameters.

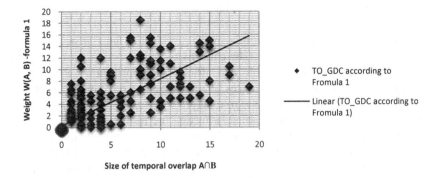

Fig. 6. Distribution of temporal overlaps between successive groups in Ti, and Ti+1 according to weight formula 1

The distribution study of temporal overlaps (TO) between each Ti, Ti+1 according to corresponding arcs weight W(A, B) and previous weights |A∩B|, shows practically (Fig.6) the previous discussed particulars cases around this weighting (formula1).

For example, there're singletons groupings with more strategic location than others that are not singletons, some other groupings are active (not null GDC) at Ti, but it's isolated at Ti+1 (or vice versa). This means that centrality and composition stability parameters are expressed by this used weighting with less dependence.

However the new TW-DAG model that should be weighted according to the formula 2, try to make more dependence between parameters in arcs weights (from 2 previous matrices M1 and R: centrality and size of local stable composition 'TO'). The distribution study of TO between each Ti, Ti+1 according to new weights W (A, B) versus |A∩B|, shows that this new weighting and |A∩B| are more addictive (more balanced). Accordingly, the singletons and no singletons elements (TO) are involved in arcs weight which will be favored following more balanced way between local stable composition size and its centrality. In this case, integrated successive temporal overlaps in the covering and heaviest detected group sequence are larger and more central. If a persistent grouping of individuals is included, it can be the largest possible structure maximizing and balanced between composition stability and centrality at each Ti. The question can be raised now about centrality of such structure, if isn't null, and about stability of its role played at each time point Ti?

Discussion: Tests will be required to validate if an identity expressed by such encapsulated grouping of individuals (N) really meets to this parameters combination. A correlation study showed that CP goes through 82% - 99% of heaviest arcs between Ti, Ti+1, (covering more stable and central overlaps). At a deeper level, the correlation study between parameters of these overlaps succession and those expressed by a persistent group N inside, showed that a largest group balanced largest stable and central composition at each Ti can be deeply imitated with 95%-97%. But, the stability of this strategic role played by such structure remains a raised question?

6   Conclusion and Future Works

Within a dynamic social context, a certain significant identity must be acquired by a structure to be qualified as a SN core. The collectivity appearance and resistance can be significantly expressed by a stable and efficient composition on the network communication flows in time. The choices of time windows resolution, the group's nature in the network over time and the role played by these groups (selected group centrality and how quantify it) are variants affecting the results. Such characterized identity can be enhanced by considering additional constraints and new parameters as the centrality stability in time balanced in an improved weighting model. Issues are surrounding the SN fragility (e.g. in epidemiological context) and the informational gain carried from such core identification in different networked environments evolving in time (e.g. illegal SN hiding fraudulent behaviors or Political, religious networks, epidemiology...etc.). On the other hand, the question is opened about such core character in dynamic context, identified on an additional dimension by considering a higher abstraction level embodied by a semantic richness of social entities and their interactions? Toward a more significant identity of core structure within dynamic and semantic context.

References

1. Memon, N., Alhajj, R.: Introduction to the first issue of social network analysis and mining journal. SOCNET 1, 1–2 (2011), doi:10.1007/s13278-010-0016-2; published online: November 13, 2010
2. Stephen, P., Borgatti, M.G.: Models of core/periphery structures. ELSEVIER - Social Networks Journal 21(4), 375–395 (2000) ISSN: 0378-8733
3. Tang, J., Musolesi, M., Mascolo, C., Latora, V., Nicosia, V.: Analyzing information flows and key mediators through temporal centrality metrics. In: SNS 2010, Paris, France, April 13. ACM (2010) 978-1-4503-0080-3
4. Wang, L., Hopcroft, J., He, J., Liang, H., Suwajanakorn, S.: Extraction the core Structure of Social Network using alpha Beta community. Internet Mathematics 9(1), 58–81 (2013)
5. Everett, M.G., Borgatti, S.P.: The centrality of groups and classes. Journal of Mathematical Sociology 23(3), 181–201 (1999)
6. Jamali, M., Haffari, G., Ester, M.: Modeling the temporal dynamics of social rating networks using bidirectional effects of social relations and rating patterns. In: International World Wide Web Conference Committee (IW3C2), WWW 2011 – Session: Temporal Dynamics, Hyderabad, India, March 28-April 1. ACM (2011) 978-1-4503-0632-4/11/03
7. Berger-Wolf, T.Y., Saia, J.: A Framework for Analysis of Dynamic Social Networks. In: KDD 2006, Philadelphia, Pennsylvania, USA, August 20-23. ACM (2006) 1-59593-339-5/06/0008
8. Fortunato, S.: Community detections in graphs. Physics and Society 486, 75–174 (2010)
9. Blondel, V., Guillaume, J.-L., Lambiotte, R., Lefebvre, E.: Fast unfolding of communities in large networks. Journal of Statistical Mechanics 2008(10) (September 2008)
10. Commetrix (Version 2.4 - 2012), http://www.commetrix.net/

11. Batagelj, V., Mrvar, A.: Pajek - Analysis and Visualization of Large Networks. In: Juenger, M., Mutzel, P. (eds.) Graph Drawing Software. Mathematics and Visualization, pp. 77–103. Springer, Berlin (2003) ISBN 3-540-00881-0

12. Pajek 3.08 Manual: short explanations of all procedures implemented in the last version of Pajek. Extracted from de Nooy W., Mrvar, A., Batagelj, V.: Exploratory Social Network Analysis with Pajek. Structural Analysis in the Social Sciences 34. Cambridge University Press (2011) ISBN: 0521602629. CUP, Amazon, Tokyo Denki University Press (2009)

13. Leskovec, J., Lang, K., Dasgupta, A., Mahoney, M.: Community Structure in Large Networks: Natural Cluster Sizes and the Absence of Large Well-Defined Clusters. Internet Mathematics 6(1), 29–123 (2009)

14. Klimmt, B., Yang, Y.: Introducing the Enron corpus. In: CEAS Conference (2004)

Clustering Heterogeneous Data Streams with Uncertainty over Sliding Window

Houda Hentech, Mohammed Salah Gouider, and Amine Farhat

BESTMOD, Université de Tunis, Institut Supérieur de Gestion de Tunis,
41 Avenue de la liberté, cité Bouchoucha, 2000 Le Bardo, Tunisia
houda.hentech@yahoo.com, {ms.gouider,farhat_amine}@yahoo.fr

Abstract. Existing methods for clustering uncertain data streams over sliding windows do not treat the categorical attributes. However, uncertain mixed data are ubiquitous. This paper investigates the problem of clustering heterogeneous data streams pervaded by uncertainty over sliding windows, so-called SWHU-Clustering. A Heterogeneous Uncertain Temporal Cluster Feature (HUTCF) is introduced to monitor the distribution statistics of mixed data points. Based on this structure, Exponential Histogram of Heterogeneous Uncertain Cluster Feature (EHHUCF) is presented as a collection of HUTCF. This structure may help to handle the in-cluster evolution, and detects the temporal change of the cluster distribution. Our approach has several advantages over existing method: 1) the higher execution efficiency benefits from its good design as it avoids the effects of old data on the final results. 2) We incorporated the k-NN into the clustering process in order to reduce the complexity of the algorithm. 3) Memory consumption can be managed efficiently by limiting the number of HUTCF in each EHHUCF. Simulations on real databases show the feasibility of SWHU-Clustering as well as its effectiveness by comparing it with UMicro algorithm.

Keywords: Data streams, uncertainty, clustering, similarity measure, sliding window model.

1   Introduction

The growth of the amount of data has been very fast due to the development and the rapid growth of the storage technologies. Streaming data are ubiquitous; it has been emerged in many applications and domains such the traffic TCP/IP, the on-line financial transactions [1,2], sensors networks [3] and so on. This large amount of high frequency data creates a great need for advanced data stream tools to process and manage efficiently. Due to the special characteristics of data streams, the traditional techniques of data mining have to be re-designed and adapted with the behavior of streaming application. Extracting meaningful knowledge is ensured by the clustering which is a well known machine learning technique to discover groups and identify interesting distributions in the considered data. The clustering is an unsupervised task which aims to obtain

A. Cuzzocrea and S. Maabout (Eds.): MEDI 2013, LNCS 8216, pp. 162–175, 2013.

homogeneous partitions of objects while promoting the heterogeneity between these partitions. Webster [4] defines cluster analysis as *"A statistical classification method for discovering whether the individuals of a population fall into various groups by making quantitative comparisons of multiple characteristics"*.

Since data stream mining is applied with limited memory, so it is not feasible to store the sequence of stream in its entirety. Thus the approximate results [5] are required rather than exact answers. many approaches believe that it is important to concentrate only on the most recent data points. Based on this observation, we proposed the clustering of uncertain mixed data streams over sliding window. This model is useful for eliminating the outdated data as they affect the clustering results. In this paper, we propose the so-called Exponential Histogram of Heterogeneous Uncertainty Cluster Feature(EHHUCF) which is used to store the distribution character of recent mixed data and summarizing the online-evolution of clusters. In order to collect the uncertainty information of tuples in uncertain data streams, we define the attribute-level tuple uncertainty so that the probability information of each dimension can be quantified.

This paper is organized as follows: Section 2 introduces the related works. The description of the problem and the parameters of our approach are respectively proposed in section 3. The algorithm and the analysis of the different phases are described in section 4. Finally, section 5 presents the experimental results and the their analysis.

2   Related Work

Most of the existing works and available approaches of clustering data streams have not explicitly dealt with the uncertainty of the input data. They are based on a fundamental assumption that the training data sets contain only certain information and they focus on handling precise data. However, when dealing with real-world applications, the massive amounts of data are inseparably connected with imperfection. Uncertain data management has seen revived interest in recent years because of the huge number of fields which cannot be described exactly in one state. Several algorithms lack the mining of recent uncertain data streams since they adopt the pyramidal time frame model as LuMicro [6] and UMicro [7] which they leveraged the general model of uncertainty to track the information uncertainty. However, Changzhen Hu et al[8] proposed new algorithm SWCUStreams which focuses on tracking clusters over sliding window. All the above algorithms manage the uncertain numerical data streams efficiently but they don't tackle the heterogeneous attributes in their clustering process. That is why, Huang et al. [9] introduced a new approach, so called, HUClustering to deal with the uncertainty of mixed data streams. Recently, Lisa Serir et al. [10], introduced a new algorithm called E2GK (Evidential Evolving Gustafson-Kessel) to cluster uncertain data streams using belief function theory [11], which improves good results on detecting outliers and handling uncertain data.

Processing mixed data using the sliding window model has not taken into account in all the related works. For these reasons, we propose to develop an approach based on the classical probability theory with the conjunction of the sliding window to deal with large mixed data streams. Our method tackles the problem encountered in the HU-Clustering by processing only recent records. We concentrate only on the recent data since it is impossible to store all the data in memory. This technique allows processing all the incoming data by satisfying the constraint of limited available memory. Since new record comes, the obsolete data will be discarded.

3 Parameters Definition

Generally, objects that belong to the training set are known with accuracy and the value of each one of its attributes is certain. Unlike the standard structure, we assume that the training set may contain data where there is some uncertainty in the knowledge of the attribute values. We propose to represent the uncertainty on the attributes values of the instances by a probability assigned to the set of possible values considered in the clustering problem.

3.1 Structure of Data Stream

Assume that heterogeneous data streams with uncertainty are a set of (c+b)-dimensional tuples $X_1, X_2, ...X_n$ arriving at time $T_1, T_2, ..T_n$ for any $i < n$, $T_i < T_n$ and each tuple has a probability $P_1(X_1), P_2(X_2), .., P_n(X_n)$ respectively. Each heterogeneous tuple is a vector containing c-dimensional numerical attributes and $b-$dimensional categorical attributes. It is defined as $X_i = C_i :$ $B_i = (x_i^1, x_i^2, .., x_i^c, y_i^1, y_i^2, y_i^b)$. For each tuple X_i, each dimension of numerical attributes has $N^p (1 < p < c)$ possible instances and the occurrence probability of each instance is $p(x_{ij}^p)$. Each dimension of categorical attributes has $N^{p'}$ $(1 < p' < b)$ possible instances and the occurrence probability of each instance is $p(y_{ij}^{p'})$.

3.2 Heterogeneous Tuple Uncertainty

The uncertainty of each tuple must be quantified based on the probability of each one. The probability distribution of each instance indicates that the uncertainty of tuple and the probability of tuple are inverse proportion. As described in [9] the uncertainty of the mixed record is:

$$U(X_i) = 1/(2(U(x_i) + U(y_i))) \tag{1}$$

The uncertainty of each numerical and categorical attribute is defined as $U(x) = \sum_{p=1}^{c} U(x_i^p)/c$ and $U(x_i^p)$ describes the uncertainty of each dimensional attribute. It is defined as follows:

$$U(x_i^p) = -\sum_{j=1}^{N^p} p(x_{ij}^p) * \log_2 p(x_{ij}^p) \tag{2}$$

The uncertainty of each record is characterized by the following properties: Non-negativity which means tha the uncertainty measure is always positive. In the case of complete knowledge each dimensional attribute has one possible value so $p(x_i) = 1$ and $p(y_i) = 1$. As a result, U(X)=0, otherwise U(X)>0. Furthermore, U reaches the upper bound in the case of total ignorance when the probability is uniformly distributed.

3.3 Heterogeneous Uncertainty Temporal Cluster Feature

The Heterogeneous Uncertainty Temporal Clustering Feature of (c+b) dimensional tuples sets $X_1, X_2, ..X_n$ arriving at time $T_1, T_2, ..T_n$ is defined as a $(2.c + \sum_{p'=1}^{b} F^{p'} + 3) - dimension$ vector $((\overline{CF2^x})(C), (\overline{CF1^x})(C), U(C), t(C), n(C), H)$. Wherein, each entry in tuple is defined in [9]. Heterogeneous uncertainty temporal clustering feature is used for tracking the summarization of uncertainty information of tuples and as well as it represents the change of the cluster distribution. Similar to the additive property of the traditional temporal clustering feature in [12], heterogeneous uncertainty temporal clustering feature also satisfies this property. HUTCF($C1 \cup C2$) can be created according to HUTCF (C1) and HUTCF(C2), wherein, C1 and C2 are two sets of uncertainty tuples. The merging process of two HUTCF can be obtained directly by summing up all the entries of each one. Furthermore, the merging process leads to a new HUTCF which is defined by three entries $(\overline{CF1^x})(C)$, $(\overline{CF2^x})(C)$, n and U. They can be obtained directly from the HUTCF(C1) and HUTCF(C2) by summing them. However, the time stamp of the new HUTCF corresponds to the maximum of time stamp in HUTCF (C1) and HUTCF (C2). In addition, probability frequency histogram of categorical attributes H satisfies also this property as well as the frequency of each possible value is an addition of the two $f_k^{p'}$ of each HUTCF. However, the probability of each one is the the mean of the two $p_i^{p'}$.

In uncertain data streams, Exponential Histogram of Uncertain Cluster Feature (EHHUCF) is a set of HUTCF, wherein, each HUTCF corresponds to a bucket, described as G1, G2, and G3... Therefore, EHHUCF is a set of buckets with different time sequence. Each bucket satisfies the following conditions:

- When $i < j$, the arrival time of all tuples in the bucket G_i is less than that of all tuples in the bucket G_j.
- Let L(G) express the size of the bucket G, then L (G_1)=1. For any set G_i (i>1), has either the same size or as twice as its previous set $L(G_i) = L(G_{i-1})$ or $L(G_i) = 2L(G_{i-1})$. If the size of the bucket is 2^i, then the level of the bucket is defined as $i \in [0, L]$, wherein, the highest level of the bucket is L.
- $\lceil 1/\epsilon \rceil$ or $\lceil 1/\epsilon \rceil + 1$ l-level HUTCFs can be found for each l($0 \leq l < L$) except for the L-level, where L is the highest level of HUTCFs in the EHHUCF and ϵ is a user-specified parameter. We can conclude that the number of the outdated tuples are limited in the interval $[0, \epsilon n]$ where n indicates the number of tuples in the EHHUCF. Since the EHHUCF is well structured as described above, the expired points are situated only in the last HUTCF

which it may contain at most ϵn records[1]. As a conclusion, the number of expired records is in the interval $[0, \epsilon n]$.

3.4   Dissimilarity Measure between Two Tuples

Clustering uncertain hetregeneous data streams needs the definition of new similarity measure which takes into account both the categorical attributes and numerical attributes as proposed in [9]. We will discuss how dissimilarity can be computed for objects described by numerical variables. Since each dimension numerical attribute contains several possible instances, so we have to define the expected value in order to compute the distance between two points. So the expected value of each record is computed as follows:

$$x_i^p = \sum_{j=1}^{N^p} x_{i_j}^p * p(x_{i_j}^p)$$

The most popular distance measure is Euclidean distance which is used as a dissimilarity measure between two numerical attributes. However, The similarity between two categorical attributes [9] is obtained by:

$$Sim(B_i, B_j) = \sum_{p'=1}^{b} \Psi(y_i^{p'}, y_j^{p'}) \tag{3}$$

Where:

$$\Psi(y_i^{p'}, y_j^{p'}) = \sum_{i=1}^{N^{p'}} p'_i * \frac{1 - \delta(y_i^{p'}, y_j^{p'})}{b} \quad And : \delta(y_i^{p'}, y_j^{p'}) = \begin{cases} 1 & \text{if } y_i^{p'} \neq v_j^{p'} \\ 0 & \text{otherwise} \end{cases}$$

3.5   Dissimilarity Tuple-Cluster

In order to assign the new arriving point, we have to compute the dissimilarity between the new tuple and the center of each existing EHHUCF. So we use the heterogeneous distance measure [9].

$$Sim(X_i, C_j) = Sim(X_i, (CF1^x(C))/n) + \theta Sim(B_i, H) \tag{4}$$

Where $(CF1^x(C))/n$ indicates the center of the cluster over numerical attributes. The similarity between the numerical attributes of two tuples is described as above. However, in the case of categorical attributes the similarity is adjusted by the weight $\theta \in [0, 1]$ which can affect the range of similarity over categorical attributes.

$$Sim(B_i, H) = \sum_{p'=1}^{b} \Psi(h_{p'}, y_{p'})/n \tag{5}$$

---

[1] We suppose that the last HUTCF contains m records so $\frac{1}{\epsilon}(1+2+4, .. +m) \leq n$, we can prouve that $m \leq \epsilon n$.

4   Clustering Heterogeneous Uncertain Data Streams over Sliding Window

In this section we will detail our proposed method by presenting the algorithm and the different steps. The clustering process is divided into three main phases: initialisation, online micro-cluster maintenance and the offline macro-clustering to generate the final clusters.

4.1   Initialization Step

In the beginning we need to create the first EHHUCFs and store them in the memory. It is done by using an offline algorithm which is the K-prototype [13] algorithm. It is designed to cluster the heterogeneous data and find out homogeneous partitions during the sliding window. After obtaining the desired number of EHHUCF, the two phases framework [14] are applied: online and offline components.

4.2   Online Maintenance of EHHUCFs

Find the Cluster. During this phase, the statistical information about the data points is collected. Once these initial EHHUCFs have been created, the online process of updating the EHHUCF is started in order to preserve the fixed number of EHHUCF and respecting the sliding window by discarding the obsolete points.

Considering a set S of partitions, whenever a new tuple is arrived, the EHHUCFs are updated incrementally in order to reflect the changes. The new tuple needs to be absorbed by an existing EHHUCF, or creating a new one for its own. The clustering process begins by computing the distance between the new tuple and each existing cluster. The algorithm then checks whether the record X_i can be absorbed by the nearest EHHUCF or not. A simple approach is to compare the distance between X_i and EHHUCF $(Sim(X_i, C_i) \leq \gamma)$ with the user-defined parameter γ. The cluster that meets the condition $D \leq \gamma$ is regarded as a candidate and it will be added to the set S'. As a result, we obtain in the set S' the partitions that have a distance lower than the user specified threshold.

In traditional methods, the appropriate cluster is selected based on the distance metric and they do not take into account the uncertainty of the clustering result. However, when the data is uncertain such single criterion cannot find the best cluster efficiently. That is why we should incorporate the information quality, which is quite important, into the clustering process. The uncertainty of each cluster is defined in the previous section. This measurement can give us an overview about the quality of information in the cluster. In other words, smaller uncertainty of the data leads to greater quality of the cluster. Based on this assumption, the quality of the appropriate cluster in S' should benefit a lot after absorbing the new point. So, a crucial method is to select the cluster, which reduces the uncertainty the most. In other words, we select one cluster with the maximum value of $\Delta U(C) = U(C) - U(C \cup \{x_t, u_t\})$, where C is any cluster in S'. To do so, we have to compute the variation of the uncertainty in all the clusters after absorbing the new point. But, if the size of the set S' is very large, a lot of useless computation is performed.

To cope with the problem of useless computation, we propose to use the K-NN model which is considered as the appropriate solution for that. We keep only the most K-nearest neighbors clusters in another set S" and then the EHHUCFs in the new set are leveraged to continue the clustering process by ignoring the other clusters. After that, the uncertainty of each EHHUCF in the set S" is computed. We measure the new value of uncertainty after integrating the new point. Accordingly, we select the cluster which, profits a lot after including this record, as the suitable EHHUCF.

Given a set S, if any cannot meet the condition $D \leq \gamma$, new cluster is added to the set S as a single cluster containing only the new point (Line 19-20). But before that, the number of fixed clusters in set S must be maintained, when the number is equal and greater than n (Line 15-17), an old cluster is removed according to the update time of each cluster, wherein, the update time can be derived from the last added HUTCF. Therefore, the number of synopses will be decreased by 1 and new EHHUCF synopsis is then generated for record x, and the size of the set S is increased by 1.

Maintenance of EHHUCF. Whenever new tuple is arrived, a new HUTCF will be created to collect the information statistic. After assigning the record in the appropriate EHHUCF, the update process is not launched immediately to merge the HUTCFs but just a 0-level HUTCF is created for each new point. That is why we define a process Update EHHUCF in line 25 to arrange the HUTCFs in the corresponding EHHUCF. This operation is invoked repeatedly whenever a new record arrives, at most one EHHUCF (denoted as hi if existed) contains expired records at any time. Most of the time, the target EHHUCF has accumulated many 0-level HUTCFs. So, when Update EHHUCF is called all the assembled 0-level HUTCFs will be merged. Before introducing the fast computational method proposed in [15], theorem should be considered first.

Theorem 1. *Given an EHHUCF synopsis of N points, there is at least $(1/\epsilon) \log(\epsilon N + 1)$ HUTCFs synopsis in the EHHUCF.*

This theorem indicates that the memory consumption can be managed better when we fix a limit to the number of 0-level HUTCFs in each EHHUCF. As a consequence of that, this method relieves the pressure of the maintenance of EHHUCF.

Proof. **If** $\epsilon = 1$, the HUTCFs are a geometric progression as the common ratio 2, and the sum is N.

However, **If** $\epsilon \in (0, 1)$: as mentionned above we just get one number from each level so that the sequence which we obtain is still a geometric progression as the common ratio is 2. So, the minimum sum that we obtain is $(\epsilon.N)$. As a result, the sum of the geometric progression is $2^n - 1$ Acoording to the two formulas, we can conclude that $\epsilon.N \leq 2^n - 1$, where n is the number of terms. To find out the the total number of levels, we apply the logarithm:

$$\log(\epsilon.N + 1) \leq \log(2^n) \Rightarrow n \geq \log(\epsilon.N + 1)$$

As a consequence of that, we note that there is at least $\frac{1}{\epsilon} \log(\epsilon.N + 1)$ HUTCFs synopsis in the EHHUCF.

We assume that an EHHUCF contains N points, so n 0-level HUTCFs will be created by these points. While the HUTCFs are highly structured and the total number of points is known, so it is easy to fix the structure of the EHHUCF. The update process of the target EHHUCF is detailed as follows:

1. Based on the previous theorem, the maximum number of levels is $L_{max} = n \geq \log(\epsilon.N + 1)$. We suppose that L_{max} be the minimum value and we fill $1/\epsilon$ HUTCFs in each bucket. So, $L_{max} = \lfloor \log(\epsilon.N + 1) \rfloor$.
2. The number left over is $R = N - (1/\epsilon)(2^{L_{max}} - 1)$
   •If $R > 2^{L_{max}}$, so we affect $R/2^{L_{max}}$ buckets into the last level and then we split the remainder number R mod $2^{L_{max}}$ to binary format $2^0 + 2^1... + 2^i$.
   •If $R < 2^{L_{max}}$ R will be divided to binary format $2^0 + 2^1... + 2^i$. We can put a bucket into corresponding level based on item's exponent. For example, 2^0 means that allocate one bucket into 0-level.
3. The structure of the EHHUCF is ready. The different buckets contains each one soe HUTCFs so our task is merging them to the assigned level according to the structure of the HUTCFs as described in the section 3.3.

However, if the target EHHUCF is updated at least once, so the update process will be the same as cited above. But the little difference is that in the step 3 the different HUTCFs will be assigned to different levels to preserve the structure. In addition, the old HUTCFs with high level will be merged with th new ones.

4.3   Cluster Generation

When a clustering request arrives, clusters are calculated from all EHHUCF synopses, as shown on Lines 32-33. For each EHHUCF synopsis h_i, all the HUTCF synopses in h_i are summed up to generate a large HUTCF synopsis H_i. To generate the clusters, the solution employed involves treating the EHHUCF h_i as a representative point locating at the center of h_i with weight mi, where m_i is the number of records in h_i. To find out the final clusters of all pseudo points the k-prototype algorithm is employed.

5   Experimental Results

In this section, we provide all necessary parts related to the evaluation of the SWHU-Clustering. We start by providing a description of the used data sets.

Algorithm 1. SWHU-Clustering

Data: UDS, γ,n, k

1 **Begin**
2 S is the initial set of cluster. S contains at most n clusters. { Initially, apply k-prototypes to create a set of S containing n clusters and Create a new EHHUCF for each cluster   ;
3 count=|EHHUCF| ;
4 **while** *data stream DS is not discontinue* **do**
5   Receive new data point X at current time t from stream DS
6   Calculate the uncertainty of each tuple
7   **for** *each EHHUCF* **do**
8   Compute $Sim(X_i, C_i)$ according to the HUTCF of X_i and $C_i \in S$
9   **end**
10   **if** $(Sim(X_i, C_i) \leq \gamma)$ **then**
11   Add C_i to the set of candidate cluster S '
12   Constitute k-NN candidate set S"
13   return the cluster C in S" with maximum value of $\Delta U(C) = U(C) - U(C \cup \{x_t, u_t\})$
14   **end**
15   **else**
16   **if** $|EHHUCF| > n$ **then**
17   Compute $\Delta T = T - T(C_i)$ and remove the cluster Ci with the maximum value of ΔT
18   count=count-1
19   **end**
20   Create a new EHHUCF containing only HUTCF(X)
21   count=count+1
22   **end**
23   **for** *i= 1 to | EHHUCF|* **do**
24   **if** *hi containing expired HUTCF* **then**
25   **begin**
26   Update EHHUCF(hi)
27   Remove expired HUTCFs(hi,t_c, W)
28   **if** *hi has no HUTCF* **then**
29   delete hi
30   **end**
31   **end**
32   **end**
33   **end**
34   **if** *Clustering request arrived* **then**
35   Calculate clusters based on all h_i of EHHUCFs
36   **end**
37 **end**
38 **End**

Then, we explain how artificially those uncertain data sets are created. Different performance criteria are proposed for the evaluation of SWHU-Clustering. We have performed several tests and simulations on real databases obtained from the U.C.I. repository [16]. Different results carried out from these simulations will be presented and analyzed in order to evaluate the obtained results. We compare the SWHU-Clustering algorithm with UMicro algorithm, which ignores the categorical attributes and the sliding window model.

5.1   Artificial Uncertainty Creation in the Training Set

Training sets are generally composed with certain objects described by known attribute values and classes. Instances with partially known values are usually eliminated from the databases and they are not considered in learning process, probably because it is not easy to know what to do with these objects since the users are in pain to describe their characteristics exactly.

The SWHU-Clustering method is essentially developed to handle uncertain objects. So, the question is how construct these probabilities to obtain uncertain data sets, since there is not real databases within uncertainty. To deal with this constraint, we need to create artificially the uncertain data set as proposed in [8]. The parameter of SWHU-Clustering is set as follows: W is the size of sliding windows; the similarity threshold γ is equal to 1.6; the error parameter $\epsilon = 0.1$ and $\theta=1$.

To illustrate the ability of SWHU-Clustering, synthetic data sets are generated to test the scalability and the efficiency of the method. We have performed several tests and simulations on real databases obtained from the U.C.I. such as Adult and KDD Cup. We have modified these databases by introducing uncertainty in the attributes values of their instances using a gaussian distribution. In order to evaluate the SWHU-Clustering approach, for each data set, we run the algorithm several times. The accuracy of our results is measured according to the purity, the efficiency and the scalability tests of the obtained ones.

5.2 Scalability Test

We measured the efficiency of the uncertain stream clustering method. This efficiency was tested using the number of data stream points processed per second, when the algorithm was run continuously. This provides us an idea of the maximum throughput that can be processed by the algorithm.

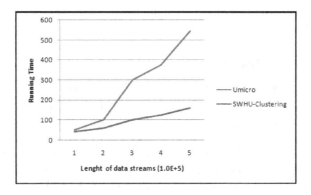

Fig. 1. Execution time versus length of stream

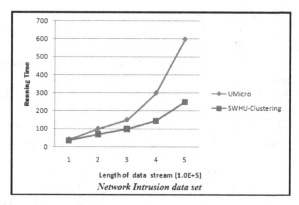

Fig. 2. Execution time versus length of stream

The comparison of clustering processing time for our approach and UMicro is conducted on different data sets. We can note that the processing time of SWHU-Clustering and UMicro grows linearly with the change of the length of data streams. However, the processing time of SWHU-Clustering is less than that of UMicro for the same length of data streams. So SWHU-Clustering has higher execution efficiency.

The higher execution efficiency of SWHU-Clustering benefits from its good design. In the first place, the sliding windows model enables SWHU-Clustering to not store the snapshot of each tuple. The use of the EHHUCF structure help to maintain the EHHUCF structure every time and preserve only the HUTCF that belongs to the sliding window by discarding the expired records. On the contrary, UMicro adopts pyramidal time frame model, which requires storing snapshot for each new arriving tuple regularly; whereas the frequency of storing affects the execution efficiency of algorithm. Finally, the K-NN was leveraged in the clustering process in order to reduce the complexity of useless computation. Consequently, the processing time of SWHU-Clustering is decreased in the process of clustering.

5.3   Effectiveness Test

The purity is used to evaluate the effectiveness of SWHU-Clustering and UMicro, which measures the quality of the obtained clusters. The figure. 3 shows the purity of the two methods for both adult and network intrusion data sets with increasing progression of the streams. The clustering quality of SWHU-Clustering is compared with that of UMicro for different window sizes at different time stamps. We illustrate in the figure 3 (first figure) the purity of clusters obtained using the adult data set within the sliding window w=100. The purity of the final clusters is measured as well as the length of the data streams increases. So, we note that SWHU-Clustering improves good results with higher quality better than the UMicro method. It can be seen that SWHU-Clustering clearly outperforms UMicro while the purity of SWHU-Clustering is always above 80.

For example, at time stamp 4000 the purity of SWHU-Clustering is about 93 and 13 times larger than UMicro. The results on the Network Intrusion data set show that SWHU-Clustering produces better clustering output than UMicro in the scenario of sliding windows.

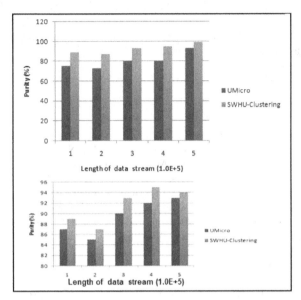

Fig. 3. Quality comparison

The quality of clustering of SWHU-Clustering comes from EHHUCF's ability of capturing the distribution of recent records. The old records in EHHUCFs are iteratively eliminated. This mechanism may help to preserve the radius of an EHHUCF smaller when its cluster center drifts, which leads to keep them with finer granularity than UMicro. The UMicro adopts the pyramidal time frame in the clustering process which allows rising the granularity of the obtained micro-clusters since the old data are kept in memory. This model can be appropriate to keep the traces and highlight the history within different time horizons but it reduces the clustering quality when the micro-clusters grow linearly as the stream proceeds.

6   Conclusion

Datasets containing uncertain information are common in real life data mining applications. However, standard versions of clustering methods are badly adapted to such environment. Thus, the development of appropriate appraoches which support this kind of applications is crucial. This paper has contributed to the development of one clustering method for data streams under uncertainty. The experimental results are witnesses of the feasibility and the effectiveness of our algorithm where an EHHUCF structure is introduced by combining exponential histogram with heterogeneous uncertainty of cluster feature to record the evolution of each cluster and to capture the distribution of recent records. Comparing with UMicro algorithm, we find that our SWHU-Clustering algorithm has high quality, fast processing rate and efficiently fitting in with the streaming setting. These tests have shown that SWHU-Clustering performs well and better than the UMicro.

It will be interesting to extend our method by introducing the possibility theory to handle the uncertainty pervaded in the attributes' values and show its strengths and weaknesses.

References

[1] Chen, J., DeWitt, D.J., Tian, F., Wang, Y.: Niagaracq: A scalable continuous query system for internet databases. In: Chen, W., Naughton, J.F., Bernstein, P.A. (eds.) Proceedings of the 2000 ACM SIGMOD International Conference on Management of Data, Dallas, Texas, USA, May 16-18, pp. 379–390. ACM (2000)

[2] Zhu, Y., Shasha, D.: Statstream: statistical monitoring of thousands of data streams in real time. In: Proceedings of the 28th International Conference on Very Large Data Bases, VLDB 2002, pp. 358–369. VLDB Endowment (2002)

[3] Bonnet, P., Gehrke, J., Seshadri, P.: Towards sensor database systems. In: Tan, K.-L., Franklin, M.J., Lui, J.C.-S. (eds.) MDM 2001. LNCS, vol. 1987, pp. 3–14. Springer, Heidelberg (2000)

[4] Online, M.W.: Merriam-webster online dictionary (2009)

[5] Considine, J., Li, F., Kollios, G., Byers, J.: Approximate aggregation techniques for sensor databases. In: Proceedings of the 20th International Conference on Data Engineering, ICDE 2004, pp. 449–460. IEEE Computer Society, Washington, DC (2004)

[6] Zhang, C., Gao, M., Zhou, A.: Tracking high quality clusters over uncertain data streams. In: Proceedings of the 2009 IEEE International Conference on Data Engineering, pp. 1641–1648. IEEE Computer Society (2009)

[7] Aggarwal, C.C., Yu, P.S.: A framework for clustering uncertain data streams. In: Proceedings of the 2008 IEEE 24th International Conference on Data Engineering, ICDE 2008, pp. 150–159. IEEE Computer Society (2008)

[8] Guoyan, H., Dapeng, L., Jiadong, R., Changzhen, H.: An algorithm for clustering uncertain data streams over sliding windows. In: 2010 6th International Conference on Digital Content, Multimedia Technology and its Applications (IDC), pp. 173–177. IEEE Computer Society (2010)

[9] Huang, G.Y., Liang, D.P., Hu, C.Z., Ren, J.D.: An algorithm for clustering heterogeneous data streams with uncertainty. In: Proceedings of the International Conference on Machine Learning and Cybernetics, ICMLC 2010, Qingdao, China, July 11-14, pp. 2059–2064. IEEE (2010)

[10] Serir, L., Ramasso, E., Zerhouni, N.: Evidential evolving gustafson kessel algorithm for online data streams partitioning using belief function theory. Int. J. Approx. Reasoning 53, 747–768 (2012)

[11] Dempster, A.P.: Upper and lower probabilities induced by a multivalued mapping. Annals of Mathematical Statistics 38, 325–339 (1967)

[12] Zhou, A., Cao, F., Qian, W., Jin, C.: Tracking clusters in evolving data streams over sliding windows. Knowl. Inf. Syst. 15, 181–214 (2008)

[13] Huang, Z.: Clustering large data sets with mixed numeric and categorical values. In: The First Pacific-Asia Conference on Knowledge Discovery and Data Mining, pp. 21–34 (1997)

[14] Aggarwal, C.C., Han, J., Wang, J., Yu, P.S.: A framework for clustering evolving data streams. In: Proceedings of the 29th International Conference on Very Large Data Bases, vol. 29, pp. 81–92. VLDB Endowment (2003)

[15] Liu, W., OuYang, J.: Clustering algorithm for high dimensional data stream over sliding windows. In: Proceedings of the 2011 IEEE 10th International Conference on Trust, Security and Privacy in Computing and Communications, pp. 1537–1542. IEEE Computer Society (2011)

[16] Murphy, P., Aha, D.: Uci repository databases (1996)

Schema Extraction and Integration of Heterogeneous XML Document Collections

Prudhvi Janga and Karen C. Davis

University of Cincinnati, Cincinnati, Ohio, USA
jangapi@mail.uc.edu, karen.davis@uc.edu

Abstract. The availability of vast amounts of heterogeneous XML web data motivates finding efficient methods to search, integrate, query, and present this data. The structure of XML documents is useful for achieving these tasks; however, not every XML document on the web includes a schema. We discuss challenges and accomplishments in the area of generation and integration of XML schemas. We propose and implement a framework for efficient schema extraction and integration from heterogeneous XML document collections collected from the web. Our approach introduces the Schema Extended Context Free Grammar (SECFG) to model XML schemas, including detection of attributes, data types, and element occurrences. Unlike other implementations, our approach supports the generation of XML schemas in any XML schema language, e.g., DTDs or XSD. We compare our approach with other proposed approaches and conclude that we offer the same or better functionality more efficiently and with greater flexibility.

Keywords: XML schema, schema integration, schema extraction, schema discovery.

1 Introduction

XML supports a wide range of web applications from intelligent web searching to web-based e-commerce. The availability of large amounts of heterogeneous and distributed web data from multiple XML data sources adds new challenges for the integration of XML data. In typical clustering or integration approaches, the structure or schema of the XML document should be known. However, most of the XML documents over the web have no accompanying schema. XML schema extraction helps not only in integration but also in efficient storage and querying of XML data [GGR+00, PLM+02, XP11]. Automatic schema extraction from XML documents also assists schema designers by letting them analyze schema patterns and find new ones [C02]. Extraction and integration of XML schemas facilitates XML data transformations to different formats such as relational data [MAC03]. Hence, there are several reasons to develop algorithms and methods for efficient automated generation and integration of XML schemas from a heterogeneous collection of XML documents.

Merged schemas should be concise but should also be able to completely represent the XML documents under consideration. As these two requirements are sometimes contradictory, finding an optimal tradeoff is a challenging task [C02, GGR+00]. XML

A. Cuzzocrea and S. Maabout (Eds.): MEDI 2013, LNCS 8216, pp. 176–187, 2013.

schema extraction also involves using XML schema languages such as DTD or XSD which incorporate the full expressive power of regular expressions, contributing to the complexities of efficient and accurate schema extraction.

In addition to the complexity, many of the research efforts that have proposed XML schema extraction techniques yield incomplete results. In our work we have proposed techniques for efficient extraction of XML schemas which not only generate schemas that are complete but are also capable of producing XML schemas in both popular schema languages, XSD or DTD, and could be extended easily to support other schema languages. Unlike other research efforts that only support schema generation on homogeneous collections, our techniques also support heterogeneous collections where the XML documents can have widely varying structures and content.

We develop the Schema Extended Context-Free Grammar (SECFG) that uses extended regular expressions to model an XML schema, thereby making the schema extraction process schema-language independent. We propose an algorithm that integrates individual schemas by merging SECFG grammars. The algorithms we propose for XML schema generation and integration address challenges such as data type, attribute, and property detection, as well as schema completeness and support for multiple schema languages. We propose a framework for our algorithms that outlines the process of extraction, clustering, integration, storage, and querying of XML web data.

The reminder of this paper is organized as follows. Section 2 describes related research. Section 3 discusses our approach for XML schema extraction from individual XML documents. Section 4 describes the schema unification/merge algorithm proposed for merging individual schemas. In Section 5 we present experimental results and conclude with a discussion of future work in Section 6.

2   Related Research

XML schema generation for a given XML document normally involves three main steps: extraction of XML elements, simplification/generalization to obtain the structure of the document, and transformation of the structure into an XML schema definition. Simplification or generalization of elements to generate good DTDs using regular expressions [GGR+00, AR05] only works with DTDs and does not address complete schema generation. Simplification or generalization of elements using tree construction has been proposed [JOK+02, MLN00], but there are no individual XML document schemas available except for the merged final schema after the process is complete. Several research efforts [C02, PV00, W95] use extended context-free grammars for modeling XML document structure. However, this approach does not produce a complete XML schema that represents the XML document collection and the extraction and integration of XML schemas are combined into a single stage. Min et al. [MAC03] propose a schema extraction system that supports the generation of a DTD and XSD from XML documents, but it does not guarantee the completeness of the generated schema. Xing et al. [XP11] focus on schema extraction from a large collection of XML documents, but it does not support complete XML schema generation, heterogeneous collections, and multiple schema languages.

XML schema integration merges the XML schemas into a single XML schema. If a single XML schema cannot be achieved, this step returns the merged schema along with other independent schemas that could not be merged. The XML schema integration step aims at generating a schema that is adequate to describe the collection of XML documents but not so generic that it could describe many other XML documents not under consideration [GGR+00]. There are many research efforts that have proposed techniques that work well with homogenous collections. Integration of XML schemas over a heterogeneous collection of XML documents is much more complicated than schema integration on a homogenous collection of XML documents.

The Xtract system proposed by Garofalakis et al. [GGR+00] uses factorization and the MDL principle to integrate candidate DTDs. The MDL principle [R78] states that the best theory or language (in this case, a DTD) that can be inferred from data (in this case, collection of XML documents) that follows some patterns is the one that minimizes the sum of the number of bits needed to describe the theory itself and the number of bits needed to encode data using that theory. Moh et al. [MLN00] use spanning graph construction to merge individual XML schemas that are represented by document trees; they do not detect attribute types and entity references or handle processing hyperlinks and multimedia data. Jung et al. [JOK+02] integrate XML schemas from homogenous XML document collections. Chidloviskii [C02] proposes schema induction from a set of range extended context free grammars. The author uses content and context similarity measures to merge non-terminal symbols present in the context-free grammars. Min et al. [MAC03] generate either a DTD or XSD schema which is the integrated schema of the XML documents collection.

Most of the previous techniques, summarized in Table 1, combine XML schema generation with schema integration. However, we perform XML schema generation as a separate step in our framework to avoid repeating it during both XML schema integration and clustering. Some of the research efforts discussed above do not yield a complete XML schema that represents the XML documents under consideration. The technique that we propose is capable of extracting XML schemas that are complete. Most of the research efforts are only capable of representing the extracted schema in either one of the schema languages (XSD or DTD). Since our approach for XML schema extraction is modular, the extracted schema information can be represented in any of the XML schema languages. All of the proposed integration techniques [JOK+02, C02, MAC03] suffer from the same problem. These techniques incur processing overhead in real time and cannot be used for large collections of XML documents. Many techniques work well with homogenous collections and do not address heterogeneous collections. The framework that we have proposed works well with large collections of both homogenous and heterogeneous data and produces an integrated view of the XML data by clustering similar XML document data together. The integration technique that we propose can produce one or more merged schemas from a given collection of XML documents based on the structure of documents present in a given collection. This helps to avoid over-fitting the given collection or failing to represent all the documents. Our framework also separates the extraction and integration of XML schemas into two different stages to achieve better real-time performance and guarantee reusability.

Table 1. Analysis of Research Efforts for Extraction and Integration of XML Schemas

	[GGR+00]	[JOK+02]	[MLN00]	[AR05]	[C02]	[XP11]	[MAC03]	Our Approach
schema type	DTD	DTD	DTD	DTD	XSD	DTD	DTD, XSD	DTD, XSD & others
complete schema	○	●	○	●	○	○	○	●
technique	Regular Expr. & Factoring	N-ary Trees	Document Trees & Spanning Graph	Regular Expr. & Factoring	Extended Context-Free Grammars	NFA to Lazy DFA	Restricted Content Model	Schema Extended Context-Free Grammars
accuracy or conciseness	MDL Theory	○	○	MDL Theory	○	MDL Theory	○	MDL Theory
heterogeneous collections	●	○	○	●	●	○	●	●
tag/attribute similarity	○	○	○	○	○	○	○	●
similarity measure	○	○	○	○	○	Edit Distance	○	Edit Distance
reusability of schemas	○	○	○	○	○	○	○	●

yes=●, no=○

3   XML Schema Generation

There are three main steps in our XML schema generation process. XML schema generation starts by ordering XML documents by search rank so that the most relevant schemas are extracted first. However, this is an optional step if XML schema generation is being carried out offline independently of a user search. Once that step is complete, for each XML document, the XML schema is obtained. The three main steps for XML schema generation are (1) structured example creation, (2) generation of an SECFG grammar, and (3) generalizing the grammar. Each of these steps is explained below.

3.1   Generation of Structured Examples

We represent XML documents as structured examples of an unknown SECFG to aid in the process of XML schema inference. Structured examples are derivation trees where all non-terminal labels are removed [C02]. We define a recursive algorithm that generates a structured example for a given element (E) present in an XML document. This algorithm initializes a temporary set of nodes TN to store the generated nodes of the derivation tree. The element E that has been supplied to the algorithm is parsed and all the sub-elements of E are extracted into S. If there are no sub-elements, the element is considered to be a simple element and the node for the element is generated using start and end tags of the element. However, if E is a complex element with sub-elements then the nodes for each of the sub-elements are generated recursively until the deepest level is reached. Once all the nodes for sub-elements inside the complex element have been generated, the algorithm then generates the node for the complex element itself and links it to the nodes of the sub-elements present in the temporary set, *TN*. Thus, for a given XML document, *GenerateStructuredExample(E)* creates a derivation tree that is a combination of unknown nodes (that become non-terminal symbols in the grammar) as well as element nodes called the structured example of the document.

3.2   Schema Extended Context-Free Grammars

We model an XML schema by creating a new grammar called the Schema Extended Context-Free Grammar (SECFG), an extension of ECFG [C02]. We associate features of an XML schema with components of an SECFG as shown in Table 2. The SECFG grammar addresses features such as attribute detection, order of child elements, number of child elements and detection of default, fixed, and substitution group values for elements and attributes, along with all other features already addressed using ECFG modeling.

Regular expressions used to represent SECFG are called extended regular expressions because they support both the minimum and maximum number of occurrences as well as several other attributes of a given element with a properties tag. The properties inside a properties tag are defined as a semicolon-delimited list of strings where each string is denoted by $P=a$, where P represents the name of the property (attribute name) and a represents the value of the property. A properties tag that accompanies a terminal symbol summarizes features such as order, number of child elements, data type, default value, and fixed values.

Formally, a Schema Extended Context Free Grammar is defined by a 5-tuple $G = (T, N, P, \delta, start)$ where T, N, and P are disjoint sets of terminals, non-terminals, and properties, respectively. Each property in P is defined over an empty set or an enumeration or a range of values it can accept. When a property is defined over an empty set it can accept any values. The symbol *start* is an initial non-terminal and δ is a finite set of production rules of the form $A \rightarrow \alpha$ for $A \in N$, where α is an extended regular expression over terms, where each term is a terminal-properties-nonterminal-terminal sequence such as *tpBt'* where *t*, *t'* are a pair of opening and closing tags respectively, $t, t' \in T$, $B \in N$ and $p \in P$. The expression *tpBt'* can be abbreviated as *tp:B* without loss of information.

Table 2. Correspondence between XML Schema Language Features and SECFG Components

XML Schema Language	SECFG
Element name (tag)	Terminal
Element definition	Production
Element attributes (includes data types and occurrences)	Properties tag
Named complex type	Non-terminal
Abstract complex type	Non-terminal
Complex type definition	One or more productions
Sequence element group	Sequential pattern in a production
Choice element group	Disjunction pattern in a production

We induce an SECFG from a structured example by traversing the tree in a depth-first approach. Every time we encounter an unknown node in the structured example tree, we add a production to the SECFG being generated and traverse the unknown node under consideration to complete the right side of the production. Since the grammar represents the complete document structure, there are numerous productions that are structurally identical. To achieve conciseness, generalization removes duplicate productions and merges productions with similar content and context [C02].

3.3   Generalization of SECFG

Algorithm : $GeneralizeSECFG(G_i)$
Input: grammar passed by reference: G_i
1: BEGIN
2: In G_i merge the nonterminal symbols having similar names and structure
3: Determine data types for terminals present in G_i
4: Determine and merge attributes for terminals present in G_i
5: Generalize content sets present in nonterminal productions of G_i into regular expressions.
6: Determine ranges(min,max occurence) of the generalized content sets in G_i
7: Generate extended regular expressions for content sets in G_i
8: END

Fig. 1. Generalization of an SECFG

This algorithm takes an SECFG G_i that has not been generalized. A generalized grammar is one in which data types, order, and other properties are defined and the nonterminal symbols with the same name are merged to yield a concise grammar that describes the structure of the XML document. When translated into a grammar, all the non-terminal and terminal tags are unique at this stage. Hence, there is no need for using tag similarity in generalizing a given SECFG. However, in the integration stage where multiple schemas are merged, we cannot guarantee uniqueness of elements and sub-elements among different schemas, so we measure tag similarity. The algorithm shown in Fig. 1 performs the generalization of an SECFG. Once the generalization is complete, we use an SECFG-to-schema mapping algorithm that associates the features of an XML schema with an SECFG as shown in Table 2 to derive an XML schema definition in any XML schema language such as DTD or XSD.

4   XML Schema Integration

XML schema integration involves merging multiple individual schemas into a final schema. We propose the algorithm shown in Fig. 2 for XML schema integration. We merge the grammars to produce an integrated SECFG. Any grammars that could not be merged in this stage are marked as independent grammars. Once the merging process is complete, we transform the integrated SECFG into an XML schema.

Algorithm : *XML Schema Integration*

Input: Collection of schema definitions: S
Output: Merged XML schema as XSD or DTD

1: BEGIN
2: Order the collection of XML schemas S by rank
3: Initialize an empty grammar G which holds the integrated schema grammar
4: **for each** schema S_i in S **do**
5:     Derive a schema extended context-free grammar G_i for S_i
6:     $MergeGrammar(G_i, G)$ where G is the base grammer
7:     Generate XML schema definition S_{def} from G
8:     Transform S_{def} to desired schema language XSD or DTD
9: **end for**
10: END

Fig. 2. XML Schema Integration

Algorithm : *MergeGrammar(G_i, G)*

Input: grammars passed by reference: G_i and G

1: BEGIN
2: Initialize an empty grammar G_{temp}
3: Calculate similarity measure $Sim_{G_i,G}$ ▷ Edit distance is used to calculate similarity
4: **if** $Sim_{G_i,G} \geq Sim_{threshold}$ **then**   ▷ $Sim_{threshold}$ is max. edit distance allowed
5:     Add productions of G to G_{temp}
6:     Add productions of G_i to G_{temp}
7:     $GeneralizeSECFG(G_{temp})$
8:     $G \leftarrow G_{temp}$
9: **else**
10:     $G_i.IsIndependent$=true
11: **end if**
12: END

Fig. 3. Merge Grammar G_i into G

The algorithm shown in Fig. 3 merges a given grammar G_i into a base grammar G (the grammar that holds the integrated structure) and also generalizes the merged grammar. It starts by initializing a grammar G_{temp} that stores all the productions of G_i and base grammar, G. The grammar G_{temp} is generalized to give a compact structure stored as G. Since we consider a set of heterogeneous XML documents, the grammar G_i produced by the XML document X_i might be structurally different from the base grammar, G. We calculate the edit distance between the base grammar G and the grammar to be merged, G_i. If the edit distance is less than or equal to the maximum edit distance parameter, we merge the two grammars. We define edit distance as the minimum cost of the edit scripts such as insert a non-terminal, delete a non-terminal, or replace a non-terminal that transform the individual SECFG grammar to conform to the base grammar. As the edit distance might differ based on the size of the document, we use a normalized edit distance measure to compare to the maximum edit distance. Once the similarity between the base grammar and the grammar G_i is calculated, we check whether it is above the threshold defined by the end user. If it is, then we merge the two grammars.

5   Experimental Results

In this section we discuss results of experiments carried out to test the validity and efficiency of our approach.

5.1   Comparison of an Actual versus Generated XML Schema

We generate XML schemas from a number of different XML datasets that have been automatically created using Altova XMLspy. We use synthetic as well as real world schemas in our experiments. Fig. 4 shows an example of an actual XML schema that represents a collection of XML documents and the one that is generated from our system by extracting and integrating schemas from the collection of XML documents. We can observe that both the schemas are very close to each other, differing mainly in the number of maximum occurrences of the element *<Title>* (10 in the original and 6 in ours.) The exact number of minimum and maximum occurrences cannot be guaranteed by any approach if the collection of XML documents does not fully represent the schema under consideration. Results from the experiments are discussed in the next section.

```xml
<?xml version="1.0" encoding="ISO-8859-1" ?>
<xs:schema xmlns:xs="http://www.w3.org/2001/XMLSchema">

<!-- definition of simple elements -->
<xs:element name="Instructor" type="xs:string"/>
<xs:element name="Capacity" type="xs:positiveInteger"/>
<xs:element name="Room" type="xs:string"/>
<xs:element name="Title" type="xs:string"/>

<!-- definition of attributes -->
<xs:attribute name="courseid" type="xs:string"/>

<xs:element name="Course">
  <xs:complexType>
    <xs:sequence>
      <xs:element ref="Title" minOccurs="0" maxOccurs="10"/>
      <xs:element ref="Instructor" minOccurs="0" maxOccurs="1"/>
      <xs:element ref="Capacity" minOccurs="0" maxOccurs="1"/>
      <xs:element ref="Room" minOccurs="0" maxOccurs="1"/>
    </xs:sequence>
    <xs:attribute ref="courseid" use="required"/>
  </xs:complexType>
</xs:element>

<xs:element name="Courses">
  <xs:complexType>
    <xs:sequence>
      <xs:element ref="Course" minOccurs="1" maxOccurs="1000"/>
    </xs:sequence>
  </xs:complexType>
</xs:element>

</xs:schema>
```

Fig. 4(a). Example of an Actual XSD

```
◢ <xs:schema xmlns:xs="http://www.w3.org/2001/XMLSchema">
    <#comment/>
    <xs:element name="Title" type="xs:TextOnly"/>
    <xs:element name="Instructor" type="xs:TextOnly"/>
    <xs:element name="Capacity" type="xs:TextOnly"/>
    <xs:element name="Room" type="xs:TextOnly"/>
    <#comment/>
    <xs:attribute name="courseid" type="xs:Text"/>
    <#comment/>
  ◢ <xs:element name="Course" type="xs:ElementsOnly">
      ◢ <xs:complexType>
          ◢ <xs:Sequence>
              <xs:element ref="Title" maxOccurs="6" minOccurs="0"/>
              <xs:element ref="Instructor" maxOccurs="1" minOccurs="0"/>
              <xs:element ref="Capacity" maxOccurs="1" minOccurs="0"/>
              <xs:element ref="Room" maxOccurs="1" minOccurs="0"/>
            <xs:attribute ref="courseid" use="required" default="String"/>
  ◢ <xs:element name="Courses" type="xs:ElementsOnly">
      ◢ <xs:complexType>
          ◢ <xs:Sequence>
              <xs:element ref="Course" maxOccurs="1000" minOccurs="1"/>
```

Fig.4(b). Our Generated XSD

5.2   Datasets and Quality of Inferred Schemas

To validate our approach and also show the advantages of it, we compare the schemas generated using our approach with XTRACT [GGR+00], DDbE [LA01], DTDXtract [AR05], and the restricted element content model [MAC03]. Although there are some other systems that also discuss XML schema generation, we do not consider them for comparison because they either do not discuss their algorithms in detail or they do not present experimental details. We have implemented our approach using Microsoft Visual Basic and the .Net framework. We use the same real-life DTDs in the experiments with XTRACT [GGR+00]. For each DTD for a single element, we generate an XML file containing 1000 instantiations of the element using Altova XMLspy. The regular expressions that represent the original DTDs used to generate the datasets are shown in the first column of Table 3. We refer to the regular expression representing a DTD as the DTD itself from here on. The DTDs from other approaches such as XTRACT, DDbE, and DTDXtract were obtained from Min et al. [MAC03]. The results from our approach are shown in the rightmost column in Table 3. Our approach generates all the schemas that match the original DTDs, demonstrating that our approach is accurate and valid. One noteworthy difference is that our approach produces schemas (can be represented in XSD or DTD or any other schema language) that match the original DTDs while other approaches just produce DTDs.

Table 3. Comparison of Actual Versus Generated DTDs

Original DTD	XTRACT	DTDXtract	DDbE ver2	Restricted Element Content Model	Our Approach
a|b|c|d|e	a|b|c|d|e	a|b|c|d|e	a|b|c|d|e	a|b|c|d|e	a|b|c|d|e
(a|b|c|d|e)*	(a|b|c|d|e)*	(a|b|c|d|e)*	((a|(e|b|c|a|d|(d+c))|(e|a|(e|c|d|(e+b+))|c|b|(e+b+)|d|(d+c))|d|e|b|c|(e+b+)|(dcb)|(d+c))*)	(a|b|c|d|e)*	(a|b|c|d|e)*
ab*c*	ab*c*	ab*c*	(a(b|c)+)	ab*c*	ab*c*
a*b?c?d?	a*b?c?d?	a*b?c?d?	(((a|b)|c|d|a|((b|c)|d|b|c)|b)+)	a*b?c?d?	a*b?c?d?
(a(bc)+d)*	(a(bc)*d)*	(a(bc)+d)*	---------	(a(bc)+d)*	(a(bc)+d)*
(ab?c*d?)*	---------	(ab?c*d?)*	((((ac+ac+d)|(a+b)|a)| . . . |(c+dab))*)	(ab?c*d?)*	(ab?c*d?)*

5.3   Normalized Time Comparison of XML Schema Extraction Techniques

We compare the time taken to extract XML schemas from datasets among different systems such as XTRACT, DDbE, and our system. We exclude DTDXtract from the normalized time comparisons because this system uses the same algorithm used by XTRACT apart from an extension to support Kleene plus (+) expressions. Fig. 5 shows a normalized time comparison of different systems with respect to the different DTDs. We consider a normalized time comparison because the time taken to extract various DTDs by different systems such as XTRACT have been implemented using a computer configuration which is different from the configuration that we have used to

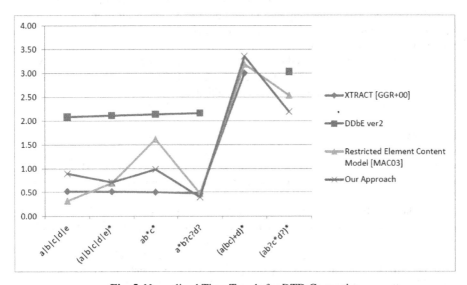

Fig. 5. Normalized Time Trends for DTD Generation

develop our system [MAC03]. Fig. 5 shows the standard scores (how many standard deviations an observation is above or below the mean). The time taken for XSD as well as DTD generation for different DTD/XSD data sets in our system is significantly less when compared to other systems such as XTRACT and DDbe ver2. Our system is not only comparable to the XTRACT system but also handles one additional case. Our system performs as well as or better than the element content model. It should also be noted that the time taken by our system is comparable or better than other systems even though it produces both DTD and XSD schemas. This result validates the efficiency of the approach we have taken as well as the system we have implemented.

6   Conclusions and Future Work

We introduce the problem of extraction and integration of XML schemas from heterogeneous collections of XML documents. We propose a grammar to represent the structure of the XML document (SECFG) and implement algorithms to extract and integrate XML schemas. We describe experimental studies that evaluate the effectiveness of our schema extraction and integration algorithms. We perform experiments using synthetic as well as real-life datasets and compare results from our approach against other systems that have already been proposed.

We discuss challenges involved in the extraction and integration of XML schemas and techniques to overcome those challenges. However, we have not addressed challenges involved in the location or clustering of XML web data. We use normalized edit distance to calculate the similarity between an individual schema and the base schema (to be the final schema) during schema integration. Future work could be done on enhancing our schema integration algorithm by incorporating some hybrid similarity measures (schema mapping techniques) that have been proposed for XML document clustering purposes. We are also working on using SECFG model for XML to relational schema mapping.

We expect to obtain additional experimental results as evidence of the validity and scalability of our approach; we plan to release our datasets to support reproducibility of our results as well as further research when this is complete.

References

[AR05] Leonov, A.V., Khusnutdinov, R.R.: Study and Development of the DTD Generation System for XML Documents. Programming and Computer Software (PCS) 31(4), 197–210 (2005)

[C02] Chidlovskii, B.: Schema extraction from XML collections. In: Proceedings of the 2nd ACM/IEEE-CS Joint Conference on Digital Libraries, Portland, Oregon, USA, June 14-18, pp. 291–292 (2002)

[GGR+00] Garofalakis, M.N., Gionis, A., Rastogi, R., Seshadri, S., Shim, K.: XTRACT: A system for extracting document type descriptors from XML documents. In: Proceedings of the 2000 ACM SIGMOD International Conference on Management of Data, Dallas, Texas, USA, May 16-18, pp. 165–176 (2000)

[JOK+02] Jung, J.-S., Oh, D.-I., Kong, Y.-H., Ahn, J.-K.: Extracting Information from XML Documents by Reverse Generating a DTD. In: Proceedings of the 1st EurAsian Conference on Information and Communication Technology (EurAsia ICT), Shiraz, Iran, October 29-31, pp. 314–321 (2002)

[LA01] Berman, L., Diaz, A.: Data Descriptors by Example (DDbE), IBM alphaworks (2001), http://www.alphaworks.ibm.com/tech/DDbE

[MAC03] Min, J.-K., Ahn, J.-Y., Chung, C.-W.: Efficient Extraction of Schemas for XML Documents. Information Processing Letters 85(1), 7–12 (2003)

[MLN00] Moh, C.-H., Lim, E.-P., Ng, W.K.: DTD-Miner: a tool for mining DTD from XML documents. In: Proceedings of the Second International Workshop on Advance Issues of E-Commerce and Web-Based Information Systems (WECWIS 2000), Milpitas, California, USA, June 8-9, pp. 144–151 (2000)

[PLM+02] Passi, K., Lane, L., Madria, S.K., Sakamuri, B.C., Mohania, M., Bhowmick, S.S.: A model for XML Schema Integration. In: Bauknecht, K., Tjoa, A.M., Quirchmayr, G. (eds.) EC-Web 2002. LNCS, vol. 2455, pp. 193–202. Springer, Heidelberg (2002)

[PV00] Papakonstantinou, Y., Vianu, V.: DTD Inference for Views of XML Data. In: Proceedings of the 19th ACM SIGMOD-SIGACT-SIGART Symposium on Principles of Database Systems (PODS), Dallas, Texas, USA, May 15-17, pp. 35–46 (2000)

[R78] Rissanen, J.: Modeling by shortest data description. Automatica 14(5), 465–471 (1978)

[W95] Wood, D.: Standard Generalized Markup Language: Mathematical and Philosophical Issues. In: van Leeuwen, J. (ed.) Computer Science Today. LNCS, vol. 1000, pp. 344–365. Springer, Heidelberg (1995)

[XP11] Xing, G., Parthepan, V.: Efficient Schema Extraction from a Large Collection of XML Documents. In: Proceedings of the 49th Annual Southeast Regional Conference, Kennesaw, GA, USA, March 24-26, pp. 92–96 (2011)

Structural Entities of an Ontology-Driven Unifying Metamodel for UML, EER, and ORM2

C. Maria Keet[1] and Pablo Rubén Fillottrani[2,3]

[1] School of Mathematics, Statistics, and Computer Science, University of
KwaZulu-Natal and UKZN/CSIR-Meraka Centre for Artificial Intelligence Research,
South Africa
keet@ukzn.ac.za

[2] Departamento de Ciencias e Ingeniería de la Computación, Universidad Nacional
del Sur, Bahía Blanca, Argentina
prf@cs.uns.edu.ar

[3] Comisión de Investigaciones Científicas, Provincia de Buenos Aires, Argentina

Abstract. Software interoperability may be achieved by using their respective conceptual data models. However, each model may be represented in a different conceptual data modelling language for the tool's
purpose or due to legacy issues. Several translations between small subsets of language features are known, but no unified model exists that
includes all their language features. Aiming toward filling this gap, we
designed a common and unified, ontology-driven, metamodel covering
and unifying EER, UML Class Diagrams v2.4.1, and ORM2. This paper
presents the static, structural, components of the metamodel, highlighting the common entities and summarizing some modelling motivations.

1 Introduction

The need for, and reality of, complex software system design and integration
of information from heterogeneous sources is motivated by upscaling of scientific collaboration in the life sciences [36], e-government initiatives [31], company
mergers [4], and the Semantic Web. Therefore, establishing connections between
multiple conceptual models has become an important task, as the system's conceptual data models may be available in, mainly, UML, EER and ORM. However,
this capability is not common in traditional information systems development
and management other than at the physical schema layer [6] and for conceptual models represented in the same language [2,12]. Subtle representational
and expressive differences (e.g., [17]) in the languages are primarily due to their
different origins and purposes, and makes this task very difficult, and even within
one language family there are differences in meaning of an element [14,24].

The state of the art in this area has only incidentally gone beyond a single
Conceptual Data Modelling (CDM) language and only for UML and ORM (e.g.,
[14,24,25]). It is unclear to what extent the languages agree on their underlying
ontological foundations to model information. This limits mapping and transformation algorithms for CASE tools to let one work in parallel on conceptual data
models represented in different languages that otherwise could be highly useful in

A. Cuzzocrea and S. Maabout (Eds.): MEDI 2013, LNCS 8216, pp. 188–199, 2013.

information integration and complex system development. Moreover, a more detailed insight in the overlap and underlying modelling principles will contribute to investigating the effect of language features on modelling information.

To solve these issues, it first should be clear what entities and constraints exist in each language and how the differences can be reconciled without changing the languages. We achieve this by developing a single integrated metamodel inclusive of all language features; in particular, we describe in this work such a unifying metamodel for the static, structural components of UML 2.4.1 class diagrams, EER, and ORM2/FBM, which, to the best of our knowledge, is the first of its kind. We use insights from Ontology and ontologies during the metamodel development rather than the argument of convenience to fit with an *a priori* chosen logic language. The unification brings afore the differences and commonalities: 1) they agree on Relationship, Role (/association end), and Object type (/class/entity type), and 2) they differ in coverage of, among others, attributes. We provide an overview of related works in Section 2, describe the metamodel in Section 3, and conclude in Section 4.

2   State of the Art

Within CDM and software engineering, CDMs are compared through their metamodels (in ORM) highlighting their differences in [17], which is useful before unifying them. Most other works take a formal approach only. This can be by means of a single formalisation in a chosen logic by first formalizing a language (among others, [1,5,18,21,22,34]), and optionally in the scope of partial unification [8,27]. Perhaps due to this approach, different logics have been used for different CDM languages, therewith still not providing the sought-after interoperability for either of the languages or among each other; e.g., the Description Logic $\mathcal{ALUNI}$ is used for a partial unification [8] but *DL-Lite* and $\mathcal{DLR}_{ifd}$ are used for partial formalisations to stay within the chosen decidable fragment [1,5,23], omitting features that render the language undecidable [23], so they cannot simply be linked up and implemented.

Other approaches include [41,6,7,2,3], which are more advanced in the notion of a common language. Venable and Grundy designed [41] and implemented a unification [13,42] for a part of ER and a part of NIAM (a precursor to ORM), omitting, mainly, value types, nested entity types, and composite attributes, and NIAM is forced to have the attributes as in ER. Bowers and Delcambre [6] present a framework for representing schema and data information coming from several data models, mainly relational, XML and RDF. Its main characteristic is a flat representation of schema and data, and the possibility of establishing different levels of conformance between them. However, its representational language ULD only includes ordinal, set and union class constructs, and cardinality constraints. Boyd and McBrien [7] use a Hypergraph Data Model to relate schemas represented in ER, relational, UML, and ORM, and includes transformation rules between them. It has the features inclusion, exclusion and union class constructs, and mandatory, unique and reflexive constraints, and various notions of cardinality constraints and keys, but roles, aggregation, and weak entity types are missing.

Atzeni et al [2,3] describe an automatic approach that translates a schema from one model to another by means of a small set of "metaconstructs"—entities (called "abstracts"), attributes (called "lexicals"), relationships, generalization, foreign keys, and complex attributes—that can be used to characterize different models. Automatic translations between schemas are produced in Datalog, but translations from a rich representational language may require a sequence of such basic translations, if possible. Guizzardi [14] proposes a Unifying Foundational Ontology (UFO) which is used to redefine UML metamodel for structural conceptual modelling concepts.

Our approach is different regarding scope and methodology. We aim to capture *all* the languages' constructs and *generalise* in an ontology-driven way so that the integrated metamodel subsumes the static elements of EER, UML Class Diagrams v2.4.1, and ORM2 without changing the base languages. Methodologically, our metamodel is ontological rather than formal, compared to all other known works that present first a formal common language for translations that leave aside important particular aspects of each language. We first develop a conceptual model of all possible entities and their relations in the selected languages, and will devise a formalization for their translations afterward. The main benefit is that it allows one to have a clear comprehension of the meaning(s) of an entity in each language whilst coping with the broader scope. This is an essential step towards achieving the full potential of information sharing.

3   Ontology-Driven Metamodel

The metamodel is a conceptual model about the selected CDM languages that covers all their native features and is still consistent. Whether a particular feature is a good feature is beyond the scope, because we aim at representing in a unified way what is already present in the language. We do, however, use Ontology (philosophy) and ontologies (artifacts in IT and computing) to enhance understanding of the features and to unify perceived differences through generalization, and to improve the quality of the metamodel.

The principal entities (cf. constraints) are depicted in Fig. 1 in UML Class Diagram notation, where a white fill of a class icon indicates that that entity is not present in either of the three languages, a single diagonal fill that it is present in one language, a double diagonal that it is present in two, and a dark fill that it is present in all three groups of languages (EER, UML v2.4.1, ORM2); naming conventions and terminological differences and similarities of the entities are listed in the appendix at the end of the paper. Although UML Class Diagrams have limited expressiveness, we prefer a more widely known graphical notation for the purpose of communication (it will be formalised in a suitable logic anyway). The remainder contains explanations of the metamodel fragments, being roles, relationship, and attributes, class/entity type, nested and weak entity type, subsumption, and aggregation.

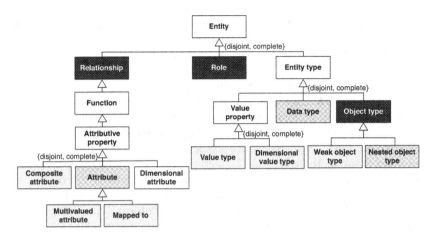

Fig. 1. Main static, structural, entities of the metamodel; see text for details

3.1   Classes, Concepts, Types

CDMs use terms such as entity type, object type, and class. In philosophy, distinctions are made between classes, concepts, types, and universals. The meaning of these terms do not coincide, so in order to be more precise in the characterisation of these of core entities, we shall first briefly summarise a selection of the general, mostly agreed-upon, meanings, principally examined in Ontology (its aim is to clarify some possible terminological confusion and we take them at face-value, but will not debate which one is 'better' or how to formulate their description more precisely).

- *Class* is associated with set theory and the extension—a set of actual objects as members. Two distinct classes must have different extensions.
- *Concept* generally refers to a mind-dependent entity that may, or may not, have instances, and where there is not a membership relation between the individual object and its concept, but an instantiation relation between the object and the concept it instantiates [11].
- *Universals* are mind-independent entities, which do have at least one instance, hence, also uses the instantiation relation, not membership [30].
- *Properties* are "(also called 'attributes,' 'qualities,' 'features,' 'characteristics,' 'types') are those entities that can be predicated of things or, in other words, attributed to them." [39], which can be relational or unary.
- *Type* denotes a 'kind' of thing, and is closely associated with mathematics.
- *Unary predicate* is used in logic, and may have instances associated to it through the interpretation function (assuming a model-theoretic semantics).
- *Entity* means whatever can be deduced from the context in which the term is used, but such that that thing is a discrete unit, therewith it can refer to an instance or object, but also to a universal or concept or class.

In contrast to the extensional view and grouping similar things together into a class or set, concepts and universals concern the intension; informally: they are the descriptions, or a set of properties, that those entities that instantiate them, have. For instance, that each Computer has a CPU and memory, and has the function to compute, or that Apple is a kind of fruit that has a certain shape and colour. The main philosophical difference lies in the mind (in-)dependence and, with that, whether there is such thing as reality.

ORM, EER, and UML use different terminology, which might indicate different ontological commitments regarding the subject domain we wish to represent in the conceptual data model. In UML, "The purpose of a class is to specify a classification of objects and to *specify the features* that characterize the structure and behavior of those objects." (p49) (emphasis added) [32]. For ORM, the draft ISO standardisation [10] declares that object type is a "concept used to classify the objects in the universe of discourse into different kinds" (p5), which is divided into non-lexical object type—an "object type, each of whose instances are non-lexical objects" (p5)—and lexical object type, which "is a metaclass each instance of which represents a concept that is used to represent values" (p12). The original ER diagram uses "entity sets" [9], known as entity types since soon thereafter [38], into which entities are classified and "we know that it has the properties common to the other entities in the entity set" (p11) [9] and "An *entity type* E defines a collection of entities that have the same attributes." (p1004) [38], hence, both extension and intension are considered. EER generally follows the same line, although it is formulated differently by [40]: "Entity types conceptualize structuring of things of reality through attributes." and "$E \doteq (attr(E), \Sigma_E)$ where E is the entity type defined as a pair – the set $attr(E)$ of attribute types and the set Σ_E of integrity constraints that apply to E." (p1084), i.e., definitely the intension, and it comprises both attributes and constraints explicitly. Despite the differences in formulation, practically, it does not make a real difference: in the conceptual data model, each one is used to denote a kind of thing where the relevant aspects of its intension is described, and will have an extension in the software (e.g., as object in OO software, or tuples in a database table) and each of those objects represents an instance in reality. However, one just as well can design a database about [mind-dependent] deities in the Stone Age. From the ontological viewpoint, we thus can postulate that the conceptual data models' entity type or class, is, mostly, a universal, but sometimes may be a concept and one can let them be subsumed by Entity. The terminology we use henceforth for those entities in conceptual data models that describe the intension, is Object type. Although UML is more widely used than either EER or ORM, hence, the term 'class' more familiar, what actually is being modelled/represented, is the intension with respect to the application domain, not a placeholder for the extension, and that term does not clash in intention with terminology in ontology.

Finally, Weak object type is included thanks to ER and EER's weak entity type that has an identification that is a combination of one or more of its attributes and the identifier of its related strong entity type. Depending on the ontological status of weak entity type [14,25], it is possible to approximate its meaning in UML with the Identifier profile or use ORM's compound reference scheme, but there is no icon for it in UML and ORM.

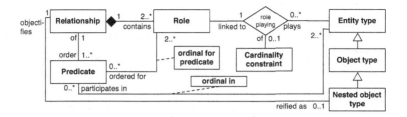

Fig. 2. Relationships between Relationship, Role, and Entity type; see text for details

3.2   Roles and Relationships

There are many points that can be discussed about roles and relationship, but we shall restrict ourselves to their definition, and differences among them and with a object type, how to deal with the aggregation associations, and subsumption.

Distinguishing Roles, Relationships, and Predicates. A relationship, or relational property in ontology [39], is an entity that relates entities, hence, it requires at least two entities to participate in it. Thus, there are no unary relationships, whereas there can be unary predicates and object types are unary. Second, a relationship is composed of at least two *roles*, or: "association ends" or "member ends" in UML [32], ORM/FBM use "roles" [18,19,10], and EER's roles may be called components of a relationship [9,40]. A role is something that an object plays in a relationship, therewith characterising relationship and committing to the *positionalist* ontological commitment of relations and relationships as to what they are (see also [29,24]). The three CDM languages agree on this and therefore they appear in the metamodel (recall Fig. 1), including the disjointness between Relationship, Role, and Entity Type and their interaction is depicted in Fig. 2. The ternary role playing enforces that each role must have exactly one entity type with no or one cardinality constraint (the minimum and maximum cardinality are part of the Cardinality constraint), and each entity type may play zero or more roles.

ORM's predicates are an addition to roles and relationships and adheres to the so-called "standard view" of relations [29]. They have an intricate relation with roles and relationships: 1) an ordered for between roles, 2) a predicate can exist only if there is a relation between those roles that compose the relationships, and the relationship that that predicate is an ordering of (i.e., it is a join-subset), and 3) entities that participate in the predicate must play those roles that compose the relationship of which that predicate is an ordered version of.

Nested Object Types. A Nested object type (see Fig. 1) is also called association class, associative entity, or objectified fact type. Although documentation of CDM languages discuss the notion of a "duality" of nested object types as both being a relationship and an object type, and therewith indicating that one could have multiple inheritance of Nested object type to two supertypes, Relationship and Object type (e.g., [15]), this is not correct. A nested object type is

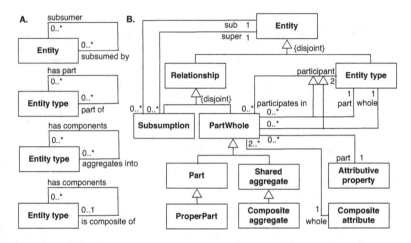

Fig. 3. Subsumption and aggregation. A: short-hand notation; B: more detailed representation, where there is an additional constraint on the two associations of subsumption such that the participating entities must be of the same type, and an attributive property participates only in a part-whole relation if it is part of a composite attribute.

composed of a relationship or the outcome of a *transformation of* or *reification of* a relationship, each one of which is certainly distinct from *being* a relationship. Therefore, the metamodel relates them through a normal association.

The constraints regarding nested object types are rather basic, which reflects the flexibility concerning reification/objectification in UML and ORM. No restrictions are mentioned in the UML standard regarding objectifying an association into an association class [32], and although ORM initially had some restrictions on when one would be allowed to objectify a fact type [19], these restrictions have been lifted more recently [16].

Subsumption and Aggregation Relationships. Considering relationships in more detail, we have to address subsetting relationships versus subtyping, and aggregation. The two relationships in Fig. 3 are represented twice: once as recursive relationship, and once as being a kind of relationship that has two participating entities, each providing a different perspective on the relationship.

Subsumption. Subsumption of entities is included in all languages except ER. Some argue against allowing multiple inheritance [35,37], but there it is assumed that there are no real relationships (an OBO-language limitation) and/or that subtypes must always be disjoint (an Aristotelean left-over), which need not be the case for some subject domain and, moreover, CDM languages permit it. Thus, the constraints in the metamodel reflects this.

Subsumption for relationships and roles is more interesting. UML 2.4.1 distinguishes between subsetting—the association ends and/or participating classes are sub-ends/sub-classes of those participating in the super-association or indirectly through an association's attributes—and "specialization" of associations

[32]. Specialization is not set-oriented, but because of the differences in intension of the association [32], although the UML standard does not describe how that is supposed to work. The only way to change an association's intension, is to restrict the relational properties of an association, as recognised in ontology [26]; e.g., each relationship that is asymmetric is also irreflexive. Only few such subsumptions exists [19], however, and little is known about its practicality other than the few experiments reported in [26] for ontologies. Nevertheless, it may become more relevant in the near future, and therefore we keep this option available. Both ways of relationship subsumption are captured in the metamodel with the more general Subsumption, and both UML and ORM include subsumption of roles, therefore, the participating entities for Subsumption are Entity.

Aggregation. Much has been written about UML's shared and composite aggregation (among many, [14,28,33]), yet the UML standard still does not offer any more clarity on what they really are. Shared aggregation tends to be mapped loosely onto parthood and composite aggregation to proper parthood, yet aggregation is also used for meronymic associations in UML Class Diagrams, such as *member-of* (see [28] for an overview); hence, one can neither draw a subsumption relation between the aggregations and parthood nor adorn the subsumption from PartWhole with a disjointness axiom. The UML standard's description of shared and composite aggregation also indicates behavioural characteristics or lifecycle semantics of the part and whole, but its inclusion in the metamodel is beyond the scope of the static components.

Finally, observe the possible participation of attributes in a PartWhole relationship, which is added to accommodate ER/EER's Composite attribute. Given that the entity that plays the part-role is Attributive property, it entails that it is still possible to include uncommon representations, such as nested composite attributes or a composite attribute with a multivalued attribute.

Attributes and Value Types. Ontological aspects of attributes deserve a separate paper; here we only summarise the outcome. Formally, an *attribute* (A) is a binary relationship between a *relationship* or *object type* ($R \cup E$) and a *data type* (D, sometimes called 'concrete domains'), i.e., $A \mapsto R \cup E \times D$; e.g., an attribute hasColour $\mapsto$ Flower $\times$ String.

The different attributes in Fig. 1 reflect their differences in meaning in the CDM languages and it can be motivated by Ontology and ontologies. An attribution, or quality (in ORM called Value types), such as the Colour of an apple or its Shape, 'inheres in' (needs a) bearer to exist and is formalised as a unary predicate, not a binary. They differ from what we call here Object Type, and philosophers agree on this. This distinction is also reflected in the foundational ontologies; e.g., GFO has Property (the attribution) and Presential/Occurrent (the object or relation), which is refined into atomic and non-atomic attributes [20] that resemble EER's simple and composite attributes.

UML uses the standard definition and meaning of attribute and it is normally modelled 'inside' a class- or association-icon as, e.g., "hasColour:String", although hasColour may be drawn also as an association with at the far end a class-icon for the data type [32]. ER and EER have partial attributes: no ER or EER

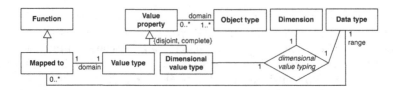

Fig. 4. Value properties, distinguishing between plain and dimensional value types

diagram notation lets the modeller specify the data type of an attribute, be-cause declaring datatypes is carried out at the physical design stage of database development. Although the 'bubble notation' of EER could give an impression that an attribute is an unary entity of itself, the understanding from its formal foundation [9,40] is that the attribute is alike UML's attribute. ER and EER contain two additional types of attributes: composite and multivalued attributes even though both can be remodelled as basic attributes.

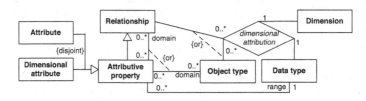

Fig. 5. Simple and dimensional attributes; Dimensional attribute is reified version of the ternary relation dimensional attribution

ORM is said to be "attribute-free" [19], but it does have attributes in the strict sense of the meaning. ORM's value type differs from object type (ORM entity type) in that there is a behind-the-scenes software-generated "mapped to" relationship [10], being mapped_to ↦ ValueType × DataType; e.g., hasColour is asserted between Flower and Colour, and then a mapped_to ↦ Colour × String. The crucial differences between UML's and ORM's attributes, are that ORM uses three entities with two binary relationships where the unary attribution (value type) can be reused, whereas UML collapses it all into one binary rela-tionship and keeps the attribute 'inside' the class.

Finally, ORM's CASE tools lets one specify not only the data type when declaring a value type, but also, if desired, the dimension of the measurement, such as cm or day; thus, adding meaning to the values. This has not been specified in a metamodel or formalised yet. One can model this as a ternary—e.g., as hasHeight ↦ Flower × Integer × cm—or as three relations between object type, and value type, value type and data type, and data type and dimension. For our metamodel, we chose for the more precise ternary relation dimensional value typing, as shown in Fig. 4. For symmetry, we also added its analogue for attributes (Fig. 5), although the UML standard does not mention dimensions explicitly.

4   Conclusions

We presented a unifying metamodel capturing ORM, EER, and UML v2.4.1 with respect to their static, structural, entities and their relationships. Strictly, the only intersection of features among all these CDM languages are role, relationship (including subsumption), and object type. Attributions are represented differently, but, ontologically, they aim to represent the same. Several implicit aspects, such as dimensional attribute and its reusability and relationship versus predicate, have been made explicit.

The complete metamodel with the section for the constraints has been developed, but not described here due to space limitations, and likewise for more detailed justifications for the modeling decisions taken. We will use the metamodel for the formalisation, where it will aid in the comprehension of differences between CDM languages and in the development of tools.

Acknowledgements. This work is based upon research supported by the National Research Foundation of South Africa (Project UID: 80584) and the Argentinian Ministry of Science and Technology.

References

1. Artale, A., Calvanese, D., Kontchakov, R., Ryzhikov, V., Zakharyaschev, M.: Reasoning over extended ER models. In: Parent, C., Schewe, K.-D., Storey, V.C., Thalheim, B. (eds.) ER 2007. LNCS, vol. 4801, pp. 277–292. Springer, Heidelberg (2007)
2. Atzeni, P., Cappellari, P., Torlone, R., Bernstein, P.A., Gianforme, G.: Model-independent schema translation. VLDB Journal 17(6), 1347–1370 (2008)
3. Atzeni, P., Gianforme, G., Cappellari, P.: Data model descriptions and translation signatures in a multi-model framework. AMAI 63, 1–29 (2012)
4. Banal-Estanol, A.: Information-sharing implications of horizontal mergers. International Journal of Industrial Organization 25(1), 31–49 (2007)
5. Berardi, D., Calvanese, D., De Giacomo, G.: Reasoning on UML class diagrams. Artificial Intelligence 168(1-2), 70–118 (2005)
6. Bowers, S., Delcambre, L.M.L.: Using the uni-level description (ULD) to support data-model interoperability. Data & Knowledge Engineering 59(3), 511–533 (2006)
7. Boyd, M., McBrien, P.: Comparing and transforming between data models via an intermediate hypergraph data model. In: Spaccapietra, S. (ed.) Journal on Data Semantics IV. LNCS, vol. 3730, pp. 69–109. Springer, Heidelberg (2005)
8. Calvanese, D., Lenzerini, M., Nardi, D.: Unifying class-based representation formalisms. Journal of Artificial Intelligence Research 11, 199–240 (1999)
9. Chen, P.P.: The entity-relationship model—toward a unified view of data. ACM Transactions on Database Systems 1(1), 9–36 (1976)
10. Committee Members: Information technology – metamodel framework for interoperability (MFI) – Part xx: Metamodel for Fact Based Information Model Registration (Draft release date: April 18, 2012) iSO/IEC WD 19763-xx.02
11. Earl, D.: The classical theory of concepts. In: Internet Encyclopedia of Philosophy (2005), http://www.iep.utm.edu/c/concepts.htm
12. Fillottrani, P.R., Franconi, E., Tessaris, S.: The ICOM 3.0 intelligent conceptual modelling tool and methodology. Semantic Web Journal 3(3), 293–306 (2012)
13. Grundy, J., Venable, J.: Towards an integrated environment for method engineering. In: Proceedings of the IFIP TC8, WG8.1/8.2 Method Engineering 1996 (ME 1996), vol. 1, pp. 45–62 (1996)

14. Guizzardi, G.: Ontological Foundations for Structural Conceptual Models. Phd thesis, University of Twente, The Netherlands. Telematica Instituut Fundamental Research Series No. 15 (2005)
15. Guizzardi, G., Wagner, G.: Using the unified foundational ontology (UFO) as a foundation for general conceptual modeling languages. In: Theory and Applications of Ontology: Computer Applications, pp. 175–196. Springer (2010)
16. Halpin, T.: Objectification of relationships. In: Proc. of EMMSAD 2005, Porto, Portugal, June 13-14. CEUR-WS, pp. 13–14 (2005)
17. Halpin, T.A.: Comparing Metamodels for ER, ORM and UML Data Models. In: Advanced Topics in Database Research, vol. 3, pp. 23–44. Idea Publishing Group, Hershey (2004)
18. Halpin, T.: A logical analysis of information systems: static aspects of the data-oriented perspective. Ph.D. thesis, University of Queensland, Australia (1989)
19. Halpin, T.: Information Modeling and Relational Databases. Morgan Kaufmann Publishers, San Francisco (2001)
20. Herre, H.: General Formal Ontology (GFO): A foundational ontology for conceptual modelling. In: Theory and Applications of Ontology: Computer Applications, ch. 14, pp. 297–345. Springer (2010)
21. ter Hofstede, A.H.M., Proper, H.A.: How to formalize it? formalization principles for information systems development methods. Information and Software Technology 40(10), 519–540 (1998)
22. Kaneiwa, K., Satoh, K.: Consistency checking algorithms for restricted UML class diagrams. In: Dix, J., Hegner, S.J. (eds.) FoIKS 2006. LNCS, vol. 3861, pp. 219–239. Springer, Heidelberg (2006)
23. Keet, C.M.: Prospects for and issues with mapping the Object-Role Modeling language into $\mathcal{DLR}_{ifd}$. In: Proc. of DL 2007. CEUR-WS, vol. 250, pp. 331–338 (2007)
24. Keet, C.M.: Positionalism of relations and its consequences for fact-oriented modelling. In: Meersman, R., Herrero, P., Dillon, T. (eds.) OTM 2009 Workshops. LNCS, vol. 5872, pp. 735–744. Springer, Heidelberg (2009)
25. Keet, C.M.: Enhancing identification mechanisms in UML class diagrams with meaningful keys. In: Proc. of SAICSIT 2011, Cape Town, South Africa, October 3-5. ACM Conference Proceedings, pp. 283–286 (2011)
26. Keet, C.M.: Detecting and revising flaws in OWL object property expressions. In: ten Teije, A., Völker, J., Handschuh, S., Stuckenschmidt, H., d'Acquin, M., Nikolov, A., Aussenac-Gilles, N., Hernandez, N. (eds.) EKAW 2012. LNCS, vol. 7603, pp. 252–266. Springer, Heidelberg (2012)
27. Keet, C.M.: Ontology-driven formal conceptual data modeling for biological data analysis. In: Biological Knowledge Discovery Handbook: Preprocessing, Mining and Postprocessing of Biological Data, ch. 6, Wiley (in press, 2013)
28. Keet, C.M., Artale, A.: Representing and reasoning over a taxonomy of part-whole relations. Applied Ontology 3(1-2), 91–110 (2008)
29. Leo, J.: Modeling relations. Journal of Philosophical Logic 37, 353–385 (2008)
30. MacLeod, M.C., Rubenstein, E.M.: Universals. In: The Internet Encyclopedia of Philosophy (2005), http://www.iep.utm.edu/u/universa.htm
31. Mendes Calo, K., Cenci, K.M., Fillottrani, P.R., Estevez, E.C.: Information sharing-benefits. Journal of Computer Science & Technology 12(2) (2012)
32. Object Management Group: Superstructure specification. Standard 2.4.1, Object Management Group (2012), http://www.omg.org/spec/UML/2.4.1/
33. Odell, J.: Advanced Object-Oriented Analysis & Design using UML. Cambridge University Press, Cambridge (1998)
34. Queralt, A., Teniente, E.: Decidable reasoning in UML schemas with constraints. In: Bellahsène, Z., Léonard, M. (eds.) CAiSE 2008. LNCS, vol. 5074, pp. 281–295. Springer, Heidelberg (2008)

35. Rector, A.: Modularisation of domain ontologies implemented in description logics and related formalisms including OWL. In: Proc. of K-CAP 2003, pp. 121–129 (2003)
36. Rosenthal, A., Mork, P., Li, M.H., Stanford, J., Koester, D., Reynolds, P.: Cloud computing: a new business paradigm for biomedical information sharing. Journal of Biomedical Informatics 43(2), 342–353 (2010)
37. Smith, B.: Beyond concepts, or: Ontology as reality representation. In: Varzi, A., Vieu, L. (eds.) Proc. of FOIS 2004, pp. 73–84. IOS Press, Amsterdam (2004)
38. Song, I.Y., Chen, P.P.: Entity relationship model. In: Liu, L., Özsu, M.T. (eds.) Encyclopedia of Database Systems, vol. 1, pp. 1003–1009. Springer (2009)
39. Swoyer, C.: Properties. In: Zalta, E.N. (ed.) The Stanford Encyclopedia of Philosophy. Stanford, winter 2000 edn. (2000), http://plato.stanford.edu/archives/win2000/entries/properties/
40. Thalheim, B.: Extended entity relationship model. In: Liu, L., Özsu, M.T. (eds.) Encyclopedia of Database Systems, vol. 1, pp. 1083–1091. Springer (2009)
41. Venable, J., Grundy, J.: Integrating and supporting Entity Relationship and Object Role Models. In: Papazoglou, M.P. (ed.) ER 1995 and OOER 1995. LNCS, vol. 1021, pp. 318–328. Springer, Heidelberg (1995)
42. Zhu, N., Grundy, J., Hosking, J.: Pounamu: a metatool for multi-view visual language environment construction. In: IEEE Conf. on Visual Languages and Human-Centric Computing (2004)

Appendix: Naming Conventions. The following naming conventions are used, in the order of Metamodel, UML v2.4.1, EER, ORM/FBM. Where no value is given, that element is absent.

- Relationship; association, can be 2-ary according to the MOF 2.4.1, but also >2-ary [32]; relationship, ≥2-ary; atomic/compound fact type, ≥1-ary.
- Predicate; ; ; predicate.
- Role; association end / member end; component of a relationship; role.
- Entity type; classifier; ; object type.
- Object type; class; entity type; non-lexical object type / entity type.
- Attribute; attribute; attribute, but without a data type in the diagram; (represented differently).
- Dimensional attribute; (no recording of dimension); ; (represented differently).
- Composite attribute; a property can be a composite of another property ; composite attribute; implicitly present by adding new roles.
- Multivalued attribute; ; multivalued attribute; .
- Value type; ; ; lexical object type / value type, without dimension.
- Dimensional value type; ; ; lexical object type / value type, with dimension.
- Data type; Data type, LiteralSpecification; ; data type.
- Object subtype; subclass; subtype; subtype.
- Sub-relationship; subsetting or subtyping of association; subtyping the relationship ; subset constraint on fact type.
- Nested object type; association class; associative entity type; objectified fact type.
- Weak object type; ; weak entity type; .
- Composite aggregate; composite aggregation; ; .
- Shared aggregate; shared aggregation; ; .

The Foundational Ontology Library ROMULUS

Zubeida Casmod Khan and C. Maria Keet

School of Mathematics, Statistics, and Computer Science,
University of KwaZulu-Natal and UKZN/CSIR-Meraka Centre for Artificial
Intelligence Research, South Africa
zkhan@csir.co.za, keet@ukzn.ac.za

Abstract. A purpose of a foundational ontology is to solve interoperability issues among domain ontologies and they are used for ontology-driven conceptual data modelling. Multiple foundational ontologies have been developed in recent years, and most of them are available in several versions. This has re-introduced the interoperability problem, increased the need for a coordinated and structured comparison and elucidation of modelling decisions, and raised the requirement for software infrastructure to address this. We present here a basic step in that direction with the Repository of Ontologies for MULtiple USes, ROMULUS, which is the first online library of machine-processable, modularised, aligned, and logic-based merged foundational ontologies. In addition to the typical features of a model repository, it has a foundational ontology recommender covering features of six foundational ontologies, tailor-made modules for easier reuse, and a catalogue of interesting mappable and non-mappable elements among the BFO, GFO and DOLCE foundational ontologies.

1   Introduction

It has been 15 years since the introduction of the notion of ontology-driven information systems [1], which entails ontology-driven conceptual data modelling [2,3,4,5]. Ontology-driven conceptual data modelling uses principles and solutions from Ontology (philosophy) and ontologies (as artifacts) to improve the quality of a conceptual data model and refine its language, which therewith improves the quality of the information system. This can be applied to individual aspects by devising solutions to modelling problems in conceptual data models—e.g., part whole relations in conceptual models, aided by a foundational ontology [4]—as well as more broadly to modify a conceptual data modelling language's metamodel thanks to a foundational ontology (e.g., [3]). However, one solution or extension may use, say, the DOLCE foundational ontology [6] for refining UML's aggregation association [4], another could be informed by the UFO foundational ontology [3], and yet another by GFO [7], but it is not clear whether DOLCE, UFO, and GFO are compatible. Proliferation of modelling improvements, then, end up to be incompatible if the improvements rest on different philosophical assumptions represented in different foundational ontologies. Moreover, besides DOLCE, GFO, and UFO, other foundational ontologies have been developed over the years, such as SUMO [8], YAMATO [9], and BFO

A. Cuzzocrea and S. Maabout (Eds.): MEDI 2013, LNCS 8216, pp. 200–211, 2013.

[http://www.ifomis.org/bfo]. This potential for incompatibilities for ontologically well-founded conceptual data models has been recognised in the field of ontologies where they serve integration of domain ontologies, and it has been observed already within the Semantic Web setting, where ontology developers use their preferred foundational ontology that differ in various aspects, which therewith exhibit a semantic interoperability problem for domain ontologies.

A solution to such semantic issues has been proposed as the "WonderWeb Foundational Ontologies Library" (WFOL) in 2003, so that one should be able to commit to different but systematically related (modules of) foundational ontologies [6]. However, this library has not been implemented due to theoretical and implementation limitations. The main theoretical hurdle is alignment of foundational ontologies. Implementation limitations were primarily due to the absence of a common representation language, and there was scant stable software infrastructure for ontologies. Thanks to a range of advances in the meantime, the solvability of the implementation issues is within reach but has not yet been realised, whilst foundational ontology alignment and mapping is at the early stages. The creation of a software-based model repository is a necessary first step to manage these issues so as to have a one-stop shop for foundational ontologies and therewith foster coordinated, or at least interchangeable, ontology-driven conceptual data modelling with broadly usable results, as well as enabling examination of interchangeability of a foundational ontology that is mapped to a domain ontology.

We propose to solve practical shortcomings through the creation of the first such online library of machine-processable, aligned and merged, foundational ontologies: the Repository of Ontologies for MULtiple USes ROMULUS. ROMULUS has features typical of Open Ontology Repositories [10], such as browsing the ontology and standardized metadata. Moreover, it incorporates a new web-based version of ONSET [11] that helps selecting a foundational ontology, it contains the included foundational ontologies' OWLized version in whole and as various types of modules, and it contains both the logic-based pairwise alignments of DOLCE, BFO, and GFO, as well as a catalogue of individual alignments that are not mappable due to other axioms. ROMULUS is online accessible at http://www.thezfiles.co.za/ROMULUS/.

In the remainder of the paper, we first describe several motivating examples for conceptual data models in Section 2. The design and features of ROMULUS are presented in Section 3, and compared with related works on model repositories with respect to ontologies in Section 4. We discuss ROMULUS and the relevance of some mappings for ontology-driven conceptual data modelling in Section 5 and we conclude in Section 6.

2   A Selection of Motivating Examples

In the following motivating examples, the purpose is not to discuss which way is better for modelling a universe of discourse or refining a modelling language, but instead to demonstrate *i)* consequences of a modelling choice, *ii)* the need for systematically related elements of foundational ontologies, and *iii)* that a foundational ontology library such as ROMULUS does assist with this.

Let us take as first example UML classes and EER or ORM entity types on the one hand, and a foundational ontology's counterpart to that, which may be subsumed by Particular for instances or Universal for kinds or 'classes' of particulars. For instance, DOLCE is a foundational ontology of particulars that has entities (categories), such as Endurant (an entity wholly present at a time), Process, and Amount of Matter (stuff, like water and gold) [6]. BFO is an ontology of universals, which has, Independent Continuant (alike Endurant), Process, and Fiat Object Part. UFO [3] and GFO [7] are ontologies of particulars *and* universals: one of the first distinctions in the hierarchy is between Particular/Individual and Universal, where the former subsumes, among others, gfo:Presential, gfo:Role, ufo:Set, and ufo:Quality, and the latter gfo:Persistant and ufo:RigidSortal. Does it matter for conceptual data modelling? It can, and, moreover, does in the case where one wants to align ontological principles of a conceptual data modelling language to a foundational ontology. For instance, UFO has Quality (the ontological version of an attribute) as a subclass of Moment, and a Quality Universal as subclass of Moment Universal [3]. GFO's Property is similar in idea, but is a subclass of Individual, and is unrelated to moments. That is, similar ideas are actually quite distinct. A different issue is that of GFO's Amount_of_substrate (like water, gold) and DOLCE's Amount of Matter, which convey a similar notion as Guizzardi's "stuff universal" for which was proposed a stereotype ≪quantity≫ that is a sortal that is a universal in [12], but UFO—used in another extension [3]—does not consider amounts of matter, and nor does BFO, i.e., stuff does not exist according to UFO and BFO, so we cannot identify and model it. This results in a situation where aligning EER or UML to DOLCE or GFO would permit us to create a stereotype to denote such entities and relate them with subQuantityOf [4,12], but not with UFO or BFO.

These examples may seem confusing to a reader, for one does not have an overview at hand of each of the foundational ontologies' content and structure. And, perhaps, for some alignments, it does not make a difference which foundational ontology is chosen because not all its entities are used in such an alignment. However, we only can know this for sure if we have insight in the systematically assessed mappings between the entities in the various foundational ontologies. For instance, DOLCE's and GFO's notion of amounts of matter are comparable also when taking into account the structure of the ontology, but seemingly similar entities can end up not to be so: mapping dolce:set to gfo:Set results in an inconsistency, because DOLCE has it as a type of Abstract that is a Particular (equivalent to gfo:Individual), whereas gfo:Set is disjoint from gfo:Individual. UFO's Set is alike DOLCE's set—an AbstractParticular—so, by transitivity, one can infer that ufo:Set and gfo:Set are ontologically distinct entities as well.

In addition to the need for a systematic investigation into possible alignments and mappings to foster the possibility that the various extensions to conceptual data modelling languages are practically compatible, we need ways to at least quickly check that, and, where relevant for the application scenario, swap between one or the other foundational ontology where possible. Although this can be carried out and maintained on paper, software-based mapped ontologies where the mappings are at least guaranteed not to lead to any inconsistency simplify this process. This, then, could feed into a software-based content negotiation method. Likewise, a catalogue of entities that cannot be mapped serves as an easy online reference of incompatibilities.

3   A Repository of Ontologies for MULtiple USes

In line with our goal of creating a foundational ontology repository, we have designed and implemented a web-based software system ROMULUS in order to allow modellers to publicly access and benefit from all the functionality of the repository. In this section, we describe the requirements, design, and features of the Repository of Ontologies for MULtiple USes.

Before the actual design, requirements were formulated. The functional requirements are briefly described here, of which the first three are adapted from the original WFOL proposal in [6]. The library must provide a high-level view of the foundational ontologies with only the most general entities common to all implemented foundational ontologies, it must provide a comparison of implemented foundational ontologies, and ontology metadata must be available [6]. In addition, to serve interoperability and interchangeability, basic ontology mediation must be present, including alignment, mapping, and merging of the foundational ontologies. To facilitate usability, the foundational ontologies in the repository must be modularised, there must be easy and effective online ontology browsing and searching, renderings in human-readable views of each foundational ontology module must be available, and there must be an ontology download facility.

3.1   Design of ROMULUS

The three main components of ROMULUS are the web server (used to execute HTML pages and PHP scripts), the Tomcat server (used to execute JSP pages) and the MySQL database (used to store ontology alignments, ontology metadata and users' ontology selection results and to assist with search functions). The interaction of the components in ROMULUS is shown in Fig. 1, and we describe here the four conceptually different aspects of the design: the front-end features, ontology metadata, the ontologies themselves that have been modularised to meet and anticipate further requests for partial foundational ontologies suitable for a task, and ontology selection.

Front-End Features. The modular design of the foundational ontology library is met through different tabs in the user interface of the repository. For online ontology browsing, WebProtégé [13] is used, which requires a tomcat server. There are separate HTML pages with tables and lists for the comparison of foundational ontologies for the different categories of criteria[1], for the

---

[1] There is a page for each category: ontological commitments, representation languages, software engineering properties, subject domains and applications.

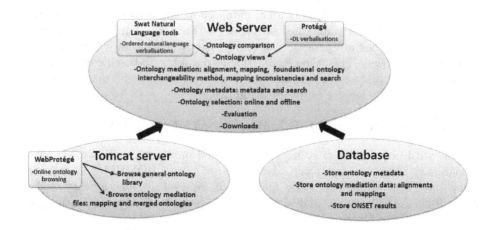

Fig. 1. The interaction of ROMULUS's components

user-readable version of the alignments of the ontologies and, for the metadata. SWAT Natural Language tools [14] was used to generate the HTML pages of the verbalisation of each ontology module in a structured natural language format. The Protégé-generated Description Logic axioms of each ontology module are available as pdf files. ROMULUS's alignments and mappings are stored in a database and rendered as HTML tables. Similar to the ontology browsing page, WebProtégé is used to easily access all the mappings and the merged ontologies. The foundational ONtology Selection and Explanation Tool ONSET [11] has its own tab where it may be executed online and downloaded for offline usage. The experimental foundational ontology interchangeability method listed in Fig. 1 can be accessed at ROMULUS's foundational ontology interchangeability page.

Ontology Metadata. Additional data pertaining to foundational ontologies are required to assist ontology developers with reusing an ontology effectively. Metadata values for each original, modularised, mapped and merged ontology module are provided in ROMULUS. In order to facilitate interoperability with other ontology repositories, we considered the Ontology Metadata Vocabulary (OMV) [15], which is a general OWL-formalised metadata vocabulary, and OM^{2}R metadata model [16], which is aimed at ontology mapping reuse. ROMULUS uses OMV and OM^{2}R, as well as its own metadata for each foundational ontology. The additional metadata not available in OMV and OM^{2}R concerns modularity with module type (e.g., OWL 2 profile; see below) and original ontology, and mediation with original ontologies that are mediated and alignment type. For this first version of ROMULUS, we store the metadata in ROMULUS's centralised back-end database together with the alignments and mappings (Fig. 2), which we render to human-readable pages describing the metadata for each ontology. Storing the metadata in a database makes it easier to search through it, and we hope to minimise duplication. We intend to integrate the OWL version of the metadata in the ontologies in a future version.

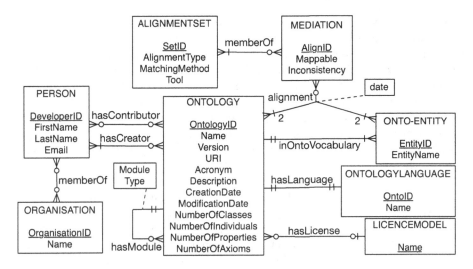

Fig. 2. ER diagram of ROMULUS's database regarding ontology mediation, extending (a subset of) OMV and OM^{2}R on, notably, mediation, entity, and module

Modularised Ontologies. Ontology modularisation deals with creating or altering an ontology to be broken down into modules for specific functions. The idea behind it is to hide unnecessary detail when not required. Modularity is important in that it aids in ontology maintenance, publication, validation and processing. Factors pertaining to modularization are discussed elsewhere [17,18], and modules are created to organise and manage domain coverage, isolate branches of a taxonomy, extract a particular subject domain and/or theory, to isolate patterns, assist with scalable automated reasoning, or to reduce the cognitive overload. Such modularization ideas have been incorporated in ROMULUS on an experimental basis.

The following types of modules have been created:

- *Separate branches of 3D and 4D entities in the ontologies*: For when one wants to keep the entities that exist as a whole at all times (3D entities) separate from entities with temporal parts that unfold over time (4D entities);
- *Isolated branches of taxonomies of the ontologies for available subject domains support*: A module can be used for a specific subject domain; e.g., biomedical, business.
- *More/less detailed versions of the ontologies*: For when one does not need the entire functionality of the ontology, variants of an ontology with fewer/more entities, properties, and axioms; e.g., gfo-basic and gfo-full.
- *OWL 2 profiles*: For when one wants to improve the efficiency of reasoning, modules in different expressive fragments of OWL 2; e.g., OWL 2 EL.

OWL Module extractor [19], Swoop [20] and Protégé have been considered for ontology modularisation of the foundational ontologies. OWL Module extractor and Swoop use a logic based analysis of the axioms only and this resulted in large modules similar to the original ontologies. For this reason, we could not apply

OWL Module extractor and Swoop to create modules. In DOLCE, endurant and perdurant are linked by a participation relation, making it difficult to separate them into separate hierarchies. In order to create modules of these types, it was necessary to manually remove some of the axioms relating the two entities. We encountered a similar problem when modularising DOLCE to be a module without quality and qualia. Protégé generated smaller modules according to the user's input, in most cases, but some unnecessary entities were still present after using Protégé and they were manually modularised.

In addition to the 'full' versions of the three ontologies, the following ones were newly created:

- New DOLCE modules: DOLCEEndurants, DOLCE-Perdurants, DOLCENo-QualityAndQualia, DOLCE-EL (trimmed to what can be represented in OWL 2 EL and DOLCE-QL);
- New BFO modules: BFOContinuants, BFOOccurrents, BFO-EL-QL-RL;
- New GFO modules: GFOATO (based on the Abstract Top Level layer), GFOACO (based on the Abstract Core Level), GFONoOccurrents, GFONoPersistantsAndPresentials, GFOBasicEL, GFOBasicQL.

Given that these modules are proper fragments of the original ones that were aligned, mapped, and merged, their respective remaining mappings for the modules are also available in ROMULUS.

Foundational Ontology Selection. It is worthwhile to include an ontology selector tool in ROMULUS in order to bridge the process of foundational ontology selection with the features offered by the repository. ONSET is such a—and, to date, the only—foundational ontology selection and explanation tool that was designed to aid the user with the task of selecting an appropriate foundational ontology for domain ontology development [11]. Significant changes and improvements have been made to v2.0 of ONSET, with an aim to integrate it in ROMULUS. Instead of a stand-alone jar file, there is now a web-based version, which has access to ROMULUS's centralised database (Users still can download the offline version v1.2 of ONSET, without linkage to ROMULUS's features, available in ROMULUS's ontology selection page). This also provides for the new feature that users can save their ontology selection results both locally in a CSV file format, and to let ONSET store a copy of it in ROMULUS's database, which can be used for further analysis and investigation with regard to foundational ontology usage and selection. A condensed conceptual data model for this is displayed in Fig. 3 (the details of Results and ConflictingReasons are not shown due to space limitations). ONSET v2.0 also provides links to features in ROMULUS, such as its modules and metadata for a particular foundational ontology. Finally, we added the YAMATO and GIST foundational ontologies to ONSET v2.0, therewith providing the user with more possible foundational ontology choices (the other ones in v1.2 are BFO, DOLCE, GFO, and SUMO). Use cases of ONSET can be found at ROMULUS's ontology selection page.

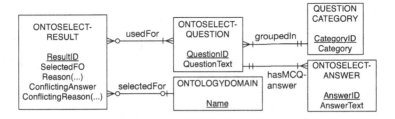

Fig. 3. Summarised ER diagram of ONSET's saved data

4   Related Works

We compare ROMULUS to several other ontology repositories, and subsequently discuss some considerations for a foundational ontology library. A comparison was conducted with other repositories, including OOR [10], BioPortal [21], TONES [22], COLORE [23] and Ontohub [24], which is summarised in Table 1.

In terms of repository vision, ROMULUS is a repository of foundational ontologies. It is closed in that users cannot upload their own ontologies or data, but they are encouraged to download the ontologies and data on the repository. BioPortal, OOR and Ontohub are an open repositories where users are encouraged to upload their ontology projects, contributions, and download resources. BioPortal is specifically a repository of biomedical ontologies. TONES is aimed at being a central location for ontologies that will be helpful for application developers for testing purposes. It is a closed repository where users are only allowed to download the ontologies and view some metadata. COLORE aims to be an open repository of Common Logic ontologies to aid in ontology evaluation and integration techniques, and to support the design, evaluation, and application of ontologies in first-order logic.

From the comparison of functionality, ROMULUS provides advanced functionality in most of the criteria used in this evaluation. It also provides features that were not available in other repositories, which therefore merited the development of a new repository. These include complete metadata for each ontology that also includes metadata about modularity and ontology mediation beyond the standard metadata vocabularies, carefully analysed alignments and merged ontologies, and a foundational ontology selection and explanation tool for guidance to select the most relevant one.

5   Discussion

ROMULUS combines various technologies to provide a range of features and it is the first realisation of the "WFOL" envisioned since 2003. It meets the main goals of the WFOL [6], described in Section 3: 1) it provides a higher-level ontology, FFO, containing only the common entities of DOLCE, BFO and GFO ontologies, which could be used as a starting point for ontology development;

Table 1. Comparison of ROMULUS's features with those of other repositories

	ROMULUS	BioPortal and OOR	TONES	COLORE	Ontohub
Browse	Uses WebProtégé. Hierarchical ontology view. Displays classes, object properties, individuals and annotations of an ontology.	Hierarchical ontology view. Displays classes local and class neighbourhood. Has advanced visualization support.	Browsing is currently unavailable.	No support.	Sequential ontology view. Lists of classes, properties, individuals and sentences.
Mediation	Alignments and mappings between its ontologies, merged and higher-level foundational ontologies, mapping inconsistencies and a method for foundational ontology interchangeability.	Some mappings between ontologies. Users may specify mappings.	No support.	No support.	No support.
Metadata	Metadata lists for ontologies based on OMV, OM²R, and own model.	Metadata lists for ontologies based on OMV, but some missing metadata.	Metadata for metrics of each ontology.	Metadata exists in the ontology files.	Metadata lists for ontologies, but some missing metadata.
Ontology selection	ONSET, a foundational ontology selection tool, available to download and execute locally.	An ontology recommender system that allows one to calculate which ontologies are most relevant for a corpus.	No support.	No support.	No support.
Search	Allows a user to search for alignments, mappings and metadata.	Advanced search. Allows a user to search for entity names, ids, synonyms, properties and filter search.	No support.	No support.	Search for ontology name and ontology symbol.
Ontology view	Views in description logics and natural language.	No support.	No support.	Views in common logic.	No support.
Comparison	Ontology comparison in terms of different categories of criteria.	No support.	No support.	No support.	No support.
Ontology access	Users can view and download ontologies and tools.	Users can upload, edit own ontologies and download ontologies.	Users can download ontologies.	Users can view and download ontologies.	Users can upload, edit own ontologies and download ontologies.

2) it is a reference point for comparisons between different ontological approaches of selected foundational ontologies; 3) it provides a common framework for analyzing, harmonizing and integrating existing ontologies and metadata standards thanks to its criteria comparison of selected foundational ontologies, alignments, mapping and merged ontologies, and extensive metadata for each ontology. Also, it is rigorous, including a logic-based approach, and extensively researched. In addition to these WFOL requirements, ROMULUS provides modular and mediated foundational ontologies, online browsing of the ontologies, online and offline foundational ontology selection and download facilities.

The results of the ontology mediation are partially based on a preliminary ontological analysis and partially based on the formalizations of the respective foundational ontologies. Nevertheless, there were still unexpected inconsistencies of entities and of relationships that one would consider well-established ontologically, such as a mathematical set. We do not aim to solve such inconsistencies here. Instead, ROMULUS with its ontology mediation results is meant as a systematic foundation for such an investigation, and it provides starting points for deeper ontological analyses to possibly resolve them. To aid such investigations, additional features could be added to ROMULUS, such as a wiki-like discussion page for each 'alignment with issues'.

From an ontology engineering viewpoint, ROMULUS is a major step toward foundational ontology interchangeability, because a prerequisite for this are the mapped ontologies. Meaning negotiation between two domain ontologies that each are linked to a different foundational ontology through a merged ontology of those two foundational ontologies has now become something within reach. Although the technologies might seem 'pedestrian' now, they were not until recently, and it is principally the realisation of OOR features extended for foundational ontologies that makes ROMULUS a novelty.

Revisiting FO Interoperability for Conceptual Data Models. Instead of cumbersome manual analyses as described in Section 2, we now can conduct a quick look-up in ROMULUS. For instance, Set is in the list of logical inconsistencies, so we do not have to look further. This is true for parthood as well, or: whichever foundational ontology one chooses, it is never truly the same with any of the others. This information is available now at one's fingertips, compared to reading through the foundational ontology's respective documentation: UML's aggregation association is typically mapped into a part-whole relation, which can be parthood in the sense of mereology or meronymy [4]. Considering for the sake of example only the mereology usage of the aggregation association, we would have to specify which mereological theory it would fit in with. DOLCE uses the AGEM theory where proper parthood is irreflexive, asymmetric and transitive, BFO's Relation Ontology [25] has only transitivity as characteristic of proper parthood, and the higher-order logic version of BFO itself is founded on a constellation of parthood theories. Then, if we were to refine UML's metamodel, it does make a difference which foundational ontology we use for the exercise, because the (logical) implications will be different.

Conversely, DOLCE's Amount of Matter does not appear in the list of inconsistencies, but instead is in the mappings with GFO. If one is willing to be slightly lenient on the particular versus universal issue, then the foundational ontologies' version of attributes can be matched among all three foundational ontologies, using the equivalences among Quality and Property. This is now readily available with the pairwise mapped, online, ontologies and searchable mappings and inconsistencies.

6   Conclusions

We presented a core step in the direction of addressing interoperability issues with the Repository of Ontologies for MULtiple USes, ROMULUS, software infrastructure. This is the first online library of machine-processable, modularised, aligned, and logic-based merged foundational ontologies. In addition to the typical features of a model repository, ROMULUS has a foundational ontology recommender covering features of six foundational ontologies that is integrated with ROMULUS' features and it has tailor-made modules for easier reuse. Most important for the actual ontology-driven conceptual data modelling, are its features and site content with a catalogue of interesting mappable and non-mappable elements among the BFO, GFO and DOLCE foundational ontologies, and the pairwise machine-processable mapped ontologies.

We are currently adding extended search features, and the preliminary user evaluation of the alignments (available in ROMULUS already), will be extended with community discussion pages. Also, we hope to gather sufficient voluntarily saved ontology selections to analyse them and find patterns in selection criteria.

Acknowledgements. This work is based upon research supported by the National Research Foundation of South Africa (Project UID: 80584) and the Argentinian Ministry of Science and Technology.

References

1. Guarino, N.: Formal ontology and information systems. In: Proc. of FOIS 1998. IOS Press (1998)
2. Guarino, N., Guizzardi, G.: In the defense of ontological foundations for conceptual modeling. Scandinavian Journal of Information Systems 18(1), 9 (2006)
3. Guizzardi, G., Wagner, G.: Using the unified foundational ontology (UFO) as a foundation for general conceptual modeling languages. In: Theory and Applications of Ontology: Computer Applications, pp. 175–196. Springer (2010)
4. Keet, C.M., Artale, A.: Representing and reasoning over a taxonomy of part-whole relations. Applied Ontology 3(1-2), 91–110 (2008)
5. Keet, C.M.: Ontology-driven formal conceptual data modeling for biological data analysis. In: Biological Knowledge Discovery Handbook: Preprocessing, Mining and Postprocessing of Biological Data. Wiley (in press, 2013)
6. Masolo, C., Borgo, S., Gangemi, A., Guarino, N., Oltramari, A.: Ontology library. WonderWeb Deliverable D18 (ver. 1.0, 31-12-2003) (2003), http://wonderweb.semanticweb.org
7. Herre, H.: General Formal Ontology (GFO): A foundational ontology for conceptual modelling. In: Theory and Applications of Ontology: Computer Applications, pp. 297–345. Springer (2010)

8. Niles, I., Pease, A.: Towards a standard upper ontology. In: Proc. of FOIS 2001, Ogunquit, Maine, October 17-19, IOS Press (2001)

9. Mizoguchi, R.: YAMATO: yet another more advanced top-level ontology. In: Proc. of AOW 2010. CRPIT, pp. 1–16. ACS, Sydney (2010)

10. Baclawski, K., Schneider, T.: The open ontology repository initiative: Requirements and research challenges. In: Proceedings of the Workshop on Collaborative Construction, Management and Linking of Structured Knowledge, Washington DC, USA, October 25. CEUR-WS, vol. 514 (2009)

11. Khan, Z., Keet, C.M.: ONSET: Automated foundational ontology selection and explanation. In: ten Teije, A., Völker, J., Handschuh, S., Stuckenschmidt, H., d'Acquin, M., Nikolov, A., Aussenac-Gilles, N., Hernandez, N. (eds.) EKAW 2012. LNCS, vol. 7603, pp. 237–251. Springer, Heidelberg (2012)

12. Guizzardi, G.: On the representation of quantities and their parts in conceptual modeling. In: Proc. of FOIS 2010, Toronto, May 11-14. IOS Press (2010)

13. Tudorache, T., Vendetti, J., Noy, N.F.: Web-Protege: A lightweight OWL ontology editor for the web. In: Proc. of OWLED 2008. CEUR-WS, vol. 432 (2008)

14. Third, A., Williams, S., Power, R.: OWL to English: A tool for generating organised easily-navigated hypertexts from ontologies. In: Proc. of ISWC 2011(Poster/Demo), Bonn, Germany, October 23-27. Springer (2011)

15. Hartmann: J., Sure, Y., Haase, P., Palma, R., del Carmen Suárez-Figueroa, M.: OMV - Ontology Metadata Vocabulary. In: Ontology Patterns for the Semantic Web (OPSW), Galway, Ireland (November 2005)

16. Thomas, H., Brennan, R., O'Sullivan, D.: Using the OM2R meta-data model for ontology mapping reuse for the ontology alignment challenge - A case study. In: 7th Intl. Ws. on Ontology Matching (OM 2012). CEUR-WS, vol. 946 (2012)

17. d'Aquin, M., Schlicht, A., Stuckenschmidt, H., Sabou, M.: Criteria and evaluation for ontology modularization techniques. In: Stuckenschmidt, H., Parent, C., Spaccapietra, S. (eds.) Modular Ontologies. LNCS, vol. 5445, pp. 67–89. Springer, Heidelberg (2009)

18. Borgo, S.: Goals of modularity: A voice from the foundational viewpoint. In: Proc. of WoMO 2011. FAIA, vol. 230, pp. 1–6. IOS Press (2011)

19. Cuenca Grau, B., Horrocks, I., Kazakov, Y., Sattler, U.: Modular reuse of ontologies: Theory and practice. J. of Artificial Intelligence Research 31, 273–318 (2008)

20. Kalyanpur, A., Parsia, B., Sirin, E., Grau, B.C., Hendler, J.A.: Swoop: A web ontology editing browser. Journal of Web Semantics 4(2), 144–153 (2006)

21. Whetzel, P.L., et al.: Bioportal: enhanced functionality via new web services from the national center for biomedical ontology to access and use ontologies in software applications. Nucleic Acids Research 39(Web-Server-Issue), 541–545 (2011)

22. Vale, D.C., et al.: The TONES ontology repository, http://owl.cs.manchester.ac.uk/repository/browser (accessed on December 22, 2012)

23. Gruninger, M.: COLORE: Common logic ontology repository (2009), http://ontolog.cim3.net/file/work/OOR-Ontolog-Panel/2009-08-06Ontology-%?Repository-Research-Issues/Colore--MichaelGruninger20090806.pdf

24. Lange, C., Mossakowski, T., Kutz, O., Galinski, C., Grüninger, M., Couto Vale, D.: The distributed ontology language (DOL): Use cases, syntax, and extensibility. In: Proc. of Terminology and Knowledge Engineering, TKE 2012 (2012)

25. Smith, B., et al.: Relations in biomedical ontologies. Genome Biol. 6(5), 46 (2005)

Transforming Formal Specification Constructs into Diagrammatic Notations

Kobamelo Moremedi[1] and John Andrew van der Poll[2]

[1] School of Computing, University of South Africa, Pretoria, South Africa
kobamelomoremedi@yahoo.com
[2] Graduate School of Business Leadership, University of South Africa, Midrand, South Africa
vdpolja@unisa.ac.za

Abstract. Specification plays a vital role in software engineering to facilitate the development of highly dependable software. Various techniques may be used for specification work. Z is a formal specification language that is based on a strongly-typed fragment of Zermelo-Fraenkel set theory and first-order logic to provide for precise and unambiguous specifications. While diagrammatic specification languages may lack precision, they may, owing to their visual characteristics be a lucrative option for advocates of semi-formal specification techniques. In this paper we investigate to what extent formal constructs, e.g. Z may be transformed into diagrammatic notations. Several diagrammatic notations are considered and combined for this purpose.

Keywords: Diagrammatic notation, Formal specification, Euler diagrams, Spider diagrams, Venn-Pierce diagrams, Z.

1 Introduction

The correctness of software has a significant impact in controlling and delivering the essential, and often safety critical services that we depend on, such as health care; transport (airlines and railways); and telecommunication [1]. Specification is a vital activity aimed at producing a system that will meet the user requirements stated during the initial stages of software development. The resultant specification is used in software development to provide a clear communication of requirements documentation and system objects among stakeholders involved in the software project. Hence, it is desirable that a specification be accessible to intended users in order to facilitate the development of quality software.

Various specification techniques have been developed to specify software systems. The Z notation is a formal text-based language that has a successful history of being able to provide for precise specifications in the development of critical systems [2]. The IBM CICS system is one of the large projects in which Z was used successfully [17]. The use of Z increased the quality and reliability of the system [21]. Z is based on first-order logic and a strongly typed fragment of Zermelo-Fraenkel set theory [19]. Its basic construct is the schema which is used to structure the specification. System operations are collected into schemas to describe the state of the system and how it changes [6], [20], [21].

A. Cuzzocrea and S. Maabout (Eds.): MEDI 2013, LNCS 8216, pp. 212–224, 2013.
© Springer-Verlag Berlin Heidelberg 2013

Diagrams, as a semi-formal notation are widely applicable in conveying important ideas, and in Computer Science they can be used to specify software. For example, 'spider diagrams' have been used in the specification of failures of safety critical systems, ontology representations, database search queries and file system management [5], [7], [10], [12].The familiar Venn diagram has often been used as a heuristic tool in mathematics and logic, facilitating the formalization of the relevant idea. However, Shin challenged the view that diagrams could not yield formal specifications by developing two sound and complete reasoning systems of Venn diagrams [4], [7].

Although diagrams (as a semi-formal notation) lack the precision of a formal notation, e.g. spider diagrams, their value has been recognized recently, in aspects of software specification, reasoning and information visualization. Consequently, this paper is aimed at investigating the extent to which diagrams can capture the structures and operations of discrete structures omnipresent in Z specifications. Translating semi-formal notations (e.g.) UML to variants of Z have been done before [18], but since UML may be viewed as being at a 'higher' level than the core set-theoretic structures and operations on which a Z specification is based, our translations are based on closed-curve constructs, namely, Euler-, Venn-, Spider- and Pierce diagrams.

The layout of the paper follows: Different types of diagrams are discussed briefly in Section 2 and a small Z example is given in Section 3. Section 4 identifies a number of set-theoretic structures and operations in Z and we show how these may be specified using diagrams. Section 5 presents an analysis and directions for future work in this area.

2   Diagrammatic Notations

Different types of diagrammatic languages can be used for specifying software and in this paper we focus on diagrams based on closed curves.

2.1   Euler Diagrams

Euler diagrams were introduced in the 17th century by Leonard Euler. This notation uses 'contours' to represent the relationship between sets [7], [15]. A contour is a closed circle used in a diagram to represent a set. Most diagrammatic languages emerged from Euler diagrams [12]. **Fig.1** denotes that sets A and B are disjoint and C is a subset of A. The non-existence of elements is used to indicate an empty set. For example, no elements are indicated for set C, hence it's empty.

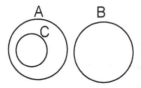

Fig. 1. An Euler diagram

2.2   Venn Diagrams

In 1880, John Venn developed Venn diagrams that are similar to Euler diagrams. Instead of missing elements, Venn diagrams use shading to denote an empty set. Venn diagrams use overlapping circles for representing relationships among sets [3]. **Fig.2** shows an example of Venn diagrams drawn with three overlapping contours. For example, the region C – (A ∪ B) could be shaded, indicating it is empty. Venn diagrams may become hard to interpret or draw once the diagram contains more than three contours.

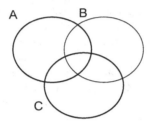

Fig. 2. A 3-contoured Venn diagram

2.3   Pierce Diagrams

Pierce introduced existential graphs by adding X-sequences on Venn diagrams to represent disjunctive information [7], [9]. Pierce diagrams, also known as 'Venn-Pierce diagrams', extend Venn diagrams by adding syntax that represents existential statements in diagrams. Pierce used 'x' instead of the existence of elements, and 'o' instead of shading, to represent an empty set [13]. The Pierce diagram in **Fig.3** shows that A – B = ∅ and A ∩ B ≠ ∅.

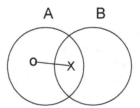

Fig. 3. A Pierce diagram

2.4   Spider Diagrams

Spider diagrams were inspired by Pierce-, Venn- and Euler diagrams. A 'spider' denotes the presence of one or more elements in a set. Spiders are nodes connected with straight lines [7]. Spider diagrams use non-overlapping contours of Euler diagrams, spiders, which generalize Pierce's X-sequences and shading from Venn diagrams [5], [9], [11]. The spider diagram in **Fig.4** has three contours labeled A, B and C. The contours are represented as A ∪ C and B ⊂ A.

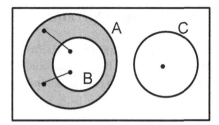

Fig. 4. A Spider diagram

3   The Z Notation

Z was developed by the Programming Research Group (PRG) at the University of Oxford. Its basic construct is the schema, containing mathematical text and being surrounded by natural language prose. Basic types to be used are specified early on in the specification document.

Below is an example specification showing two basic types, a state space (*File*) and one partial operation (*FileRead*) on the state. The example is modeled on specifications in [19] and [8].

The basic types are:

[KEY, RECORD]

The abstract state of the file system is shown below:

$$\begin{array}{|l}\hline \textit{File}\_\!\!\!\_\!\!\!\_\!\!\!\_\!\!\!\_\!\!\!\_ \\ \hline \textit{file}: \textit{KEY} \nrightarrow \textit{RECORD} \\ \hline \end{array}$$

The relationship between *KEY* and *RECORD* is defined by a partial function ($\nrightarrow$). State variables (*file* above) in Z are known as components.

The below schema specifies an operation on the state. Ξ *File* specifies that the *Read* operation will not change the state of the system (in contrast, a 'Δ' before a state name is used to indicate a possible state change). The operation receives the input $k?$ and produces output $r!$ The symbols '?' and '!' are used to decorate input and output variables respectively. Predicates are specified below the short dividing line in a schema and further constrain the state components and any additional variables. The *key?* should be known to the system and a record ($r!$) is returned for a correct key.

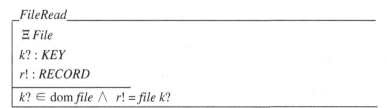

4   Specification Structures and Operators

In this section we present a number of Z specifications from the literature and transform each such construct into a diagram. The specifications shown stem mainly from [8]. The first operation considered is domain restriction, indicated by $\triangleleft$.

4.1   Domain Restriction

Consider the above file system. **Fig.5** below gives a diagrammatic representation of the state, *File*. The 'rectangles' in the diagram are used to indicate the basic types in the specification. Closed circles called contours, represent sets in the specification. The curved arrow connecting two contours denotes a relation. The name of the relation (*file*) appears above the curve, and its type is labeled below the curve. It is a partial function (*pf*).

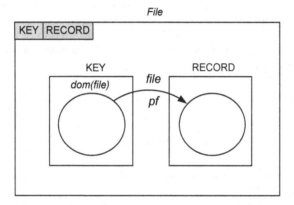

Fig. 5. The abstract state: File system

Next we consider an operation, *SelectRecord* to restrict the file system to just one record for which a key ($k?$) is provided:

$$
\begin{array}{l}
\underline{\;SelectRecord\;}\underline{} \\
\;\Delta\,File \\
\;k? : KEY \\
\underline{} \\
\;k? \in \text{dom}\,file \\
\;file' = \{k?\} \triangleleft file \\
\end{array}
$$

The file system is changed to just the record matching $k?$. Note, in practice one would define a variable for this purpose instead of removing all other records from the state.

Fig.6. shows how the above operation may be translated into a contoured diagram.

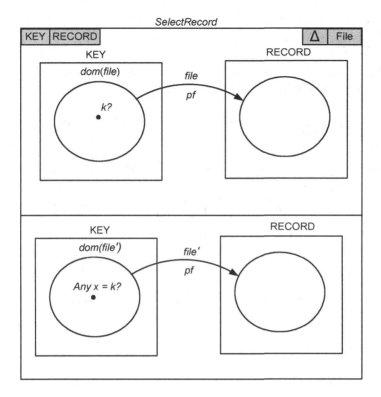

Fig. 6. Operation *SelectRecord*

The top part of the diagram (called a *before* diagram) represents the precondition to the operation. It indicates that the key k? should exist in the *file* domain. The after (bottom) diagram specifies that k? is the only key left in the file. The dot • indicates that there is at least one element in the set (a syntax taken from spider diagrams). Having restricted the domain of *file* to just $\{k?\}$, leaves but one record in the file. The key of any such record equals k? In the absence of further information one assumes *file'* $(k?) = file\ (k?)$, being a traditional proof obligation arising from the specification.

Note that our diagrammatic notation allows us to abstract away from the set connotation $\{k?\}$ specified in the schema, simply because we are working with a singleton, and the only element of the singleton is explicitly instantiated.

4.2   Overriding Operator

Consider a symbol table containing symbols with associated values. *SYM* and *VAL* are basic types used to represent, respectively, the set of symbols and associated values. The state, *ST*, consists of one component, *st*, a partial function.

$$\underline{ST}$$
$$st : SYM \nrightarrow VAL$$

Fig.7 below gives a diagrammatic representation of the above state. Note that we may omit the denotation '*dom(st)*', since it may be inferred from the diagram.

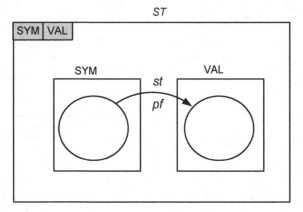

Fig. 7. The abstract state of symbol table

The following operation associates a value *v*? with symbol *s*? The operation gives feedback to the user.

$$\underline{Replace}$$
$$\Delta\, st$$
$$s? : SYM$$
$$v? : VAL$$
$$rep! : REPORT$$
$$\rule{7cm}{0.4pt}$$
$$s? \in\ \text{dom } st$$
$$s' =\ st \oplus \{\, s? \mapsto v? \}$$
$$rep! = OK$$

The overriding operator '$\oplus$' is used to replace the value (if any) of a variable in the symbol table with a new value. Its definition for any two relations $R : X \leftrightarrow Y$ and $S : X \leftrightarrow Y$ (say) is given by: $R \oplus S = ((\text{dom } S) \vartriangleleft R) \cup S$.

Fig.8 denotes the operation to update a symbol in the table in line with the above schema. The before diagram indicates that *s*? is to exist in the symbol table, while *v*?, the input to the system, may either be in the range of *st*, or not. The after diagram indicates that *s*? maps to *v*? and variable *rep*! has the value 'Ok' after the operation.

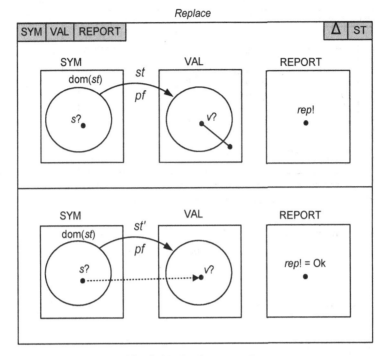

Fig. 8. The Replace operation

4.3   Domain Subtraction

Consider the next higher level of the above file system to model file identifiers mapped to files. Each file has a unique identifier. The schema below depicts the state of such a file storage system (*SS*). The abstract state denotes a partial function from *FID* to *FILE* [8].

_SS_____

$fstore: FID \nrightarrow FILE$

Fig.9 shows the abstract state of SS. It specifies *fstore* as a partial function.

The schema below specifies the operation of deleting a file [8]. Only files that exist in the system can be deleted.

_destroySS_____

ΔSS

$fid? : FID$

$fid? \in \operatorname{dom} fstore$

$fstore' = \{fid?\} \lhd fstore$

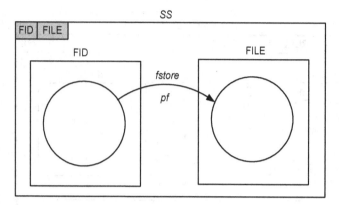

Fig. 9. The abstract state of *SS*

The domain subtraction operator '◁' is used to remove *fid?*; the state of the system is changed as indicated. After the operation, *fid?* no longer exists as a valid file identifier in the system.

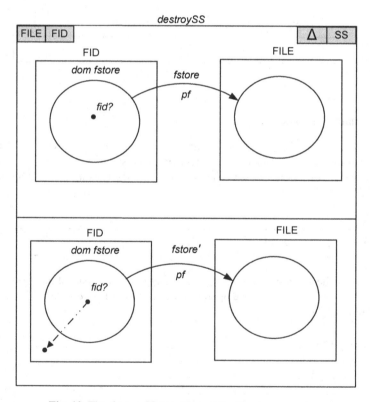

Fig. 10. The *destroySS* operation of the file storage system

Fig. 10 captures operation *destroySS*. The before diagram specifies that the file to be deleted should exist in the system and the after diagram states that the file identifier has been removed from the set of valid file identifiers. A dashed line indicating the movement is used for this purpose.

4.4   Range Subtraction

A simplified banking system stores the details of customers with the corresponding branches they belong to. A customer can be registered with only one branch. The state of the system is given by *bankSystem*.

_*bankSystem*_____

$bank : CUSTOMER \nrightarrow BRANCH$

The contour diagram for the above state is similar to that of the other operations shown above.

An operation to delete an entire branch from the system is similar to the domain subtraction operation shown earlier, and is given by:

_*deleteBranch*_____

$\Delta \, bankSystem$

$branch? : BRANCH$

$branch? \in \text{ran } bank$

$bank' = bank \vartriangleleft \{branch?\}$

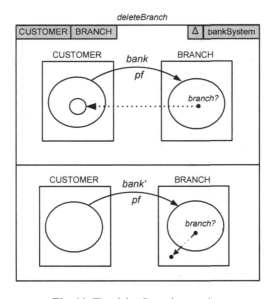

Fig. 11. The *deleteBranch* operation

The above schema is a simplified version of a real life situation. In practice customers would be moved to another branch before their branch is closed. The corresponding diagram follows.

4.5   Specifying Non-Singleton Sets

So far we have removed from a set, or restricted the domains or ranges of relations to a set containing one element only. We were able to abstract away from the complexities of sets and showed in such cases a single item only, instead of a singleton containing only that item.

The following operation removes a set containing an unspecified number of items from a domain and also overrides the relation with one of the same type. The state of the system is given in Section 3 and the operation is specified by *FileUpdate* below.

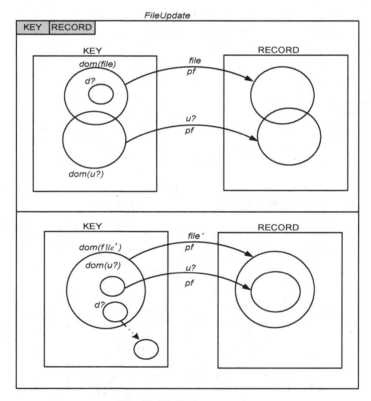

Fig. 12. FileUpdate operation

$\underline{\textit{FileUpdate}}$_____

Δ *File*

$d? : \mathbb{P} KEY$

$u? : KEY \nrightarrow RECORD$
_____

$d? \subseteq \text{dom} \textit{file}$

$d? \cap \text{dom } u? = \{\}$

$\textit{file}' = (d? \lhd \textit{file}) \oplus u?$

The set of keys to be deleted is specified by $d?$ Only valid keys may be deleted. The predicate $d? \cap \text{dom } u? = \{\}$ indicates that a record cannot be deleted and updated at the same time. The file is updated as indicated.

FileUpdate is modeled by Fig. 12.

5   Conclusions and Future Work

This paper considered the feasibility of translating Z constructs to the language of contour diagrams. The formality of Z lends itself to precise specifications and it has been applied successfully to specify systems where the quality and reliability are critical. Z may also be used as a documentation tool to increase a specifier's understanding of system operations. A possible disadvantage of a formal notation is that specialist knowledge of the underlying mathematics is required before the real benefits of formal specification can be realized [2]. This steep learning curve is often the reason cited why formal notations are not used more widely in the software industry.

Diagrams model a system by using contours to represent the relationships between mathematical structures. The use of diagrammatic languages is perceived as a way whereby software specifications are made more accessible to stakeholders and potential users of the system [7]. In the past diagrams were often excluded as contenders of formality; however the research done by Shin challenged the view that diagrams could not be used in the arena of formal specification work [4].

As part of future work, our notation will be applied to more complex operations and structures, e.g. distributed unions, bags, etc. The feasibility of reasoning about the properties of our diagrams has to be considered and the scalability of the notations has to be investigated. To this end, tools for industrial applications have to be further developed. We also plan to combine Z constructs with our diagrams to generate a comprehensive specification language to cater for clear specifications that may also be accessible to a wide range of users.

References

1. Alagar, V.S., Periyasamy, K.: Specification of Software Systems, pp. 3–14. Springer, New York (1998)
2. Bowen, J.: Formal Specification and Documentation using Z – A Case Study Approach, pp. 3–11 (2003); C.A.R. Hoare Series Editor
3. Chow, S., Ruskey, F.: Drawing Area-Proportional Venn and Euler Diagrams. In: Liotta, G. (ed.) GD 2003. LNCS, vol. 2912, pp. 466–477. Springer, Heidelberg (2004)
4. Dau, F.: Types and Tokens for Logic with Diagrams. In: Wolff, K.E., Pfeiffer, H.D., Delugach, H.S. (eds.) ICCS 2004. LNCS (LNAI), vol. 3127, pp. 62–93. Springer, Heidelberg (2004)
5. Delaney, A., Stapleton, G.: On the Descriptional Complexity of a Diagrammatic Notation. In: Proceedings of the 13th International Conference on Distributed Multimedia Systems, September 6-8 (2007)
6. Diller, A.: Z: An Introduction to Formal Methods, 2nd edn. Wiley, Chichester (1994)
7. Gil, J., Howse, J.: Formalizing Spider Diagrams. In: IEEE Symposium on Visual Languages, pp. 130–137 (1999)
8. Hayes, I.: Specification Case Studies. Prentice Hall International, UK (1992)
9. Howse, J., Molina, F., Taylor, J.: Reasoning with Spider Diagrams. In: IEEE Symposium on Visual Languages, September 13-16, pp. 138–145 (1999)
10. Howse, J., Taylor, J., Stapleton, G., Simpson, T.: The Expressiveness of Spider Diagrams Augmented with Constants. Journal of Visual Languages and Computing 20, 30–49 (2009)
11. Howse, J., Taylor, J., Stapleton, G., Simpson, T.: What Can Spider Diagrams Say? In: Blackwell, A.F., Marriott, K., Shimojima, A. (eds.) Diagrams 2004. LNCS (LNAI), vol. 2980, pp. 112–127. Springer, Heidelberg (2004)
12. Howse, J., Taylor, J., Stapleton, G.: Spider Diagrams. LMS Journal of Computation and Mathematics 2980, 154–194 (2005)
13. Molina, F.: Reasoning with Extended Venn-Pierce Diagrammatic Systems. PhD Thesis, University of Brighton (2001)
14. Potter, B., Sinclair, J., Till, D.: An Introduction to Formal Specification and Z, 2nd edn. Prentice Hall, Upper Saddle River (1996)
15. Stapleton, G., Rodgers, P., Howse, J., Taylor, J.: Properties of Euler diagrams. Layout of (Software) Engineering Diagrams 7, 1–15 (2007)
16. Stapleton, G.: A Survey of Reasoning Systems Based on Euler Diagrams. In: Proceedings of the First International Workshop on Euler Diagrams, Brighton, UK, June 1, vol. 134, pp. 127–151 (2005)
17. Spivey, J.M.: The Z Notation: A Reference Manual, 2nd edn. Prentice Hall (1992)
18. Kim, S.-K., Carrington, D.A.: A Formal Mapping between UML Models and Object-Z Specifications. In: ZB Conference, pp. 2–21 (2000)
19. Van der Poll, J.A.: Formal Methods in Software Development: A Road Less Travelled. South African Computer Journal (SACJ) (45), 40–52 (2010)
20. Wordsworth, J.B.: Software Development with Z. Addison-Wesley, IBM United Kingdom (1992)
21. Woodcock, J., Davies, J.: Using Z: Specification, Refinement and Proof. Prentice-Hall (1996)

A Markov Chain Based Model to Predict HIV/AIDS Epidemiological Trends

Andrea Nucita[1], Giuseppe M. Bernava[2], Pietro Giglio[3], Marco Peroni[3],
Michelangelo Bartolo[4], Stefano Orlando[3],
Maria Cristina Marazzi[5], and Leonardo Palombi[6]

[1] University of Messina, Italy
anucita@unime.it
[2] IFC-CNR, Italy
massimo.bernava@gmail.com
[3] DREAM Program, Italy
{piero.giglio,peronimarco,steorlando}@gmail.com
[4] San Giovanni Hospital, Rome, Italy
michelebartolo@gmail.com
[5] LUMSA University, Rome, Italy
marazzi@lumsa.it
[6] Tor Vergata University, Rome, Italy
leonardo.palombi@gmail.com

Abstract. The emerging and growing use of electronic medical records (EMRs) nowadays gives the possibility of exploiting the huge amount of collected clinical data for epidemiological research purpose, together with the opportunity to address and verify intervention policies and facility management. In this paper we present a Markov chain based model that makes use of real clinical data to simulate epidemiological scenarios for HIV epidemic at a district level. Ad hoc original software has been used, that can be adopted in every similar scenario. This research project is conducted within the Drug Resource Enhancement Against AIDS and Malnutrition (DREAM) Program to fight HIV/AIDS in sub-Saharan Africa. The results of this paper show in a clear and robust fashion how the proposed Markov chain based model can be helpful to predict epidemiological trends and hence to support decision making to face the diffusion of HIV/AIDS and other sexually transmitted diseases.

Keywords: Mathematical model, HIV epidemic, Antiretroviral.

1 Introduction

Drug Resources Enhancement against AIDS and Malnutrition (DREAM) [17] was created by the Community of Sant'Egidio to fight AIDS in sub-Saharan Africa. The project takes a holistic approach, combining Highly Active Anti-Retroviral Therapy (HAART) with the treatment of malnutrition, tuberculosis, malaria and sexually transmitted diseases. It also strongly emphasises health education at all levels. DREAM aims to achieve its goals in line with the gold standard for HIV treatment and care. Started in 2002, DREAM Program has

A. Cuzzocrea and S. Maabout (Eds.): MEDI 2013, LNCS 8216, pp. 225–236, 2013.
© Springer-Verlag Berlin Heidelberg 2013

now spread to 10 African countries: Mozambique, Malawi, Tanzania, Kenya, the Republic of Guinea, Guinea Bissau, Cameroon, Congo RDC, Angola and Nigeria.

The rapid expansion of the Program, and therefore the need to deal with a vast amount of clinical data, has led to the creation of specific software in order to manage the patients' medical files and their diagnostic data [13] that has become rapidly an essential instrument for treatment and for epidemiological analyses. A large part of the work on DREAM Software has been dedicated to the design of a relational database for the management of data contained in clinical files. This is an important resource both for the management of the clinical data of patients, as well as for the possibility it gives to analyse information found therein, from a clinical and organisational point of view. In facts, the large amount of clinical data collected within the Program during more than ten years of activity revealed itself to be a crucial mine of information about clinical histories of HIV/AIDS affected patients. Trough these data it is indeed possible to assess the disease evolution in a treated patient. Hence, taking advantage of this opportunity, we generated a new model and assessed its validity in the sub-Saharan Africa context [15], based on actual cohort data from the DREAM Program.

This paper presents our Markov chain based model for predicting HIV/AIDS epidemiological trends, that exploits real clinical data to model the disease evolution in a single patient, together with a sexual network that models the spread of epidemic in the whole population. Moreover, we present experimental results showing the flexibility of our model, which gives the possibility of making simulations in different scenarios by tuning several parameters such as population composition, sexual network definition, retention level etc.

The rest of the paper is organised as follows. In section 2 we briefly review research efforts related to our research. In section 3 our Markov chain based model is presented, while in section 4 we show some features of the simulation software and the experimental results. Finally, section 5 discusses conclusions and future work of our research.

2   Related Work

The relevance of mathematical modelling for HIV/AIDS epidemiology has been recognised at the very beginning of HIV research studies. [2] reviews the pioneering use of mathematical models in the study of HIV and epidemiology and the demographic impact of AIDS. The author analyses the validity of mathematical models, though recognising the lack, at that stage, of quantitative data and the poor understanding of key parameters about transmission, course of infection, incubation period and so on.

More recently, [9] analysed the application of different mathematical models to the spread of infectious diseases, focusing in particular on the basic reproduction number R_0, defined as the average number of secondary infections produced when one infected individual is introduced into a host population where everyone is susceptible. The author highlights how modelling HIV/AIDS spread is a challenging task, due to the heterogeneity among subjects at risk. Moreover, HIV/AIDS progression traverses many infectious classes with different infectivity [10], thus producing a more complicated modelling of the disease transmission.

In [6], the authors compare twelve different mathematical models. Some of these models are agent-based, while the remaining are deterministic. That comparison shows that the analysed models give similar results in the short period, while they differ more sensibly in the long period. Nevertheless, the noticeable fact is that all these studies agree that antiretroviral therapy, at high levels of access and with high adherence, is capable of reducing new HIV infections.

In [1], authors use a deterministic model based on ordinary differential equation in order to better assess the impact of combining prevention intervention strategies in a hyper-endemic community. [19] highlights the necessary use of mathematical models to predict the impact of new interventions, though arguing that the scale-up of any single intervention should be evaluated in practical settings, since unexpected difficulties may affect significantly the impact of intervention.

As we already mentioned, in our model we considered real clinical data as a base to describe the HIV/AIDS progression in a single patient, combined with a model to evaluate relationships among individuals and then infectivity. In [8], the authors present different stochastic models for sexual networks. They show that a general behavioural model for the formation of sexual networks is lacking, and thus evaluate the fitting of different models adopting a likelihood framework to estimate model parameters and to compare models to each other. In our study we decided to adopt the model presented in [11], where concurrency is taken into account, that is the propensity to form simultaneous partnerships. This model allowed us to consider different scenarios, from monogamy to multiple partnership, by tuning sexual network parameters. Recently, [7] tested, through a mathematical model, the hypothesis that universal voluntary testing and treatment represents a chance to eradicate the HIV epidemic in an acceptable period of time. Our Markov chain based model, which we present in the next sections, differs from that of [7], in that we use an agent-based model, rather than a deterministic model. Moreover, we use real clinical data to model the agent behaviour and disease progression. In addition, we assumed a scenario in which antiretroviral therapy (ART) is initiated using the World Health Organization (WHO) CD4 (lymphocyte cells) count threshold of 350 $cells/mm^3$, with the intent to extend treatment to the entire HIV-infected population within a short period of time. Our assumption was also that all new HIV infections would be immediately treated and retained in treatment through annual testing.

3   An Agent Based Model

3.1   Model Architecture

To model the diffusion of HIV we built an agent-based model that simulates the interactions between individuals among a district level population. Each agent thus represents an adult individual, which has a probability of being infected through sexual acts that is related to its age and sex. Moreover, an infected individual is capable of infecting other agents, with a variable infectivity that is calculated on the basis of the agents illness stadium.

Therefore, we combined two different models in order to obtain a realistic simulation framework. The first model, the *patient model*, is related to the behaviour of individuals. It is based on a Markov chain that defines the probabilities of passing from a disease stadium into another during agents' life. This is the novelty of our method, since the Markov chain is built on the basis of real life clinical data, rather than describing the evolution of the disease only by a mathematical model. The second model, we call it *epidemic model*, describes the diffusion of the disease among the whole population. Since we assume that the virus is transmitted only by sexual contacts, this model makes use of a sexual network in order to describe the relationships among agents and hence the probability for an agent to infect other individuals. Figure 1 shows the architecture of our model. The core part of the model relates to building the Markov chain matrix of probabilities. As we already mentioned, these probability values are inferred from real clinical data. For the present study, we used a dataset from the DREAM Program, consisting of clinical data from thousands of patients treated by the Program in different Sub-Saharan countries. This dataset will be better described in the experiment section. Subsequently, the epidemic model simulates the interaction between agents, by means of two key concepts: i) the probability that an agent has of establishing a relationship with another agent (sexual network); ii) the probability that an agent has of infecting another agent through a sexual act (infectivity). In the following of this section we describe more in detail these two models.

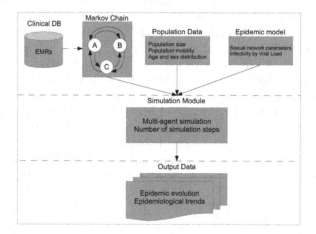

Fig. 1. Model Architecture. A database containing patients data is used to generate the probability matrix of the Markov chain. The model for patient evolution is combined with the sexual network model to simulate HIV spread.

3.2   Patient Model

To generate the patient model, DREAM Program data from adult patients who visited DREAM medical centres in Mozambique and Malawi from January 2002 through July 2009 were used. Clinical progression was monitored (with measurement of CD4 lymphocytes cell counts quarterly and viral loads every six months, clinical visits every three months, and follow-up every three months) in individuals receiving antiretroviral therapy (ART) (eligible per WHO guidelines) and those who did not reach clinical or laboratory thresholds for ART initiation. In this way, it was possible to calculate measures of survival time, annual mortality rate, patients lost to follow-up, and refusal rates in the population. These parameters were introduced in a Markov chain prediction model for the analysis of disease progression in treated and untreated patients.

A Markov process is a stochastic process in which the probability of migrating from one state to another depends on the current state, irrespective of the previous path. Therefore the Markov chain is a discrete random process which uses the Markov property. Considering a state space S of a Markov chain, the elements $X_i \in S$ are random variables and the probability P of state transition is expressed as follows:

$$P(X_{n+1} = x_{n+1} | X_n, X_{n-1}, ..., X_0) = P(X_{n+1} = x_{n+1} | X_n) \tag{1}$$

Therefore, the probability of transition from state X_n to state X_{n+1} is independent of the previous path, and only depends on the current state X_n. In the present study, each state of the Markov chain was represented by the health status of a patient. Markov chains can have graphical representations, where the nodes represent the states, and the edges the transition probabilities. The probability matrix expresses the transition probabilities for all the possible state transitions. More precisely, given the probability matrix Q, the matrix element q_{ij} represents the probability of transition from state i to state j. The probability matrix originating from patient data was calculated in the following manner: in the first step, individual clinical histories were characterised as a sequence of health states. For patient a, clinical history would be characterised as:

$$a \to < S_1, ..., S_n > \tag{2}$$

where $S_i (i = 1, ..., n)$ are health states and the whole duration of the observation is $n/2$ years, being patient observations carried out with a six-month frequency. Subsequently, the clinical histories of the patients are described as states sequences, and the transition probabilities are extracted for all possible state transitions. This probability matrix is used for the Markov process as seen in figure 2.

Parameters needed to classify disease states were categorised as shown in Table 1.

Viral load thresholds were selected based on prior infectivity studies [18,16,4,5,12], and CD4 cell count categories were based on clinical survival thresholds [3,20]. The clinical evolution of patients was assessed every six months,

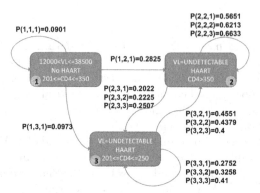

Fig. 2. A small portion of the Markov chain used in the model. Each rectangle represents a patient state, characterised by a viral load value, a CD4 cell count value and a boolean value indicating whether or not the patient is under triple ART. The arcs represent the probability of a patient changing state, e.g. $P(i, j, k)$ means the probability that a patient will pass from state i to state j after k semesters.

Table 1. Clinical parameters used to classify disease stages

Param	Ranges			
CD4 cell counts $(cells/mm^3)$	< 200 200-350 350			
HIV-1 virus load	NA < 1, 700	1,700-12,000	12,000-38,500	
ART use	YES NO			

to coincide with the timing of complete blood cell counts. At each step, the health status of a patient was determined by the combination of viral load and CD4 cell count values and ART parameters. Consequently, 31 health states were possible, including death. Health states were modelled in a Markov chain as shown in figure 2, with patients modelled as agents in a complex simulation system.

3.3   Epidemic Model

This model describes disease evolution in the whole population. Patient infectivity by viral load value was determined according to prior studies [18]. The probability of infection was assigned according to viral load ranges, and it was possible to assess infectivity risk per coital act at any point of observation. Relationships among individuals, including multi-partner relationships, were modelled according to Kretzschmar and Morris [11]. In that model, given two individuals x and y, the probability that a relationship had been established was calculated by the following equation (in case of assortative mixing):

$$\phi(x, y) = (1 - \xi) + \xi \times \frac{partner(x) \times partner(y)}{d^2} \tag{3}$$

where $partners(x)$ and $partners(y)$ are the numbers of present partners respectively of x and y; d is the maximum value of $partners(z)$, for all individuals z in population observed at that time; $\xi \in [0, 1)$ is a parameter that describes the transition from a partnership random distribution ($\xi = 0$) and situations where individuals that already have partnerships are more likely to form new partnerships. In our experiments we showed how mixing functions affect epidemiological trends.

In the epidemic model, the evolution of the epidemic was determined by new infections caused by HIV-infected individuals having relationships with uninfected subjects. As we show later, our software gives the possibility of representing different relationships types, by tuning these factors. There is a probability that two individuals at each time step unit form a partnership, and there is also a probability that at each time step, partnerships are broken, generating the time span of relationships. Hence, the number of partnerships for each agent is a function of the population and of the probabilities of formation and breakage of relationships. In the analysis of the partnership function, the mean number of partnerships was about three for a population of 300000 at a given time step. Similarly, the frequency of sexual contacts was derived from Rakai studies [12]: number of coital acts was a function of age, sex, and health conditions.

In summary, a Markov chain was used to determine disease progression in a single patient model, and a partnership model was used to assess the probability that an infected individual would transmit HIV to a serodiscordant partner, generating the scenario depicted in figure 3.

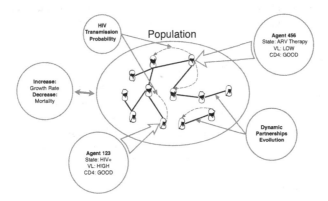

Fig. 3. Epidemic model basic representation

4   Experimental Results

In this section we describe our experimental results. All the experiments have been conducted by using an ad hoc software, which was written using Microsoft $C\#$ language. The software takes several parameters as input, most of them being modifiable by the software interface. The probability matrix, described in section 3.2, is loaded as an input file by the software, together with other model features, such as sexual network typology, age and sex population classification and possible disease stages of patients/agents. The main window of the software is shown in figure 4, even though it is possible to launch simulations from command line.

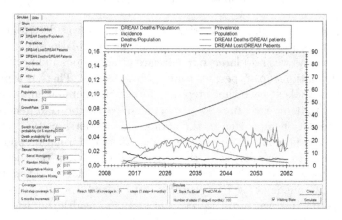

Fig. 4. Main window of simulation software. Going from the upper left corner to the bottom right, several frames show modifiable paramters: *Show*) which trends to be shown; *Initial*) initial parameters for simulation: population cardinality, prevalence, growth rate; *Lost*) percentage patients lost to follow-up and their probability of dying; *Sexual Network*) parameters that determine typology of sexual network; *Coverage*) intervention coverage parameters; *Simulate*) Buttons to start simulation and to export simulation file. In the central part of the window, the graphs resulting from simulation are shown.

As we already discussed above, data for the model were collected from a cohort of DREAM Program patients, which is described in the following. In order to assess a realistic scenario, we fed our model with demographic data from a rural district of an African country. This choice is not restrictive, since different simulations may be conducted by changing the demographic pattern.

4.1   Population Data and Parameters

Demographic parameters were used for general population models and DREAM Program data were used for the model simulation of HIV-infected patients: data from 26565 patients followed up at Mozambique and Malawi DREAM centres for > 7 years were input into the model.

A general population sample size of 300000 individuals was considered, assuming a balance of immigration and emigration flux of 3% each. The demographic pattern of a typical rural district in Malawi was assumed, and age distributions were determined according to country data. An implementation latency time, defined as the number of months needed to achieve the full coverage of the population, was considered with three scenarios at 12, 24, and 36 months, respectively. At three years, full coverage of the candidate population was assumed. The demographic variables used in the model were based on country statistics [14]. The initial HIV prevalence rate was estimated at 12%. In addition, the model assumed annual universal voluntary testing of adults, immediate treatment of HIV-infected individuals with CD4 cell counts $< 350\ cells/mm^3$ and/or symptomatic disease (WHO categories 34), treatment of patients with CD4 cell counts $> 350\ cells/mm^3$ on reaching this CD4 cell count threshold over time, and treatment of all HIV-infected pregnant women irrespective of immunologic or virologic status. The time distribution switch between groups was a consideration in the model. Over time, 13% of patients who initially entered the model with CD4 cell counts $> 350\ cells/mm^3$ reached lower values after one year, 35% after two years and 18% after three years. The model assumed that 66% of patients with initial CD4 counts $> 350\ cells/mm^3$ would be receiving treatment after three years, and 81% after five years. The model took into consideration the mortality rate of untreated patients who would likely be receiving ART in a few years even with a good immunologic status.

4.2   Experiments

In this section some simulation are discussed, in order to show the capabilities of our model. In figure 5 the epidemiological trends, based on the parameters described above are shown. Our findings, based on these parameters, support the main conclusions of the Granich study [7], that is, treatment of all infected individuals translates into a drastic reduction in incident HIV infections and leads to the "sterilisation" of the epidemic.

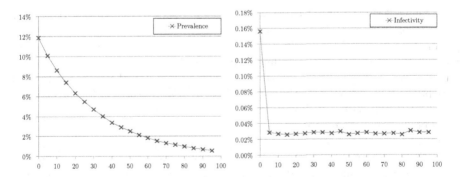

Fig. 5. Prevalence and infectivity trends. The simulation used the following parameters: population, 300000; initial prevalence, 12%; population growth rate per year, approximately 2.3%; number of 6-month simulation steps (on x axses), 100; probability that a patient will be lost to follow-up, 3%; death rate among patients lost to follow-up after 6 months, 50%; initial treatment coverage, 50%; and coverage after 1 year, 100%.

To stress our model, we conducted more simulations, by changing some assumptions on the model parameters. Given the probability matrix described in section 3, which is derived directly from patient data described above, we conducted different simulations by changing sexual network typology and the percentage of lost to follow up patients. We expected that these different scenarios would have affected the epidemiological trends, for different reasons. Changing sexual parameters from serial monogamy to multi-partnership relationships would result in a greater number of partner for infected individuals and thus in a greater probability of new infections. On the other hand, modifying the percentage of lost to follow up patients would result in a greater number of untreated patients, with a generalised growth of infectivity and then of new infections. Moreover, lost to follow up patients would have a greater probability of dying.

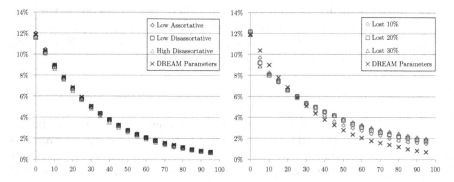

Fig. 6. Prevalence trends. The simulation used the same parameters of figure 5, except for sexual network typology (left) and percentage of lost to therapy patients (right).

In figure 6 the results of these simulations are shown, referring in particular to prevalence rate. As it is possible to notice, changes in the sexual network parameters do not affect significantly prevalence trend. Even with high level of multi partnerships the trend is almost the same of that with the first parameter set. A reason in the prevalence behaviour may be found in the fact that treated patients have a very low infectivity (see figure 5), and thus a very low probability of infecting new partners. A very different situation occurs when the number of lost to follow up patients increases sensibly. First, the prevalence rate goes down rapidly, because the number of deaths is greater among lost to follow up patients. Nevertheless, after about ten years these patients affect sensibly the prevalence trend, because of their greater infectivity. In this case, the trend of prevalence changes its slope, affecting negatively the intervention efficacy.

5   Conclusion and Future Work

In this paper we presented a Markov chain based model to evaluate HIV/AIDS epidemiological trends. Our model is agent-based and results from the combination of two different models. The first describe the evolution of the single patient, while the second models the interaction among individuals. Contrary to other known mathematical models, the patient model exploits real clinical data collected within the DREAM Programme to describe the patient evolution, thus giving a more realistic description of how the disease progresses in a treated patient. Our experimental results corroborate prior studies, confirming that expanding access to testing and therapy would affect the epidemiological evolution and limit the spread of HIV/AIDS. As part of our future work, we aim at extending our model and our software, to be more adaptable to model other infectious diseases.

References

1. Alsallaq, R.A., Baeten, J.M., Celum, C.L., Hughes, J.P., AbuRaddad, L.J., Barnabas, R.V., Hallett, T.B.: Understanding the potential impact of a combination HIV prevention intervention in a hyper-endemic community. PLoS ONE 8(1) (2013)
2. Anderson, R.M.: The role of mathematical models in the study of HIV transmission and the epidemiology of AIDS. Journal of Acquired Immune Deficiency Syndromes 1(3), 241–256 (1988)
3. Chan, K.C., Yip, B., Hogg, R.S., Montaner, J.S., O'Shaughnessy: Survival rates after the initiation of antiretroviral therapy stratified by cd4 cell counts in two cohorts in canada and the united states. AIDS 16(12), 1693–1695 (2002)
4. Das, M., Lee Chu, P., Santos, G.M., Scheer, S., Vittinghoff, E., McFarland, W., Colfax, G.N.: Decreases in community viral load are accompanied by reductions in new HIV infections in san francisco. PLoS Med. 5(6) (2010)
5. Donnell, D., Baeten, J.M., Kiarie, J., Thomas, K.K., Stevens, W., Cohen, C.R., McIntyre, J., Lingappa, J.R., Celum, C.: Heterosexual HIV-1 transmission after initiation of antiretrovirval therapy: A prospective cohort analysis. The Lancet 375(9731), 2092–2098 (2010)
6. Eaton, J.W., Johnson, L.F., Salomon, J.A., Bärnighausen, T., Bendavid, E., Bershteyn, A., Bloom, D.E., Cambiano, V., Fraser, C., Hontelez, J.A.C., Humair, S., Klein, D.J., Long, E.F., Phillips, A.N., Pretorius, C., Stover, J., Wenger, E.A., Williams, B.G., Hallett, T.B.: HIV treatment as prevention: Systematic comparison of mathematical models of the potential impact of antiretroviral therapy on HIV incidence in south africa. PLoS Med. 9(7) (2012)
7. Granich, R.M., Gilks, C.F., Dye, C., De Cock, K.M., Williams, B.G.: Universal voluntary HIV testing with immediate antiretroviral therapy as a strategy for elimination of HIV transmission: A mathematical model. The Lancet 373(3), 48–57 (2009)
8. Handcocka, M.S., Holland Jonesb, J.: Likelihood-based inference for stochastic models of sexual network formation. Theoretical Population Biology 65(4), 413–422 (2004)
9. Hethcote, H.W.: The mathematics of infectious diseases. SIAM Review 42(4), 599–653 (2000)
10. Hollingsworth, T.D., Anderson, R.M., Fraser, C.: HIV-1 transmission, by stage of infection. The Journal of Infectious Diseases 198(5), 687–693 (2008)
11. Kretzschmar, M., Morris, M.: Measures of concurrency in networks and the spread of infectious diseases. Mathematical Biosciences 133, 165–195 (1996)

12. Lutalo, T., Gray, R.H., Wawer, M., Sewankambo, N., Serwadda, D., Laeyendecker, O., Kiwanuka, N., Nalugoda, F., Kigozi, G., Ndyanabo, A., Bwanika, J.B., Reynolds, S.J., Quinn, T., Opendi, P.: Survival of HIV-infected treatment-naive individuals with documented dates of seroconversion in rakai, uganda. AIDS 19, 15–19 (2007)
13. Nucita, A., Bernava, G.M., Bartolo, M., Di Pane Masi, F., Giglio, P., Peroni, M., Pizzimenti, G., Palombi, L.: A global approach to the management of EMR (electronic medical records) of patients with HIV/AIDS in sub-saharan africa: the experience of dream software. BMC Medical Informatics and Decision Making 9(42) (2009)
14. World Health Organization. World health statistics 2008 (2008), http://www.who.int/whosis/whostat/2008/en/index.html
15. Palombi, L., Bernava, G.M., Nucita, A., Giglio, P., Liotta, G., Nielsen-Saines, K., Orlando, S., Mancinelli, S., Buonomo, E., Scarcella, P., Doro Altan, A.M., Guidotti, G., Ceffa, S., Haswell, J., Zimba, I., Magid, N.A., Marazzi, M.C.: Predicting trends in HIV-1 sexual transmission in sub-saharan africa through the drug resource enhancement against aids and malnutrition model: Antiretrovirals for reduction of population infectivity, incidence and prevalence at the district level. Clinical Infectious Diseases (2012)
16. Palombi, L., Marazzi, M.C., Guidotti, G., Germano, P., Buonomo, E., Scarcella, P., Doro Altan, A.M., Zimba, I., Magnano San Lio, M., De Luca, A.: Incidence and predictors of death, retention, and switch to second-line regimens in antiretroviral-treated patients in sub-saharan african sites with comprehensive monitoring availability. Clinical Infectious Diseases 48(1), 115–122 (2009)
17. DREAM Programme (2013), http://dream.santegidio.org
18. Quinn, T.C., Wawer, M.J., Sewankambo, N., Serwadda, D., Li, C., Wabwire-Mangen, F., Meehan, M.O., Lutalo, T., Gray, R.H.: Viral load and heterosexual transmission of human immunodeficiency virus type 1. New England Journal of Medicine 342(13), 921–929 (2000)
19. Thiébaut, R., May, M.T.: Mathematical modelling of hiv prevention intervention. AIDS 27(3), 475–476 (2013)
20. Wood, E., Hogg, R.S., Yip, B., Harrigan, P.R., O'Shaughnessy, M.V., Montaner, J.S.: Is there a baseline cd4 cell count that precludes a survival response to modern antiretroviral therapy? AIDS 17(15), 711–720 (2003)

Pattern-Based ETL Conceptual Modelling

Bruno Oliveira[1], Vasco Santos[2], and Orlando Belo[1]

[1] ALGORITMI R&D Centre, University of Minho, Braga, Portugal
id4103@alunos.uminho.pt, obelo@di.uminho.pt
[2] CIICESI, School of Management and Technology, Porto Polytechnic, Felgueiras, Portugal
vsantos@estgf.ipp.pt

Abstract. In software development, patterns and standards are two important things that contribute strongly to the success of any system implementation. Characteristics like these ones improve a lot systems communication and data interchange across different computational platforms, integrating processes and data flows in an easy way. In ETL systems, the change of business requirements is a very serious problem leading frequently to reengineer existing populating processes implementations in order to receive new data structures or tasks not defined previously. Every time this happens, existing ETL processes must be changed in order to accommodate new business requirements. Furthermore, ETL modelling and planning suffers from a lack of mature methodology and notation to represent ETL processes in a uniform way across all implementation process, providing means to validate, reduce implementation errors, and improve communication among users with different knowledge in the field. In this paper, we used the BPMN modelling language for ETL conceptual modelling, providing formal specifications for workflow orchestration and data process transformations. We provide a new layer of abstraction that is based on a set of patterns expressed in BPMN for ETL conceptual modelling. These patterns or meta-models represent the most common used tasks in real world ETL systems.

Keywords: Data Warehousing System, ETL Systems, ETL Conceptual Modelling, Verification, and Validation, ETL Patterns and Meta-models, and BPMN.

1 Introduction

In software development, the use of standard solutions facilitates a lot the development of complex systems. In real world applications, commercial tools use them to decompose solutions based on common software patterns that define their behaviour as well as ensure communication with other patterns/systems. Patterns represent templates or sets of rules that have the ability to specify how a particular problem can be solved, considering particular applications scenarios framed in different real-world contexts. These patterns allow for reusability and improve the general quality of the system, reducing potential negative impacts or incorrect software development processes. Thus, the use of software patterns improves code reusability, minimize the impact of requirements changing, and consequently reduce development costs.

A. Cuzzocrea and S. Maabout (Eds.): MEDI 2013, LNCS 8216, pp. 237–248, 2013.

ETL (Extract-Load-Transform) systems are a very particular type of software that is considered a critical component in any data warehousing system implementation. Design and implement an ETL system imply the specification of a set of construction rules related to specific decision-making processes, which are typically very volatile in terms of base requirements, since business requisites frequently change to cover and accommodate additional operational areas, leading to an increasing business process complexity. Even with the use of standard solutions in data warehousing systems implementation, it's always necessary to provide specific decision-making processes reflecting especially business analysis metrics of agents involved. This happens simple because different people having different ways of acting and different ways of thinking, which are linked, in some way, to a specific set of particular decision-making processes [1]. Moreover, operational systems have specific data schemas supporting very different operational business requirements. The definition of specific data extraction procedures from different data sources structures will be also considered, which may represent an additional effort because extraction mechanisms can be limited by obsolete technology or extraction mechanisms that still are used. All this, make ETL components reuse a difficult task to achieve [1]. Thus, it is easy to understand Kimball, when he stated that the implementation process of a ETL system consumes usually about 70% of the resources required to implement a data warehouse [2]. Moreover, it is known that the success of a data warehousing system depends heavily on the adequacy of its populating system, which imposes an extreme care and concern by the ETL development team in its planning, design, architectures, and implementation.

Proprietary tools generally support ETL modelling and implementation tasks, providing their own methodologies and notations. The use of such tools complicates ETL implementation and maintenance, since it imposes additional efforts for the ETL team that needs to understand their own specificities, and not standard tasks and mechanisms. Proprietary notations also limit communication with non-technical users due to the fact that the models produced are generally very detailed with issues related especially to the runtime environment of the tool. Moreover, if we need to change the ETL supporting tool, the effort to do that will be considerable. It will be need to build the ETL process from scratch (or almost). With these problems in mind, several authors have made relevant efforts to provide more standard methodologies and notations for ETL modelling, which are generally based on new notations or with some meta-model extensions of existing standard notations. However, we consider that there is still a lack of a complete methodology covering the whole ETL development cycle, providing an easy and understandable notation for all user profiles, allowing its mapping for a more detailed model for execution, and providing its validation before proceeding to a final implementation of the ETL system.

This paper presents another approach to ETL conceptual modelling that help to alleviate the negative effects of a less suitable planning for the development of an ETL system, providing a very practical way for ETL conceptual modelling based on a set of patterns that were built using *Business Process Model Notation* (BPMN) [3]. These patterns represent and characterize some of the most common tasks used on real world ETL processes, providing the necessary steps to implement a specific procedure that can be applied in many different application scenarios. Each pattern acts like a black box that receives some input parameters, and produces the respective output using a set of pre-defined operations.

The choice of BPMN notation for pattern representation was mainly due to its simplicity representing and modelling business processes, coupled with its power of expressiveness, which makes BPMN notation quite easy to apply in ETL systems application contexts [4–6]. Thus, it's possible to provide very descriptive models through the use of BPMN 2.0 orchestration elements that can be mapped posteriorly into execution primitives, providing a straightforward design process into execution primitives. After a brief exposure of some related work (Section 2), we present in section 3 a pattern-based meta-model representation; based on some of the most ETL common used tasks. Next, in section 4, we present a *Data Quality Enforcement* (DQE) pattern, proposing its control elements using XPDL (XML Process Definition Language) and its data process specified in *Relation Algebra* (RA). Finally, in section 5, we present conclusions pointing out some future research lines.

2   Related Work

Using BPMN for ETL modelling has been explored by Akkaoui since 2009 [4]. In their former work, Akkaoui and Zimányi explored first the use of BPMN for ETL modelling, showing some examples how BPMN, commonly used for business processes implementation, can be used for more specific processes like ETL processes. These authors considered that existing organizational business processes must be integrated with ETL processes, since business processes can help not only to identify key data but also to identify the appropriated opportunity-window to load it into the data warehouse. They also explored how conceptual models could be implemented through the use of BPEL (*Business Process Execution Language*), showing that BPMN notation can be successfully applied to ETL processes, providing an easy way to understand mechanisms that already are used by many organizations and known by several types of users. Later, Akkaoui [5] provided a BPMN-based meta-model for an independent ETL modelling approach, exploring also the necessary bridges for a model-to-code translation, providing its execution model for some commercial tools. More recently, Akkaoui [6] proposed a more complete BPMN-based meta-model for ETL modelling based on control process mechanisms and data process operations. The first one provides process orchestration, which can be accomplished by several BPMN elements such as events and flow control gateways; the second is related to specific operations allowing for the manipulation of data among several data sources that may be coordinated by control process elements. Based on these two perspectives and on an ETL classification tree presented in the same work, the authors provided a specific meta-model covering ETL control mechanisms and data operations. Based on Akkaoui former work, we already presented [7] a pattern oriented approach for ETL conceptual modelling. Despite basing our work on the ideas originally presented by Akkaoui et al. [4–6], many other important initiatives have been taken in this field highlighting important aspects that should be considered in any ETL process modelling. For example, the work of Simitisis and Vassiliadis presented a methodology [8–11] covering the main phases of ETL modelling, namely: conceptual, logical and physical. More recently, El-Sappagh et al. [12] proposed the EMD (Entity-Mapping Diagram) framework that provide a meta-model and notation for conceptual modelling of ETL processes. In turn, Trujillo and Luján-Mora revealed an UML approach [13] proposing an extension of the notation elements through the use of a new set of constructs representing specific activities commonly used on ETL conceptual modelling. Despite the many contributions already made in this field, we believe that still is an absence in the field of a complete proposal that will permit the conceptual modelling of an ETL system, as an initial work and discussion of its main features, allowing posteriorly the generation of the corresponding logical model and the generation of a physical model with the possibility of being executed. We intend to do that, using a set of patterns, composed by a specific flow of activities, representing the most common and error prone tasks on ETL systems design and implementation.

3   A BPMN 2.0 Meta-model Extension for ETL Modelling

Using BPMN notation for ETL specification is quite interesting. It provides a useful and expressive notation for the ETL conceptualization stage, as well as supplies several orchestration mechanisms that allow for their subsequent instantiation in execution primitives. With BPMN it's possible to represent more abstract processes, hiding some specific implementation details of their practical implementation, which turns possible to map them into new models associated to some specific execution architectures. Therefore, in this paper we propose a pattern-oriented approach with the ability to represent the most common tasks used in ETL systems implementation. We formalized these patterns through the use of a set of BPMN meta-models, which are characterized using a set of pre-established activities and its correspondent data flows. These meta-models can be used for ETL conceptual modelling, contributing to improve the quality of the process, reducing potential design errors as well as the costs associated with the whole process implementation. With these purposes in mind, we propose a BPMN 2.0 meta-model extension in order to represent a family of meta-models that can be instantiated and implemented by a tool that supports BPMN specification. Through this, we can add a new layer to the existing BPMN meta-model, composed by a set of pre-defined ETL patterns - based on a specific set of input parameters representing a particular application scenario, each pattern produces the corresponding output data set based accordingly to its control and data process specification. Following the BPMN-X approach [14] proposed for BPMN extension model representation, in Fig. 1 it's presented an excerpt of the relationship between BPMN base elements and the ETL Tasks class of the ETL pattern layer extension that we are proposing here.

The BPMN-X UML-based approach complies with the base BPMN rules for meta-model extension [3], guaranteeing that original BPMN elements are not modified and ensuring compatibility with existing BPMN supporting tools. In a BPMN meta-model each activity can be characterized as atomic (*Task*) or non-atomic (*SubProcess*). The *SubProcess* class inherits the attributes and associations with other classes (model associations) from *Activity* and *FlowElementsContainer* superclass. Our proposal extends this last class, once meta-models we going to define for ETL process specification are composed by several operations and pre-established data flows. The model presented in Fig. 1 uses two stereotypes allowing for the identification of original elements (<<*BPMNElement*>>) and extended elements (<<*ExtensionElement*>>). Using the <<*ExtensionElement*>> stereotype, we present the ETLTasks superclass, which is also a subclass of the *SubProcess* class. Detailing our *ETLTasks* superclass, we present in Fig. 2 the pattern-based ETL meta-model we propose, using the Ecore model provided by EMF framework from Eclipse[1], in order to represent all concepts related to the specification of each ETL pattern.

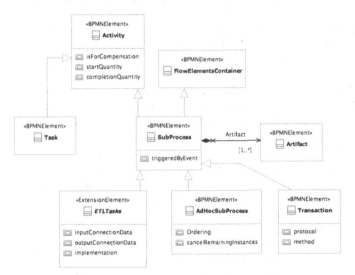

Fig. 1. The BPMN meta-model extension for ETL modelling

The meta-model of Fig. 2 presents several concepts related to pattern control elements and pattern data manipulation definition. In there, we included the *ConnectionParameters* class, which represents specific data that is used for input/output execution parameters and the *ConnectionMapping* class to specify data mappings about input parameters for data sources access and output parameters, where execution results from each pattern are stored. The *ETLTasks* class is the abstract superclass of the meta-model's classes representing here only a small example of a possible set of standard sub processes that can be included in the proposed meta-model, namely: *Load* – that represents load procedures for populating a data warehouse; DQE – which includes replace, unique, attribute decomposition and text transformation procedures; CDCLogFile – that applies for change data capture procedure based on a log file to capture relevant data that was changed on operational information systems; *SCDHistoryPreservation* – which represents a slowly changing dimension procedure that keeps records changing history in an auxiliary table; and Surrogate key procedures for a dimensional surrogate key generation process (*DimensionalSurrogateKey* class) and a surrogate key pipeline process (*SurrogateKeyPipeline* class). Each of these subclasses represents a standard ETL pattern integrating a specific set of pre-established tasks and data flow controls required for pattern definition and specification. In one of our previous articles [7] we

---

[1] http://www.eclipse.org

already presented a surrogate key pipeline pattern specification, and the necessary guidelines for its representation in a set of execution primitives. In the next section, we will describe some of most common DQE procedures, presenting its control and data process formal specification.

4   A BPMN Meta-model for Data Quality Validation

Data quality validation procedures are used to detect, remove errors and inconsistencies from data gathered on information sources. Given the nature of a data warehouse, it's critical to have correct data to feed it. This uniformity and cleaning procedures must be applied properly in some ETL's stage, in order to not affect the quality of decision-making processes. Data integration is highly influenced by the number of operational sources that participate in the ETL process as data providers, and by its schemas and inconsistencies that may exist. For that reason, specific procedures [15] must be used in all ETL transformation or cleaning steps, which allow for the specification of adequate strategies in order to eliminate problems related to data integration. Simpler tasks are typically used, such as: attribute decomposition; content attribute normalization; or duplicate elimination, as well as more complex processes that involve query ETL meta-data (mapping tables). These data dictionary tables are used for ETL support, storing necessary equivalences to support normalization and correction procedures. In order to specify these common procedures, in Fig. 3 we present the corresponding BPMN meta-model corresponding to a set of specific DQE procedures. This meta-model represents a general application of all data quality procedures presented previously in Fig. 2. However, for particular scenarios, this process can be simplified for including only a few of these procedures.

The DQE process starts by reading all necessary parameters that support the execution process: the audit table connection data in order to load and process target records, the mapping tables that contain the meta-data for ETL support, the target attributes for each table, the correspondence between all the attributes involved with, i.e. from audit table and data dictionary tables, the list of functions that will be applied and its respective attribute mappings, and the connection data of the target repository where records that were cleaned or conformed will be stored. Next, a loop sub-process (Fig. 3) starts applying specific data quality procedures. For this sub-process, two types of functions cab be identified: *pre-functions*, which are applied to a record prior the data replacement procedures; and *post-functions*, which are applied after the application of replacement procedures. Both type of functions represent simple procedures that must be applied to operational data, such as attribute decomposition and text transformations procedures. On the other way, post-functions, like duplicate elimination procedures, are only applied when replacing procedures are finished.

The replacement procedures are performed whenever it is necessary to standardize or correct (when necessary) data according to a given set of mapping rules stored in specific mapping tables. Thus, it's necessary to search these tables every time we need to get a replacement value. For a giver attribute, if no correspondences are found the process will continue following its specifications, i.e., data can be loaded to quarantine tables in order to be analysed latter, and approved automatically according to a set of specific rules when possible.

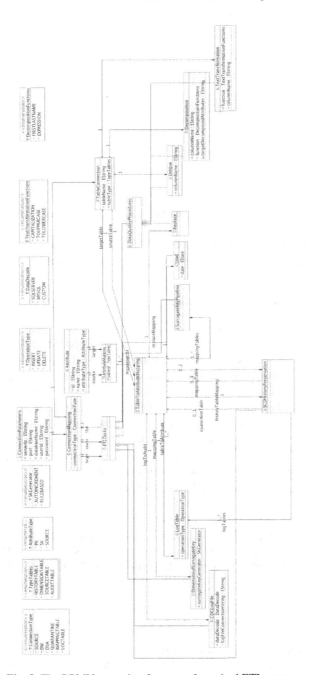

Fig. 2. The BPMN extension for a set of standard ETL patterns

The ETL conceptual model presented in Fig. 3 represents a single record for each sub process loop iteration. However, records are not necessarily pushed from external application one by one each time. The flows can be adjusted or reorganized according

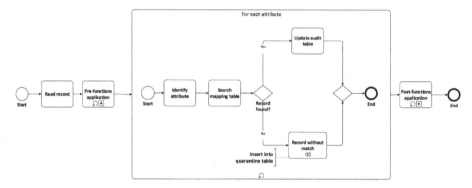

Fig. 3. A general BPMN conceptual model for a DQE procedure

to its physical implementation. However, in conceptual representation it is not needed to represent specific characteristics related to its implementation.

4.1   Workflow Control Specification

When modelling ETL processes we need to express the different control flows and data transformations between all the tasks that are embedded in them. The use of BPMN for ETL workflows, allows for a rich graphical representation of all the control flows established between activities we want to implement, as well as their own characterization and description. However, when defining a specific BPMN workflow as a standard pattern for ETL modelling, we must enforce some rules to be applied for the orchestration of flows and to allow the integration with some commercial tools. For that we selected XPDL (*XML Process Definition Language*) [16] specification, a XML based language, which can be used to formalize the process activities. Thus, we can specify how activities are executed and what is its execution sequence. Additionally, with XPDL specification we can also assure compatibility between BPMN workflow engines, which support the BPMN meta-model extension presented in Fig. 2. We must also consider that not all activities specified in a DQE pattern can be used in a real world scenario, simple because each ETL system has its own requirements. In a real process implementation, the XPDL file will be generated according to a particular pattern configuration, based on a specific application scenario.

4.2   Data Process Specification

With XDPL format we are able to formalize workflow orchestration elements and their interchanges across several BPMN-based tools. However, for each ETL workflow process we needed to specify a set of data transformations associated to the correspondent workflow tasks. Which means that BPMN allows for the specification of a number of steps (and its sequence) in order to achieve a specified goal. Data transformation procedures specify how data from operational sources will be transformed in order to complete each workflow task. Thus, we specified and modelled all transformations associated with ETL model's tasks using *Relational Algebra* (RA) [17–19], providing thus all formal transformations needed for each DQE procedure used. All transformations are presented based on the same base audit table structure. Nevertheless, transformations can be applied sequentially. In RA an audit table can be represented using a general schema for data representation such as:

$$auditData = \langle Att_1, ..., Att_n \rangle \qquad (1)$$

In Eq. 1 we can see a representation of *auditData* identifying the source audit table used on DQE procedures, and a set of attributes $Att_1, ..., Att_n$ that composes the audit table. As described before, we categorize DQE procedures in **pre-functions**, attribute decomposition and text transformation procedures; **replacement procedures**, for data correction or data normalization; and **post-functions**, for the elimination of duplicated records. For the decomposition of attributes, we defined the following RA expression:

$$auditData\_d \leftarrow \varepsilon_{[Att\_d_1 = subs(Att_n, 1), ..., Att\_d_n = subs(Att_n, n)]}(auditData) \qquad (2)$$

in which *subs* is a user-defined function that extracts a set of characters from an attribute. In this function, the first argument (Att_n) is the attribute to be parsed and the second on ($1..n$) defines which set of characters will be extracted (first, second, etc.). Lastly, the extended RA operator: ε [20] creates a new attribute based on data that is in other attributes, storing the result set in the *auditData_d* table. For text transformation procedures, such as upper, lowercase or capitalize conversion, we starting creating a new attribute based on the attribute to be transformed, for instance Att_n, and applying the respective transformation (*userFunction*) (Eq. 3). Then we remove the old Att_n attribute from table (Eq. 4) preserving the new one. Finally, we need to rename the new attribute to the old name restoring the original structure of the table:

$$Temp1 \leftarrow \varepsilon_{[Att_y = [userFunction](Att_n)]}(auditData) \qquad (3)$$

$$Temp2 \leftarrow \pi_{Att_1 ..., Att_m, Att_y}(Temp1) \qquad (4)$$

$$auditData \leftarrow \rho_{Att_n / Att_y}(Temp2) \qquad (5)$$

Next, we need to specify some normalization procedures, such as name or acronyms replacement, and values correction procedures. Both of them require an auxiliary table (Equation 6) to support mappings among user pre-defined corrections and source data.

$$mappingTable = \langle Att_n, ..., Att_{n1} \rangle \qquad (6)$$

The conforming data task is represented by the result of a join operation, identifying the conformed abbreviation/correction that will be replaced (Eq. 7, 8 and 9), in the target table:

$$Temp1 \leftarrow auditData \bowtie mappingTable \qquad (7)$$

$$Temp2 \leftarrow \pi_{Att_1, ..., Att_m, Att_{n1}}(Temp1) \qquad (8)$$

$$srcTempData \leftarrow \rho_{Att_n/Att_{n1}} (Temp2) \qquad (9)$$

Afterwards, the identification of tuples that have attribute values with no match in the auxiliary table can be loaded to specific quarantine tables for future analysis and recovering. This behavior can be specified from both data normalization and data correction procedures (Eq. 10 and 11):

$$Temp1 \leftarrow auditData \rhd mappingTable \qquad (10)$$

$$quarantine \leftarrow auditData - Temp1 \qquad (11)$$

For post-function duplicate elimination procedure, we must to identify all duplicate attributes and treated properly. Considering a particular attribute Att_n, which stores information that should be unique in the dimension, one possible method to identify duplicates is to find if the value of the attribute is in more than one tuple, not respecting the uniqueness rule (Eq. 12, 13, 14 and 15). If such records exist then they must be stored in some quarantine table for future analysis.

$$Temp1(Attn, mycount) \leftarrow Att_n \ni {}_{COUNT} Att_n (auditData) \qquad (12)$$

$$Temp2 \leftarrow \sigma_{mycount>1} (Temp1) \qquad (13)$$

$$Temp3 \leftarrow \pi_{Att_n} (Temp2) \qquad (14)$$

$$tempDataDup \leftarrow Temp3 \bowtie auditData \qquad (15)$$

After identifying the duplicates, they should be removed from the dimension table:

$$auditData\_U \leftarrow auditData - TempDataDup \qquad (16)$$

5   Conclusions and Future Work

We have presented in this paper a pattern ETL modelling proposal based on the BPMN 2.0 notation. We described a meta-model that supports our ETL practical implementation, integrating a set of patterns composed by a group of tasks that we consider as standard in any common ETL system implementation. At this point it is very important to distinguish our proposal from other BPMN conceptual modelling proposals. As we have shown in one of our past papers [7], we consider the idea of applying BPMN to ETL conceptual modelling very interesting, particularly in what is concerned with mapping of conceptual models in execution primitives, witch can be accomplished not only using BPEL but also using BPMN 2.0. Additionally, not only the familiarity of the stakeholders of the organization with the BPMN notation is a great advantage, but also the integration and communication of ETL processes developed with other organizational processes already implemented is guaranteed [21]. The approach presented in this paper was essentially settled on a set of templates (or patterns) that are composed by several atomic tasks representing standard ETL processes commonly used on regular ETL systems, which includes tasks such as: change data capture, slowly changing dimensions with history maintenance, surrogate key pipelining or DQE procedures. We think that with this approach we can reduce significantly potential inadequacies on the design and implementation of an ETL system. As an example of a pattern specification, we presented a description DQE pattern, including a set of procedures used on data integration processes. We propose a XPDL specification for process control formalization, providing its serialization and computer interpretation, allowing for the representation of all BPMN diagram concepts in an interchangeable format. Finally, and using RA, we also presented a specification of all elementary transformations that were needed to apply all data transformations associated with each DQE procedure.

In a near future we intend to provide a complete family of BPMN patterns specification at control and data process levels, in order to have the possibility to design and develop a complete ETL process, covering its main areas of planning and implementation. Additionally, we will extend our work to provide specific mapping rules allowing for BPMN–based ETL conceptual model translation to a logical model, letting its conversion and integration into existing ETL support tools, services and structures.

References

1. Weske, M., van der Aalst, W.M.P., Verbeek, H.M.W.: Advances in business process management. Data & Knowledge Engineering 50 (2004)
2. Kimball, R., Caserta, J.: The Data Warehouse ETL Toolkit: Practical Techniques for Extracting, Cleaning, Conforming, and Delivering Data (2004)
3. OMG: Documents Associated With Business Process Model And Notation (BPMN) Version 2.0. Documents Associated With Business Process Model And Notation (BPMN) Version 2.0 (2011)
4. El Akkaoui, Z., Zimányi, E.: Defining ETL worfklows using BPMN and BPEL. In: Proceedings of the ACM Twelfth International Workshop on Data Warehousing and OLAP, DOLAP 2009, pp. 41–48 (2009)
5. El Akkaoui, Z., Zimányi, E., Mazón, J.-N., Trujillo, J.: A model-driven framework for ETL process development. In: Proceedings of the ACM 14th International Workshop on Data Warehousing and OLAP, DOLAP 2011, pp. 45–52 (2011)
6. El Akkaoui, Z., Mazón, J.-N., Vaisman, A., Zimányi, E.: BPMN-Based Conceptual Modeling of ETL Processes. In: Cuzzocrea, A., Dayal, U. (eds.) DaWaK 2012. LNCS, vol. 7448, pp. 1–14. Springer, Heidelberg (2012)
7. Oliveira, B., Belo, O.: BPMN Patterns for ETL Conceptual Modelling and Validation. In: Chen, L., Felfernig, A., Liu, J., Raś, Z.W. (eds.) ISMIS 2012. LNCS, vol. 7661, pp. 445–454. Springer, Heidelberg (2012)
8. Vassiliadis, P., Simitsis, A., Skiadopoulos, S.: Conceptual modeling for ETL processes. In: Proceedings of the 5th ACM International Workshop on Data Warehousing and OLAP, DOLAP 2002, pp. 14–21 (2002)
9. Vassiliadis, P., Simitsis, A., Skiadopoulos, S.: On the Logical Modeling of ETL Processes. In: Pidduck, A.B., Mylopoulos, J., Woo, C.C., Ozsu, M.T. (eds.) CAiSE 2002. LNCS, vol. 2348, pp. 782–786. Springer, Heidelberg (2002)
10. Simitsis, A., Vassiliadis, P.: A Methodology for the Conceptual Modeling of ETL Processes. In: Eder, J., Missikoff, M. (eds.) CAiSE 2003. LNCS, vol. 2681, pp. 305–316. Springer, Heidelberg (2003)

11. Vassiliadis, P., Simitsis, A., Georgantas, P., Terrovitis, M.: A framework for the design of ETL scenarios. In: Eder, J., Missikoff, M. (eds.) CAiSE 2003. LNCS, vol. 2681, pp. 520–535. Springer, Heidelberg (2003)
12. El-Sappagh, S.H.A., Hendawi, A.M.A., El Bastawissy, A.H.: A proposed model for data warehouse ETL processes. Journal of King Saud University – Computer and Information Sciences 23 (2011)
13. Trujillo, J., Luján-Mora, S.: A UML Based Approach for Modeling ETL Processes in Data Warehouses. In: Song, I.-Y., Liddle, S.W., Ling, T.-W., Scheuermann, P. (eds.) ER 2003. LNCS, vol. 2813, pp. 307–320. Springer, Heidelberg (2003)
14. Stroppi, L.J.R., Chiotti, O., Villarreal, P.D.: Extending BPMN 2.0: Method and Tool Support. In: Dijkman, R., Hofstetter, J., Koehler, J. (eds.) BPMN 2011. LNBIP, vol. 95, pp. 59–73. Springer, Heidelberg (2011)
15. Rahm, E., Do, H.H.: Data Cleaning: Problems and Current Approaches. IEEE Data Engineering Bulletin 23, 2000 (2000)
16. Shapiro, R.M.: XPDL 2.1 - Integrating Process Interchange & BPMN (2008)
17. Codd, E.F.: A relational model of data for large shared data banks. Commun. ACM 13, 377–387 (1970)
18. Özsoyoğlu, G., Özsoyoğlu, Z.M., Matos, V.: Extending relational algebra and relational calculus with set-valued attributes and aggregate functions. ACM Trans. Database Syst. 12, 566–592 (1987)
19. Grefen, P.W.P.J., de By, R.A.: A Multi-Set Extended Relational Algebra - A Formal Approach to a Practical Issue. In: Proceedings of the Tenth International Conference on Data Engineering, pp. 80–88. IEEE Computer Society, Washington, DC (1994)
20. Baralis, E., Widom, J.: An Algebraic Approach to Rule Analysis in Expert Database Systems. In: Proceedings of the 20th International Conference on Very Large Data Bases, pp. 475–486. Morgan Kaufmann Publishers Inc., San Francisco (1994)
21. Wilkinson, K., Simitsis, A., Castellanos, M., Dayal, U.: Leveraging Business Process Models for ETL Design. In: Parsons, J., Saeki, M., Shoval, P., Woo, C., Wand, Y. (eds.) ER 2010. LNCS, vol. 6412, pp. 15–30. Springer, Heidelberg (2010)

Towards OntoUML for Software Engineering: From Domain Ontology to Implementation Model

Robert Pergl[1], Tiago Prince Sales[2], and Zdeněk Rybola[1]

[1] Department of Software Engineering,
Faculty of Information Technology,
Czech Technical University in Prague, Czech Republic
{robert.pergl,zdenek.rybola}@fit.cvut.cz
[2] Ontology and Conceptual Modeling Research Group (NEMO),
Computer Science Department,
Federal University of Esprito Santo, Brazil
tpsales@inf.ufes.br

Abstract. OntoUML is a promising method for ontological modelling. In this paper, we discuss its possible use for software engineering. We propose a method of transformation of an ontological model into a software-engineering object-oriented class model in UML and its instantiation. Our approach is based on the following best practices: pure object-oriented paradigm and approach of dividing state and identity as introduced in the Clojure programming language.

Keywords: OntoUML, Sortals, UML, object-oriented modelling, models transformation.

1 Introduction

Software engineering is a demanding discipline that deals with complex systems. The goal of software engineering is to ensure a quality software implementation of these complex systems. Various reports (e.g. Standish Group's) show that the success rate of software projects is far from satisfactory. We see the transformation of an ontological conceptual model into an implementation model as an engineering method that may contribute to better results and higher quality of the resulting software. We address the topic related to the *preservation of information between the successive software-engineering project phases* as discussed e.g. in [1]. We discuss the transformation of a structural conceptual model (in OntoUML) into a structural implementation model (in UML) during the design phase.

2 Goals and the Structure of the Paper

On one hand, we want to present our original method of transformation of ontologically well-founded conceptual models, written in OntoUML, into a pure

A. Cuzzocrea and S. Maabout (Eds.): MEDI 2013, LNCS 8216, pp. 249–263, 2013.

object implementation model described by the UML class diagrams. To achieve that, we determine the following subgoals:

1. To develop a basic transformation of a conceptual OntoUML model into an implementation object-oriented model (section 4).
2. To develop a transformation of individual OntoUML entity types: We will limit ourselves to Sortal types in this paper (section 5).
3. To present a complete example of transformation of a sample model (section 6).

3   Methods and Materials

3.1   OntoUML

OntoUML is an ontology-based conceptual modelling language, initially proposed in Guizzardi's PhD Thesis [2] as a lightweight extension of UML (using the notion of Profiles). The language is based on the cognitive science achievements of understanding specifics of our perception and on modal logic and related mathematical foundations (sets and relations).

Unlike other extensions of UML, OntoUML does not build on the UML's ontologically vague "class" notion, rather it constitutes a complete system independent of the original UML elements. It uses some aspects (like classes), however, it omits a set of other problematic concepts (for instance aggregation and composition) and replaces them with its own ontologically correct concepts.

OntoUML is designed to comply with the *Unified Foundational Ontology* (UFO) and because of that, it provides expressive and precise constructs for modellers to capture a domain of interest. OntoUML addresses many problems in conceptual modelling, such as part-whole relations [3], and Roles and the counting problem [4].

The language has been successfully applied in different contexts. In [5], the authors developed an ontology using OntoUML for the domain of electrophysiology, which was used to provide semantic interoperability for medical protocols. Another application was for a domain of transport networks, in which it was applied to evaluate an ITU-T standard for transport networks [6].

OntoUML Sortals. The notion of *Sortals* incorporated in OntoUML is the very same of the one in UFO, so in order to explain it, we must come back to the foundational ontology. One can understand UFO as a theory regarding individuals and universals. In conceptual modelling, universals are known as classes and individuals as objects, which instantiate these classes. Sortal universals are a special type of classes whose individuals follow the same identity principle, in contrast to Non-Sortal universals, which do not. Examples of Sortal universals are Person, Student and Child. Examples of Non-Sortal universals are Customer (can be a Person or a Corporation – different kinds) and Insurable Item (can be a Car, a House or even a Person).

Identity principle is the feature that makes possible for one to count and distinguish individuals. The universal Person, for example, if understood from a social perspective, could define that its identity principle is one's social security number, whilst in a more biological perspective, it could be one's fingerprint. Some Sortal universals define the identity principle for their instances, whilst others just inherit it.

Another important ontological property of Sortals is *rigidity*. Some Sortals are rigid, which means that for every individual who instantiates the Sortal, they must always do so in every moment during its life cycle (e.g. Man, Company, Apple). On the other hand, some Sortals are anti-rigid, which means that an individual can instantiate it in a given moment and not do so in another one (e.g. Student, Employee, Child).

Kinds and Subkinds. In UFO there are three types of Sortals that define the identity principle for their instances (named Substance Sortal Universals): Kinds, Quantities and Collectives. Since the principle of identity of an individual must never change, these are also rigid types. In addition, every individual must have an (exactly one) identity principle, so all individuals must be an instance of exclusively one such universal. Subkinds represent another type of Sortals, which are rigid and they inherit the identity principle from other types. For that reason, they must always have a Substance Sortal as an ancestor. In this paper, we focus only on the Kinds and Subkinds Substance Sortals.

Roles. The Role Sortal defines an entity type of a Role an object plays when in a relation to other objects. Similar to Subkind, Role inherits the ontological identity from its Substance Sortal ancestor. It is an anti-rigid and *relationally dependent* concept. This means at the instance level that for an individual to play a given Role, i.e. to be a Role instance, it must participate in a relation with some other object. The anti-rigid property of Roles requires that we handle it dynamically in the implementation – the object can start to play the Role and stop playing the Role during its life.

Phases. In UFO, a Phase universal is a type whose instantiation is characterized by a change in an intrinsic property of an individual. Since it is out of the scope of this paper to discuss properties, it is sufficient to say that intrinsic properties are the opposite of relational properties. An intrinsic property can be structured, such as person's age, or unstructured, like one's headache.

Phases are anti-rigid and they inherit their identity principle from their Substance Sortal ancestor. An additional constraint on the Phase type is that it must be represented in partitions, i.e. Phases must belong to a disjoint and complete generalization set. An example of a Phase partition is phases of a person's life: A person can be a child, an adult or an elder. Each phase is characterized by a certain range of age and every person must be in exactly one of these phases.

According to the features of OntoUML mentioned above, we consider OntoUML very suitable for conceptual modelling as it can distinguish many various types of entities. Therefore, we also consider a tranformation of such a model into an implementation model very important to support the use of OntoUML in software engineering.

3.2 Object Model and UML

Object model started as a notion of programming paradigm in 1960s. It first appeared in the Simula programming language and it was nurtured in many following languages since then. Along the object-oriented programming (OOP), the object-oriented analysis (OOA) and the object-oriented design (OOD) together with object-oriented modelling (OOM) were established [7]. Today, object-oriented approaches dominate the software engineering and programming practice.

In this paper, we stick to pure object-oriented model which is exemplified e.g. in the Smalltalk programming language [8]. We utilize the following concepts:

Object – an entity that has encapsulated *inner state* in the form of **attributes** and reacts to **messages** sent by other objects by invoking **methods**, which are the only external representation of the object.

Class – a "template" that contains a structure of attributes and methods code. A class can spawn its **instances** – objects. In pure object model, class *is an object as well* and thus it may receive messages.

Constructor – a special *class* method for spawning instances (**new** in Smalltalk). By redefining the constructor, we may achieve special initialization of a new instance. This approach differs in many hybrid object languages (like C++), where the constructor is an *instance method* that is called *after* a new instance is created, thus having limited control over instance spawning.

Collection – a special object that can compose an unspecified (conceptually unlimited) number of instances. In pure object-oriented approach, the **members** of a collection may be of *heterogeneous* classes (which is unfortunately not true for hybrid languages like Java or C++).

We consider two basic relations between classes:

Inheritance – the *is-a*, or generalization-specialization relation. Here we deal with inheritance of classes, although inheritance of objects (without a class system) is also possible.

Aggregation [1] – the *part-of* relation between *objects*, where the aggregating object contains an aggregated object as its part. This is technically achieved by putting the object to an attribute. In the class diagram, aggregation is represented by a directed association (arrow) from the aggregating object's class to the aggregated object's class.

---

[1] In UML, apart from aggregation, *composition* is discussed as another term for part-whole relations. For our purpose, we will use the term aggregation in its broader meaning including composition and also other flavours of part-whole relationships as discussed by Guizzardi in [9].

As for the notation, we will stick to the Unified Modeling Language (UML), a standardized general-purpose modelling language that was created for object-oriented software engineering. It includes a set of graphic notation techniques to create visual models of object-oriented software-intensive systems. Although UML was designed to be a conceptual modelling language as well, it is better suited for implementation modelling, as it misses (and messes) crucial conceptual concepts [2]. We use a subset of *class diagram* notation for our purpose of the transformation of an OntoUML conceptual model into a UML implementation model here. For further information, see numerous literature available, we recommend [10].

3.3   The Concept of *State* and *Identity*

The concept of state and identity was introduced[2] in the Clojure programming language, a pure functional language coming from Lisp. However, its importance spans to conceptual modelling, as well. In our work we use it in the transformation to build completely dynamic object hierarchies that may be changed on-the-fly.

"Clojure introduces a philosophical and conceptual paradigm shift in its treatment of things. It takes the standard notion of a thing (an object or a variable) and decomposes it into two separate concepts - *state* and *identity*. Every thing has both a state and an identity. State is a value associated with an identity at a particular moment in time, whereas identity is the part of a thing that does not change, and creates the link between many different states at many different times. The value of each state is immutable and cannot change. Rather, change is modelled by the identity being updated to refer to a different state entirely." – [11].

In this approach the notion of *value* is very close to OntoUML's notion of *Quality Value*, where Quality is a sort of "identity" and Quality Value is its "state".

Hickey states that *state and identity are usually unified in object-oriented languages*, however, he also states that it does not have to be so.

In our approach, we apply the distinction of state and identity in pure object-oriented paradigm, as we discern *identity objects* and *value objects*. Identity objects are not allowed to hold any values, they just refer to the associated states. This enables us to build dynamic object hierarchies that may be changed on-the-fly. This could be especially useful when dealing with the history aspect of the data – for instance to capture the relations and attributes of an object in some history moment before changing its Phase or Role. We exemplify this approach in section 6.

---

[2] Here we do not want to go into philosophical roots of this concept, though we do not doubt that a discussion of this would be both deep and useful.

4   Transformation of OntoUML into Object Model

In this section, we present the foundations of a transformation. The transformation is well-known and very similar to the transformation of UML conceptual models. Therefore we emphasize the most important aspects of the tranformation into an object implementantion model. For details about specific Sortals transformation, see section 5.

An object model is very near to human thinking [12] and thus to OntoUML as well, so the transformation is rather straightforward (compared to – for example – a relational model). The object model contains less constructs than OntoUML. That means an OntoUML model thus needs to "collapse" into object-oriented concepts introduced in the previous subsection:

- Object (class) with attributes and methods,
- Object aggregation,
- Inheritance.

Various types of entities in OntoUML (Kind, Subkind, Role, ...) are transformed into object model **classes**. So, the discussion leads to the question how not to loose semantics during the transformation. Unfortunately, the space limitation does not allow us to discuss the issue in detail. We, however, redirect the interested reader to [1], where this issue is discussed.

4.1   Transformation of Attributes

An example of an OntoUML entity type with attributes is in Figure 1.

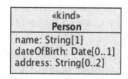

Fig. 1. An example of OntoUML entity type with attributes

The transformation of attributes is one-to-one with respect to the following:

- We may map types to a concrete object-oriented language or let them be general.
- Maximal multiplicities 0..1 of the attributes lead to instance variables.
- Maximal multiplicities * of the attributes lead to **collections**.
- For mandatory attributes with multiplicities 1..1, it is necessary to ensure non-empty value of instance variable.
- For mandatory attributes with multiplicities 1..*, it is necessary to ensure non-empty collection.

Ensuring Mandatory Attributes. An object model contains no support for declarative specification of mandatory attributes. The mandatory attributes thus need to be handled *in methods*. The suggest the following two options:

1. *"Hard method"*: Enforce a value insertion when creating or updating the instance. Prevent inserting empty value (*null* in most languages) in constructor and other methods by throwing an error.
2. *"Soft method"*: Do not prevent inserting empty values but implement consistency checks when required – i.e. before persisting to a database.

4.2 Implementation of Associations

Association is a **bidirectional** relation between classes that has a name and **"multiplicity" values at both sides, i.e. 4 characteristics** (2x lower bound, 2x upper bound).

An example of OntoUML association is shown in Figure 2.

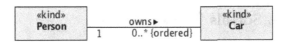

Fig. 2. An example of an OntoUML association

The following types of multiplicities are distinguished [7]:

1:1 – every instance of class A has (at maximum) one instance to which at most one instance of class B is associated.

1:N – every instance of class A may have one or more instances of class B associated (it corresponds to UML's 1..* multiplicity).

M:N – an instance of class A may have more instances of class B associated and the instance of class B may have more instances of class A associated (corresponds to UML's *..* multiplicity).

The most direct implementation of an association is by *aggregation* (*part-of* relation between objects). Aggregation in object model is, however, a **unidirectional** relation. This is quite a complex issue and it may be solved by various approaches, as discussed e.g. in [13] or [14]. For the simplicity of concepts' explanations in this paper, we will limit ourselves to just *one-direction references* approach to transforming associations to object model – see Figure 3 for an example of 1:N-type association transformation. The direction of the aggregation is chosen according to primary navigation needs in this situation and we do not assume backward navigation.

As the aggregation leads to ordinary attributes, the issue of ensuring the minimal multiplicities of *1* at the opposite side of arrow – the target – is equivalent with ensuring the mandatory attributes described in section 4.1. Ensuring the mandatory presence of the instance on the arrow side – the source – is not trivial, as may be seen in [13], [14] or [15] and we will thus not discuss it here.

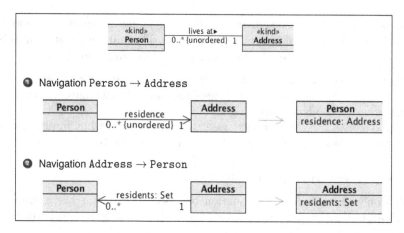

Fig. 3. Transformation of a 1:N bidirectional association into an unidirectional aggregation

5   OntoUML Sortals Transformation

This section discusses the main principles of transformations of individual Sortals into an object model classes. For each Sortal, we briefly and informally summarize its features that are important from the software-engineering point of view. We present the transformation into a class model in UML and we provide additional comments.

5.1   Kind and Subkind

The *Kind* type defines an object's identity and its attributes. According to our approach of dividing identity and state – see subsection 3.3, the <<kind>> entity type is transformed into two classes – one to hold the identity and the other to hold the state.

The *Subkind* type defines additional features of other Kinds and Subkinds, and thus forms a specialization hierarchy. It also makes the identity more accurate. Therefore, both the *identity* and the *state* parts have to be transformed along with the hierarchy. An example of the *Kind* and *Subkind* hierarchy is shown in Figure 4. For simplicity, we will not include the identity and state separating in the following parts describing the transformation of other OntoUML concepts.

5.2   Role

The most straightforward transformation of a Role type is to implement each <<role>> class in the OntoUML model by its own class in the UML model. However, because of the anti-rigidity, this class cannot be a specialization of its supertype from the OntoUML model because the specialization is rigid in UML models and OO implementation languages – it cannot be changed during the life

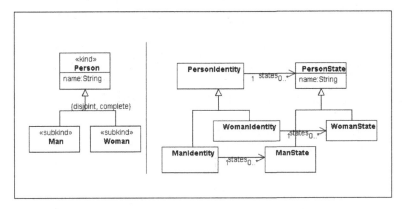

Fig. 4. Transformation of a Role type into a UML model

of the instance. Therefore, the generalization from the OntoUML model must be transformed into an *aggregation* that can be easily modified during the life of the instance without changing the identity provided by the associated rigid supertype. An example of such a transformation is shown in Figure 5.

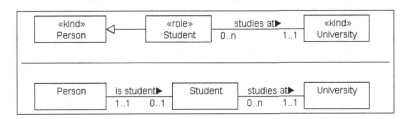

Fig. 5. Transformation of a Role type into a UML model

5.3 Phase

The transformation of the *Phase* entity type is similar to the transformation of Roles. Each <<role>> class in the OntoUML model is transformed into a UML class. To preserve the anti-rigidity of Phases in a UML model where the specialization and the generalization are rigid, the Phase partition hierarchy cannot be implemented by specialization. Instead, it is realized as an aggregation. However, compared to Roles, an entity may be in *just one* Phase of the Phase partition. We may denote this using XOR constraint, as shown in Figure 6, where an OntoUML model of various restaurant table states is transformed into a pure object implementation model in UML.

XOR constraint means that an instance of the *Person* type composes an instance of one of the phases in its **Phase** attribute. Additionally, the target multiplicity constraint is *1*; that means that each instance of the *Person* type must contain an instance of just one of the phases.

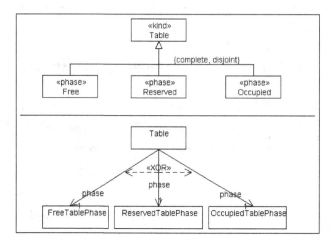

Fig. 6. Example of the Phase transformation

In fact, the transformation is platform-dependent. In dynamically-typed object-oriented languages (Smalltalk, Python, ...) a programmer is able to put objects of various types into the same attribute. However, in static object-oriented programming languages (Java, C++, C#, ...), all attributes must define its type. To be able to put all the phases to the same attribute, an abstract supertype or an interface is necessary, as shown in Figure 7.

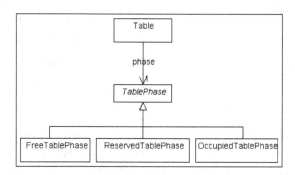

Fig. 7. Example of the Phase transformation for static object-oriented languages

6   Example of Transformation

In the example, we will include *history* information in the UML model, i.e. we track not just the current world, but all the worlds that happened to exist in the past. As in [16], we "assume that the only thing specified in the domain ontology is how many times a certain substantial may play the same Role universal simultaneously, not throughout lifetime".

Figure 8 presents a sample model containing rigid and anti-rigid types. Figure 9 presents a transformed model according to the principles described above, where we need to:

1. Separate rigid and anti-rigid parts into distinct composed objects.
2. Separate identity and state (subsection 3.3).

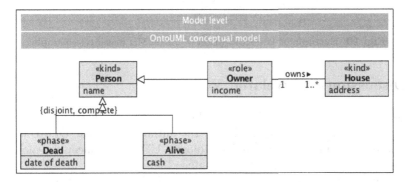

Fig. 8. Example of transformation – OntoUML conceptual model

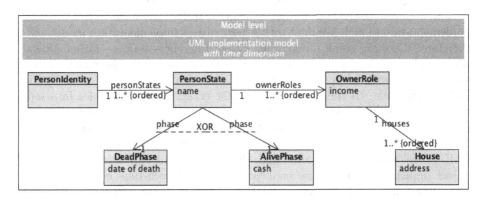

Fig. 9. Example of transformation – UML implementation model

As for the instance level, Figure 10 depicts a sample OntoUML instances in two different worlds. Having unlimited dynamic behaviour of entity types at instance-level OntoUML, we perceive just the resulting identities and their attributes, while in the object model's instance world in Figure 11 the information is divided into the corresponding instances of classes[3].

---

[3] We use a slightly simplified notation for collections here – *personStates* and *houses* collections are represented by a forked line leading to its members.

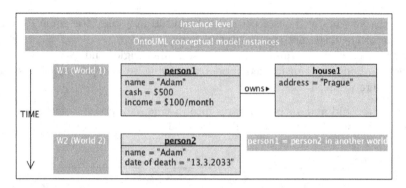

Fig. 10. Example of transformation – OntoUML instances example

7   Discussion and Related Work

The issue of conceptual modelling and domain ontologies have been discussed in many publications and papers. In [2], the author defines the OntoUML language based on Unified Foundational Ontology – UFO – for conceptual modelling without discussing its use in software engineering.

The use of OntoUML for software engineering is discussed in [16]. The author discusses the conceptual modelling at two levels – the ontological and the informational. He also suggests a transformation of an OntoUML model into an object-oriented UML implementation model. However, our approach differs in some aspects: In [16], the author presents transformation for object-oriented implementation model. We deal with a pure object implementation model and, therefore, there are some differences. These differences become rather crucial when dealing with anti-rigid types like Roles and Phases. Furthermore, the author transforms Role types from the OntoUML model into associations in the UML model. We, on the other hand, prefer transforming the Roles into separate UML classes in order to capture Role attributes. Consequently, we also use methods in the implementation to achieve the best quality object design. Moreover, we consider using aggregation of Phase classes and Role classes in the UML model to be more dynamic and, therefore, it conforms better to the pure object implementation. It also enables more flexible run-time manipulation of Roles and Phases. Additionally, we also deal with another OntoUML and UFO concept – Phases – that are not discussed in [16]. On the other hand, Carraretto deals with other entity types (Relators, Non-Sortals) that we do not cover here.

The problem of object Roles and its transformation has also been discussed in many publications and papers – for instance in [17], [18] and [19] and others. The transformation of relationships has been also discussed in [15] in the context of relational databases and multiplicity constraints where the reader may find thorough discussion of the topics.

There are books and papers started to be written about the Clojure programming language (e.g. [20], [11], [21]). It is a pure functional language inspired by traditional Lisp and it provides several interesting ideas related to the topic of

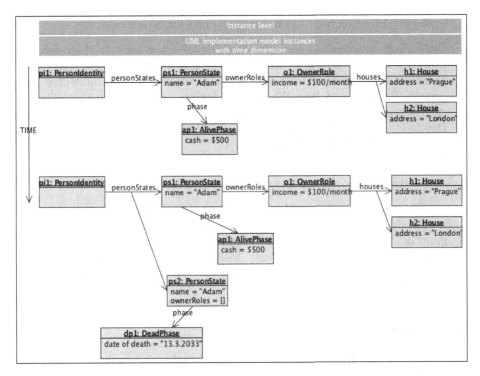

Fig. 11. Example of transformation – object instances example (UML)

the paper. In this paper, we discussed the concept of separation of state and identity. However, the concept of *immutability* is also relevant to the topic of implementing OntoUML models – by implementing immutability of data structures, we get a complete separation of OntoUML worlds and so the mechanism shown in Figure 11 is maintained automatically by the interpreter.

8   Conclusions

Transformation of OntoUML (ontological) models into software engineering models is not a trivial issue, as we face limitations in current technologies. We discussed mostly a pure object-oriented technology here. It is perceived today as the most advanced technology for implementing business information systems. Moreover, pure object-oriented paradigm is language-agnostic, as it may be (with more or less limitations) applied not only in pure object-oriented languages as Smalltalk, but also in hybrid ones like Java or C++.

With respect to OntoUML models, we see the following issues as crucial:

- Achieving maximum dynamic of systems – we prefer *aggregation* instead of static *inheritance*.
- Separating *state* from *identity* – here, we see Clojure's approach as very promising.

We see the following issues as important topics for future research:

- Generating automatic constraints checking for the transformed models for various paradigms and programming languages, as shown e.g. in [15].
- Transformations of OntoUML Non-Sortal entity types and other types (especially Relators and Part-Whole relations are very important in software engineering).
- Development of open, flexible and yet user-friendly and practical CASE tools supporting the transformations.

Acknowledgements. This paper was elaborated under the cooperation of:

- *The Centre for Conceptual Modelling* http://ccm.fit.cvut.cz supported by Faculty of Information Technologies, Czech Technical University and grant no. SGS13/099/OHK3/1T/18 of the Czech Technical University.
- *The Ontology and Conceptual Modeling Research Group (NEMO)* http://nemo.inf.ufes.br supported by FAPES (PRONEX grant #52272362)

References

1. Pícka, M., Pergl, R.: Gradual modeling of information system: Model of method expressed as transitions between concepts. In: Proceedings of the ICEIS 2006 - 8th International Conference on Enterprise Information Systems, vol. ISAS, pp. 538–541 (2006)
2. Guizzardi, G.: Ontological Foundations for Structural Conceptual Models, vol. 015. University of Twente, Enschede (2005)
3. Guizzardi, G.: The problem of transitivity of part-whole relations in conceptual modeling revisited, Amsterdam, The Netherlands (2009)
4. Guizzardi, G.: Agent roles, qua individuals and *the counting problem*. In: Garcia, A., Choren, R., Lucena, C., Giorgini, P., Holvoet, T., Romanovsky, A. (eds.) SELMAS 2005. LNCS, vol. 3914, pp. 143–160. Springer, Heidelberg (2006)
5. Goncalves, B., Guizzardi, G., Pereira Filho, J.G.: Using an ECG reference ontology for semantic interoperability of ECG data. Special Issue on Ontologies for Clinical and Translational Research (2011)
6. Barcelos, P.P.F., Guizzardi, G., Garcia, A.S., Monteiro, M.: Ontological evaluation of the ITU-T recommendation g.805, vol. 18. IEEE Press, Cyprus (2011)
7. Booch, G., Maksimchuk, R.A., Engel, M.W., Young, B.J., Conallen, J., Houston, K.A.: Object-Oriented Analysis and Design with Applications, 3 edn. Addison-Wesley Professional (April 2007)
8. Hunt, J.: Smalltalk and Object Orientation: An Introduction, 1st edn. Springer (July 1997)
9. Guizzardi, G.: Representing collectives and their members in UML conceptual models: An ontological analysis. In: Trujillo, J., et al. (eds.) ER 2010. LNCS, vol. 6413, pp. 265–274. Springer, Heidelberg (2010); WOS:000289184200033
10. Fowler, M.: UML Distilled: A Brief Guide to the Standard Object Modeling Language, 3rd edn. Addison-Wesley Professional (September 2003)
11. VanderHart, L., Sierra, S.: Practical Clojure, 1st edn. Apress (June 2010)

12. Kay, A.C.: The early history of smalltalk. SIGPLAN Not. 28(3), 69–95 (1993)
13. Gessenharter, D.: Mapping the UML2 semantics of associations to a java code generation model. In: Czarnecki, K., Ober, I., Bruel, J.-M., Uhl, A., Völter, M. (eds.) MODELS 2008. LNCS, vol. 5301, pp. 813–827. Springer, Heidelberg (2008)
14. Gessenharter, D.: Implementing UML associations in java: a slim code pattern for a complex modeling concept. In: Proceedings of the Workshop on Relationships and Associations in Object-Oriented Languages, RAOOL 2009, pp. 17–24. ACM, New York (2009)
15. Rybola, Z., Richta, K.: Transformation of special multiplicity constraints - comparison of possible realizations. In: FedCSIS 2012, Wroclaw, Poland (September 2012)
16. Carraretto, R.: Separating Ontological and Informational Concerns: A Model-driven Approach for Conceptual Modeling. Master thesis, Federal University of Espírito Santo (2012)
17. Gottlob, G., Schrefl, M., Röck, B.: Extending object-oriented systems with roles. ACM Trans. Inf. Syst. 14(3), 268–296 (1996)
18. Cabot, J., Raventós, R.: Conceptual modelling patterns for roles. In: Spaccapietra, S., Atzeni, P., Chu, W.W., Catarci, T., Sycara, K. (eds.) Journal on Data Semantics V. LNCS, vol. 3870, pp. 158–184. Springer, Heidelberg (2006)
19. Bierman, G., Wren, A.: First-class relationships in an object-oriented language. In: Gao, X.-X. (ed.) ECOOP 2005. LNCS, vol. 3586, pp. 262–286. Springer, Heidelberg (2005)
20. Mark Volkmann, R.: Clojure - functional programming for the JVM
21. Halloway, S.: Programming Clojure, 1st edn. Pragmatic Bookshelf (2009)

Model Engineering as a Social Activity:
The Case of Business Processes

Gottfried Vossen[1,2]

[1] European Research Center for Information Systems (ERCIS)
University of Münster
Leonardo-Campus 3, D-48149 Münster, Germany
[2] Waikato Management School
The University of Waikato
Private Bag 3105, Hamilton, New Zealand
vossen@uni-muenster.de

Traditionally, model engineering is about the construction of technical artifacts, which can range from sketchy drawings to complete physical assemblies. Translated into computer science terms, model engineering occurs in such fields as requirements engineering, software engineering, data modeling, or business process modeling (BPM), to mention just a few. In each case, the task is to establish a model, i.e., an abstraction of some real-world application, scenario, or case in such a way that it becomes amenable to a computer-based solution, mostly in data structures, algorithms, and software [1]. Such an abstraction eliminates irrelevant details and focuses on those parts of the given application that are essential for a solution. As a result, designers come up with models such as use-case diagrams, data models, class diagrams, entity-relationship diagrams, graph models, state charts, or various forms of Petri nets (this is not an exhaustive list) [2, 3, 5]. An important step once a model has been established is to verify that it captures the given reality appropriately, and that it is of "acceptable" quality.

Although model engineering typically requires high expertise in the respective area, its results often lack the quality originally intended, so that software projects based on the modeling result do not drive home the desired benefit or even fail. This has been a theme recurring over many years in computer science and information technology (IT), and over time many proposals have been made to cope with this situation, including layered architectures, object-orientation, or service-orientation. These suggestions typically follow a "separation of concerns" or a "divide and conquer" approach.

A different suggestion has recently been made by various communities based on the observation that it is often the case that IT people, i.e., the model engineers, hardly understand what users (e.g., the marketing or sales department, the back-office) mean when they express their desires, and that it is therefore reasonable to make design a social activity [4, 5]. Indeed, since often a number of participants with different backgrounds, goals, and capabilities are (or should be) involved, in a design or modeling tasks, the idea is to bring them all to the same table. An area where this has already proved a fruitful approach is the less

A. Cuzzocrea and S. Maabout (Eds.): MEDI 2013, LNCS 8216, pp. 264–265, 2013.
© Springer-Verlag Berlin Heidelberg 2013

technical area of business process modeling (BPM), which is why this talk takes a closer look at the case of BPM.

From a global perspective, business processes increasingly form the crux of any organization, since changes in the global market are common for the daily agenda: Companies are increasingly forced to adapt to new customers, competitors, and business partners. Competitive edges are achieved more frequently not by better products, but by efficient and cost-effective processes. In short: Business processes have developed into an additional factor of production and hence into an engineering artifact. The design of business processes has quite some history already, yet over time the originally purely experiential approach has been augmented by an engineering component so that it is common today to speak of business process engineering (BPE). This circumscribes the design and layout, the analysis, improvement, optimization as well as the documentation of operational activities and their basic conditions. The benefits of a business process model is greatest when the knowledge and creativity reflects all people involved, whether they are internal employees of an enterprise, employees of partner enterprises, or generally people whose knowledge can contribute to the design of the business process, either directly or indirectly. Social BPE attempts to provide a response to these issues. This talk will start from early modeling activities regarding business processes and will draw a bow from there to recently identified challenges in social BPM.

References

1. Aho, A., Ullman, J.D.: Foundations of Computer Science. W.H. Freeman, San Francisco (1992)
2. Batini, C., Navathe, S.B., Ceri, S.: Conceptual Database Design: An Entity-Relationship Approach. Bejamin/Cummings Publ. Co., Redwood City (1992)
3. Pohl, K., Rupp, C.: Requirements Engineering Fundamentals; Rocky Nook Computing, Santa Barbara, CA (2011)
4. Pflanzl, N., Vossen, G.: Human-Oriented Challenges of Social BPM; Technical Report, ERCIS, University of Münster (June 2013)
5. Schönthaler, F., Vossen, G., Oberweis, A., Karle, T.: Business Processes for Business for Communities. Springer, Berlin (2012)

A Transformation-Driven Approach to Automate Feedback Verification Results*

Faiez Zalila, Xavier Crégut, and Marc Pantel

Université de Toulouse, IRIT – France
{firstname.lastname}@enseeiht.fr

Abstract. The integration of formal verification methods in modeling activities is a key issue to ensure the correctness of complex system design models. In this purpose, the most common approach consists in defining a translational semantics mapping the abstract syntax of the designer dedicated Domain-Specific Modeling Language (DSML) to a formal verification dedicated semantic domain in order to reuse the available powerful verification technologies. Formal verification is thus usually achieved using model transformations. However, the verification results are available in the formal domain which significantly impairs their use by the system designer which is usually not an expert of the formal technologies.

In this paper, we introduce a novel approach based on Higher-Order transformations that analyze and instrument the transformation that expresses the semantics in order to produce traceability data to automatize the back propagation of verification results to the DSML end-user.

Keywords: Domain specific modeling language, Formal verification, Model checking, Translational semantics, Traceability, Verification feedback, Fiacre.

1 Introduction

Model-Driven Engineering (MDE) provides powerful techniques and tools to define *Domain-Specific Modeling Languages* (DSMLs) adapted for given user dedicated domains. These techniques rely on the DSML metamodel that describes the main concepts of the domain and their relations. MDE allows system designers (DSML end-users) working closer to the system domain as they will manipulate concepts from the real system.

Model validation and verification (V&V) activities are key features to assess the conformance of the future system to its behavioral requirements. In order to apply them, it is required to introduce an execution semantics for the DSMLs to verify whether built models behave as expected. This one is usually provided as a mapping from the abstract syntax (metamodel) of the DSML to an existing semantic domain, generally a formal verification dedicated language, in order to reuse powerful tools (simulator or model-checker) available for this language [1,2].

---

* This works was funded by the french Ministry of Industry through the ITEA2 project OPEES and openETCS and the french ANR project GEMOC.

A. Cuzzocrea and S. Maabout (Eds.): MEDI 2013, LNCS 8216, pp. 266–277, 2013.

One key issue is that system designers are not supposed to have a strong knowledge on formal languages and associated tools. Thus, the challenge for the DSML designer is to leverage formal tools so that the system designer does not need to burden with formal aspects and then to integrate them in traditional Computer Assisted Software Engineering (CASE) tools, like the Eclipse platform.

MDE already provides means to define metamodels (e.g. Ecore tools, Emphatic) along with static properties (e.g. OCL) and to generate either textual syntactic editors (e.g. xTEXT, EMFTEXT) or graphical editors (e.g. GMF, Spray, Sirius). Additionally, the DSML designer should extend the DSML framework with required elements to perform V&V tasks relying on translational semantics from the DSML to formal languages (e.g. Petri nets, automata, etc.).

Translational semantics for DSMLs into formal semantic domains allows the use of advanced analysis tools like model-checkers. It introduces the executability aspect for DSMLs and can provide execution paths in case of verification failures. However, this approach has a strong drawback: the verification results are generated in the formal technical space, whereas DSML end-users are not supposed to have a strong knowledge on formal languages and associated tools. Therefore, these results should be lifted to the user level (i.e. the DSML level) automatically.

The DSML designer does not only provide the translational semantics but must also implement a backward transformation that bring back the formal verification results to the DSML level so that they are understandable by the system designer (DSML end-user). Bringing back formal results to the DSML level can be complex. It is thus mandatory to assist the DSML designer by providing methods and tools to ease the implementation of result back propagation.

In this work, we propose a generic approach to integrate hidden formal verification through model-checking for a DSML. We rely on the Executable DSML pattern [3] to define all concerns involved in the definition of DSML semantics while its translational semantics is defined using a model-to-model transformation. Then, we define a higher-order transformation (HOT) to manipulate the translational semantics in order to generate the mandatory tools to ensure the back propagation of verification results. We rely on the FIACRE intermediate language [4] to help DSML designers to use formal methods by reducing the semantic gap between DSMLs and formal methods.

To illustrate our proposal, we consider as running example the xSPEM executable extension of the SPEM process modeling language [5]. It was designed in order to experiment V&V in the TOPCASED toolkit [6] using an MDE approach.

The paper is structured as follows: section 2 presents the *Executable DSML pattern* illustrated with SPEM [5] and the FIACRE metamodel. Section 3 explains our approach to generate the DSML verification framework. Section 4 presents the overview of the use of the generated DSML verification framework by the system designer. Section 5 gives some related work in the domain of user level verification results. Finally, Section 6 concludes and gives some perspectives.

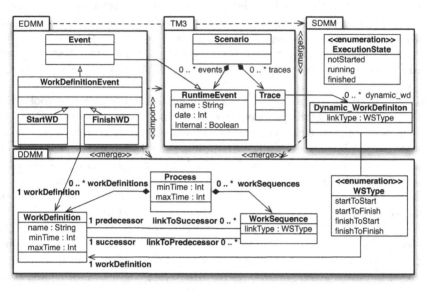

Fig. 1. *Executable DSML pattern* applied into the SPEM metamodel

2   The *Executable DSML pattern* for V&V

When dealing with an executable DSML, the usual metamodel generally does not model the notions manipulated at runtime such as dynamic information or stimuli that make the model evolve. To address this issue, Combemale et al. have proposed the *Executable DSML pattern* [3]. In the context of formal verification, the pattern is applied both on the source DSML and the formal target DSML to help in leveraging to the DSML side the results obtained on the formal side.

2.1   xSPEM as an Executable DSML

The *Executable DSML pattern* applied on SPEM metamodel is shown in Figure 1.

The classical DSML metamodel is shown as the *Domain Definition Meta-Model (DDMM)*. It provides the key concepts of the language (representing the considered domain) and their relationships. It is the usual metamodel used to define the modeling language in standardization organisations. It is usually endowed with structural constraints. For instance, the SPEM metamodel defines the concepts of *Process* composed of (1) *workDefinitions* that model the activities performed during the process, (2) *workSequences* that define temporal dependency relations (causality constraints) between activities.

During the execution of a model, additional data are usually mandatory for expressing the execution itself. A first extension, named *State Definition Meta-Model (SDMM)*, stores dynamic data in the form of metatype instances. For example, each workdefinition is in one of the states: *notStarted, running or finished*.

The state attribute should be defined in the *Dynamic_WorkDefinition* metatype. The second extension, *Event Definition MetaModel (EDMM)*, reifies the concrete stimuli of the DSML as subtypes of the common abstract RuntimeEvent metatype. Concrete EDMM events add properties in relation to, and/or redefine properties of, events related to the formal semantics to be supported. As an illustration, runtime events for xSPEM include "start a workdefinition" and "finish a workdefinition". Thus, two metatypes *StartWD* and *FinishWD* will be defined.

Finally, the *Trace Management MetaModel (TM3)* allows to define a scenario as a sequence of runtime events usually interleaved with the state of the model between triggered previous and next events. The TM3 is independent of any DSML.

2.2   The Fiacre Formal Language

FIACRE [4] is a french acronym for an *Intermediate Format for Embedded Distributed Components Architectures*. It was designed as the target language for model transformations from different DSMLs such as Architecture Analysis and Design Language (AADL), Ladder Diagram (LD), Business Process Execution Language (BEPL) and some UML diagrams (sub-languages).

The FIACRE formal language allows representing both the behavioral and timing aspects of systems, in particular embedded and distributed systems, for formal verification and simulation purposes. Fiacre is built around two notions:

- Processes describe the behavior of sequential components. A process is defined by a set of control states, each associated with a piece of program built from deterministic constructs available in classical programming languages (assignments, conditionals, repetitions, and sequential compositions), non deterministic constructs (non deterministic choice and non deterministic assignments), communication events on ports, and transitions to next state.
- Components describe the composition of processes, possibly in a hierarchical manner. A component is defined as a parallel composition of instantiated components and/or processes communicating through ports and shared variables. The notion of component also allows restricting the access mode and visibility of shared variables and ports, associating timing constraints with communications, and defining priority between communication events.

Verification results are obtained at the formal level and must be leveraged at the DSML level. This feedback is made easier thanks to the *Executable DSML pattern* [3] applied not only at the DSML level but also at the formal one.

In this work, our aim is to build DSML events out of the FIACRE ones provided by verification failures. We are thus interested only in the FIACRE EDMM. It contains specific events [7]: instances of processes entering or leaving a state, variables changing values, communications through ports and tagged statements occurring in process instances.

3   Generation DSML Verification Framework

Our approach is based on two model-based concepts: 1) **traceability** and 2) **higher-order transformation**. It relies on the Atlas Transformation Language (ATL) [8].

3.1   Traceability Mechanism

The model transformation traceability consists in storing a set of relations (also named mappings) between corresponding source and target model elements in order to reuse them to verify and validate software life-cycle.

Several traceability approaches are proposed in the literature [9]. For example, in [10], authors introduce an approach named embedded traceability. In this latter, the traceability elements are embedded inside the target models. For [11], the traceability information are considered as a model, more precisely as an additional target model of a transformation program. We have chosen the last because it avoids polluting source and target models with traceability information. Traceability information are generated while running the model transformation (*Source2Target model transformation*) as illustrated in Fig. 2.

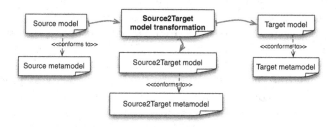

Fig. 2. The traceability mechanism

3.2   Higher-Order Transformation

A higher-order transformation is a model transformation that manipulates other model transformations. It means that the input and/or output models are themselves model transformations. Fig. 3 gives a technical overview of the application of a higher-order transformation where both inputs and outputs are model transformations [12]. A first step parses the textual syntax and builds a model conforming to the ATL metamodel. Then, the higher-order transformation (*ATL Higher-Order transformation*) manipulates the input model and generates another transformation model (*ATL output model*). It generally adds some information. We use it to easily extend the translational semantics to support traceability data generation. Finally, the textual representation (*ATL output transformation*) was generated from the generated ATL model.

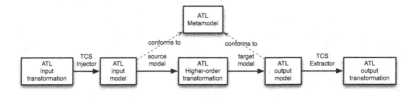

Fig. 3. An overview of Higher-Order transformation

3.3 The Approach Architecture

The figure 4 shows the overall organization of our approach. It explains different steps performed by the DSML designer in order to prepare the verification framework used by the DSML end-user. It also introduces the capability of our approach to simplify the DSML designer task in order to facilitate the integration of a verification framework for a new DSML.

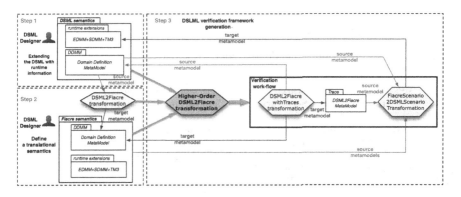

Fig. 4. Scheme of different steps to generate the DSML verification framework

Step 1. The DSML designer extends the DSML abstract syntax (DDMM) with the runtime information conforming to the *Executable DSML pattern*. It consists in defining different events (EDMM) and snapshots (SDMM) to be captured.

Step 2. The DSML designer defines the translational semantics (*DSML2Fiacre transformation*) from DSML DDMM into the formal FIACRE language. In our case, it is defined as a model-to-model transformation implemented with ATL.

In our example, the translational semantics consists in transforming a SPEM model into a FIACRE specification. Here are some rationale behind this translational semantics. Each workdefinition is translated into one FIACRE process. Such a process contains three states (*notStarted*, *running* and *finished*) and two transitions (from *notStarted* to *running* and then from *running* to *finished*). The transitions are guarded (conditional statement) according to the dependencies defined between workdefinitions (the previous activities must have reached the expected state). As a FIACRE process cannot inspect the current state of other processes, the process takes as argument an array containing the state of each workdefinition (derived from the XSPEM SDMM). Each transition includes an assignment to update variables which store the state of the activities.

In addition, the transformation must integrate the information to capture the DSML events. FIACRE allows to annotate the FIACRE model with tag statements "#ident". So, the DSML designer must extend the translational semantics with tag statements in order to capture the corresponding event in the DSML scenario.

The listing 1.1 shows an application of this extension for the *StartWD* event which is a workdefinition event. A tag declaration named *"StartWD"* is defined (lines 12-13) in order to capture the *StartWD* event defined in the SPEM EDMM. A tag statement is initialized with the corresponding tag declaration (lines 9-10). This statement is inserted in the first FIACRE transition (*from not-Started ... to running*) just before the assignment which updates the state variable of the activity (lines 6-7). These elements are also defined for the *FinishWD* event.

```
1   WorkDefinition2Fiacre {
2       from
3           workdefinition: SpemMetaModel!WorkDefinition
4       to
5           ...
6       sequence_statement_start: FiacreMetaModel!StatementSequence(
7           statements <− Sequence{start_tag_statement, assignment_is_started}
8       ),
9       start_tag_statement: FiacreMetaModel!TaggedStatement(
10          tag <− tag_start_wd
11      ),
12      tag_start_wd: FiacreMetaModel!TagDeclaration(
13          name <− 'StartWD'
14      )
15      ...
```

Listing 1.1. Extending the translational semantics with tagged statements

Step 3. The *DSML2Fiacre transformation* defined by the DSML designer provides the proposed translational semantics extended with bindings which allow implementing DSML events. Based on this model-to-model transformation, a higher-order transformation (*Higher-Order DSML2Fiacre transformation*) allows to generate different elements to extend the DSML verification framework. Let's detail the generated elements.

DSML2Fiacre Metamodel : It is the traceability metamodel. It defines a meta-class for each traceable element.

Definition 1. *A traceable element is a DSML element extended at least with an event in the DSML EDMM.*

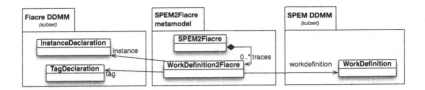

Fig. 5. SPEM2Fiacre trace metamodel

The generated meta-class contains references to record the traceable element (*workdefinition*), the tag declaration (*tag*) and its corresponding process instance (*instance*). In the case of xSPEM, only *WorkDefinition* is a traceable element. The generated trace metamodel, SPEM2Fiacre, is shown in Figure 5.

Therefore, a meta-class named *WorkDefinition2Fiacre* was generated to store the workdefinition and the corresponding tag event containing the tag declaration and its instance. The traceability metamodel is generated in order to be referenced by the translational semantics enriched with traceability rules.

DSML2FiacrePlusTraces Transformation : It adds traceability rules to the translational semantics proposed in the *DSML2Fiacre transformation*. Traceability elements are created into the rule which translates the traceable element.

Typically, the traceability information consists in saving a tag event information (Fiacre side) and the traceable element (DSML side).

Listing 1.2 introduces elements into the *WorkDefinition2Fiacre* rule (line 1). According to the generated *DSML2Fiacre* metamodel, this rule produces a target pattern element (lines 6-9) to create *WorkDefinition2Fiacre* instance (line 6) with the tag declaration (line 7) and the generated Fiacre process instance (line 8). Saving traceability source information in ATL consists in adding a single-statement imperative block to initialize the source element, *workdefinition*, with the traceable element (lines 10-13).

```
1   rule WorkDefinition2Fiacre{
2      from
3         workdefinition : SpemMetaModel!WorkDefinition
4      to
5         ...
6      start_trace : SpemMetaModel2FiacreMetaModel!WorkDefinition2Fiacre (
7         tag <- tag_start_wd,
8         instance <- process_instance
9      )
10     do {
11        start_trace.refSetValue('workdefinition', workdefinition);
12        ...
13     }
14     ...
```

Listing 1.2. The generation of traceability target pattern elements

FiacreTM32SpemTM3 Transformation : It defines the backward transformation which allows to back propagate the Fiacre formal scenario into the DSML scenario. Listing 1.3 shows some elements in this ATL transformation.

It defines an ATL helper (lines 1-5) for each traceable element (*WorkDefinition* in this case) to request from a tag event the corresponding trace element (*WorkDefinition2Fiacre*). An ATL rule (lines 7-14) is defined for each DSML event to generate from a tag event (lines 8-10) using the trace element a corresponding DSML event (lines 11-13).

```
1   helper context FiacreSemanticsMetaModel!"fiacreSemantics::fiacreEDMM::TagEvent"
2   def: getTraceabilityElement() :
3       Spem2FiacreMetaModel!WorkDefinition2Fiacre =
4       Spem2FiacreMetaModel!WorkDefinition2Fiacre.allInstances()
5       −>select(trace|trace.tag=self.tag and trace.instance=self.instance)−>first();
6
7   rule TagEvent2StartEvent{
8     from fcr_event:
9       FiacreSemanticsMetaModel!"fiacreSemantics::fiacreEDMM::TagEvent"
10        (fcr_event.tag.name='StartWD')
11    to spem_event:
12      SpemSemanticsMetaModel!"spemSemantics::spemEDMM::StartWD"(
13          workdefinition <− fcr_event.getTraceabilityElement().workdefinition)
14  }
```

Listing 1.3. A subset of the backward transformation

4   The Use of the DSML Verification Framework

Once the previous steps have been performed, the DSML verification framework is generated. Figure 6 shows an overview of the generated DSML verification framework connected to both modeling and formal levels.

This framework allows the DSML end-user to define models (xSPEM *model*) conforming to the DSML abstract syntax (xSPEM DDMM) and to verify behavioral properties while hiding formal methods and tools.

The defined model is translated with *SPEM2FiacrewithTraces* transformation into a Fiacre program (*fiacre model*). Additionally, a traceability model (*spem2fiacre* model) is also generated which saves mappings between both models.

Next, the existing tools around the Fiacre language (Frac compiler[1] and Selt[2], the Tina [13] model-checker) perform the formal verification and generate the formal results (*counter-example* in case of failure). In the same spirit defined in this paper, we have transformed these formal results at the Petri nets level to more abstract results at the Fiacre level (*fiacre scenario*) [14]. Finally, the backward transformation (*FiacreScenario2SPEMScenario* transformation) is performed in order to generate the expected scenario (xSPEM *scenario*).

---

[1] http://projects.laas.fr/fiacre/manuals/frac.html
[2] http://projects.laas.fr/tina/manuals/selt.html

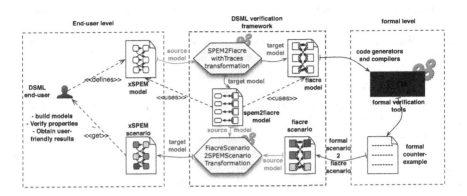

Fig. 6. The use of the generated DSML verification framework

5   Related Work

The problem of integrating formal verification into the design of DSMLs has been widely addressed by the MDE community. However, the analysis feedback at the DSML level problem is typically either ignored or resolved by defining ad-hoc or hard-coded solutions. For example, in [15], authors propose an approach, named *Metaviz*, based on the real-time systems specification and validation tool set IFx-OMEGA. It is designed to ease the visualization of simulation trace. The goal is to assist the user in the Interactive Simulation task by refining this step with a diagnosis process built around visualization concepts. It consists in feeding back verification results at OMEGA level. Thus, It can be considered as an ad-hoc approach.

On the other hand, a few number of works handling the feedback with general solutions exists in the literature.

Hegedüs et al. [16] propose a technique for the back propagation of simulation traces based on change-driven model transformations from traces generated by SAL model checking framework to the specific animator named BPEL Animation Controller. So, they define a change-driven model transformation which consumes changes of the Petri nets simulation run and produces a BPEL process execution using traceability information generated while running the translational semantics defined previously. In this case, after defining the runtime extension for both levels (BPEL and Petri nets) and the translational semantics, the DSML designer is invited to define 1) a change command metamodel for Petri nets and BPEL and also 2) the back-ward change-driven transformation. In our approach, we try to generate automatically the mandatory data required to feedback verification results without introducing additional information.

In [17], authors introduce an algorithm requiring the DSML's semantics to be defined formally, and a relation R to be defined between states of the DSML and states of the target language. The DSML designer must provide as input a natural-number bound n, which estimates a difference of granularity between the semantics of the DSML and the semantics of the target language. However, we don't think that DSML designer, for who it is difficult to use formal methods and verification, can define this important information to feedback verification results.

The most advanced work about back propagation problem is defined in [18]. A *Triple Graphical Pattern (TGP)* is defined to introduce how a result generated in the formal domain can be shown in the DSML level. TGP is defined to resolve the problem of 1-to-1 restriction on back propagation. It allows to handle the 1-to-n case which means that several events in the formal verification results may correspond to one event in the DSML level and m-to-n case which considers mappings as a set of events in the both levels. These cases occur due to the mismatch between trace granularity between the DSML and formal levels caused by the semantic gap between both levels. In our case, the use of the intermediate language FIACRE allows to reduce this semantic gap and therefore the 1-to-n and m-to-n mapping are usually not occurring. Also, the DSML designer does not need to extend the translational semantics with any additional information to ensure the back-annotation task. Finally, as a technical viewpoint, defining a Triple Graph Transformation Systems (TGTS) is typically more complicate task than an ATL transformation.

6   Conclusion

In this paper, we have presented an approach to integrate formal tools into the verification of DSMLs. It consists in generating a DSML verification framework containing the necessary elements to map the DSML abstract syntax into a semantic domain and also to feed verification results — generated in the formal level — back to the DSML level.

Our solution is a generic tool implementing a higher-order transformation that requires a translational semantics defined between the DSML and the FIACRE intermediate language. The translational semantics is extended with tagged statements which trigger DSML events. This additional information allows identifying which elements are concerned with the back propagation task. Therefore, all required elements are generated automatically. It has been illustrated on XSPEM as DSML and FIACRE as the formal language.

This approach has been designed for domain specific languages. It is currently being experimented for several significantly different DSMLs like Architecture Analysis and Design Language (AADL), Business Process Engineering Language (BPEL) and Ladder Diagram (LD).

References

1. Merilinna, J., Pärssinen, J.: Verification and validation in the context of domain-specific modelling. In: Proceedings of the 10th Workshop on Domain-Specific Modeling, DSM 2010, pp. 9:1–9:6 (2010)

2. Harel, D., Rumpe, B.: Meaningful Modeling: What's the Semantics of "Semantics"? Computer 37(10), 64–72 (2004)
3. Combemale, B., Crégut, X., Pantel, M.: A Design Pattern to Build Executable DSMLs and associated V&V tools (short paper). In: Asia-Pacific Software Engineering Conference (APSEC), Hong Kong, China (2012)
4. Berthomieu, B., Bodeveix, J.-P., Filali, M., Farail, P., Gaufillet, P., Garavel, H., Lang, F.: FIACRE: an Intermediate Language for Model Verification in the TOP-CASED Environment. In: ERTS 2008 (2008)
5. Software & Systems Process Engineering Metamodel (SPEM) 2.0, Object Management Group (October 2007)
6. Farail, P., Gaufillet, P., Canals, A., Camus, C.L., Sciamma, D., Michel, P., Crégut, X., Pantel, M.: The TOPCASED project: A Toolkit in OPen source for Critical Aeronautic SystEms Design. In: Embedded Real Time Software (ERTS 2006), Toulouse, January 25-27 (2006)
7. Abid, N., Dal Zilio, S.: Real-time Extensions for the Fiacre modeling language (2010), http://automata.rwth--aachen.de/movep2010/index.php?page=about
8. Jouault, F., Kurtev, I.: Transforming Models with ATL. In: Bruel, J.-M. (ed.) MoDELS 2005. LNCS, vol. 3844, pp. 128–138. Springer, Heidelberg (2006)
9. Galvao, I., Goknil, A.: Survey of traceability approaches in model-driven engineering. In: 11th IEEE International Enterprise Distributed Object Computing Conference (EDOC), p. 313 (October 2007)
10. Kolovos, D.S., Paige, R.F., Polack, F.A.C.: Merging models with the epsilon merging language (EML). In: Wang, J., Whittle, J., Harel, D., Reggio, G. (eds.) MoDELS 2006. LNCS, vol. 4199, pp. 215–229. Springer, Heidelberg (2006)
11. Jouault, F.: Loosely coupled traceability for ATL. In: Proceedings of the European Conference on Model Driven Architecture (ECMDA) Workshop on Traceability (2005)
12. Tisi, M., Jouault, F., Fraternali, P., Ceri, S., Bézivin, J.: On the use of higher-order model transformations. In: Paige, R.F., Hartman, A., Rensink, A. (eds.) ECMDA-FA 2009. LNCS, vol. 5562, pp. 18–33. Springer, Heidelberg (2009)
13. Berthomieu, B., Ribet, P.-O., Vernadat, F.: The tool TINA – construction of abstract state spaces for Petri nets and time Petri nets. Int. Journal of Production Research 42(14), 2741–2756 (2004)
14. Zalila, F., Crégut, X., Pantel, M.: Verification results feedback for FIACRE intermediate language. In: Conférence en Ingénierie du Logiciel, CIEL (June 2012), http://gpl2012.irisa.fr/?q=node/31
15. Aboussoror, E.A., Ober, I., Ober, I.: Seeing errors: model driven simulation trace visualization. In: France, R.B., Kazmeier, J., Breu, R., Atkinson, C. (eds.) MODELS 2012. LNCS, vol. 7590, pp. 480–496. Springer, Heidelberg (2012)
16. Hegedüs, Á., Bergmann, G., Ráth, I., Varró, D.: Back-annotation of simulation traces with change-driven model transformations. In: SEFM 2010, pp. 145–155 (2010)
17. Combemale, B., Gonnord, L., Rusu, V.: A generic tool for tracing executions back to a DSML's operational semantics. In: France, R.B., Kuester, J.M., Bordbar, B., Paige, R.F. (eds.) ECMFA 2011. LNCS, vol. 6698, pp. 35–51. Springer, Heidelberg (2011)
18. Guerra, E., de Lara, J., Malizia, A., Díaz, P.: Supporting user-oriented analysis for multi-view domain-specific visual languages. Information and Software Technology 51(4), 769–784 (2009)

Allegories for Database Modeling

Bartosz Zieliński, Paweł Maślanka, and Ścibor Sobieski

Department of Theoretical Physics and Computer Science
Faculty of Physics and Applied Informatics
University of Łódź
ul. Pomorska nr 149/153, 90-236 Łódź, Poland
{bzielinski,pmaslan,scibor.sobieski}@uni.lodz.pl

Abstract. Allegories are categories modeled upon the category of sets and binary relations (where sets are objects and binary relations are morphisms composed using joins). In this paper we present a new conceptual data modeling formalism based on the language of allegories. We show that allegories provide more convenient framework for modeling data than more traditional categorical approaches in which arrows are interpreted as functional dependencies and in which many to many or partial relationships have to be represented as spans. Finally, we demonstrate that by using allegories different than the allegory of sets and binary relations, for example the allegory of sets and lattice valued relations, one can model replicated data or data stored in a valid time temporal database.

1 Introduction

Conceptual database modeling is an important part of database design process. Existence of a conceptual model not only assists in creating better database schema and applications, but it also helps in integrating data from various sources, some of which might be XML, object-oriented or graph instead of relational. For some modeling formalisms there exist tools capable of generating relational schemas and queries from a conceptual description. A recent rise of semantic web only emphasizes the need for semantics rich data models.

Many conceptual data models were proposed. Among the most popular are ER diagrams [3] and UML [1], some more obscure ones include Object Role Modeling [10] and some of the models mentioned in the survey [11]. Most of these modeling formalisms are pictorial in nature and they lack a strict mathematical semantics [5]. Therefore a lot of research was devoted to creating semantic models with sound mathematical basics (see e.g., [5], [6], [7], [12], [13], [17], [18], [19]) or retrofitting a sound mathematical interpretation into an existing formalism (see e.g. [15]). A popular choice of mathematical base for those efforts (in particular a choice made by all the papers cited above) is category theory, not the least because of it using pictorial (diagrammatic) language itself. This approach was successfully used in tackling the view update problem ([14],[16]). The way the categories are used in most cases is modeled upon the category of sets and

A. Cuzzocrea and S. Maabout (Eds.): MEDI 2013, LNCS 8216, pp. 278–289, 2013.

functions, that is arrows in a category are interpreted as generalized functions — the relationships which are functional in nature. For example it is natural to view foreign keys as arrows between tables in a relational schema. If many to many relationships are needed, they can be implemented using spans or powersets.

A main contribution of this paper is to propose a new conceptual modeling formalism, which is based on allegories instead of usual categories. The only other place where the authors could find a suggestion of using allegories instead of usual categories for data modeling was a remark in [6]. Allegories are enriched categories (there are additional operations on arrows in addition to composition) modeled upon the category of sets and binary relations (where sets are objects and binary relations are morphisms composed using joins). Hence in allegories any generalized (binary) relations are represented directly, rather then through additional constructions. A conceptual data model is specified in our formalism using construction resembling an algebraic sketch (see e.g. [2]). This is similar to some other formalisms like the ones in [13] and [6], though they use only the language of usual categories. A specification is meant to be interpreted in some allegory, where the interpretation is understood to describe the actual state of a specified database realization. A basic target of interpretation is obviously the category of sets and binary relations corresponding to the usual single node database. Had this been the only viable target, we would gain little by abstracting from the algebra of binary relations, and the idea of using binary relations as the basis of conceptual modeling is not exactly new (see e.g. [11]). We demonstrate however, that by using the allegories of fuzzy relations (see e.g.[9]) we can interpret the model in replicated and valid time temporal databases.

2   Preliminaries

While we assume the reader to be familiar with basics of category theory, these preliminaries should provide sufficient background to understand the content of this paper. Book [2] provides more in-depth introduction. First we recall some basic definitions in order to fix the (slightly nonstandard) notation. The bulk of these preliminaries is taken by the basics of allegories which are not widely known and for which [8] is the basic (and about the only) textbook.

A graph $\mathcal{G}$ consists of a set[1] of vertices $\mathrm{Obj}[\mathcal{G}]$, a set of arrows $\mathrm{Arr}[\mathcal{G}]$, and a pair of functions $\overleftarrow{(\cdot)}, \overrightarrow{(\cdot)} : \mathrm{Arr}[\mathcal{G}] \longrightarrow \mathrm{Obj}[\mathcal{G}]$, called source and target, respectively. For any $A, B \in \mathrm{Obj}[\mathcal{G}]$ we denote by $\mathrm{Arr}_\mathcal{G}(A, B)$ the set of arrows (hom-set) with source A and target B. A graph morphism $F : \mathcal{G} \to \mathcal{H}$ from a graph $\mathcal{G}$ to a graph $\mathcal{H}$ is a pair of maps

$$F_o : \mathrm{Obj}[\mathcal{G}] \longrightarrow \mathrm{Obj}[\mathcal{H}], \quad F_a : \mathrm{Arr}[\mathcal{G}] \longrightarrow \mathrm{Arr}[\mathcal{H}]$$

such that $\overleftarrow{F_a(f)} = F_o(\overleftarrow{f})$, $\overrightarrow{F_a(f)} = F_o(\overrightarrow{f})$, for all $f \in \mathrm{Arr}[\mathcal{G}]$.

---

[1] Because we will not encounter any set theoretical problems in this paper we will not distinguish between sets and classes

A category $\mathcal{C}$ is a graph with associative arrow composition $f; g \in \mathrm{Arr}_{\mathcal{C}}(\overleftarrow{f}, \overrightarrow{g})$ defined whenever $\overrightarrow{f} = \overleftarrow{g}$ (note the diagrammatic order), and identity arrows id_A for each object $A \in \mathrm{Obj}[\mathcal{C}]$ satisfying $f; \mathrm{id}_B = \mathrm{id}_A; f = f$ for all $f \in \mathrm{Arr}_{\mathcal{C}}(A, B)$. When using single letter morphism names we will often omit the semicolon composition operator abbreviating $fg := f; g$. We reserve the usual composition operator $\cdot \circ \cdot$ for the composition of actual maps when they are not understood as arrows in categories, and then $(f \circ g)(x) = f(g(x))$. A graph morphism $F : \mathcal{C} \to \mathcal{D}$ between categories is called a functor when it maps identity arrows to identity arrows and respects composition, i.e., $F_a(f; g) = F_a(f); F_a(g)$.

An *allegory* [8] $\mathcal{A}$ is a category with two additional operations on the hom-sets called intersection and reciprocation, respectively:

$$\cdot \sqcap \cdot : \mathrm{Arr}_{\mathcal{A}}(A, B) \times \mathrm{Arr}_{\mathcal{A}}(A, B) \to \mathrm{Arr}_{\mathcal{A}}(A, B),$$
$$(\cdot)^{\circ} : \mathrm{Arr}_{\mathcal{A}}(A, B) \to \mathrm{Arr}_{\mathcal{A}}(B, A), \tag{1}$$

where $A, B \in \mathrm{Obj}[\mathcal{A}]$. The operators are required to satisfy the following conditions. First, intersection operators should satisfy the axioms making each hom-set a meet semi-lattice (see e.g. [4]). We denote the associated partial order by $\sqsubseteq$, i.e., $R \sqsubseteq S :\equiv R \sqcap S = R$, for all $R, S \in \mathrm{Arr}_{\mathcal{A}}(A, B)$. In addition $\cdot \sqcap \cdot$ and $(\cdot)^{\circ}$ have to satisfy the following formulas, for all $R, S, T \in \mathrm{Arr}[\mathcal{A}]$ such that the formulas are well defined:

$$R^{\circ\circ} = R, \quad (RS)^{\circ} = S^{\circ}R^{\circ}, \quad (R \sqcap S)^{\circ} = R^{\circ} \sqcap S^{\circ},$$
$$R(S \sqcap T) \sqsubseteq RS \sqcap RT, \quad RS \sqcap T \sqsubseteq (R \sqcap TS^{\circ})S. \tag{2}$$

Allegories generalize the category $\mathcal{R}$ (which is also an allegory) in which objects are sets and arrows between sets A and B are binary relations $R \subseteq A \times B$. Because of it we will often refer to arrows in any allegory as "relations". It is customary in $\mathcal{R}$ to write aRb iff $(a, b) \in R$. The composition of relations $R \in \mathrm{Arr}_{\mathcal{R}}(A, B)$ and $S \in \mathrm{Arr}_{\mathcal{R}}(B, C)$ is just the natural join. More precisely:

$$a(RS)c \quad :\equiv \quad \exists b \in B . aRb \wedge bSc. \tag{3}$$

The unit of composition in $\mathcal{R}$ is $\mathrm{id}_A := \{(a, a) | a \in A\}$ for all $A \in \mathrm{Obj}[\mathcal{R}]$. The intersection operator in $\mathcal{R}$ is the set intersection, i.e., $R \sqcap S := R \cap S$, and the reciprocation is defined by $aR^{\circ}b :\equiv bRa$.

Another allegory which will feature prominently in this paper is the allegory $\mathcal{R}[L]$ of locale valued relations (see e.g. [8]). A locale [8] L is a complete lattice [4] (that is a lattice where all, not just finite infima and suprema exist) in which $a \wedge \bigvee_i b_i = \bigvee_i (a \wedge b_i)$, for any $a \in L$ and $\{b_i\}_i \subseteq L$ Note that, because L is complete, it contains top ($\top$) and bottom ($\bot$) elements. In $\mathcal{R}[L]$ objects are sets and arrows are L-valued relations, that is, for any $A, B \in \mathrm{Obj}[\mathcal{R}[L]]$, the hom-set $\mathrm{Arr}_{\mathcal{R}[L]}(A, B)$ consists of functions $R : A \times B \to L$. Composition, for $R \in \mathrm{Arr}_{\mathcal{R}[L]}(A, B)$ and $S \in \mathrm{Arr}_{\mathcal{R}[L]}(B, C)$ is defined by

$$(RS)(a, c) \quad := \quad \bigvee_{b \in B}\big(R(a, b) \wedge S(b, c)\big). \tag{4}$$

It is easy to see that for all $A \in \mathrm{Obj}[\mathcal{R}[L]]$ the identity morphisms can be defined explicitly by $\mathrm{id}_A(a, b) := \top$ if $a = b$ and $\mathrm{id}_A(a, b) := \bot$ if $a \neq b$.

The intersection and reciprocation operators are defined in $\mathcal{R}[L]$ by

$$(R \sqcap S)(a, b) := R(a, b) \wedge S(a, b), \quad R^\circ(a, b) := R(b, a). \tag{5}$$

Note that $\mathcal{R}[\{\top, \bot\}]$ is isomorphic with $\mathcal{R}$.

The arrows in $\mathcal{R}[L]$ should be interpreted as "fuzzy" relations (see e.g. [9]), where the value $R(a, b)$ gives the degree of how much the relation R holds between a and b, with $\bot$ meaning it does not hold and $\top$ meaning it completely holds, and the possibility of (potentially incomparable) intermediate degrees.

We distinguish the following classes of arrows $R \in \mathrm{Arr}_{\mathcal{A}}(A, B)$:

- If $\mathrm{id}_A \sqsubseteq RR^\circ$ then R is called *total*.
- If $R^\circ R \sqsubseteq \mathrm{id}_B$ then R is called *functional*.
- If R is functional and total it is called a *map*.
- If $RR^\circ \sqsubseteq \mathrm{id}_A$ then R is called *injective*.
- If $\mathrm{id}_B \sqsubseteq R^\circ R$ then R is called *surjective*.

A class of all maps in an allegory $\mathcal{A}$ is denoted by $\mathrm{Map}[\mathcal{A}]$. A family $\{r_i\}_i \subseteq \mathrm{Map}[\mathcal{A}]$ with a common source A is called *jointly monic* if $\sqcap_i r_i r_i^\circ = \mathrm{id}_A$. For any maps $h, h' \in \mathrm{Map}[\mathcal{A}]$ with target A, if $h; r_i = h'; r_i$ for all i then $h = h'$.

For any $A, B \in \mathrm{Obj}[\mathcal{A}]$ we denote by $\top_{A,B}$ and $\bot_{A,B}$ the top and bottom elements of $\mathrm{Arr}_{\mathcal{A}}(A, B)$, respectively, if they exist. In $\mathcal{R}$ we have $\top_{AB} := A \times B$, $\bot_{AB} := \varnothing_{AB}$, and in $\mathcal{R}[L]$ $\top_{AB}(a, b) := \top$, $\bot_{AB}(a, b) := \bot$ for all $a \in A$, $b \in B$.

Let $A, B \in \mathrm{Obj}[\mathcal{A}]$. Suppose that the top element $\top_{AB} \in \mathrm{Arr}_{\mathcal{A}}(A, B)$ exists. An object C together with maps $\pi_A, \pi_B \in \mathrm{Map}[\mathcal{A}]$ (called *projections on components*) typed as $A \xleftarrow{\ \pi_A\ } C \xrightarrow{\ \pi_B\ } B$ is called a *relational product* if

$$\pi_A; \pi_A^\circ \sqcap \pi_B; \pi_B^\circ = \mathrm{id}_C, \quad \pi_A^\circ; \pi_B = \top_{AB} \tag{6}$$

Relational products are products in $\mathrm{Map}[\mathcal{A}]$ and they are unique up to an isomorphism. In an allegory $\mathcal{A}$ there might be a canonical choice of relational product of each $A, B \in \mathrm{Obj}[\mathcal{A}]$. In such a case we denote the canonical product object by $A \otimes B$ and the projections by π_A^{AB} and π_B^{AB}. The relational product is usually not associative, but $A \otimes (B \otimes C)$ and $(A \otimes B) \otimes C$ are isomorphic.

In particular, in $\mathcal{R}$ the canonical relational product is the usual cartesian product with the projections on the components as projections. Similarly, in $\mathcal{R}[L]$, the canonical relational product of objects A and B is also their cartesian product $A \times B$, and the projections π_A^{AB} and π_B^{AB} are defined by:

$$\pi_A((a, b), a') = \begin{cases} \bot & \text{if } a \neq a' \\ \top & \text{if } a = a' \end{cases}, \quad \pi_B((a, b), b') = \begin{cases} \bot & \text{if } b \neq b' \\ \top & \text{if } b = b' \end{cases}. \tag{7}$$

3   Conceptual Data Model with Allegories

In this section we introduce a conceptual model based on allegories, which involves domains (sets of values) and generalized binary relations between domains. The model requires the use of allegories with slightly more structure:

Definition 1. *A PTB(product, top and bottom) allegory is an allegory $\mathcal{A}$ such that for all $A, B \in \mathrm{Obj}[\mathcal{A}]$ there exist top and bottom arrows $\top_{AB}, \bot_{AB} \in \mathrm{Arr}_{\mathcal{A}}(A, B)$ and the canonical choice of relational product.*

In particular $\mathcal{R}$ and $\mathcal{R}[L]$ are PTB allegories. Before we can define the model, we first need the following auxilliary notion:

Definition 2. *Let $\mathcal{G}$ be a graph. Denote by $\overline{\mathrm{Obj}[\mathcal{G}]}$ the closure of $\mathrm{Obj}[\mathcal{G}]$ with respect to $\cdot \otimes \cdot$ (the canonical choice of relational products). A set $\mathcal{T}_{\mathcal{G}}$ of allegorical terms associated to $\mathcal{G}$ is defined as the smallest set of expressions such that:*

- *$R \in \mathcal{T}_{\mathcal{G}}$ for all $R \in \mathrm{Arr}[\mathcal{G}]$,*
- *$\mathrm{id}_A, \top_{AB}, \bot_{AB}, \pi_A^{AB}, \pi_B^{AB} \in \mathcal{T}_{\mathcal{G}}$ for all $A, B \in \overline{\mathrm{Obj}[\mathcal{G}]}$,*
- *if $t \in \mathcal{T}_{\mathcal{G}}$, then $(t)^\circ \in \mathcal{T}_{\mathcal{G}}$,*
- *if $t_1, t_2 \in \mathcal{T}_{\mathcal{G}}$ are such that $\overrightarrow{t_1} = \overleftarrow{t_2}$ then $(t_1); (t_2) \in \mathcal{T}_{\mathcal{G}}$,*
- *if $t_1, t_2 \in \mathcal{T}_{\mathcal{G}}$ are such that $\overleftarrow{t_1} = \overleftarrow{t_2}$ and $\overrightarrow{t_1} = \overrightarrow{t_2}$, then $(t_1) \sqcap (t_2) \in \mathcal{T}_{\mathcal{G}}$.*

We will omit unnecessary parentheses when writing elements of $\mathcal{T}_{\mathcal{G}}$. In the above conditions we used the functions $\overleftarrow{(\cdot)}, \overrightarrow{(\cdot)} : \mathcal{T}_{\mathcal{G}} \longrightarrow \overline{\mathrm{Obj}[\mathcal{G}]}$ defined using induction on the structure of terms as the extension of source and target functions:

$$\overleftarrow{\mathrm{id}_A} = A = \overrightarrow{\mathrm{id}_A}, \quad \overleftarrow{\top_{AB}} = A = \overleftarrow{\bot_{AB}}, \quad \overrightarrow{\top_{AB}} = B = \overrightarrow{\bot_{AB}},$$

$$\overleftarrow{\pi_A^{AB}} = \overleftarrow{\pi_B^{AB}} = A \otimes B, \quad \overrightarrow{\pi_A^{AB}} = A, \quad \overrightarrow{\pi_B^{AB}} = B,$$

$$\overleftarrow{t^\circ} = \overrightarrow{t}, \quad \overrightarrow{t^\circ} = \overleftarrow{t}, \quad \overleftarrow{t_1; t_2} = \overleftarrow{t_1}, \quad \overrightarrow{t_1; t_2} = \overrightarrow{t_2}, \quad \overleftarrow{t_1 \sqcap t_2} = \overleftarrow{t_1}, \quad \overrightarrow{t_1 \sqcap t_2} = \overrightarrow{t_1},$$

where t, t_1, t_2 are terms.

We are now ready to formulate the definition of our conceptual model.

Definition 3. *An allegorical conceptual data model $(\mathcal{G}, \mathcal{E})$ consists of a finite graph $\mathcal{G}$ and a finite set $\mathcal{E}$ of equations of the form $t_1 = t_2$, where $t_1, t_2 \in \mathcal{T}_{\mathcal{G}}$.*

We will often write the equation $t_1 \sqcap t_2 = t_1$ as $t_1 \sqsubseteq t_2$, for any terms t_1 and t_2 (and still call it equation). The graph part of the allegorical conceptual model can be depicted using pictures, like Fig. 1, which give accessible overview of the conceptual data elements. Equations allow us to specify constraints and dependencies between data elements. The model is intended to be interpreted in some PTB allegory. In order to formulate the precise definition of interpretation we first need the following simple observation:

Lemma 4. *Let $\mathcal{G}$ be a graph, and let $\mathcal{A}$ be a PTB allegory. Let $F : \mathcal{G} \to \mathcal{A}$ be a graph morphism. Then F_o can be extended naturally to a map $\hat{F}_o : \overline{\mathrm{Obj}[\mathcal{G}]} \to \mathrm{Obj}[\mathcal{A}]$ (defining $\hat{F}_o(A \otimes B) := \hat{F}_o(A) \otimes \hat{F}_o(B)$), and F_a can be extended to a map $\hat{F}_a : \mathcal{T}_{\mathcal{G}} \to \mathrm{Arr}[\mathcal{A}]$ using induction on the structure of terms in $\mathcal{T}_{\mathcal{G}}$, that is by defining for all $t_1, t_2 \in \mathcal{T}_{\mathcal{G}}$:*

$$\hat{F}_a(\mathrm{id}_A) = \mathrm{id}_{\hat{F}_o(A)}, \quad \hat{F}_a(\top_{AB}) = \top_{\hat{F}_o(A)\hat{F}_o(B)}, \quad \hat{F}_a(\bot_{AB}) = \bot_{\hat{F}_o(A)\hat{F}_o(B)},$$

$$F_a(\pi_A^{AB}) = \pi_{\hat{F}_o(A)}^{\hat{F}_o(A)\hat{F}_o(B)}, \quad F_a(\pi_B^{AB}) = \pi_{\hat{F}_o(B)}^{\hat{F}_o(A)\hat{F}_o(B)},$$

$$\hat{F}_a(t_1^\circ) = \hat{F}_a(t_1)^\circ, \quad \hat{F}_a(t_1; t_2) = \hat{F}_a(t_1); \hat{F}_a(t_2), \quad \hat{F}_a(t_1 \sqcap t_2) = \hat{F}_a(t_1) \sqcap \hat{F}_a(t_2).$$

Definition 5. *Let* $(\mathcal{G}, \mathcal{E})$ *be an allegorical conceptual data model and let* $\mathcal{A}$ *be a PTB allegory. A graph morphism* $H : \mathcal{G} \rightarrow \mathcal{A}$ *is called an* interpretation *of* $(\mathcal{G}, \mathcal{E})$ *if for all equations* $(t_1 = t_2) \in \mathcal{E}$ *the equality* $\hat{H}_a(t_1) = \hat{H}_a(t_2)$ *holds in* $\mathcal{A}$.

Each interpretation corresponds to some actual realization and state of the database. The choice of allegory determines the kind of database, different interpretations in the same allegory may be interpreted as different states of the same database. Interpretation of the allegorical conceptual model in $\mathcal{R}$ is the typical (in fact motivating) choice sufficient for, say, single instance, transactional databases. The model is not, however, bound to $\mathcal{R}$, one can use other allegories. This freedom allows to describe, for instance, replicated or temporal database realizations.

We can reason about data within the conceptual model $(\mathcal{G}, \mathcal{E})$ by deriving new equations specifying properties of data from equations $\mathcal{E}$ and allegory axioms. Just treat the terms as elements of some unspecified PTB allegory, and perform the usual derivation. Such new equalities will hold in any interpretation. Here is the precise (semantic) definition of a derived equality in the model:

Definition 6. *Let* $(\mathcal{G}, \mathcal{E})$ *be an allegorical conceptual model. We write* $(\mathcal{G}, \mathcal{E}) \models_F t_1 = t_2$ *if* $\hat{F}_a(t_1) = \hat{F}_a(t_2)$ *holds for an interpretation* F *of* $(\mathcal{G}, \mathcal{E})$. *We say that the equality* $t_1 = t_2$ *holds in* $(\mathcal{G}, \mathcal{E})$ *(writing* $(\mathcal{G}, \mathcal{E}) \models t_1 = t_2$*) if* $(\mathcal{G}, \mathcal{E}) \models_F t_1 = t_2$ *for any interpretation* F.

We will now consider a concrete example $(\mathcal{G}, \mathcal{E})$ of an allegorical conceptual model. The graph $\mathcal{G}$ is depicted in Fig. 1 and equations $\mathcal{E}$ in Fig. 2. The reader should verify that the semantics of the equations is as described below by considering their meaning in $\mathcal{R}$. The first of equations (a) says that employed-in is just a reciprocal of employs. The second defines sibling-of in terms of child-of: sibling is a child of common parent. Note that this definition implies that sibling-of is symmetric (i.e., $(\mathcal{G}, \mathcal{E}) \models$ sibling-of $=$ sibling-of$^\circ$) as it should, but it also allows for a person to be a sibling of herself.

A unique code called PESEL is assigned to every citizen of Poland. Accordingly, the equations (b) in Fig. 2 declare the pesel relation to be an injective map, which forces all Person-s to be polish in all interpretations of $(\mathcal{G}, \mathcal{E})$.

Consider now the domain Address. Relations country, city, street and street-no are attributes of any entity in the Address domain. It follows that they should be maps: functionality is specified in equations (c2) and (c3) and totality follows from (c1). In addition those attributes uniquely specify the address, hence they are declared as the monic collection of arrows in equation (c1). Note that we do not assume here that Address is a relational product of Countries, Cities, Streets and Street No. The Adress domain may contain other fields not considered here, and, more importantly, the Adress domain should contain only valid (existing) adresses, and not every combination of country, city, street and street number is valid. We treat similarly domains Product and Production in equations (d1)–(e2).

Observe that domains such as Production let us overcome the limitations of using only binary relations — we cannot express directy the naturally ternary (that is normalised as much as possible) relation "employer produces some amount of product", we have to use auxilliary domain Production.

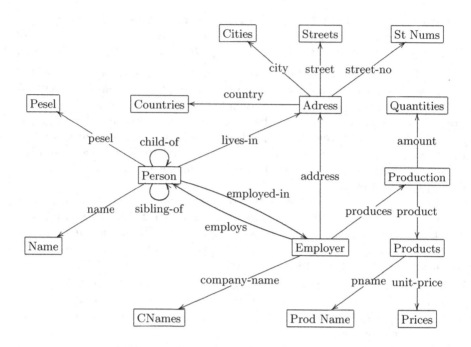

Fig. 1. Graph $\mathcal{G}$ of the example allegorical conceptual model

Consider now the Person domain and the employed-in relation, which is neither functional (as person might be employed by more then one employer) nor total (as person, perhaps an underage child, might not be employed). In a more functionally oriented model we might be forced to introduce subobject Employees of Person consisting of employed people:

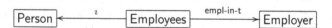

This is unnecessary in our formalism, but one can do it, complementing the above picture with equations declaring $\imath$ to be an injective map, empl-in-t to be a total relation, and defining employed-in in terms of $\imath$ and empl-in-t::

$$\imath; \imath^\circ = \mathrm{id}_{\mathsf{Employees}}, \quad \imath^\circ; \imath \sqsubseteq \mathrm{id}_{\mathsf{Person}}, \quad \mathrm{id}_{\mathsf{Employees}} \sqsubseteq \mathsf{empl\text{-}in\text{-}t}; \mathsf{empl\text{-}in\text{-}t}^\circ,$$
$$\mathsf{employed\text{-}in} = \imath^\circ; \mathsf{empl\text{-}in\text{-}t}. \tag{8}$$

In addition to sentences related to semantics of relations in the conceptual model one can also use the language of allegories to express business rules or constraints. For example, equation (f) in Fig. 2 expresses the rule that the child cannot work for the same employer as the parent. Indeed, in $\mathcal{R}$ equation (f) can be equivalently expressed in the language of first order logic, by

$$\neg \exists e, p_1, p_2 \,.\, p_1 \text{ child-of } p_2 \wedge p_1 \text{ employed-in } e \wedge p_2 \text{ employed-in } e. \tag{9}$$

$$\text{employed-in} = \text{employs}^{\circ}, \quad \text{sibling-of} = \text{child-of}; \text{child-of}^{\circ}, \qquad \text{(a)}$$

$$\text{pesel}; \text{pesel}^{\circ} = \text{id}_{\text{Person}}, \quad \text{pesel}^{\circ}; \text{pesel} \sqsubseteq \text{id}_{\text{Pesel}}, \qquad \text{(b)}$$

$$\text{country}; \text{country}^{\circ} \sqcap \text{city}; \text{city}^{\circ} \sqcap \text{street}; \text{street}^{\circ} \sqcap \text{street-no}; \text{street-no}^{\circ} = \text{id}_{\text{Adress}}, \qquad \text{(c1)}$$

$$\text{country}^{\circ}; \text{country} \sqsubseteq \text{id}_{\text{Countries}}, \quad \text{city}^{\circ}; \text{city} \sqsubseteq \text{id}_{\text{Cities}}, \qquad \text{(c2)}$$

$$\text{street}^{\circ}; \text{street} \sqsubseteq \text{id}_{\text{Streets}}, \quad \text{street-no}^{\circ}; \text{street-no} \sqsubseteq \text{id}_{\text{St-nums}}, \qquad \text{(c3)}$$

$$\text{product}; \text{product}^{\circ} \sqcap \text{amount}; \text{amount}^{\circ} = \text{id}_{\text{Production}}, \qquad \text{(d1)}$$

$$\text{product}^{\circ}; \text{product} \sqsubseteq \text{id}_{\text{Products}}, \quad \text{amount}^{\circ}; \text{amount} \sqsubseteq \text{id}_{\text{Quantities}}, \qquad \text{(d2)}$$

$$\text{pname}; \text{pname}^{\circ} \sqcap \text{unit-price}; \text{unit-price}^{\circ} = \text{id}_{\text{Products}}, \qquad \text{(e1)}$$

$$\text{pname}^{\circ}; \text{pname} \sqsubseteq \text{id}_{\text{Prod Name}}, \quad \text{unit-price}^{\circ}; \text{unit-price} \sqsubseteq \text{id}_{\text{Prices}}, \qquad \text{(e2)}$$

$$(\text{child-of}; \text{employed-in}) \sqcap \text{employed-in} = \bot_{\text{Person Employees}}. \qquad \text{(f)}$$

Fig. 2. Set of equations $\mathcal{E}$ for the example allegorical conceptual model

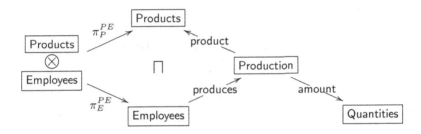

Fig. 3. Construction of a query using relational product

4 Queries in Allegories

Let $(\mathcal{G}, \mathcal{E})$ be an allegorical conceptual model. Any term $t \in \mathcal{T}_{\mathcal{G}}$ may be interpreted as a query to the conceptual model. Indeed, let F be an interpretation of $(\mathcal{G}, \mathcal{E})$ in an allegory $\mathcal{A}$ corresponding to the, say, current database state. Then the relation $\hat{F}_a(t) \in \text{Arr}[\mathcal{A}]$ (see Lemma 4) can be understood as the answer to this query. Such a conceptual queries can be very useful, as the designers can specify not only the data model but also typical application queries already during the conceptual database design. It might seem a limitation that our queries can return only binary relations. However, as the example below demonstrates, the use of relational products allows us to represent queries with n-ary answers.

Consider the allegorical conceptual model $(\mathcal{G}, \mathcal{E})$, where $\mathcal{G}$ is depicted in Fig. 1 and equations $\mathcal{E}$ are listed in Fig. 2. Suppose that we want the query $t \in \mathcal{T}_{\mathcal{G}}$ relating the product and employer with the amount of product produced by this employer. Let us abbreviate $P := \text{Product}$, $E := \text{Employer}$ in the sub/sup-scripts. One proves that (see also Fig. 3):

$$t \quad := \quad \left((\pi_P^{PE}; \text{produces}) \sqcap (\pi_E^{PE}; \text{product}^{\circ}) \right); \text{amount}. \qquad \text{(10)}$$

Let $p \in$ Products, $e \in$ Employees and $q \in$ Quantities. Under the interpretation $F : \mathcal{G} \to \mathcal{R}$ of $(\mathcal{G}, \mathcal{E})$ the sentence $(p, e)\hat{F}_a(t)q$ is equivalent with

$$\exists c \in \text{Production} . \ e \ \hat{F}_a(\text{produces}) \ c \wedge c \ \hat{F}_a(\text{product}) \ p \wedge c \ \hat{F}_a(\text{amount}) \ q \quad (11)$$

which is exactly what we want. The advantage of the formula (10) is that it makes sense in other contexts, where we do not interpret our conceptual model in $\mathcal{R}$.

5   Cuts for Fuzzy Relations

Let L be a locale. Let $u \in L$. A u-cut (c.f. [9]) graph morphism $F^u(R) : \mathcal{R}[L] \to \mathcal{R}$ is defined, for all $A \in \text{Obj}[\mathcal{R}[L]]$ and $R \in \text{Arr}[\mathcal{R}[L]]$ by

$$F_o^u(A) := A, \qquad aF_a^u(R)b :\equiv R(a, b) \geqslant u, \quad \text{for all } a \in \overleftarrow{R}, \ b \in \overrightarrow{R}. \quad (12)$$

The result on u-cuts we present in this section is probably known but we were unable to find a reference so we present it anyway as it will be crucial in what follows. First we need an auxiliary definition:

Definition 7. *Let $\mathcal{A}$ and $\mathcal{B}$ be a PTB allegories. We call a functor $F : \mathcal{A} \to \mathcal{B}$ a PTB allegory functor if it preserves the structure of a PTB allegory, i.e., $F_a(R \sqcap S) = F_a(R) \sqcap F_a(S)$, $F_a(\perp_{AB}) = \perp_{F_o(A)F_o(B)}$, etc.*

Recall that an element u of lattice L is called *join irreducible* if $u \neq \perp$ and whenever $u = a \vee b$ for some $a, b \in L$ then $u = a$ or $u = b$. We denote the set of all join irreducible elements in a lattice L by $\mathcal{J}(L)$. If a lattice L contains $\perp$ then an element $a \in L$ is called *an atom* if it covers $\perp$, that is if $a > \perp$ and if $b < a$ then $b = \perp$ for all $b \in L$. We denote the set of all atoms in L by $\mathcal{A}(L)$.

Proposition 8. *Let L be a locale and let $u \in L$. Then the u-cut graph morphism $F^u : \mathcal{R}[L] \to \mathcal{R}$ is a PTB allegory functor if u is an atom or L is finite and u is join irreducible. If F^u is a functor and L is finite then u is join irreducible.*

In the proof of the above proposition we use the following well known results:

Lemma 9. *If lattice L is finite then $u \in L$ is join irreducible if and only if*

$$\bigvee_i a_i \geqslant u \quad \equiv \quad \exists i . a_i \geqslant u \qquad \text{for any family } \{a_i\}_i \subseteq L \quad (13)$$

Lemma 10. *If an element u of a (not necessarily finite) lattice L is an atom then the property 13 holds.*

Proof (of Proposition 8). The nontrivial part is to prove that F_a preserves composition. Let $R, S \in \text{Arr}[\mathcal{R}[L]]$ be such that $\overrightarrow{R} = \overleftarrow{S}$. Let $x \in \overleftarrow{R}$, $y \in \overrightarrow{S}$. Then

$$\begin{aligned}
xF_a^u(R; S)y \quad &\equiv \quad \left(\bigvee_{z \in \overrightarrow{R}} \left(R(x, z) \wedge S(z, y) \right) \right) \geqslant u \\
&\overset{*}{\equiv} \quad \exists z \in \overrightarrow{R} . \left(R(x, z) \wedge S(z, y) \right) \geqslant u \\
&\equiv \quad \exists z \in \overrightarrow{R} . \left(\left(R(x, z) \geqslant u \right) \wedge \left(S(z, y) \geqslant u \right) \right) \\
&\equiv \quad \exists z \in \overrightarrow{R} . \left(\left(xF_a^u(R)z \right) \wedge \left(zF_a^u(S)y \right) \right) \\
&\equiv \quad x \left(F_a^u(R); F_a^u(S) \right) y. \quad (14)
\end{aligned}$$

Here, by Lemma 9 and Lemma 10, the starred equivalence holds always if u is an atom or L is finite and u is join irreducible. On the other hand if L is finite and the starred equivalence is valid for any relations R, S, then by Lemma 9 u is join irreducible. We leave the rest of the proof to the readers as an exercise.

6   Fuzzy Relations for Temporal Databases

Let $\mathbb{T}$ denote the time domain. In many cases we can define $\mathbb{T} := \mathbb{R}$ but we want to keep it general. In this section we show that interpreting the allegorical conceptual model in $\mathcal{R}[2^{\mathbb{T}}]$ allows us to transparently apply the model to data which will be stored in a valid time temporal database. Here the intended semantics of $\mathcal{R}[2^{\mathbb{T}}]$ is that $R(a, b)$, for any $R \in \mathrm{Arr}_{\mathcal{R}[2^{\mathbb{T}}]}(A, B)$ and $a \in A$, $b \in B$ is the set of those moments of time when the relation R between a and b holds. In another words, we say that a relation R holds between a and b at time $t \in \mathbb{T}$ if and only if $t \in R(a, b)$, or equivalently, if $R(a, b) \supseteq \{t\}$.

Let $(\mathcal{G}, \mathcal{E})$ be an allegorical conceptual model and let H be an interpretation of $(\mathcal{G}, \mathcal{E})$ in allegory $\mathcal{R}[2^{\mathbb{T}}]$. Proposition 8 implies that for any $t \in \mathbb{T}$ the $\{t\}$-cut graph morphism $F^{\{t\}} : \mathcal{R}[2^{\mathbb{T}}] \to \mathcal{R}$ is a PTB allegory functor. Then, the following remark, which is immediate to prove, implies that for any $\{t\}$ we have an interpretation $F^{\{t\}} \circ H : \mathcal{G} \to \mathcal{R}$.

Remark 11. Let $G : \mathcal{G} \to \mathcal{A}$ be an interpretation of an allegorical conceptual model $(\mathcal{G}, \mathcal{E})$ and let $K : \mathcal{A} \to \mathcal{B}$ be a functor of PTB allegories. Then $K \circ G : \mathcal{G} \to \mathcal{B}$ is an interpretation of $(\mathcal{G}, \mathcal{E})$.

The interpretation $F^{\{t\}} \circ H$ of $(\mathcal{G}, \mathcal{E})$ in $\mathcal{R}$ corresponds to the knowledge stored in the temporal database, the state of which is represented by H, about facts valid at $t \in \mathbb{T}$. Furthermore, because $F^{\{t\}} \circ H$ is an interpretation, we can say that $(\mathcal{G}, \mathcal{E})$ models properties valid at any moment of time. In order to specify the properties of changes of data, which requires relating properties of data at different times, one would need to extend the specification language.

7   Fuzzy Relations for Replicated Databases

In this section we will use $\mathcal{R}[L]$, for an appropriate choice of a finite distributive lattice L, to interpret our allegorical conceptual model in the context of replicated databases. First we need to recall some notions from the theory of finite lattices.

For any poset P we denote by $\mathcal{O}(P)$ the set of down sets of P. $A \subseteq P$ is a down set if whenever $p \in A$ and $q \leqslant p$ then $q \in A$. For any $p \in P$ we denote

$$\downarrow p := \{q \in P \mid q \leqslant p\} \in \mathcal{O}(P). \tag{15}$$

$\mathcal{O}(P)$ is a lattice with set union and intersection serving as join and meet. Birkhoff's Representation Theorem says that every finite distributive lattice L is isomorphic with $\mathcal{O}(\mathcal{J}(L))$.

Here, let P be a set of replicated database servers partially ordered with respect to their authority. In particular the discrete order on the set of servers corresponds to completely decentralized replication (and then $\mathcal{O}(P) = 2^P$), and the order defined by the diagram below, corresponds to one master server with the authoritative information and a number of equally unreliable slaves:

Because $A \in \mathcal{O}(P)$ (where P is finite) can be represented as the set of maximal elements in A, it follows that for any $R \in \mathrm{Arr}[\mathcal{R}[\mathcal{O}(P)]]$, it makes sense to let $R(a, b)$ represent statement "the most authoritative servers in $R(a, b)$ agree that a and b are in relation R. In this way the $\mathcal{O}(P)$-valued relations represent the state of the replicated database on all nodes at the same time. Because for all $p \in P$ the downsets $\downarrow p \in \mathcal{O}(P)$ are join irreducible, it follows by Proposition 8 that the $\downarrow p$-cut graph morphism $F^{\downarrow p} : \mathcal{R}[\mathcal{O}(P)] \to \mathcal{R}$ is an PTB allegory functor, and hence, by Remark 11, for any $p \in P$ and any interpretation $H : \mathcal{G} \to \mathcal{R}[\mathcal{O}(P)]$ of the allegorical conceptual model $(\mathcal{G}, \mathcal{E})$ we have interpretation $F^{\downarrow p} \circ H$ of $(\mathcal{G}, \mathcal{E})$ in $\mathcal{R}$ which corresponds to the local database state on node p. As in the previous section we infer from it that the equations $\mathcal{E}$ hold on each local node p.

8   Conclusion

We have presented the new conceptual modeling formalism based on allegories, with a sketch-like flavour, which, because of the richer language available we believe to be better suited and accessible then other category based formalisms proposed in the past. Our model when interpreted in the allegory $\mathcal{R}$ of binary relations can be understood as using binary relations and relation algebra to model and specify data, and the variations of this idea underly many existing modeling formalisms (see e.g. [11]). We show, however, that using a much more abstract language of general allegories, rather than relations directly, allows us to apply our model to the specification of temporal and distributed systems. So far the specification formalism allows us to define only those properties which are independent of the particulars of the representation, like the properties of data in the temporal database which hold for all moments of time. In the future work we will extend our specification language so that we are able to declare the properties of the data model specific to a class of interpretations, like dependecies between different copies of replicated data.

References

1. Uml and data modeling. A Rational Software Whitepaper (2003)
2. Barr, M., Wells, C.: Category Theory for Computing Science. Prentice-Hall international series in computer science. Prentice Hall (1995)

3. Chen, P.P.S.: The entity-relationship model – toward a unified view of data. ACM Trans. Database Syst. 1(1), 9–36 (1976)
4. Davey, B., Priestley, H.: Introduction to Lattices and Order. Cambridge mathematical text books. Cambridge University Press (2002)
5. Diskin, Z.: Formalizing graphical schemas for conceptual modeling: Sketch-based logic vs. heuristic pictures. In: 10th International Congress of Logic, Methodology and Philosophy of Science, pp. 40–41 (1995)
6. Diskin, Z.: Generalised sketches as an algebraic graph-based framework for semantic modeling and database design. LDBD research report, Frame Inform Systems (May 1997)
7. Diskin, Z., Kadish, B.: Algebraic graph-oriented = category theory based – manifesto of categorizing database theory. LDBD research report, Frame Inform Systems (December 1994)
8. Freyd, P., Scedrov, A.: Categories, Allegories. North-Holland Mathematical Library. Elsevier Science (1990)
9. Furusawa, H.: Algebraic Formalisations of Fuzzy Relations and Their Representation Theorems. Ph.D. thesis, Kyushu University (1998)
10. Halpin, T.: Object-role modeling (ORM/NIAM). In: Handbook on Architectures of Information Systems, pp. 81–102. Springer (1998)
11. Hull, R., King, R.: Semantic database modeling: survey, applications, and research issues. ACM Comput. Surv. 19(3), 201–260 (1987)
12. Johnson, M., Kasangian, S.: A relational model of incomplete data without nulls. In: Proceedings of the Sixteenth Symposium on Computing: the Australasian Theory, CATS 2010, vol. 109, pp. 89–94. Australian Computer Society, Inc., Darlinghurst (2010)
13. Johnson, M., Rosebrugh, R.: Sketch data models, relational schema and data specifications. Electronic Notes in Theoretical Computer Science 61, 51–63 (2002); Computing: the Australasian Theory Symposium, CATS 2002
14. Johnson, M., Rosebrugh, R.: Fibrations and universal view updatability. Theor. Comput. Sci. 388(1-3), 109–129 (2007)
15. Johnson, M., Rosebrugh, R., Wood, R.J.: Entity-relationship models and sketches (1996) (preprint)
16. Johnson, M., Rosebrugh, R., Wood, R.J.: Lenses, fibrations and universal translations. Mathematical. Structures in Comp. Sci. 22(1), 25–42 (2012)
17. Lippe, E., ter Hofstede, A.H.M.: A category theory approach to conceptual data modeling. Informatique Theorique et Applications 30(1), 31–79 (1996)
18. Rosebrugh, R., Wood, R.J.: Relational databases and indexed categories. In: Proceedings of the International Category Theory Meeting 1991. CMS Conference Proceedings, vol. 13, pp. 391–407. American Mathematical Society (1992)
19. Spivak, D.I.: Simplicial databases. CoRR abs/0904.2012 (2009)

Author Index